**Agnostic Capability**  How can multi-purpose service logic be made effectively consumable and composable?

 **Agnostic Context**  How can multi-purpose service logic be positioned as an effective enterprise resource?

 **Agnostic Sub-Controller**  How can agnostic, cross-entity composition logic be separated, reused, and governed independently?

 **Asynchronous Queuing**  How can a service and its consumers accommodate isolated failures and avoid unnecessarily locking resources?

 **Atomic Service Transaction**  How can a transaction with rollback capability be propagated across messaging-based services?

 **Brokered Authentication**  How can a service efficiently verify consumer credentials if the consumer and service do not trust each other or if the consumer requires access to multiple services?

 **Canonical Expression**  How can service contracts be consistently understood and interpreted?

 **Canonical Protocol**  How can services be designed to avoid protcol bridging?

 **Canonical Resources**  How can unnecessary infrastructure resource disparity be avoided?

 **Canonical Schema**  How can services be designed to avoid data model transformation?

**Canonical Schema Bus**

 **Canonical Versioning**  How can service contracts within the same service inventory be versioned with minimal impact?

 **Capability Composition**  How can a service capability solve a problem that requires logic outside of the service boundary?

 **Capability Recomposition**  How can the same capability be used to help solve multiple problems?

 **Compatible Change**  How can a service contract be modified without impacting consumers?

 **Compensating Service Transaction**  How can composition runtime exceptions be consistently accommodated without requiring services to lock resources?

 **Compositi...**  be implemen... ...loss of autonomy?

 **Concurrent Contracts**  How can a service facilitate multi-consumer coupling requirements and abstraction concerns at the same time?

 **Content Negotiation**  How can a service capability accommodate service consumers with different data format or representation requirements?

 **Contract Centralization**  How can direct consumer-to-implementation coupling be avoided?

 **Contract Denormalization**  How can a service contract facilitate consumer programs with differing data exchange requirements?

 **Cross-Domain Utility Layer**  How can redundant utility logic be avoided across domain service inventories?

 **Data Confidentiality**  How can data within a message be protected so that it is not disclosed to unintended recipients while in transit?

 **Data Format Transformation**  How can services interact with programs that communicate with different data formats?

 **Data Model Transformation**  How can services interoperate when using different data models for the same type of data?

 **Data Origin Authentication**  How can a service verify that a message originates from a known sender and that the message has not been tampered with in transit?

 **Decomposed Capability**  How can a service be designed to minimize the chances of capability logic deconstruction?

 **Decoupled Contract**  How can a service express its capabilities independently of its implementation?

 **Direct Authentication**  How can a service verify the credentials provided by a consumer?

 **Distributed Capability**  How can a service preserve its functional context while also fulfilling special capability processing requirements?

**Domain Inventory**  How can services be delivered to maximize recomposition when enterprise-wide standardization is not possible?

# SOA with Java

*Realizing Service-Orientation*
*with Java Technologies*

## Thomas Erl, Andre Tost, Satadru Roy, and Philip Thomas

PRENTICE
HALL

PRENTICE HALL

UPPER SADDLE RIVER, NJ • BOSTON • INDIANAPOLIS • SAN FRANCISCO

NEW YORK • TORONTO • MONTREAL • LONDON • MUNICH • PARIS • MADRID

CAPE TOWN • SYDNEY • TOKYO • SINGAPORE • MEXICO CITY

For information about buying this title in bulk quantities, or for special sales opportunities (which may include electronic versions; custom cover designs; and content particular to your business, training goals, marketing focus, or branding interests), please contact our corporate sales department at corpsales@pearsoned.com or (800) 382-3419.

For government sales inquiries, please contact governmentsales@pearsoned.com.

For questions about sales outside the U.S., please contact international@pearsoned.com.

Visit us on the Web: informit.com/ph

Library of Congress Control Number: 2014939738

ISBN-13: 978-0-13-385903-4

ISBN-10: 0-13-385903-7

Text printed in the United States on recycled paper at Courier in Westford, Massachusetts.

First printing: June 2014

**Editor-in-Chief**
Mark Taub

**Senior Acquisitions Editor**
Trina MacDonald

**Development Editor**
Teejay Keepence

**Managing Editor**
Kristy Hart

**Copy Editors**
Teejay Keepence
Maria Lee

**Senior Indexer**
Cheryl Lenser

**Proofreader**
Maria Lee

**Publishing Coordinator**
Olivia Basegio

**Cover Designer**
Thomas Erl

**Compositor**
Jasper Paladino

**Photos**
Thomas Erl

**Graphics**
Jasper Paladino

*To my family and friends.*
—Thomas Erl


*Thanks go to my wife and my boys for their*
*continued understanding, patience and support.*
—Andre Tost


*I'd like to express my sincere thanks to Thomas Erl for giving me the*
*opportunity to work on this book. It has been a privilege to be associated*
*with him and along the way, I have learned a lot about service-orientation.*
*I'd also like to thank Mark Taub at Pearson for supplying technical*
*books supporting my work.*
—Satadru Roy


*To my wife, Sarah, for her tireless support.*
—Philip Thomas

# Contents at a Glance

# Contents

# PART I: FUNDAMENTALS

# PART II: SERVICES

# PART III: SERVICE COMPOSITION AND INFRASTRUCTURE

# Foreword
# by Mark Little

Over the past decade SOA has moved out of the hype and into mainstream development, becoming a standard part of any architect's repertoire. Although its roots go back beyond CORBA, SOA came to the forefront with the advent of two technology waves: Web Services and the Enterprise Service Bus (ESB). As REST picked up adoption beyond the Web, so it too became useful within the SOA paradigm. Of course, with the rise of cloud and mobile industries, SOA's applicability has continued to grow and we are seeing more and more business-critical deployments that are examples of good SOA implementations.

In parallel to the evolution and adoption of SOA, the Java language and platform have grown in maturity and dominance within the industry. In fact, the first ESB was written in Java and so are the most popular Web service stacks, such as Apache CXF. As relevant standards have evolved, such as Java Enterprise Edition, so too have they embraced more and more service-orientation principles, offering new APIs and development approaches. It is therefore no surprise that SOA and Java appear together more often than not in real-world deployments across a range of industry sectors.

Building good service-oriented applications is often a challenge, not just for individual developers but also at the organizational level. Even with a range of interfaces, frameworks, and other tools aimed at making SOA development easier, it is often difficult to know which to use and when. In terms of open standards, Java offers the richest suite of such aids, but at the same time can complicate a developer's life by their sheer number.

As Shakespeare once said: "We suffer a lot the few things we lack and we enjoy too little the many things we have."

The authors of this book have created a great resource for anyone new to Java to learn how to translate SOA practices into reality. Likewise, it's a must-have book for Java developers to see how they can use their Java experiences when developing service-oriented applications. Rather than just throw out example code for this or that framework in isolation, the authors have pulled together some wonderful case studies. These case studies are used throughout the book and help put everything into perspective.

It's nice to see that the authors have also made this book self-contained. Far too often we are introduced to books, particularly those in a series, that can only be read if you've also purchased other books that came before and perhaps even some that come afterwards. Not so here. We have introductory chapters that spend a lot of time ensuring that even the most novice reader has all of the information they need at their fingertips. Very refreshing, especially when you consider that some of these chapters could be books in their own right! So whether you are a Java expert who needs to learn about SOA, or an SOA expert who needs to learn about Java, this book has all of the details you need. The Java background text covers the latest Java EE 7 specification, including topics such as JTA/JCA, EJB3, CDI, JPA, and JMS.

One of the dominant SOA implementation approaches today remains SOAP-based Web services. The WS-* standards are the most widely adopted cross-vendor standards relevant to SOA and are used extensively in enterprises both inside and outside of the cloud. This book pulls together the often confusing plethora of standards and implementation approaches in a coherent manner, offering the reader an easier on-ramp to this critical area than is available elsewhere. In terms of how Java interfaces with Web-based services, the authors cover standards such as JAX-WS, JAX-RS and their Spring equivalents. Copious amounts of code are used to help illustrate critical points such as how to get the best throughput or security for your applications. The chapter called Service-Orientation Principles with Java Web-Based Services is one of the best of its kind, covering details such as WSDL, data mapping with REST and how to achieve loose coupling.

What also helps to positively differentiate this book from others in this area are chapters on how to build specific types of services in Java following service-orientation principles and getting them to perform well at the same time: this isn't a book that is just heavy on theory, but it more than complements any theory with a very heavy practical aspect, making it ideal for architects and developers alike. If you're looking for how to build individual services or, more likely as your applications grow, composite services in a way that does not break service-orientation principles, then the authors have created a book that you need to have on your shelf, well read, or next to your computer. The code in chapters such as Service Composition with Java is presented in such a way and with the right context that you should be able to use much of it as a template for you and your teams.

Another technology which is often used within SOA deployments, but also just as often misunderstood, is the Enterprise Service Bus. Like REST, some people love the ESB whilst others believe they bring nothing of value. This book helps to shed some light on the ESB and inject some much needed reality to the debate, allowing you to select the right tool for the right job. ESBs aren't a global panacea for everything SOA-related. But neither are they something which should be ignored, and the authors help to make this clear in a succinct manner.

Whether you're a Java developer looking for a book to explain SOA or an SOA expert looking for something to help you turn those ideas into a Java reality, this is the book for you. It also doesn't matter whether you are a software developer, an architect, working in a team, or by yourself, this book works on many levels and is relevant to you as you move through the SOA design and development phases.

Dr. Mark Little, Red Hat

# Acknowledgments

- Claude Baillargeon, La Capitale

- Chris Barran

- Antonio Bruno, UBS Wealth Management

- Jason Burrows, Pacific Blue Cross

- David Chou, Microsoft

- Leonid Felikson

- Olaf Heimburger, Oracle

- Khanderao Kand, Guavus

- Anish Karmarkar, Oracle

- Kris Kothumb

- Dennis Lamarre, System Science Corporation

- Briana Lee

- Beth Liang, HeathWallace

- Karl Lopes

- Anil Luthra

- Damian Maschek, Deutsche Bahn Systel GmbH

- Veeru Mehta

- Paulo Merson

- Prakash Narayan

- Songlin Qiu

- Antony Reynolds, Oracle

- Rich Rosen

- Sam Rostam

- Sanjay Singh

- Dennis Sosnoski

- Kanu Tripathi

- Sameer Tyagi

- Clemens Utschig, Boehringer Ingelheim Pharma

- Matt Wright, Oracle

- Kareem Yusuf PhD, IBM

# Chapter 1

# Introduction

## 1.1 About This Book

The Java platform has evolved significantly over the past decade and has become a preferred platform for building Web-based enterprise applications. The service-orientation paradigm introduces a number of requirements and design principles that formalize the application of Java platforms and technologies in support of the strategic goals of service-oriented computing. This book explores service-oriented solution design and implementation through the application of techniques and best practices that utilize Java technology advances.

### Objectives of This Book

This book was written with the following primary goals in mind:

- to provide coverage of contemporary Java distributed technologies and modern service technologies

- to document the application of service-orientation principles to the Java technology platform

- to explore the application of SOA design patterns to various Java technologies and solutions built with these technologies

- to provide coverage of Java infrastructure extensions relevant to service-oriented solutions

### Who This Book Is For

This book can be used as a tutorial and reference text intended for the following types of readers:

- experienced Java developers and architects who want to learn how to apply service-orientation principles and select SOA design patterns in order to create shared services and service-oriented solutions

- enterprise architects that want to learn more about how to position and establish Java platforms and technologies within an IT enterprise that has or will undergo SOA adoption

- developers who want to build solutions using modern Java service technologies

**What This Book Does Not Cover**

This is not a "how-to" book for Java. Although the chapters in Part I contain a great deal of introductory coverage of Java distributed technologies, the overall purpose of this book is to explore the intersection of Java technologies and the application of service-orientation principles and SOA design patterns. You should not proceed to read this book if you are new to Java.

## 1.2 Prerequisite Reading

This book assumes you have a basic knowledge of:

- Java technologies, APIs, and standards
- fundamental XML concepts
- fundamental service-orientation

If you have not yet worked with XML, you can read some of the brief tutorials published at www.servicetechspecs.com. If you are new to SOA, you can get a basic understanding of service-oriented computing, service-orientation, and related design patterns by studying the content at the following Web sites:

- www.serviceorientation.com
- www.soapatterns.org
- www.soa-manifesto.com

To ensure that you have a clear understanding of key terms used and referenced in the upcoming chapters, you can also visit the online master glossary for this book series at www.soaglossary.com to look up definitions for terms that may not be fully described in this book.

Here are some recommendations for additional books that elaborate on key topics covered by this title:

- *SOA Principles of Service Design* – A comprehensive documentation of the service-orientation design paradigm with full descriptions of all of the principles referenced in this book. Concise profiles of these principles are provided in Appendix B.

- *SOA Design Patterns* – This is the official SOA design pattern catalog containing descriptions and examples for most of the patterns referenced in this book. You can also look up concise descriptions for these patterns at www.soapatterns.org and in Appendix C.

- *Web Service Contract Design & Versioning for SOA* – Any content pertaining to WSDL, SOAP, and XML Schema development and design, development, and versioning will be aided by the detailed coverage in this title.

- *SOA with REST: Principles, Patterns & Constraints for Building Enterprise Solutions with REST* – REST service development and implementation is covered from various perspectives in the upcoming chapters. This book provides detailed coverage of associated REST technology, architecture, and design constraints.

- *Service-Oriented Architecture: Concepts, Technology, and Design* – The coverage of service-oriented analysis and design processes in this title supplements the technology-centric focus of this book with methodology-related topics.

For more information, visit www.servicetechbooks.com.

## How This Book Is Organized

This book begins with Chapters 1 and 2 providing introductory content and case study background information respectively. All subsequent chapters are grouped into the following parts:

- Part I: Fundamentals
- Part II: Services
- Part III: Service Composition and Infrastructure
- Part IV: Appendices

## Part I: Fundamentals

The four chapters in this part cover introductory topics related to SOA, service-orientation, Web-based services technology, and Java. Note that these chapters do not contain case study content.

*Chapter 3: Fundamental SOA Concepts*

This chapter provides an overview of key terms and concepts associated with SOA, service-orientation, and service-oriented computing.

*Chapter 4: Basic Java Distributed Technologies*

With an emphasis on Java EE, this chapter introduces Java technologies and APIs relevant to this book. Open-source and commercial Java vendor platforms are further referenced.

*Chapter 5: Web-Based Service Technologies*

This chapter provides a concise overview of the industry standards and conventions that form the basis for SOAP-based Web services and REST services. A series of examples is provided for each service implementation medium.

*Chapter 6: Building Web-Based Services with Java*

This chapter focuses on the JAX-WS standard for SOAP-based Web services and the JAX-RS standard for REST services, and provides numerous examples that demonstrate basic design and implementation.

## Part II: Services

This part of the book contains a set of chapters that highlight key Java design considerations introduced by service-orientation principles, and further explores their application to the creation of Java-based utility and entity services.

*Chapter 7: Service-Orientation Principles with Java Web-Based Services*

This chapter documents each of the eight service-orientation design principles as they affect and relate to the use of Java-based technology for both SOAP-based Web services and REST services.

*Chapter 8: Utility Services with Java*

The unique design considerations that come with building utility services with Java are addressed in a series of sections that explore architecture, design, and implementation, further supported by a number of examples.

*Chapter 9: Entity Services with Java*

This chapter discusses the development of entity services with Java with an emphasis on service contract and message standardization, data access, and processing.

## Part III: Service Composition and Infrastructure

The final set of chapters build upon Parts I and II to tackle the design and implementation of entire Java-based service-oriented solutions. Topics covered range from service composition to ESB-related infrastructure considerations.

*Chapter 10: Task Services with Java*

This chapter discusses the characteristics, design, and implementation considerations of building task services with Java and further addresses preliminary service composition issues in preparation for Chapter 11.

*Chapter 11: Service Composition with Java*

This chapter covers a spectrum of topics that pertain to and further expand upon many of the areas already covered in preceding chapters to focus on the design, implementation, and performance of services aggregated into Java-based service compositions.

*Chapter 12: ESB as SOA Infrastructure*

This chapter highlights the use of ESB-based middleware and infrastructure in relation to service-oriented solution and service composition architecture and implementation.

## Part IV: Appendices

*Appendix A: Case Study Conclusion*

This appendix provides a conclusion of the case study storylines first established in Chapter 2.

*Appendix B: Service-Orientation Principles Reference*

This appendix provides the profile tables (originally from *SOA Principles of Service Design*) for the service-orientation design principles referenced in this book.

*Appendix C: SOA Design Patterns Reference*

This appendix provides the profile tables from the design patterns documented in the books *SOA Design Patterns* and *SOA with REST: Principles, Patterns & Constraints for Building Enterprise Solutions with REST*.

*Appendix D: The Annotated SOA Manifesto*

This appendix provides the annotated version of the SOA Manifesto declaration, which is also published at www.soa-manifesto.com.

## 1.3  How Principles and Patterns Are Used in This Book

As part of its exploration of service-orientation in relation to Java technologies and platforms, this book references and uses established design principles and patterns throughout its chapters.

Service-orientation design principles and SOA design patterns are always capitalized, as follows:

*"...the Service Loose Coupling principle is supported via the application of the Decoupled Contract pattern..."*

Note, as also demonstrated in this sample statement, a principle or a pattern can be referenced with or without being qualified. In other words, the statement *"..when the Decoupled Contract pattern is applied..."* has the same meaning as *"...when Decoupled Contract is applied..."*

## 1.4  Symbols and Figures

This book contains a series diagrams that are referred to as *figures*. The primary symbols used throughout all figures are individually described in the symbol legend located on the inside of the front cover.

Symbol legend posters can also be downloaded from www.arcitura.com/notation.

## 1.5  Additional Information

These sections provide supplementary information and resources for the *Prentice Hall Service Technology Series from Thomas Erl*.

### Updates, Errata, and Resources (www.servicetechbooks.com)

Information about other series titles and various supporting resources can be found at the official book series Web site: www.servicetechbooks.com. You are encouraged to visit this site regularly to check for content changes and corrections.

### Referenced Specifications (www.servicetechspecs.com)

This site provides a central portal to the original specification documents created and maintained by primary industry standards organizations.

### The Service Technology Magazine (www.servicetechmag.com)

The Service Technology Magazine is a monthly publication provided by Arcitura Education Inc. and Prentice Hall and is officially associated with the *Prentice Hall Service Technology Series from Thomas Erl*. The Service Technology Magazine is dedicated to publishing specialized articles, case studies, and papers by industry experts and professionals.

### Service-Orientation (www.serviceorientation.com)

This site provides papers, book excerpts, and various content dedicated to describing and defining the service-orientation paradigm, associated principles, and the service-oriented technology architectural model, including online access to the service-orientation principle profiles published in Appendix B.

### What Is REST? (www.whatisrest.com)

This Web site provides a concise overview of REST architecture and the official constraints that are referenced throughout this book.

### What Is Cloud? (www.whatiscloud.com)

A reference site dedicated to fundamental cloud computing topics.

### SOA and Cloud Computing Design Patterns (www.soapatterns.org, www.cloudpatterns.org)

The official SOA and cloud computing design pattern catalogs are published on these sites. The www.soapatterns.org site provides online access to the pattern profiles published in Appendix C.

### SOA Certified Professional (SOACP) (www.soaschool.com)

The official site for the SOA Certified Professional (SOACP) curriculum dedicated to specialized areas of service-oriented architecture and service-orientation, including analysis, architecture, governance, security, development, and quality assurance.

### Cloud Certified Professional (CCP) (www.cloudschool.com)

The official site for the Cloud Certified Professional (CCP) curriculum dedicated to specialized areas of cloud computing, including technology, architecture, governance, security, capacity, virtualization, and storage.

### Big Data Science Certified Professional (BDSCP) (www.bigdatascienceschool.com)

The official site for the Big Data Science Certified Professional (BDSCP) curriculum dedicated to specialized areas of data science, analytics, data analysis, machine learning, and Big Data solution engineering.

### Notification Service

To be automatically notified of new book releases in this series, new supplementary content for this title, or key changes to the aforementioned resource sites, use the notification form at www.servicetechbooks.com or send a blank e-mail to notify@arcitura.com.

# Chapter 2

# Case Study Examples

## 2.1 How Case Study Examples Are Used

Case study examples effectively provide consistent, real-world context to the abstract concepts discussed. This book incorporates examples related to the background on the two financial institutions established in this chapter. Appendix A concludes this book by ending the storylines of both case study examples and explores the results of the organizations' respective transitions to SOA.

### Style Characteristics

In order to more easily identify these sections, a light gray background has been applied to case study examples subsequent to this chapter.

> Initially, there was no concern around this approach, as each application delivered its promised set of features and solved its corresponding business problems. However, since no strategy was used to ensure that XML and Web services were being applied in a standardized manner in support of SOA, there was nothing in place to prevent the resulting design disparity...

### Relationship to Abstract Content

For those of you *not* interested in learning with case study examples, consider these parts of the book as voluntary reading. None of the abstract descriptions reference or rely on the examples as they are provided only to further assist in communicating the purpose and meaning behind the concepts, technologies, and processes covered. Feel free to bypass shaded areas or perhaps only reference them when needing further elaboration on a given subject.

### Code Samples

Many of the following chapters contain numerous case study examples with Java code. Some of the samples shown are code listings while others have code fragments that illustrate the key concepts covered in previous sections. These code samples are used to demonstrate many of the technologies discussed.

## 2.2 Case Study Background: NovoBank

NovoBank is a well-known, large-scale retail bank in North America that offers a variety of products, such as deposit accounts, loans, mortgages, and lines of credit. It has a strong presence on the east coast and is now planning to expand aggressively on the west coast, introducing new product lines to attract new customers. As part of the expansion plans, NovoBank management is also considering acquiring local banks or credit institutions with a strong presence in the local market.

NovoBank was established in the early nineties as a retail bank offering deposit account products. It acquired a number of smaller banks over the years and expanded its product offering to include loans, mortgage portfolios, and lines of credit to become one of the top-tier retail banks in North America.

### Technical Infrastructure

In the early nineties, the NovoBank IT division started with ten people. Over the last decade, rapid technology changes resulted in the introduction of new delivery channels to serve a growing number of customers of different demographic and financial backgrounds. Different groups of customers preferred different self-serve channels that ranged from Internet banking and interactive phone banking to kiosks. The advent of these new channels led to the creation of different types of user-interface applications intended for different user groups, such as customers and call center employees.

At the same time, acquisition of smaller banks meant a steady increase in the number of systems. The IT environment became more complex and heterogeneous as the number of applications grew, with tens of applications and hundreds of interfaces implemented in a variety of platforms and technologies. As a consequence, the IT division has now evolved to an organization with over a hundred staff members working on different systems across different groups. IT development is outsourced to a large system integration firm, but updates and maintenance releases are handled by the in-house IT staff.

### Automation Solutions

The current application landscape at NovoBank is a combination of a variety of in-house and acquired systems that provide deposit account, loans, mortgage, and lines of credit functionality. The back-end applications include the following:

- a Deposit Account application implemented in CICS, COBOL, and DB2 operating on a mainframe system (z/OS)

- a Loans and Mortgage application implemented on an AS/400 system

- a Line of Credit application based on COBOL and VSAM also operating on a mainframe system (z/OS)

In addition, many customer or staff-facing applications, such as channel applications, allow customers to perform self-serve or assisted banking. The channel applications include:

- a Java EE-based Internet banking application using proprietary technology to integrate with the CICS/COBOL-based back-end applications and WebSphere MQ-based messaging to communicate with the AS/400-based back-end system

- an internal branch-based banking system used only by the bank tellers to assist customers with their banking needs made up of a combination of 3270 and 5250 emulator applications that allow access to the mainframe and AS/400 systems

- ATM applications that use proprietary financial messaging standards (ISO-based) over TCP/IP to communicate with the back-end systems

- call center applications that use 3270 and 5250 emulation to access the mainframe and AS/400 systems

## Business Obstacles and Goals

The IT budget has dramatically increased over the years with a large portion spent on system integration efforts. Nearly 70% of the overall IT budget is spent on maintenance overheads. Over the years, new product development efforts are hampered by the complexity of legacy system integration and an accidental architecture accumulating a large number of stove-pipe applications. Many of these systems were never meant to operate with each other and have ended up creating their own islands of customer views and data with inevitable duplication and inconsistencies. The main problems can be summarized as follows:

- Each channel application is a silo using complex custom coding to integrate with the back-end systems. Much of the back-end system integration logic is duplicated across the channels in different technologies and platforms.

- Each channel application is tightly coupled with the back-end systems, and the simplest modifications often result in ripple effects that cascade out to the channel applications.

- With no consolidated customer view that offers a summary of the customer's account holdings, the customer information is fragmented and often duplicated across the channels. The NovoBank IT executives have now been tasked by upper management to reduce on-going maintenance costs by at least 30% and improve time-to-market for new product launches. Faced with such critical challenges, IT management has decided to overhaul the current architecture.

### Future IT Roadmap

After a careful assessment of the existing infrastructure and available technologies, NovoBank decides to re-engineer the IT system to a componentized, service-oriented architecture that will preserve legacy assets, simplify integration, facilitate rapid business process changes, and improve channel experience for branch tellers to meet the demands of reduced operational cost as well as rapid business turnaround. The architects at NovoBank have proposed a phased adoption of a service-oriented architecture in the following incremental steps:

*1. Build Reusable Business Services*

A layer of reusable Web services will be built to encapsulate and hide the implementation details of business logic located in the back-end systems. Services will be described via industry standards-based service interface contracts. The access details of any business logic on a mainframe or midrange system will be completely hidden from the service consumer applications.

There was considerable debate around using SOAP-based Web services or REST Web APIs. After evaluating the capabilities of the legacy systems and packaged integration middleware, it was decided SOAP-based Web services will be leveraged to build the business service layer. The services will be built on the Java EE platform, and service implementations will use appropriate legacy integration technologies, such as Java Connector Architecture (JCA) and Java Messaging Service (JMS), to communicate with the legacy systems.

In the future, when the back-end systems are ready to move on to more modern technologies, the channel applications will not be impacted by these changes because the service interfaces will remain the same. In addition, any channel should be able to consume core business services, such as the Balance Enquiry service or a Balance Transfer service. Such channel-independent business services will enable the delivery of information from the back-end systems in a consistent and technology-neutral way to both current and future channel applications.

*2. Consolidate Information*

A consolidated customer information system will be built to centralize all customer-related data and maintain the relationships between customers and their accounts. As part of the re-engineering effort, the customer information system will be stored in a relational database, and a set of business services will be built to facilitate access to the customer information from any channel. As an example, a Customer Summary service can be used by any channel to retrieve all the deposit, loan, mortgage, and line of credit information for a customer. The consolidated customer information system will be built from the ground up using Java EE as the implementation platform.

*3. Improve Channel Experience*

New Java EE-based branch and call center applications will be built to interface with the back-end systems via the business service interfaces. The direct data access on the mainframe and AS/400 systems from the green screen terminals will be eliminated as these Web applications will consume a set of business services without any knowledge of where and how they are implemented. The Balance Enquiry service or Balance Transfer service can be leveraged from the Internet banking application, branch application, ATMs, and call centers.

*4. Build Services Infrastructure*

SOA infrastructure software, such as an enterprise service bus (ESB), will be introduced to help mediate the interaction between the service providers and service consumers. An ESB will act as a service hosting platform that fulfills the role of an intermediary between the service providers and service consumers to perform message routing, data structure transformation, format translation, and enforcement of policies. In addition, an ESB will also help facilitate monitoring and management of the service-level agreements (SLAs).

## 2.3  Case Study Background: SmartCredit Co.

SmartCredit was established in the late nineties. Its presence has traditionally been limited to major cities on the west coast, but its low interest rate credit cards have become increasingly very popular among new immigrants and students. The company has gradually grown from a staff of fifteen to thirty-five with on-going steady revenue growth. It is now ready to enter into a new era of expansion.

## Technical Infrastructure

The company has a small IT division of ten full time employees and one manager. IT development is managed in-house. The development team follows a process that allows them to quickly build, test, and release new features.

## Automation Solutions

The company's Credit Application Processing System (CAPS) is a typical multi-tier application that consists of the following components:

- Internally, the Web application uses Java APIs (RMI/IIOP) to communicate with the component hosting the business logic.

- An in-house Java EE component accepts customer information and leverages a COTS engine to determine what offers can be made to the customer.

A COTS credit and risk engine carries out the following steps:

1. Accept a credit application.

2. Create an applicant profile.

3. Interface with one or more credit bureaus to retrieve credit reports.

4. Assign a score to the applicant by evaluating a set of rules.

5. Perform risk assessment.

6. Determine credit-worthiness of an applicant.

7. Reject or approve application and assign credit limit based on score.

8. Generate reports.

9. Create a database tier to store persistent customer and product data.

## Business Goals

As part of its expansion plans, SmartCredit is entering into a reseller business arrangement with a large local retail store that will offer re-branded credit cards to customers. The retail store offers different levels of membership programs for its customers to enjoy bonuses like special discounts and cash-back programs. With the new business partnership in place, the retail store customers who sign up for the premium membership will be offered an opportunity to apply for a credit card.

Retail store clerks signing up premium members will use iOS or Android mobile applications on tablets or mobile phones to submit credit card applications to the SmartCredit CAPS. The majority of applications will be adjudicated at point of sale within minutes. A small number of applications may require evaluation by credit and loan department staff at SmartCredit. Once a decision is made, the results will be communicated to the customer by mail. The retail store would also like the ability to check the status of pending credit applications using the SmartCredit CAPS.

### Future IT Roadmap

The new partnership poses a challenge for the SmartCredit IT department, as the current Web-based user-interface is a staff-only application inaccessible outside the SmartCredit network. Credit application business services must be exposed to external applications, such as the retail store mobile applications as well as other internal applications. Given the diverse and rapidly changing nature of the mobile applications, selecting a universally accessible and efficient integration mechanism is important.

REST APIs offer the functionality SmartCredit requires. A quick evaluation of the CAPS application identifies that, with some effort, services with REST-based uniform interfaces can be leveraged to offer core credit application functionality to both internal and external applications. The team also determines it would be simpler for onboard partners to use and scale out future operations with a REST-based CAPS architecture.

# Part I

# Fundamentals

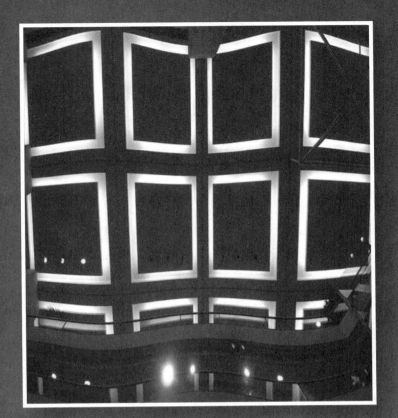

# Chapter 3

# Fundamental SOA Concepts

This chapter describes fundamental terms and concepts associated with service-oriented computing.

## 3.1  Basic Terminology and Concepts

Definitions for the following terms used throughout this book are provided in this section:

- Service-Oriented Computing
- Service-Orientation
- Service-Oriented Architecture (SOA)
- SOA Manifesto
- Services
- Cloud Computing
- Service Models
- Service Inventory
- Service Portfolio
- Service Candidate
- Service Contract
- Service-Related Granularity
- SOA Design Patterns

### Service-Oriented Computing

*Service-oriented computing* is an umbrella term that represents a distinct distributed computing platform. As such, it encompasses many things, including its own design paradigm and design principles, design pattern catalogs, pattern languages, and a distinct architectural model, along with related concepts, technologies, and frameworks.

Service-orientation emerged as a formal method in support of achieving the following goals and benefits (Figure 3.1) associated with service-oriented computing:

- *Increased Intrinsic Interoperability* – Services within a given boundary are designed to be naturally compatible so they can be effectively assembled and reconfigured in response to changing business requirements.

- *Increased Federation* – Services establish a uniform contract layer that hides underlying disparity, allowing them to be individually governed and evolved.

- *Increased Vendor Diversification Options* – A service-oriented environment is based on a vendor-neutral architectural model, allowing the organization to evolve the architecture in tandem with the business without being limited to proprietary vendor platform characteristics.

- *Increased Business and Technology Alignment* – Some services are designed with a business-centric functional context, allowing them to mirror and evolve with the business of the organization.

- *Increased ROI* – Most services are delivered and viewed as IT assets that are expected to provide repeated value that surpasses the cost of delivery and ownership.

- *Increased Organizational Agility* – New and changing business requirements can be fulfilled more rapidly by establishing an environment in which solutions can be assembled or augmented with reduced effort by leveraging the reusability and native interoperability of existing services.

- *Reduced IT Burden* – The enterprise as a whole is streamlined as a result of the previously described goals and benefits, allowing IT itself to better support the organization by providing more value with less cost and less overall burden.

These goals collectively represent the target state we look to achieve when we consistently apply service-orientation to the design of software programs.

---

**NOTE**

The strategic goals of service-oriented computing are also commonly associated with SOA, as explained in the *SOA Manifesto* section.

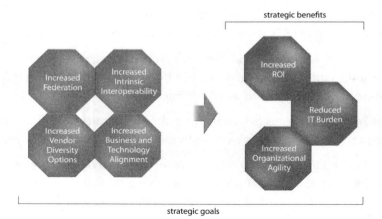

**Figure 3.1**

The three goals on the right represent the target strategic benefits achieved when attaining the four goals on the left.

## Service-Orientation

*Service-orientation* is a design paradigm intended for the creation of solution logic units that are individually shaped to be collectively and repeatedly utilized in support of the realization of the specific strategic goals and benefits associated with service-oriented computing.

Solution logic designed in accordance with service-orientation can be qualified with "service-oriented," and units of service-oriented solution logic are referred to as "services." As a design paradigm for distributed computing, service-orientation can be compared to object-orientation or object-oriented design. Service-orientation has many roots in object-orientation and has been influenced by other industry developments, as seen in Figure 3.2.

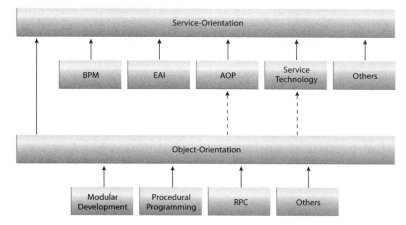

**Figure 3.2**

Service-orientation is an evolutionary design paradigm that owes much of its existence to established design practices and technology platforms.

The service-orientation design paradigm is primarily comprised of eight specific design principles (Figure 3.3):

- *Standardized Service Contract* – "Services within the same service inventory are in compliance with the same contract design standards."

- *Service Loose Coupling* – "Service contracts impose low service consumer coupling requirements and are themselves decoupled from their surrounding environment."

- *Service Abstraction* – "Service contracts only contain essential information and information about services is limited to what is published in service contracts."

- *Service Reusability* – "Services contain and express agnostic logic and can be positioned as reusable enterprise resources."

- *Service Autonomy* – "Services exercise a high level of control over their underlying runtime execution environment."

- *Service Statelessness* – "Services minimize resource consumption by deferring the management of state information when necessary."

- *Service Discoverability* – "Services are supplemented with communicative metadata by which they can be effectively discovered and interpreted."

- *Service Composability* – "Services are effective composition participants, regardless of the size and complexity of the composition."

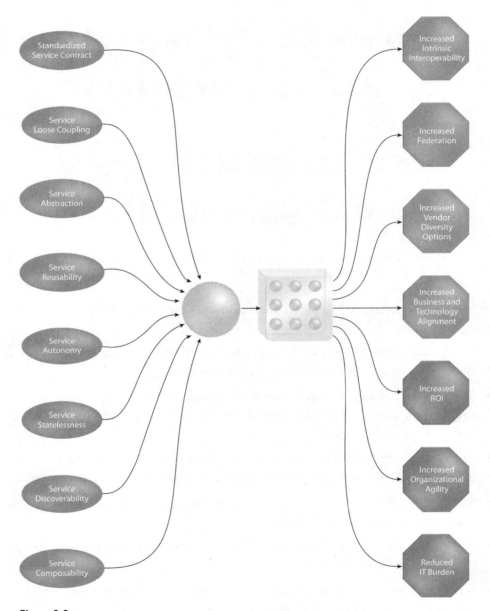

**Figure 3.3**
The repeated application of service-orientation principles to services that are delivered as part of a collection leads to a target state based on the manifestation of the strategic goals associated with service-oriented computing. Note that the container symbol represents a "service inventory," which is defined later in this chapter.

## Service-Oriented Architecture (SOA)

*Service-oriented architecture* is a technology architectural model for service-oriented solutions with distinct characteristics in support of realizing service-orientation and the strategic goals associated with service-oriented computing. Different types of service-oriented architecture can exist, depending on the scope of its application (Figure 3.4).

As a form of technology architecture, an SOA implementation can consist of a combination of technologies, products, APIs, supporting infrastructure extensions, and various other parts. The actual complexion of a deployed service-oriented architecture is unique within each enterprise as typified by the introduction of new technologies and platforms that specifically support the creation, execution, and evolution of service-oriented solutions. As a result, building a technology architecture with the SOA model establishes an environment suitable for solution logic that has been designed in compliance with service-orientation design principles.

**Figure 3.4**

The layered SOA model establishes the four common SOA types: service architecture, service composition architecture, service inventory architecture, and service-oriented enterprise architecture. (These different architectural types are explained in detail in the *SOA Design Patterns* book.)

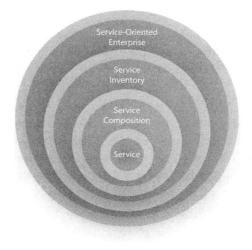

> **NOTE**
>
> Let's briefly recap the terms service-oriented computing, service-orienta-
> tion, and service-oriented architecture to clearly establish how they relate
> to each other and, specifically, how they lead to a definition of an SOA
> as follows:
>
> - A set of strategic goals representing a specific target state is associ-
>   ated with service-oriented computing.
>
> - Service-orientation is the paradigm that provides a proven method for
>   achieving this target state.
>
> - When we apply service-orientation to the design of software, we build
>   units of logic called "services".
>
> - Service-oriented solutions are comprised of one or more services.
>
> - To build successful service-oriented solutions, we need a distributed
>   technology architecture with specific characteristics.
>
> - These characteristics distinguish the technology architecture as
>   being service-oriented. This is SOA.

## SOA Manifesto

Historically, the term "service-oriented architecture" or "SOA" has been used so broadly by the media and within vendor  marketing literature that it almost became synonymous with service-oriented computing itself. The SOA Manifesto published at www.soa-manifesto.org is a formal declaration authored by a diverse working group comprised of industry thought leaders during the 2nd International SOA Symposium in Rotterdam in 2009. This document establishes, at a high level, a clear separation of service-oriented architecture and service-orientation in order to address the ambiguity that had been causing confusion in relation to the meaning of the term "SOA."

The Annotated SOA Manifesto is published at www.soa-manifesto.com and in Appendix D of this book. This version of the SOA Manifesto is recommended reading as it elaborates on statements made in the original SOA Manifesto.

**Services**

From a service-orientation perspective, a service is a unit of logic to which service-orientation has been applied to a meaningful extent. It is the application of service-orientation design principles that distinguishes a unit of logic as a service compared to units of logic that may exist solely as objects, components, Web services, REST services, or cloud-based services.

Subsequent to conceptual service modeling, service-oriented design and development stages implement a service as a physically independent software program with specific design characteristics that support the attainment of the strategic goals associated with service-oriented computing. Each service is assigned its own distinct functional context and is comprised of a set of capabilities related to this context. Therefore, a service can be considered a container of capabilities associated with a common purpose or functional context.

It is important to view and position SOA and service-orientation as being neutral to any one technology platform. By doing so, you have the freedom to continually pursue the strategic goals associated with service-oriented computing by leveraging on-going service technology advancements.

Any implementation technology that can be used to create a distributed system may be suitable for the application of service-orientation. In addition to Web services and REST services, distributed components can also be used to create legitimate service-oriented solutions (Figure 3.5).

**Figure 3.5**

These are the symbols used to represent a component. The symbol on the left is a generic component that may or may not have been designed as a service, whereas the symbol on the right highlights the embedded service contract, and is therefore labeled to indicate that it has been designed as a service.

**Cloud Computing**

*Cloud computing* is a specialized form of distributed computing that introduces utilization models for remotely provisioning scalable and measured IT resources. The primary benefits associated with cloud computing are:

- *Reduced Investment and Proportional Costs* – Cloud consumers that use cloud-based IT resources can generally lease them with a pay-for-use model that allows them to pay a usage fee for only the amount of the IT resource actually used, resulting in directly proportional costs. This gives an organization access to IT resources without having to purchase its own, resulting in reduced investment requirements. By lowering required investments and incurring costs that are proportional to their needs, cloud consumers can scale their IT enterprise effectively and proactively.

- *Increased Scalability* – IT resources can be flexibly acquired from a cloud provider, almost instantaneously and at a wide variety of usage levels. By scaling with cloud-based IT resources, cloud consumers can leverage this flexibility to increase their responsiveness to foreseen and unforeseen changes.

- *Increased Availability and Reliability* – Cloud providers generally offer resilient IT resources for which they are able to guarantee high levels of availability. Cloud environments can be based on a modular architecture that provides extensive failover support to further increase reliability. Cloud consumers that lease access to cloud-based IT resources can therefore benefit from increased availability and reliability.

When appropriate, these benefits can help realize the strategic goals of service-oriented computing by extending and enhancing service-oriented architectures and increasing the potential of realizing certain service-orientation principles.

## IT Resources

An *IT resource* is a broad term to refer to any physical or virtual IT-related artifact (software or hardware). For example, a physical server, a virtual server, a database, and a service implementation are all forms of IT resources.

Even though a service is considered an IT resource, it is important to acknowledge that a service architecture will commonly encapsulate and connect to other IT resources. This distinction is especially important in cloud-based environments, where a cloud service is classified as a remotely accessible IT resource which may encompass and depend on various additional cloud-based IT resources that are only accessible from within the cloud.

## Service Models

A *service model* is a classification used to indicate that a service belongs to one of several pre-defined types based on the nature of the logic it encapsulates, the reuse potential of this logic, and how the service may relate to domains within its enterprise.

The following three service models are common to most enterprise environments and therefore common to most SOA projects:

- *Task Service* – A service with a non-agnostic functional context that generally corresponds to single-purpose, parent business process logic. A task service will usually encapsulate the composition logic required to compose several other services in order to complete its task.

- *Entity Service* – A reusable service with an agnostic functional context associated with one or more related business entities, such as invoice, customer, or claim. For example, a Purchase Order service has a functional context associated with the processing of purchase order-related data and logic.

- *Utility Service* – A reusable service with an agnostic functional context intentionally separate from business analysis specifications and models. A utility service encapsulates low-level technology-centric functions, such as notification, logging, and security processing.

Service models play an important role during service-oriented analysis and service-oriented design phases. Although the aforementioned set of service models is well established, it is not uncommon for an organization to create its own service models that are often derived from established models.

### Agnostic Logic and Non-Agnostic Logic

The term "agnostic" originated from Greek and means "without knowledge." Therefore, logic that is sufficiently generic so that it is not specific to (has no knowledge of) a particular parent task is classified as *agnostic* logic. Because knowledge specific to single purpose tasks is intentionally omitted, agnostic logic is considered multi-purpose. Alternatively, logic that is specific to (contains knowledge of) a single-purpose task is labeled as *non-agnostic* logic.

Another way of thinking about agnostic and non-agnostic logic is to focus on the extent to which the logic can be repurposed. Because agnostic logic is expected to be multi-purpose, it is subject to the Service Reusability principle with the intention of turning it into highly reusable logic. Logic made reusable is truly multi-purpose in that, as a single software program or service, it can be used to help automate multiple business processes.

Non-agnostic logic does not have these types of expectations. It is deliberately designed as a single-purpose software program or service with different characteristics and requirements.

## Service Inventory

A *service inventory* is an independently standardized and governed collection of complementary services within a boundary that represents an enterprise or a meaningful segment of an enterprise. When an organization has multiple service inventories, this term is further qualified as *domain service inventory*.

Service inventories are typically created through top-down delivery processes that result in the definition of *service inventory blueprints*. The subsequent application of service-orientation design principles and custom design standards throughout a service inventory is of paramount importance so as to establish a high degree of native inter-service interoperability. This supports the repeated creation of effective service compositions in response to new and changing business requirements (Figure 3.6).

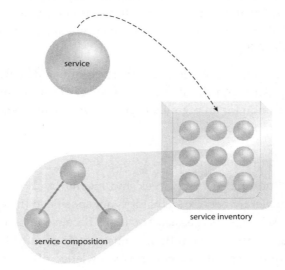

**Figure 3.6**
Services (top) are delivered into a service inventory (right)
from which service compositions (bottom) are drawn.

## Service Portfolio

*Service portfolio* (also commonly referred to as a "service catalog") is a separate term used to represent a set of the services within a given IT enterprise. The distinction between service inventory and service portfolio is important as these and related terms are used within different contexts, as follows:

- A service inventory represents a collection of implemented services that are independently owned and governed.

- The service inventory analysis is a modeling process by which service candidates are defined for a new or existing service inventory.

- A service inventory blueprint is a technical specification that represents the result of having performed a service inventory analysis. Subsequent iterations of the service inventory analysis process can expand or further refine a service inventory blueprint.

- The term "service portfolio" has a less specific definition than "service inventory" in that it can represent all or a subset of the services within an IT enterprise.

- A service portfolio often exists as a high-level documentation of services used for planning purposes.

- A service portfolio most commonly encompasses one or multiple service inventories.

*Service portfolio management* is the practice of planning the definition, delivery, and evolution of collections of services.

## Service Candidate

When conceptualizing services during the service-oriented analysis and service modeling processes, services are defined on a preliminary basis and are still subject to a great deal of change and refinement before they are handed over to the service-oriented design project stage responsible for producing physical service contracts. The term "service candidate" is used to help distinguish a conceptualized service from a service that has actually been implemented.

## Service Contract

A *service contract* expresses the technical interface of a service. It can be comprised of one or more published documents that express meta information about a service, which essentially establish an API into the functionality offered by the service via its capabilities.

When services are implemented as Web services, the most common service description documents are the WSDL definition, XML Schema definition, and WS-Policy definition. A Web service generally has one WSDL definition, which can link to multiple XML

Schema and WS-Policy definitions. When services are implemented as components, the technical service contract is comprised of a technology-specific API.

Services implemented as REST services are accessed via a uniform contract, such as the one provided by HTTP and Web media types. Service contracts are depicted differently depending on whether a uniform contract is involved.

A service contract can be further comprised of human-readable documents, such as a service-level agreement (SLA) that describes additional quality-of-service guarantees, behaviors, and limitations. Several SLA-related requirements can also be expressed in machine-readable format as policies.

Within service-orientation, the design of the service contract is of paramount importance, so much so that the Standardized Service Contract design principle and the aforementioned service-oriented design process are dedicated solely to the standardized creation of service contracts.

### Service-Related Granularity

When designing services, there are different granularity levels that need to be taken into consideration, as follows:

- *Service Granularity* – This represents the functional scope of a service. For example, fine-grained service granularity indicates that there is a small quantity of logic associated with the service's overall functional context.

- *Capability Granularity* – The functional scope of individual service capabilities is represented by this granularity level. For example, a GetDetail capability will tend to have a finer measure of granularity than a GetDocument capability.

- *Constraint Granularity* – The level of validation logic detail is measured by constraint granularity. For example, the more coarse the constraint granularity is, the less constraints (or smaller the amount of data validation logic) a given capability will have.

- *Data Granularity* – This granularity level represents the quantity of data processed. For example, a fine level of data granularity is equivalent to a small amount of data.

Because the level of service granularity determines the functional scope of a service, it is usually determined during analysis and modeling stages that precede service contract design. Once a service's functional scope has been established, the other granularity types come into play and affect both the modeling and physical design of a service contract (Figure 3.7).

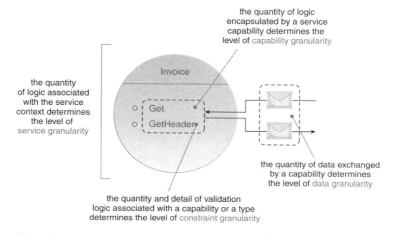

the quantity of logic encapsulated by a service capability determines the level of capability granularity

the quantity of logic associated with the service context determines the level of service granularity

the quantity of data exchanged by a capability determines the level of data granularity

the quantity and detail of validation logic associated with a capability or a type determines the level of constraint granularity

**Figure 3.7**

The four granularity levels represent various characteristics of a service and its contract. Note that these granularity types are, for the most part, independent of each other.

Granularity is generally measured in terms of fine and coarse levels. It is worth acknowledging that the use of the terms "fine-grained" and "coarse-grained" is highly subjective. What may be fine-grained in one case may not be in another. The point is to understand how these terms can be applied when comparing parts of a service or when comparing services with each other.

## Service Profiles

The document used to record details about a service throughout its lifecycle is the *service profile* (Figure 3.8). A service profile is typically maintained by the owner or custodian of a service and is based on a template that is standardized throughout a service inventory.

**Figure 3.8**

A service profile is generally created when a service is first conceptualized, and is then updated and maintained throughout subsequent lifecycle phases.

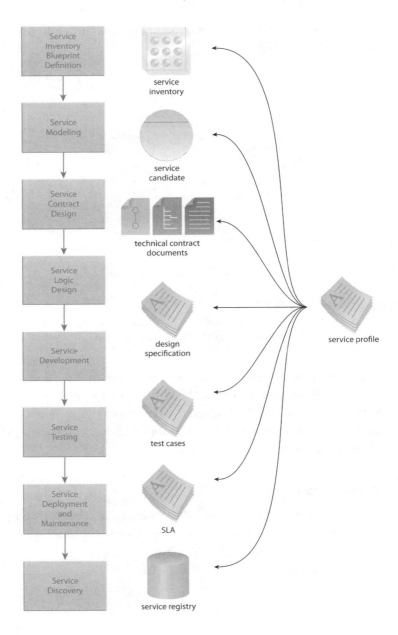

## SOA Design Patterns

A design pattern is a proven solution to a common design problem. The SOA design patterns catalog provides a collection of design patterns (Figure 3.9) that provide practices and techniques for solving common problems in support of service-orientation.

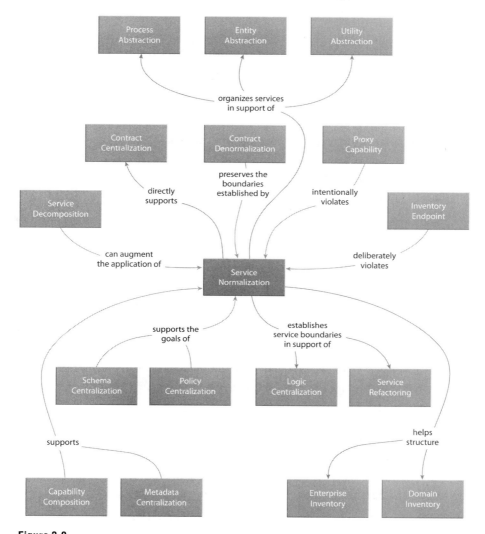

**Figure 3.9**

SOA design patterns form a design pattern language that allows patterns to be applied in different combinations and in different sequences in order to solve various complex design problems.

## 3.2 Further Reading

- Explanations of the service-oriented computing goals and benefits are available at www.serviceorientation.com and in Chapter 3 of *SOA Principles of Service Design*.

- For information about SOA types and the distinct characteristics of the service-oriented technology architecture, see Chapter 4 of *SOA Design Patterns*.

- Design principles are referenced throughout this book but represent a separate subject matter that is covered in *SOA Principles of Service Design*. Introductory coverage of service-orientation as a whole is also available at www.serviceorientation.com and all eight principle profile tables are provided in Appendix B of this book.

- For a comparison of service-orientation and object-orientation concepts and principles, see Chapter 14 in *SOA Principles of Service Design*.

- For an explanation of how SOA design patterns related to service-orientation design principles, see Chapter 5 in the *SOA Design Patterns* book.

- For general coverage of SOA project stages and associated organization roles and governance controls, see *SOA Governance: Governing Shared Services On-Premise and in the Cloud*.

- For detailed coverage of service-oriented analysis and service-oriented design process steps, see *Service-Oriented Architecture: Concepts, Technology, and Design*.

- Definitions for the terms introduced in this chapter can also be found at www.soaglossary.com.

- Read the Annotated SOA Manifesto in Appendix D (also published at www.soa-manifesto.com) for a high-level description of SOA and service-orientation (without references to specific principles or patterns).

See www.servicetechbooks.com for additional reading resources.

# Chapter 4

# Basic Java Distributed Technologies

The Java platform provides the basis for the runtime infrastructure on which many organizations worldwide host their enterprise applications. Java receives strong support for distributed applications and architectures from a number of IT vendors and open-source providers, which has been fundamental to the Java platform from its inception and predates the emergence of Web-based services standards.

This chapter introduces the pre-Web services distributed technologies of the Java platform, focusing on how these technologies can be utilized in support of building service-oriented solutions. Some of the technologies discussed also provide the basic building blocks for Web-based Java services themselves.

> **NOTE**
>
> If you are a Java professional with a working knowledge of Java distributed technologies, then you can skip this chapter.

## 4.1 Java Distributed Computing Basics

The Java platform's three distinct development and runtime platforms are based on the object-oriented Java programming language, with each targeted at a different application environment.

- *Java Platform, Standard Edition (Java SE)* – Targeted primarily at desktop applications and embedded applications, Java SE provides a range of capabilities delivered as class libraries that include several distributed computing capabilities.

- *Java Platform, Micro Edition (Java ME)* – Intended for applications running on mobile devices, such as cell phones and PDAs, Java ME aims to address some of the issues inherent in this environment, such as ensuring applications can run successfully with a small memory footprint and without continuous connectivity to external systems.

- *Java Platform, Enterprise Edition (Java EE)* – Targeted at enterprise applications, Java EE provides a robust and highly scalable runtime environment capable of hosting business-critical applications, such as quality-of-service (QoS) aspects like security and scalability. Java EE is built on Java SE, which provides all of the capabilities of the Java SE platform.

This book focuses on Java EE as the platform most relevant to the exploration of Java-based SOA. However, Java EE depends on Java SE, which in turn depends on some other basic building blocks that require attention before examining Java EE in detail.

## Java SE Architecture

Java SE is based on a layered architecture. Java applications run in a Java runtime environment (JRE). The Java Virtual Machine (JVM) included in this runtime environment insulates Java applications from the details of the operating system and provides portability between different hardware and operating system platforms. Included in the runtime environment are a number of Java classes defined within the Java SE specification and grouped as packages. These classes provide the core functionality typically required by applications, such as network access and text/math processing capabilities. Application source code is compiled using a Java Development Kit (JDK) in the byte-code running in the JVM. The JDK provides a compiler (javac) and other useful utilities and toolkits as well as the JRE.

## Java EE Architecture

We'll now introduce the Java EE platform, describing its origins and development from Java SE.

### The Beginning of Java EE

Enterprise applications often access one or more back-end systems or enterprise information systems (EISs). These could be relational database-packaged applications, such as SAP, Siebel, or components implemented in other application environments, such as CICS. Java EE applications provide business logic that interacts with these back-end systems and expose this business logic to clients requiring access.

Let's consider what is involved in starting from scratch and writing an enterprise application without the benefit of an application server. For example, providing for concurrent access by multiple clients and multi-threading capabilities is necessary. Restricting access to only authenticated clients who are authorized to access the services will require work. A solution with transactional integrity across multiple resource managers is required.

The Java EE specification defines the application architecture and runtime infrastructure onto which entire applications are deployed. Each container manages the execution of specific types of components providing a kind of contract between the application and its host runtime infrastructure. The containers also provide standard capabilities to satisfy application QoS requirements, such as multi-threading, transactional behavior, and security.

The Java EE runtime architecture is designed to support multi-tiered enterprise applications executing in different types of containers that each provide runtime support for a variety of Java EE application components. The common infrastructure platform for all containers is the Java SE runtime.

The Applet and Application Client Container (ACC) hosts client applications that execute in environments, such as desktops, browsers, and mobile devices. A Java applet hosted in an applet container, such as a browser with a Java plug-in, can access Web components over HTTP(S). The applet container services force the Java applets to execute in a restricted sandbox on the client machine.

The ACC provides services for persistence (JPA), messaging (JMS), Web services based on SOAP (Java API for XML Web services or JAX-WS, SOAP API for attachments with Java or SAAJ, and Java API for XML Registries or JAXR), REST (Java API for RESTful Services or JAX-RS), and Contexts and Dependency Injection (CDI). These APIs will be discussed in subsequent chapters.

> **NOTE**
>
> Although client applications executing in an ACC can directly use Enterprise JavaBean (EJB) services to access back-end systems, relying on Web-based services to access service-enabled applications is preferable. ACC components can also use JPA to read and write data from the database.

The Web container manages execution of and provides services for presentation-tier components, which, in a typical Java EE application, are implemented using the Java Server Pages (JSP), Servlets, or Java Server Faces (JSF) technologies. The Web container also provides various supporting services for persistence (JPA), transactions (Java Transaction API or JTA), standards-based connectivity to EIS systems based on the J2EE

Connector Architecture (JCA), security, messaging, and Web services. ACC host client applications and Web applications do not need to use EJBs to consume business services. They can be accessed over Web-based services or JPA can be used to access relational databases.

The EJB container provides a hosting environment for stateless and stateful session EJBs and message-driven beans (MDBs). As with the Web container, the EJB container must also provide additional supporting services around persistence, transactions, messaging, security, and Web services.

Starting from Java EE 5, the emphasis has shifted from building business logic in distributable and remotely accessible EJBs to building reusable, testable business logic in Plain Old Java Objects (POJOs). Open-source frameworks like Spring first popularized this model, and Java EE has embraced this philosophy encouraging Java developers to focus on building business logic in POJOs and choosing an appropriate remote protocol for distribution only when application requirements demand.

Java EE 5 first changed the EJB programming model to be based on annotated POJOs that could still benefit from container services, such as concurrency and transaction management. In Java EE 5, by default, EJBs were local components. However, even with Java EE 5, the implementations were monolithic with no way for vendors to choose to implement only a subset of the specifications and still be Java EE-compliant. In contrast with Java EE 6, the specifications emphasize the modularity of the Java EE platform by introducing the concept of a *profile* that represents a configuration of the platform suited to a particular class of applications.

An entire class of applications can be built leveraging only the services provided by the Web container as Java EE vendors now have the flexibility to implement only a subset of the Java EE specifications conforming to the requirements of a particular profile. One such profile is the Java EE Web Profile, which focuses only on Web components and a set of supporting APIs. The Web Profile leaves out some of the enterprise APIs such as JCA and JMS, which may not be required for building many typical Web applications. However, the Web Profile does include supporting services like persistence, transactions, and a lightweight local EJB-based programming model, which allow developers to build modern Web applications backed by enterprise databases.

Java EE 7 added a number of new and different specifications in each of the container areas. The one of significant interest to this book is an upward revision in the Java API for RESTful Services to version 2.0 (JAX-RS 2.0). Detailed descriptions of how REST services can be built using JAX-RS 2.0 are provided will be covered in subsequent chapters.

## Application Packaging and Deployment

Java EE applications are packaged as deployable enterprise archive files (EAR). These include compiled code (Java bytecode packaged as class files), optional source code, and any additional artifacts required by applications, such as properties files. The archive files with an `.ear` filename suffix are created using the zip file format so that they can be opened and the contents viewed using a compatible zip/unzip utility. EAR files can include EJB modules, Web modules, application client modules, and resource adapter modules, each of which can be packaged as a zip archive with a `.war` (Web applications), `.rar` (resource adapters), or `.jar` (other modules) filename suffix.

Beginning with EJB 3.1 in Java EE 6, local EJB artifacts can be packaged within a `.war` filename suffix to eliminate the need for a separate EJB jar. This greatly simplifies application development where suitably annotated EJB classes can be directly placed inside the WEB-INF/classes directory or packaged as a `.jar` file inside the WEB-INf/lib directory.

### Deployment Descriptors

The Java EE deployment unit (`.war`, `.jar`, `.ear`, or `.rar` files) can also contain deployment descriptors including the deployment settings of an application. These XML files located in a subdirectory of each module include runtime configuration settings, such as the context root used by the application server for resources like servlets and JSPs exposed using a URI. Since enterprise applications and their associated modules require access to resources outside of the Java EE environment, a way of referencing these resources is required to allow changes to be made to the external environment without recompiling and redeploying application code. In addition to allowing the occasional changes needing to be made to a production environment, such as changing the host name or IP address of a host, this also allows enterprise application code to be promoted without change through test environments and into production as part of the application lifecycle.

Deployment descriptors help insulate applications from the external environment by providing a layer of indirection through references to resources. Application code is bound to the reference defined in the deployment descriptor, and the binding of the reference to the external environment can be defined and changed at deployment time.

Java EE, from version 5 onwards, greatly simplifies deployment by removing the need for XML-based deployment descriptors with the exception of Web applications requiring a `web.xml` file. Generally, the EJB and Web service-related deployment descriptor settings can be described through code annotations. However, if required, deployment descriptor settings can be specified in XML files overriding code annotations.

**Java EE Architectural Tiers**

Java EE is based on a multi-tiered application and runtime architecture. Table 4.1 summarizes the architectural tiers with the APIs and technologies that play a key role in each tier according to the Java EE specification.

| Tier | Responsibility | Implementation Technologies |
|---|---|---|
| client | user-interface | thin client – browser<br><br>thick client – applet, stand-alone (J2SE) application, application client container |
| Web | serving of static/dynamic HTML<br><br>screen navigation/control<br><br>reusable UI components | JavaServer Pages<br><br>servlets<br><br>JavaServer Faces |
| business | business logic | Enterprise JavaBeans |
| EIS | access to EISs | packaged applications, databases, mainframe systems<br><br>accessed via JCA connectors, Java Database Connectivity, Java Message Service |

**Table 4.1**
Java EE tiers and implementation

The Java EE platform covers a range of application and runtime architectures, and provides specifications for each of the architectural tiers, components, and implementation technologies. It is entirely possible to build applications using nothing more than the base Java EE platform, such as the Java EE 6 Web Profile platform. Contemporary architectures based on Java EE can diverge from the pure Java EE model in some respects by utilizing frameworks, toolkits, and packages additional to those provided by Java EE.

### SUMMARY OF KEY POINTS

- The Java platform's three distinct development and runtime platforms, which target different application environments, are Java SE, Java ME, and Java EE.

- The Java EE specification defines the runtime architecture of a Java EE application server capable of hosting business-critical applications and provides a number of distinct containers into which different types of application components are deployed.

- The Java EE specifications define a number of distinct architectural tiers designed to support multi-tiered enterprise applications and used to structure a Java EE application, such as client, Web, business, and EISs.

## 4.2 Java Distributed Technologies and APIs

The Java language aims to provide built-in capabilities for building distributed applications. As Java has evolved into a complete platform for building distributed enterprise applications, these capabilities have been developed and extended. This section provides an overview of the technologies and APIs of the Java platform, which play an important role in building distributed applications.

### Java SE APIs

Before examining the capabilities of the Java EE platform, let's review some of the important APIs provided by Java SE.

### RMI

The Java SE platform offers the ability to communicate with remote Java objects not running within the same JVM in the form of Java Remote Method Invocation (RMI) included in the `java.rmi` package. RMI allows a Java application running in one JVM (the client) to invoke methods on a Java object running in another (the server), passing parameters as specified on the method signatures.

A number of steps are involved in exposing a Java class for remote communication. First, an interface extending `java.rmi.Remote` is defined to indicate that the implementation is to be called remotely via RMI. Next, a class that implements the interface and extends the `java.rmi.UnicastRemoteObject` is written for export via the Java Remote Method Protocol (JRMP). The stub and skeleton classes providing communication between the client and server at runtime are then generated by running `rmic`, which is the RMI compiler provided with the JDK. Now the stub can be deployed with the client application and the skeleton with the server application. The functionality provided by the Java class can now be accessed remotely via RMI.

Before a client can call methods on an object in the server, the server must create an instance of the object and register it in an RMI registry using a unique name for reference. The RMI registry can run within the server's JVM or as an external process.

To call a remote object, the client application looks up the reference to the remote object in the RMI registry using its unique name to retrieve the remote interface. The application can then call methods on the remote interface. The Java runtime handles the communications between client and server and the passing of objects as parameters between the client and the server, converting objects to a byte stream for transport via the network (marshaling) at one end and the reverse (unmarshaling) at the other. RMI supports both pass-by-value and pass-by-reference interaction styles. The objects passed must implement the serializable or remote interfaces respectively.

RMI provides a basic remote invocation mechanism. However, RMI does not address non-functional requirements, such as scalability, resilience, transactional integrity, and interoperability with non-Java platforms. Building services using this method is not preferable due to these limitations. RMI can provide the basis for other Java technologies that provide solutions to necessary non-functional requirements.

*RMI / IIOP*

RMI over IIOP takes the basic model of RMI and attempts to solve the issue of interoperability with non-Java platforms by leveraging the CORBA standards developed by the Object Management Group (OMG). CORBA is based on the approach that object request brokers (ORBs) take to facilitate communication between remote objects and provide basic QoS features, such as the ability to pass transaction and security context.

RMI, as originally developed, uses the JRMP transport protocol restricted to the Java platform. RMI/IIOP allows RMI-based remote calls using CORBA's IIOP transport protocol, enabling interoperability with CORBA objects running on other platforms. Where cross-platform communication is required, platform-independent interface definitions are specified using CORBA's Interface Definition Language (IDL). RMI/IIOP facilitates the EJB specification, as discussed later in this chapter.

### JNDI

The Java Naming and Directory Interface (JNDI) is an extension to Java SE that provides a standard way of accessing naming and directory services from Java applications. JNDI allows objects to be bound into a hierarchical directory and identified with a name. The name is then used by applications to obtain a reference to the object. The API allows access to a variety of LDAP-based directories as well as CORBA's COSNaming Service.

All JNDI names exist relative to a context defining where they are stored. When performing a JNDI lookup, an `InitialContext` object is created, defining the namespace/directory where the lookup will be performed. When a JNDI lookup is performed by a Java EE application running in a container, the environment the application is running in has its own context accessed using the `java:comp/env` prefix.

Example 4.1 illustrates the retrieval of a Java Database Connectivity (JDBC) data source to establish a connection to a database.

```
/* set up properties which specify the JNDI provider, security
credentials and other settings required for the lookup */
Properties props = new Properties();
props.put(Context.PROVIDER_URL,"myProviderURL");

// create the initial context
Context ctx = new InitialContext(props);

// name used for lookup
String jndiName = "java:comp/env/jdbc/ds1";

// perform the lookup and cast the retrieved object
DataSource ds = (DataSource)ctx.lookup(jndiName);

// create connection to database
Connection conn = ds.getConnection();
```

**Example 4.1**

The JNDI is used to locate remote objects exposed using RMI/IIOP and plays an important role in the EJB model. It is also used as a means of retrieving configuration/factory objects in application code.

*JDBC*

Enterprise applications must generally persist and retrieve data relating to business-relevant entities regardless of the architectural style adopted, and SOA is no exception. In general, relational database management systems (RDBMS) provide the technology for information storage, and the Java Database Connectivity API (JDBC) provides the technology for Java applications to work with the databases.

The JDBC API also provides a standard way of accessing relational databases from Java applications. A JDBC driver deployed on the application server provides connectivity to the database. The JDBC API defines standard interfaces or classes used to execute queries and work with the results returned by the RDBMS. Details of the connection to the database can be kept in a JDBC data source defined at deployment time and retrieved by the application using a JNDI lookup. Environment-specific configuration is left out of application code and instead specified at deployment.

## Java EE APIs

The basic distributed computing capabilities provided by Java SE are extended by the Java EE platform, which provides a number of additional APIs. This section provides an overview of the Java EE APIs for distributed applications.

*Contexts and Dependency Injection*

Contexts and dependency injection build on the dependency injection mechanism introduced in Java EE 5. Dependency injection provides loose coupling. A component implementation can vary independently of the component interface, and a particular implementation for a given interface can be chosen at deployment time without requiring any changes in code. Example 4.1 can be simplified by leveraging the Java EE container's dependency injection feature as shown in Example 4.2.

```
...
/* Datasource dependency is injected as a Resource by the container */
@Resource(name="jdbc/ds1")
private javax.sql.DataSource ds;
Connection  conn = ds.getConnection();
...
```

**Example 4.2**

> **NOTE**
>
> In Java EE 5, only container-managed components, such as EJBs, and Web components, such as servlets and servlet filters, are supported by resource injection. Java EE 6 removed the restriction to allow arbitrary dependencies to be injected like a regular Java object into a component. CDI introduces the concept of managed beans, which can be almost any type of Java class and injected as dependencies in any other object. Java EE 7 provided further enhancements with an incremental release of CDI (CDI 1.1), and makes broader, more extensive use of CDI across the platform.

### JTA

Distributed, composition-based solutions must often coordinate the invocation of multiple services within a single atomic unit of work. Java EE provides the Java Transactions API (JTA) as the standard way of handling transactions in a Java EE environment.

JTA provides a means of coordinating transactions involving multiple resource managers. The Java application server acts as a transaction manager, instructing the resource managers to begin, commit, or roll back transactions as required. JTA can achieve distributed two-phase commit across multiple resources controlled by the application server. When the transaction manager is ready to commit the transaction, it tells the resource managers to prepare to commit. The resource managers then respond and, providing no problems and no requests indicate that the transaction be aborted, a commit command is issued. If one or more of the resource managers request that the transaction be aborted, the transaction manager issues a rollback command reversing all of the actions performed within the unit of work.

In addition to allowing programming access to the JTA API to create and control user transactions, the EJB container allows access to define the transactional behavior of components with a deployment descriptor. The transactional behavior required by an operation can be stated, such as if it must be called within the scope of an existing transaction, if a new transaction must be started, or if it must not be called within transactional scope. The container then coordinates transactions based on this configuration, passing transaction context between components as needed.

Employing deployment descriptors with the JTA API has limitations. For example, not all resources provide two-phase commit support, in which case operations involving these resources must be performed outside of transactional scope. If any of these operations fail, compensating operations to reverse the action of the previous operations can be performed. Therefore, a compensation framework is needed to define compensating operations for each of the operations the application performs. The base Java EE platform does not provide a compensation framework, but future sections will explore alternative solutions.

> **NOTE**
>
> Various XA optimizations can be applied as compensating operations, such as Last Agent Commit, allowing at most one non-XA participant to participate in an XA transaction. In many application servers, the JTA implementations support this and other variants of such optimizations, but a detailed discussion is outside the scope of this book. For details please refer to *Java Transaction Processing* by Little, Pavlik, Maron et al.

### Java EE Connector Architecture

A selection of packaged applications and legacy/bespoke systems can be discovered when examining the IT landscape of any organization. It is possible, and at times preferable, to expose some of the functionality of these systems as services.

The Java EE Connector Architecture provides a standard way for Java EE applications to connect to external EISs. The JCA specification defines how the EIS connects to the Java EE application server through a service interface (SPI). JCA is the base technology for a range of connectors provided by IT vendors, as well as the standard method for integrating JMS providers with the application server.

The specification defines a common way for applications to access an EIS through a common client interface (CCI). The CCI includes a number of interfaces allowing applications to create a connection to the EIS, call functions provided by the EIS, and manipulate the results. The interfaces and programming model of the Java EE Connector Architecture follow a similar approach to other Java APIs, such as JDBC and JMS, which will seem familiar to those who have used these APIs.

### EJB

Enterprise JavaBeans (EJBs) are the Java EE components implementing application logic in the business tier of the Java EE model. Java EE 5 introduced EJB 3.0, which included some significant changes from EJB 2.1, the previous version of the specification. EJB 3.0 simplifies EJB programming, resulting in significant changes to the programming model.

The pre-EJB 3.0 versions were less user-friendly, and writing a single EJB required working with three artifacts: a component interface, a home interface, and a bean implementation class. The default choices also forced a remote programming model even with no requirements for remote communication, which resulted in unnecessary performance overhead and increased deployment complexity.

With EJB 3.0, local EJBs became the default. The old home-and-component interface views were dispensed with, and the standard deployment descriptor settings for container-value added services around transactions and security, which were captured in Java code-based annotations. However, EJBs still had to be packaged as separate EJB `.jar` files, which did not address the deployment complexity. EJB 3.1 and Java EE 6 resolved the deployment complexity with the `.war`-style packaging of EJBs, which simplified using EJB references in a Web application by distributing the artifacts as part of a packaged `.war` file. Java EE 7 released an update to the EJB specifications with EJB 3.2.

### Session EJBs

Session EJBs provide the implementation of business logic in the Java EE model. Capable of implementing the methods of a business component interface, session EJBs employ instance variables. A bean designed for instance variables required for the lifetime of a single invocation can be implemented as a stateless session bean. However, a stateful session bean is necessary if the design requires conversational state to be maintained across a sequence of invocations.

Using stateful session beans comes at the cost of additional complexity, as the server must store the state at the end of each invocation and ensure availability for subsequent invocations in a conversation. In a clustered environment, the state must be shared across multiple servers, or for server affinity to be honored by the application server, routing all of the invocations that comprise a conversation to the same server.

Stateless session beans are intended to be short-lived objects created as required and destroyed after processing an individual client request. In contrast stateful session beans are used when a client session has completed. For performance reasons, an application server might reuse session bean instances, retrieving them from a pool and returning them when a client has finished with the bean instance. This is opaque to the client. All bean instances are identical and it makes no difference whether a bean instance has been newly created or previously used.

Consider the following guidelines in support of SOA:

- As per the Service Statelessness principle, stateless logic can be implemented using stateless session EJBs to avoid some of the complexities of stateful session EJBs.

- As per the Service Abstraction principle, fine-grained interfaces should be avoided. It is possible to expose methods that accept all of the parameters required to perform some operations as a single set, which means the input and output parameters will be complex structures or objects.

- Services should favor pass-by-value rather than pass-by-reference invocation style, which fits with the EJB model of marshaling/unmarshaling parameters.

### Persistence Entities

EJB 3.0 introduced the Java Persistence API, which allows developers to model regular POJOs as lightweight persistent domain objects. The JPA runtime provides applications with a means of accessing data in persistent storage, exposing an object-oriented view of the data. Considering the capabilities offered by a typical database, the JPA provides applications with the ability to read and write data via transactions, map to a data model, and maintain integrity by enforcing constraints defined as part of the database schema.

Like any regular Java object, a persistent entity can encapsulate behavior (methods) and attributes (instance variables). As the Java application works with data by calling methods on persistence entities, the JPA runtime must translate these into calls to the underlying data store. When the data store is a typical relational database, these translated calls take the form of SQL queries that are executed against the database via JDBC. The instance variables of the entity must reflect the data in the data store. Where a relational database is used, think in terms of mapping the persistence entity's attributes (object instance variable) to columns in one or several data tables. The JPA runtime performs the object, such as relational mapping between Java objects and database tables.

---

**NOTE**

JPA evolved from the popular Hibernate persistence framework.

---

From the perspective of a Java application, persistent entities should be viewed as long-lived persistent objects. When creating an entity or changing some of its attributes, the changes are persisted to the underlying database once the transaction has committed.

EJB 3.0 introduced changes to the EJB programming model, such as annotations and persistence. Annotations are a tag, indicated with an @ prefix, which can be included in Java code to change the way the code is handled by compilers or toolkits.

A familiar example to most Java developers is the `@deprecated` annotation picked up during the Javadoc generation to indicate that a class should no longer be used. While Java 5.0 provides the ability to define unique annotations, EJB 3.0 defines some annotations with specific meaning to reduce creating excess boilerplate code when implementing an EJB. Annotations are used instead of implementing the relatively complex interfaces required by previous EJB specifications and as a simpler mechanism to indicate the developer's intent. As seen in Example 4.3, the `@Stateless` annotation can be used to implement a stateless session bean in EJB 3.0.

```
@Stateless
public class HelloWorldBean
  public String helloWorld(String name)
  {
    return ("hello "+name);
  }
}
```

**Example 4.3**

By using the `@Stateless` annotation, implementing a component interface is unnecessary as was required in previous versions of EJB. Now clients can retrieve a bean instance via a JNDI lookup of the business interface directly or by dependency injection using an `@EJB` annotation.

EJB 3.0 also changed the way persistent entities are developed, using annotations to remove the requirement to implement interfaces. In JPA, an `@Entity` annotation indicates that a Java class is a persistent entity, and additional attributes indicate the mapping of attributes to columns in the database. Clients can look up persistent entities by leveraging the JPA `EntityManager` APIs. The `EntityManager` class is used to create and remove persistent entity instances, to find entities by their primary key, and to query over entities. A persistent entity is looked up by calling a method on an `EntityManager` in Example 4.4.

```
@PersistenceContext
EntityManager em;
Account acc = em.find(Account.class, accountId);
```

**Example 4.4**

*Service-Orientation Principles and the EJB Model*

Consider the following guidelines in support of service-orientation:

- As per the Service Façade pattern, session EJBs should act as a coarse-grained service façade, and operations on the session EJB should generally reflect meaningful business use cases, such as looking up a customer's account information.

- As per the Service Statelessness principle, services should be modeled with stateless session EJBs. Each independent service operation should have a self-contained, complete transaction boundary, and a stateless session EJB operation can enforce appropriate transactional demarcation.

To illustrate this point, consider Example 4.5. An entity is implemented to represent a customer. This customer entity has a number of attributes, which are modeled as instance variables with getters and setters.

```
Integer customerNumber (primary key)
String firstname
String lastname
String title
String sex
String maritalStatus
java.util.Date birthdate
```

**Example 4.5**

Suppose Mary Smith calls to change her marital status from Miss to Mrs. With her customer number, the solution must perform the following steps:

1. Find Mary Smith's details.

2. Change her marital status.

3. Change her title.

Note the problems with carrying Steps 2 and 3 as separate service invocations. First, a stateful interaction is evident in Steps 2 and 3, which include the word "her", implying that a conversation between service consumer and service ensues. Second, multiple calls made to update each of the changing attributes indicate a fine-grained, API-like interaction.

The Service Abstraction principle states that fine-grained interfaces should be avoided, a requirement met with Java EE and JPA. A stateless session EJB can be built to expose a service operation named `updateCustomer (Customer)`, which takes an updated customer domain entity.

In contrast with previous versions of J2EE, entity beans and their wrapper data transfer objects can work directly with JPA entities and even detach them from a persistence context. In this case, after a customer entity is looked up through another service operation, such as `lookupCustomer (customerId)`, a detached customer entity is received that can then be modified and passed back to the `updateCustomer` operation. However, for more complex use cases, the use of wrapper data transfer objects can still be preferable to offer a selective view of a complex entity or even avoid exposing the underlying data model details to the service consumers.

## JMS

The Java Message Service (JMS) specification defines a set of interfaces that Java applications can use to connect to enterprise messaging systems with asynchronous messaging-based interactions. The messaging system is known as a JMS provider, and delivering one as part of every Java EE application server is mandatory. JMS interfaces are also provided by a number of independent messaging systems, such as IBM's WebSphere MQ.

JMS defines two different styles of messaging known within the specification as messaging domains. These define point-to-point and publish/subscribe models. The point-to-point model is based on the exchange of messages via queues. Sending applications or message producers connect to the messaging provider to create a JMS `message` and call `send()` to send the message to the JMS queue. We'll refer to these applications as "message producers" for the remainder of this book. Either the receiving application or message consumer can poll for messages arriving at a queue. Alternatively, a listener can be created to call user code when a message arrives at the queue, which is similar to the model used by MDBs.

JMS queue objects encapsulate the configuration parameters for a connection to a physical queue provided by the JMS provider, which acts as a route into the distributed messaging infrastructure defined within the JMS provider. Messages being forwarded to a physical queue are defined on a separate server or within a separate heterogeneous messaging infrastructure via a bridge.

The publish/subscribe model involves JMS applications registering subscriptions on particular topics represented by JMS topic destinations. Message consumers register an interest in messages on a particular topic by calling `subscribe()` on a JMS topic destination. When messages are published on this topic, performed by calling `publish()` on the corresponding JMS topic destination, each subscriber receives a copy of the message. Requests by applications to subscribe or publish a message to a topic are processed by the JMS provider's pub-sub broker. The broker is responsible for maintaining a record of subscribers to each topic and sending each publication to the appropriate subscribers.

The publish/subscribe model is well suited to situations where messages must be sent to multiple receiving applications, and/or when frequent changes to the mapping between messaging producers and messaging consumers occur. Configuration changes and having the message producer maintain knowledge of the destinations to which messages must be sent is unnecessary with the publish/subscribe model.

JMS provides for different messaging qualities of service, such as through persistent and non-persistent messages, durable and non-durable subscriptions, and by offering different options for reliable messaging. JMS can ensure messages are passed from JMS provider to application using either a transactional approach where the service supports reliable messaging or acknowledgement from the service consumer to the service.

The JMS model allows for a variety of payloads to be carried within a JMS message, each represented by a Java class inherited from `javax.jms.Message`. The JMS message types supported include:

- `TextMessage` string data

- `BytesMessage` binary data

- `ObjectMessage` a Java object (which must implement `Serializable`)

- `MapMessage` name-value pairs of primitive types identified by a `String` name

- `StreamMessage` a stream of primitive types

In addition to the message body, JMS messages also include headers carrying information beyond application data. The JMS specification defines a number of standard headers and allows user-defined headers to be included.

Beyond defining the capabilities that a messaging product must provide, the JMS specification defines the interface between the messaging provider and the Java applications. Therefore, JMS providers are not often interoperable and two heterogeneous JMS providers may not be able to be linked together. Where a messaging product supporting multiple platforms is used, JMS can provide a convenient and robust way of connecting Java applications to other non-Java systems.

Java EE 7 introduced enhancements in the revised version of the JMS specifications (release 2.0) focusing on a simplified programming model, resulting in significantly fewer lines of code required for common application tasks, such as enqueuing/ dequeuing messages.

### Message-Driven Beans

A message-driven bean is another type of EJB providing a means of exposing application logic with a JMS interface by allowing MDBs to consume messages from a JMS destination. When a message arrives at a JMS destination, the MDB container delivers the message to an MDB instance. Developing an MDB is done by implementing the `javax.jms.MessageListener` interface and invoking its `onMessage(javax.jms.Message)` method. The `onMessage` method triggers when the message delivers to the MDB.

The MDB should extract the required parameters from the JMS message and call appropriate business logic implemented in a session bean to perform the required application logic. Where supported by the JMS provider, this can be performed within the transactional scope provided by JTA so that the message can be backed out onto the JMS destination in the event of a failure.

### Security in Java EE

Service functionality should be exposed for reuse in a location-transparent and platform-independent fashion. Services must often create restricted access to only authorized service consumers. Security is of critical importance in any SOA, and Java EE provides a framework for securing Java EE components that can be leveraged when implementing services in Java EE.

Java EE provides a flexible approach to security through the Java Authentication and Authorization Service (JAAS). Resources within a Java EE application can be secured declaratively. The roles authorized to access a resource are defined in deployment descriptors. The Java EE runtime is responsible for authenticating callers and checking authorization. The granularity of Java EE security extends to individual Web resources or methods on an EJB. The application developer does not need to address security concerns through application programming. Additional work, such as restricting access to individual entity instances, is needed if greater granularity is required.

Different methods of authentication, such as basic user id, password, or certificates, are supported with pluggable authentication modules (PAMs) that the runtime is configured to use. Authorization is based on roles mapped at deployment time to users or groups defined in a user registry. Java EE provides support for different user registries used to store information, such as passwords and membership of security groups. Using an LDAP directory is a popular approach to provide a flexible and standards-compliant way of modeling complex organizational structures and associated authentication and authorization information.

Java EE provides control over the identity under which application components delegate, which is used for authenticating to external systems. In the case where Java EE server components access external systems requiring authentication, a level of indirection is provided between the application components and the external system with a JAAS authentication alias. Resources, such as data sources, are bound to an authentication alias, and the user id and password for the alias are defined at deployment time.

### SUMMARY OF KEY POINTS

- The Java SE platform provides capabilities such as remoting, database access, and directory services via a number of core APIs.

- Java EE extends the basic capabilities of Java SE with additional standards and APIs and by defining container services, which must be provided by the application server.

- The Java EE platform and specifications cover not only functional aspects but also quality-of-service considerations, such as transactionality and security.

## 4.3 XML Standards and Java APIs

This section provides brief overviews of key XML-based standards and Java APIs relevant to this book.

### XML

The Extensible Markup Language, or XML, provides a way of representing structured data in a text-based format, which includes not only a neutral data format for messages but also standards for describing message structures. As well as being one of the fundamental technologies on which Web services standards are based, XML is widely supported across numerous platforms and languages. Many industry-standard messaging formats are based on XML. For these reasons, XML is preferred to pass messages between services.

Before reviewing the Java APIs used in Java EE to work with XML messages, let's review the basics of the XML standard in Example 4.6 that illustrates how customer name and address details might be specified in XML. All XML instance documents begin with a definition.

```
<?xml version="1.0" encoding="UTF-8"?>
<customer:CustomerDetails xmlns="http://www.example.org/customer"
   xmlns:customer="http://www.example.org/customer"
   xmlns:xsi="http://www.w3.org/2001/XMLSchema-instance"
   xsi:schemaLocation="http://www.example.org/Customer.xsd">
   <Name>
     <Firstname>John</Firstname>
     <Surname>Doe</Surname>
   </Name>
   <Address addresstype="shipping">
     <Line1>1234 High St</Line1>
     <Line2>Burnaberry</Line2>
     <City>New York</City>
     <State>New York</State>
     <ZipCode>78930</ZipCode>
   </Address>
</customer:CustomerDetails>
```

**Example 4.6**

The declaration indicates that what follows is an XML document and specifies the encoding style used. UTF-8 is an encoding for Unicode characters commonly used for XML documents. The rest of the document consists of elements and attributes, which represent the data. `CustomerDetails` is the root element of the XML document shown.

Each element has a type, which can be either simple, such as a string or integer, or complex, such as a structure consisting of a number of nested elements each with its own type. Attributes, such as the `addresstype` attribute of `Address`, apply to the element on which they are specified and are always of a simple type. Both elements and attributes can be qualified by a namespace defined as a URI to avoid naming collisions between XML types defined by different organizations.

In Example 4.7, the namespace declaration:

```
xmlns:customer="http://www.example.org/customerdetails"
```

...associates a shorthand identifier prefix `customer` with the namespace `http://www.example.org/customerdetails`. The `CustomerDetails` element of this document has been namespace-qualified by prefixing it with `customer`.

The declaration:

```
xmlns="http://www.example.org/customer"
```

...on the `CustomerDetails` element defines a default namespace for all of the children of `CustomerDetails`. Unless child elements are explicitly namespace-qualified, they are assumed to belong to the default namespace.

Although a URI is used to identify namespaces, which commonly begin with an `http://` prefix, resources do not need to be available at the URI. The URI is used as an identifier, and basing the URI on an organization's registered domain name provides a way of ensuring uniqueness following a similar convention to that used for naming Java packages.

## XML Schema Definition

The XML specification includes certain rules that XML documents must follow, such as all opening tags requiring a closing tag. A document following these rules is considered well formed, and can be successfully parsed by any XML parser. XML schemas are used to specify additional constraints on the structure of an XML document based on the data represented. The schema defines, for example, the names of elements and attributes that can be included in an instance document, the order they appear in, and their possible values. A document is said to be valid if it conforms to the rules specified in its associated schema.

XML schemas themselves are specified as XML documents. The schema describing the `CustomerDetails` document is shown in Example 4.7.

```
<?xml version="1.0" encoding="UTF-8"?>
<xsd:schema xmlns:xsd="http://www.w3.org/2001/XMLSchema"
  targetNamespace="http://www.example.org/customer"
  xmlns="http://www.example.org/customer">
  <xsd:element name="State" type="xsd:string" />
  <xsd:element name="Line1" type="xsd:string" />
  <xsd:element name="Line2" type="xsd:string" />
  <xsd:element name="Surname" type="xsd:string" />
  <xsd:element name="ZipCode" type="xsd:string" />
  <xsd:element name="CustomerDetails">
    <xsd:complexType>
      <xsd:sequence>
        <xsd:element ref="Name" />
        <xsd:element ref="Address" />
```

```
        </xsd:sequence>
      </xsd:complexType>
    </xsd:element>
    <xsd:element name="Address">
      <xsd:complexType>
        <xsd:sequence>
          <xsd:element ref="Line1" />
          <xsd:element ref="Line2" />
          <xsd:element ref="City" />
          <xsd:element ref="State" />
          <xsd:element ref="ZipCode" />
        </xsd:sequence>
        <xsd:attribute name="addresstype" type="xsd:string" />
      </xsd:complexType>
    </xsd:element>
    <xsd:element name="Firstname" type="xsd:string" />
    <xsd:element name="City" type="xsd:string" />
    <xsd:element name="Name">
      <xsd:complexType>
        <xsd:sequence>
          <xsd:element ref="Firstname" />
          <xsd:element ref="Surname" />
        </xsd:sequence>
      </xsd:complexType>
    </xsd:element>
</xsd:schema>
```

**Example 4.7**

XML documents are processed by a parser, which applies the constraints defined in the XML specification itself to verify if an XML instance document is well formed. If the parser is a validating parser, the XML Schema is used to determine if the XML instance is valid as well as well formed. One validating, namespace-aware parser popular in Java circles is Xerces, an open-source project run by Apache.

> **NOTE**
>
> Prior to the emergence of XML schemas, the structure of XML documents was specified using XML DTDs. DTDs have been superseded by schemas providing a more flexible and powerful syntax for defining document structures.

## XSLT

The Extensible Stylesheet Language Transformations (XSLT) standard provides a means of transforming XML documents to other formats. Transforming an XML document to HTML to be rendered in a browser with appropriate formatting is a common example. For example, an XML document can be transformed to HTML to be rendered in a browser with appropriate formatting. To refer to different parts of an XML document, XSLT uses the XPath standard to define syntax for expressions referencing the different parts of an XML document.

The XSLT standard has several robust implementations, such as Saxon and Xalan, which provide a well-understood and widely used mechanism for specifying XML transformations.

## JAXP

The Java API for XML Processing (JAXP) provides a means of working with XML documents programmatically in Java independent of the XML parser or processor being used. Historically there were two different types of XML parser, SAX and DOM, each of which associated with a different programming model.

Simple API for XML (SAX) is an event-driven model. As an XML document is parsed, the parser invokes callback methods with user-provided implementations as each element or attribute is encountered. The application is sent the details of the XML, which include structure and data, and must decide what action to take as each part of the XML document is traversed by the parser.

SAX is stateless, and the application must keep track of the parser's current location within a document to cache any information from the XML data needed to process business logic. SAX is based on a push model in which documents are parsed in their entirety even if only part of the data is required by the application.

Document Object Model (DOM) parsers convert the entire XML document to an in-memory representation. The object representing the XML document allows applications to navigate the structure and retrieve the values of different elements and attributes.

JAXP provides support for both SAX and DOM parsers and allows XSLT transformations to be performed on XML documents. The interfaces provided can be used to access the underlying parser without using any implementation-specific APIs.

StAX provides a pull parser based on the Sun JSR 173 specification that is used in Java Web services technologies discussed in Chapter 5. The application and not the parser is in control of what part of the XML document is sent to it, as is the case for SAX. This has significant performance advantages over the memory-intensive DOM and SAX. StAX provides a pull parser that is based on the Sun JSR173 specification and used in some of the recent Java Web Services technologies discussed later in Chapter 5.

### JAXB

Manipulating XML documents with JAXP can be labor-intensive due to the complexity of the SAX and DOM APIs. The Java API for XML Binding (JAXB) is intended to provide a simpler way to work with XML by building Java classes based on the XML schemas associated with the XML document.

JAXB manages marshaling and unmarshaling between an XML document and Java objects. Default bindings are included for each of the data types defined within the XML Schema specification, although JAXB does allow these to be customized if required. Rather than working with XML APIs, the developer can ignore the conversion to and from XML documents and can focus on the generated Java objects.

#### SUMMARY OF KEY POINTS

- XML, XML Schema, and XSLT are key industry standards and common foundation technologies in SOA environments.
- JAXP and JAXB are important APIs that provide standardized interfaces for working with XML-based data.

## 4.4 Building Services with Java Components

The following section explores how services can be implemented as components using Java EE APIs and technologies. Service layers can be implemented to build services as components within each of the three distinct service layers, using the technologies and APIs available in the Java EE model.

## Components as Services

Various Java technologies can be used to build different types of services. In many instances, these technologies solve problems in areas such as orchestration, and, therefore, have relevance to certain service layers.

Java EE distributed technologies can be used to implement services in the various layers without utilizing any additional technologies, such as Web services, additional frameworks, or toolkits. Technologies introduced later in this book can help solve shortcomings or compromises highlighted in this section.

## Application Protocols

There are several common approaches to remove invocation with Java. The first approach is to use RMI in the case of POJOs or RMI/IIOP in the case of EJBs. In practice, choosing to expose POJOs using RMI offers limited quality of service. However, exposing EJBs using RMI/IIOP is a robust approach, which also offers the option of interoperability with CORBA objects.

The second approach is to provide a JMS interface, JMS is not an application protocol like HTTP, but a Java-based abstraction API over proprietary messaging engine protocols. Regardless, use of the basic JMS features of Java EE provides a basic functional implementation without a high quality of service.

With this model, the application would create a JMS `MessageConsumer` bound to a JMS destination and either call its `receive()` method to check for messages, or register a `MessageListener` that has its `onMessage` triggered when a message is received. In the Java EE model, the service would be exposed with a MDB bound to a destination.

After providing the implementation of the MDB's `onMessage(javax.jms.Message)` method, the application server's EJB container is responsible for calling when a message arrives.

On receipt of a message, the JMS wrapper or façade carries out the following steps:

1. Extract the contents of the JMS `Message`.

2. Call the service implementation (POJO or EJB) with the required input parameters.

No further steps are required for a one-way interface.

In the Java EE model, implement a servlet to provide an implementation of the doGet() and/or doPost() methods depending on which of the HTTP GET or POST methods are used.

The final approach is to expose the services using HTTP. The client will issue an HTTP request with the input message for the service and wait for the HTTP response containing the output message. On the server-side, implementing a HTTP façade is needed to receive the request and call the POJO or EJB implementation, passing it the parameters extracted from the request. For a one-way interaction, an empty response will be returned as the HTTP protocol requires.

For a request/response interaction, a response message must be constructed based on the return parameters of the POJO or EJB service implementation and returned to the waiting client as an HTTP response. In the Java EE model, implement a servlet to provide an implementation of the `doGet()` and/or `doPost()` methods depending on which of the HTTP GET or POST methods is used.

Each of these application protocols or APIs, such as JMS, has different characteristics that influence the decision on which to use when exposing service interfaces. Table 4.2 summarizes some of the key differences.

Before continuing, let's expand on the interoperability of the application protocols. First, consider RMI/IIOP, which provides interoperability with other CORBA implementations. In practice, achieving this interoperability has proven challenging due to the need to cope with the different ways CORBA providers handle security and transactions.

EJB interoperability when using RMI/IIOP between different Java EE implementations has also proven to be a source of challenges for similar reasons. Although progress has been made in this area during the lifetime of the Java EE/J2EE versions, EJBs/clients deployed in two arbitrary Java EE providers may not always interoperate.

| Characteristic | RMI/IIOP (as session EJB) | HTTP | JMS |
|---|---|---|---|
| Transactional | yes | no | depends on JMS provider |
| Firewall-Friendly | no | yes | depends on JMS provider |
| Sync/Async | sync | sync | often asynchronous depends on JMS provider |
| Interoperability | Java/CORBA only | high | depends on JMS provider |
| Contract Location | EJB specification defines | http:// URL syntax | no standard syntax use JNDI lookup or custom |
| Contract Operations | EJB specification defines | append to URL or include in message | no standard syntax JMS property or include in message |
| Contract Messages | Java objects defined by business interface | XML message defined by schema | XML message wrapped with JMS TextMessage |
| Implementation | direct exposure of EJB interface | wrap EJB with servlet façade | wrap EJB with message-driven bean façade |

**Table 4.2**
Characteristics of application protocols are listed

Looking to JMS, the degree of interoperability achieved depends on the JMS provider. Configuring external services allows communication via JMS between applications running on application servers provided by different vendors. Some messaging providers, like IBM's WebSphere MQ, provide support for additional non-Java platforms accessed using APIs other than JMS. Using these messaging providers allows interoperability with Microsoft .NET applications and other Java implementations and applications running on non-Java platforms, provided the JMS messages use an appropriate format.

## Service Contracts

The service contract must define the operations offered by the service, the input and output messages of each operation, the data types that are used in the messages, and the location of the service endpoint. A service contract can also provide additional information to a potential service consumer to judge the suitability and use of the service. These aspects are largely satisfied today with documentation written by, and intended for consumption by, humans rather than machines.

SOAP-based Web services provide a standard way of describing service operations, locations (using WSDL), and messages (SOAP). Alternatively, REST services can have the uniform interface treated as the contract or text-based special contracts, such as WADL (Web Application Description Language), in which resource representations, resource relationships, and applicable HTTP verbs for given service operations are captured in the contract.

The three aspects of the service contract are location, operations, messages, and service data representations, when building services from Java/Java EE components.

### Location

The standard way of describing the location of any Web-addressable resource is with a URI to specify the endpoint address for services exposed using any of the protocols discussed. When EJBs are exposed using RMI/IIOP, the CDI mechanism in Java EE and JNDI names facilitate obtaining a handle to the EJBs.

With a JMS interface, the service consumer must be provided with a means of sending messages to the destination to which the service is bound. Where the service consumer is a JMS client, achieve this by binding JMS-administered objects into a directory that the client retrieves with a JNDI lookup similar to retrieving an EJB home. If using JMS as a means of interoperating with non-Java clients by using a JMS provider supporting additional platforms, the details required by the client depend on the messaging product used. It is possible to specify JMS locations using URI syntax, but standards are lacking in this area and defining custom standards limits interoperability with implementations outside of direct control.

With an HTTP interface, specifying the URI of the servlet in the familiar form `http://my.host.name:<port>/context/SomeService` is necessary.

*Operations*

Following the object-oriented paradigm and features available in the Java language, the operations on the service are methods of Java classes. With a Java interface, describe the methods of the class and the input and output parameters. Where a service exposes an RMI/IIOP interface, each method of the bean implementation class is defined on the business interface of the EJB.

There is no standard way of exposing multiple operations on the JMS interface where a POJO or EJB via JMS is exposed. It is possible to create a separate destination for each operation with the JMS façade invoking the appropriate Java method based on the destination a message is received. Alternatively, use a single destination for all operations of the service, and include in the service interface a requirement that the service consumer specifies which operation it wishes to invoke in a user-defined JMS header or within the message body. The façade then extracts this property and invokes the appropriate Java method.

For HTTP, it is possible to specify the service and operation at the end of the URI. A Web container can be configured for requests to be routed to a servlet, which extracts the operation name from the URI and invokes the appropriate method on the POJO or EJB.

*Messages*

The final part of a service contract is a description of the messages supported by each service operation. The implementation of service components as POJOs or EJBs, with operations implemented as Java methods, means that the input or output parameters of the service component are Java objects or primitives. However, the format of data in these messages will depend on how the service is exposed.

When an EJB is exposed directly using RMI/IIOP, the messages act as a conduit of primitive types or, as is more common, serialized Java objects. Alternatively, passing

XML data as a Java String type, parsing the XML, and generating objects within the bean, a utility class, or façade is possible.

A range of choices remains in terms of how data is carried in the JMS messages when an API, such as JMS, is used to expose a service. Data can be transmitted in primitive forms, such as strings, streams of primitive types, raw bytes, name-value pairs, or serializable Java objects.

Where services are exposed using HTTP, different media types can be used to specify the type of data being transmitted. However, over the wire the data is shipped as a string or, in the case of attachments potentially containing binary data, MIME multipart messages. There is no standard way of mapping the media types to Java objects, but the benefits of using XML to represent the payload include the ability to:

- describe the message format in a machine-readable way using an XML schema

- use XML utility toolkits available for popular platforms and helpful in achieving interoperability with non-Java applications

- easily pass the messages in HTTP requests/responses because XML is a text-based format

For efficient representation of binary payloads, leveraging standards, such as XML Optimized Packaging (XOP) or Message Transmission Optimization Mechanism (MTOM), to capture embedded binary data in XML messages is possible. Both of these techniques are further described in Part II.

### Further Considerations

Exposing services implemented as Java components can be archived with RMI/IIOP, JMS, and HTTP. In each of these cases, various options are available for describing the service location, operations, and messages.

In the case of RMI/IIOP, the Java EE specifications provide a standard way of specifying these aspects of the service contract in the form of an EJB home or business interface. However, in order to enable a client to access an EJB, the classes required to call the EJB must be provided including generated stubs and any utility classes, such as DTOs. This tightly couples the service consumer or EJB client and service. Any changes made to the EJB's home or remote interface will generally result in having to distribute a new client JAR to service consumers.

However, in the case of JMS and HTTP, no standard way of describing the service contract exists. Custom standards must be defined, diminishing the ability to achieve interoperability with systems which have not followed the same standards, and likely resulting in a different standard for each protocol or transport.

## Components as Services and Service-Orientation

Having reviewed the available options for implementing services using basic Java EE technologies, let's consider how effectively some of the service-orientation principles can be met when implementing services as Java components.

### *Standardized Service Contract*

A service contract needs to specify the aspects of location, operations, and messages. Where services are implemented with EJBs and exposed with RMI/IIOP interfaces, these three aspects are covered by the artifacts that are created for the EJB specification. In the case of HTTP and JMS, custom specifications must be defined for the service contract. The lack of a standard service contract for JMS and HTTP services (as implemented by servlets) is inconvenient, as is the fact that no single standard covers all three of the protocols.

### *Service Loose Coupling*

In the case of EJBs and RMI/IIOP, the service consumer requires a number of specific classes for each EJB it wishes to call. These are generally delivered as an EJB client JAR containing the required classes that must be available at the time of compilation.

Making even a slight change to the EJB business interface will often break any service consumers and require recompilation, which indicates a tightly coupled implementation. However, this represents a contract-to-platform coupling because the service and the service consumer must be implemented on a common technology platform, notwithstanding the interoperability scenario between EJB services and CORBA/IIOP consumers.

In the case of JMS, the service consumer and service are loosely coupled by definitions of message structures and JMS destinations. The implementation technology of the service can change without affecting the service consumer, provided the messaging-based interface remains unchanged. Changes to the interface can also be made, provided backward compatibility with existing service consumers has been ensured, such as by adding operations or optional parameters to an operation.

Supporting backward compatibility introduces a degree of technology coupling as the message structures are linked to JMS message types and the destinations are JMS-administered objects.

A loosely coupled implementation also holds true in the case of HTTP, as a location (URI) and message format provide a reasonable level of flexibility in the possibility of making changes without affecting existing service consumers. However, use of HTTP does minimize the extent of platform and technology coupling compared with the options of using RMI/IIOP or JMS.

*Service Abstraction*

Service abstraction is determined in how the compilation is maintained while hiding the implementation details of a service. In the case of EJBs and RMI/IIOP, the interface indicates that the implementation is an EJB, although the implementation details are hidden behind the EJB remote interface. The EJB could be acting as a façade to any number of additional EJBs, Java classes, or external systems integrated using JCA, JDBC, or one of the other APIs provided by Java EE.

The same is true of JMS and HTTP interfaces, with the additional advantage that similar interfaces could be exposed with a non-Java implementation in the case where a message-oriented middleware (MOM) product with multi-platform support is used as a JMS provider.

*Service Discoverability*

For services to be discoverable, they must be described by service contracts available within a registry accessible to potential service consumers. The issues of service description and limitations imposed by the lack of widely supported standards have already been reviewed. JNDI comes closest to providing a service registry. However, this is far from an ideal solution due to a lack of interoperability and a number of other limitations.

Ideally, a service directory should include definitions of all of the services within an organization, whereas JNDI usually provides access to a namespace with the scope of a single server or a small administrative grouping of servers. For technical and organizational reasons, deploying a single enterprise-wide group of servers under common administration sharing a single namespace is not usually viable. Typically, a number of distinct, disconnected islands of servers under the control of different groups within an organization are found. If each has its own namespace, this means that multiple JNDI lookups must be performed against different naming servers with knowledge of their location/URI.

### SUMMARY OF KEY POINTS

- Services implemented as EJBs can be exposed using RMI/IIOP through JMS APIs or HTTP. Exposing services with HTTP is achieved by developing a servlet wrapper for the EJB, and a MDB wrapper with JMS.

- The input and output parameters for services implemented with base Java EE components can be passed as XML documents regardless of the transport protocols used. XML provides increased interoperability.

- Interoperability between Java EE and other heterogeneous platforms is limited using the technologies discussed so far. This is partly due to the use of standards that are not supported outside the Java world, and to the lack of widely supported standards for describing service contracts.

## 4.5  Java Vendor Platforms

This section provides an overview of some of the most popular Java EE application servers, including the open-source GlassFish application server and the commercial offerings from IBM and Oracle. As much of the functionality is dictated by the Java EE specifications, we focus on those areas differentiating the products paying particular attention to resilience, scalability, and administration.

### GlassFish Enterprise Server

GlassFish is the reference implementation of Java EE and one of the first application servers to offer a fully compliant Java EE 7 implementation. The GlassFish Open Source Server v4 is built on a modular, flexible runtime that also allows developers to build applications targeted only at a subset of the entire Java EE platform, such as the Web container. The Java EE Web Profile implementation in GlassFish v3 and v4 can be leveraged to build lightweight Web applications without requiring the full Java EE infrastructure.

However, enterprise class applications that must harness the power of advanced Java EE standards including EJB, JMS, legacy system connectivity via JCA, and various XML and Web services-related APIs, such as JAXB and JAX-WS, require the full enterprise version of GlassFish.

GlassFish configuration involves the concept of a domain, which is a logical collection of application server instances treated as one administrative unit. A Domain Administration Server (DAS), also known as the default server, is the central point of control for a single domain and all changes to the domain configuration are made through a Web-based administration console, a Web application deployed out of the box on the DAS itself.

The console also offers runtime monitoring facilities, which can be used by developers to troubleshoot problems. For administering, managing, and monitoring applications running in production, a setup through a command line interface (`asadmin`) is also offered which lends itself to scripting.

In a production setup, deploying applications on a separate set of instances controlled by the DAS is recommended. However, deploying applications on the DAS itself is sufficient for development purposes.

GlassFish 4 comes pre-installed with a messaging engine, an open-source JMS 2.0-compliant implementation named OpenMQ. GlassFish offers several deployment options for the messaging engine, including an embedded mode in which the messaging engine (message broker) runs embedded inside the application server JVM, a local mode in which the message broker process is started as a separate JVM by the application server itself, and a remote mode in which a standalone broker runs as an external process that an application server can connect to on startup.

GlassFish comes pre-installed with Project Metro, the runtime stack for the implementation of the basic and advanced SOAP-based Web services standards and associated Java Web service-related APIs, such as JAX-WS. Apart from helping developers build basic Web service applications around SOAP and WSDL, Metro also offers support for adding qualities of service to Web services in the areas of reliability, security, transactions, and policy, in compliance with the implementation of the relevant WS-* standards.

GlassFish 4 bundles another popular open-source project named Jersey, which is an implementation of the Java API for RESTful services (JAX-RS 2.0) specifications.

GlassFish is well supported by popular development IDEs, such as Eclipse and Net-Beans. Both of these IDEs allow starting and stopping GlassFish default server, deploying and un-deploying applications, and debugging applications running in the GlassFish server.

## IBM WebSphere Application Server

IBM's WebSphere brand includes a number of Java-based middleware products with WebSphere Application Server (WAS) at its core. WAS is a Java EE application server available for distributed (Linux, Unix, and Windows) and mainframe (IBM zSeries and iSeries) platforms. The 8.5.5 release provides support for Java SE 7 in addition. The codebase is common across platforms, with some differences allowing platform-specific capabilities to be utilized by the application server particularly on the mainframe.

WAS is available in various editions from an entry-level Express Edition intended for small scale use on a single server, a Network Deployment Edition allowing vertical and horizontal scaling across multiple application servers and nodes with high availability features for mission-critical applications, to a Hypervisor Edition designed to run on virtualized infrastructures important for cloud-based environments. The Liberty Profile of the WebSphere Application Server is a lightweight profile intended for Web, mobile, and OSGi applications. The Liberty Profile has a small footprint, fast startup time, and is compliant with the Java EE 6 Web Profile with the 8.5.5 release.

Additionally, WebSphere Application Server for Developers is a fully featured version of the product available for use in an application development environment free of charge, with optional chargeable support offered.

WebSphere Application Server's Naming Service is based on CORBA CosNaming, providing a distributed implementation that allows objects within a single logical cell-wide federated namespace to be looked up using the name server included with any application server within the cell. Objects can be bound into the namespace with cell, node, or server scope, which defines their visibility to applications performing JNDI lookups.

The application server supports a number of JMS providers, including a Java-based messaging infrastructure called WebSphere Default Messaging Provider. This is a high-performance messaging solution intended for production usage. It can be horizontally scaled and configured for high availability, so that messaging engines can failover to an alternative server with the contents of queues accessible. The JMS provider provides five qualities of service for messages, from best effort to assured persistent.

In order to utilize the scalability and availability features of Network Deployment Edition, servers are grouped together as part of an administrative cell, a group of nodes (physical servers) under the common control of a deployment manager. Each node can host one or more servers (J2EE application servers running in their own JVMs), with the configuration of servers in the cell controlled via the deployment manager through its Web WAS-CE is an open-source product administrative console or via a scripting interface.

All of the administrative tasks required to configure application servers and deploy/ manage applications can be performed under centralized control using the deployment manager. Flat files are used as a configuration repository, with the configuration specified as XML.

Individual servers within a cell can be grouped together in clusters, and deploying an application to a cluster allows workload to be shared between the servers (horizontal scaling). As well as scalability, clustering provides high availability for applications. An HA manager monitors resources within the application server environment, which can be configured to failover to alternative servers within a core group. This allows high availability to be achieved without the need for external HA products.

Horizontal scaling across multiple server instances can be achieved in a relatively straightforward manner for the application protocols or the abstraction APIs (HTTP, RMI/IIOP, or JMS).

In the case of HTTP, plugins are provided for a number of popular HTTP servers, allowing HTTP requests to be load balanced across a possibly clustered Web container of multiple application servers. The plugin is a Java-based filter or module that the HTTP server calls each time a request is received, passing it the URI of the resource requested.

The plugin checks to see if the request should be forwarded to an application server or left for the HTTP server to handle based on an XML configuration file generated by the deployment manager. The plugin configuration includes details of clustered servers with load-balancing policies configured, such as for simple round robin-style load balancing, or with configurable server weights to allow for scenarios where servers have unequal capacity. Should a server fail, the plugin detects the failure and stops attempting to send requests until the server has restarted. Included with the WebSphere Application Server is the IBM HTTP Server based on the Apache HTTP Server.

EJB load balancing is performed by the object request broker (ORB), and the behavior is determined by a policy configured by the application deployer. Again, round robin load balancing is the default, with optional configurable server weights. Server failures are detected and requests will not be sent to a failed server. As EJBs commonly call one another, the load-balancing behavior can be configured to "prefer-local" instances, avoiding the overhead of making a call to a remote server where possible.

JMS load balancing is achieved for incoming requests by deploying MDBs in multiple clustered application servers and binding them to a single common destination used for inbound requests. In this case, the distribution of workload between servers is determined by the rate at which each server pulls messages from the destination. Unlike the "push" model used with HTTP and EJBs using RMI/IIOP, where the proportion of the workload sent to each server is set administratively, JMS uses a "pull" model and the workload distribution is dependent on the performance of each application server and the number of MDB instances running within.

Application development tooling for the WebSphere product set is based on the popular open-source Eclipse IDE. WebSphere Developer Tools for Eclipse (WDT) is an Eclipse plugin available for free download from the Eclipse Marketplace. It provides a core set of tools for developing JEE applications for the WebSphere Application Server. Alternatively, Rational Application Developer for WebSphere Software (RAD for WebSphere) can be purchased as an integrated development environment based on the Eclipse platform and designed to offer maximum productivity when developing JEE applications for the WebSphere Application Server. RAD provides a more comprehensive set of capabilities than WDT, including test and analysis tools, and integration with the Rational Collaborative Application Lifecycle Management solution (Rational Team Concert).

## IBM WebSphere Application Server Community Edition

WebSphere Application Server Community Edition (WAS-CE) is an open-source Java EE 6 application server based on a number of well-established Apache projects (Tomcat servlet engine, Geronimo Java EE runtime, Derby database), with integration with the Eclipse IDE provided by a Web Tools Platform (WTP) plugin for WAS-CE.

All of the packages comprising the WebSphere Community Edition are available for free through the open-source community, although the additional value the IBM packaging offers to prospective users includes:

- Each release of WAS-CE combines specific releases of the constituent packages. IBM performs the integration of these releases, and the resulting combination undergoes an extensive suite of tests to ensure compatibility between the source packages and to verify the correct behavior of the product.

- Although WAS-CE is provided free of any license charge, formal product support is available for purchase as an optional service. This allows the product to be used by organizations requiring the assurance of formal, contractual support arrangements for products they deploy. Several tiers of support are available, with a range of options providing defect support and developer assistance at different service levels.

As well as providing a lightweight and low-cost entry-level application server, WAS-CE is a true open-source product that allows users access to the source code and provides them with the option of customizing the application server source code to suit their specific needs. WAS-CE includes an enterprise-messaging infrastructure based on the Apache ActiveMQ implementation, which is a JMS 1.1-compliant messaging provider. Apache OpenEJB and OpenJPA provide EJB 3.0 and JPA support respectively.

As part of the WebSphere family, WAS-CE can be administered via a Web-based administration console, via scripting interfaces, and JMX Managed Beans. Another common feature is provision for both horizontal and vertical scaling via clustering support. In addition to providing simple load-balancing capabilities to distribute workload between servers within a cluster, WAS CE uses the Web Application Distributed Infrastructure (WADI) framework to allow session state to be replicated between clustered servers, allowing failover of session state in the event of a server failure.

IBM withdrew WebSphere Application Server Community Edition from marketing in September 2013, with the WebSphere Application Server Liberty Profile offered as the strategic replacement.

**Oracle WebLogic Server**

WebLogic Server was the flagship Java application server product from BEA Systems, Inc. before they were acquired by Oracle in 2006. WebLogic is an enterprise class application server that offers a fully compliant implementation of the Java EE 6 standards.

From a QoS standpoint, WebLogic deployments can scale vertically and horizontally. In typical large-scale deployments, a clustered setup of WebLogic instances is a more common scenario. A group of WebLogic application server instances functions as a logical unit offering scalability and high availability. Instance failover options are augmented by session failover, where WebLogic server's clustering mechanism ensures session state held in the HTTP session, or in stateful session beans, is either replicated in memory across chosen peer instances or maintained in a database. In-flight transactions spanning multiple resource managers, such as databases and messaging systems, can also be recovered after server crash and a restart through a robust implementation of an XA-compliant transaction manager.

Web application deployments on WebLogic can also leverage a variety of network deployment topologies featuring a combination of Web servers, load balancers (software and hardware) and WebLogic application servers. Load balancing and failover are supported at the Web tier  and EJB tiers, although automated failover is dependent on the idempotency of the operation, which means repeating an action is guaranteed to have the same results as before regardless of the number of repetitions performed.

WebLogic administration also revolves around the concept of an administrative domain. Like GlassFish, WebLogic features a powerful administration console offering role-based access control to WebLogic administration. For example, administrators have full control over domain configuration, deployers have permission to view server configuration, and operators can view configuration and start/stop servers, whereas the monitor roles can only view server configuration. The WebLogic console also offers monitoring capabilities, although production grade troubleshooting and monitoring can be handled through the WebLogic Diagnostics Framework (WLDF) offering features around recording application performance-related information, tracking, and correlating requests through different tiers.

WebLogic JMS is a messaging engine that provides high availability and scalability through features, such as distributed destinations, where a clustered set of JMS destinations offer a logical view to the clients and handle load balancing, failover between destinations on different WebLogic server instances, and automated and manual of stored messages and transactions.

Like most application servers, WebLogic is well supported by popular IDEs, such as Eclipse and NetBeans. Various IDE plug-ins specifically targeted at WebLogic allow developers to build, deploy, and debug applications on WebLogic from their choice of IDE platform.

### SUMMARY OF KEY POINTS

- Java EE 6 and 7 specifications are implemented in both open-source and commercial application server products.

- The open-source reference implementation of Java EE 7 standards is GlassFish Open Source version 4. WebSphere Community Edition is another open-source Java EE 6 implementation.

- IBM WebSphere Application Server and Oracle WebLogic Server are the commercial application server offerings from IBM and Oracle.

# Chapter 5

# Web-Based Service Technologies

The lack of interoperability between evolving technology platforms, particularly between the Microsoft .NET and Java technology stacks, initiated the conception of the Web services standards. Interoperability between services is fundamental to an SOA, underpinning all aspects of the service-orientation paradigm. Web-based service technologies have established industry standards and conventions for realizing baseline interoperability.

---

### NOTE

The term "Web-based services" includes both SOAP and REST-style services. The terms "SOAP-based Web service" or simply "Web service" are used to refer to Web services that rely on the use of SOAP and WSDL.

---

### NOTE

This chapter provides concise introductions to the technology and syntax of SOAP-based Web services and REST services that are by no means comprehensive tutorials. If you are new to Web-based service programming, it is recommended that you study the following two series titles:

- *Web Service Contract Design & Versioning for SOA*

- *SOA with REST: Principles, Patterns & Constraints for Building Enterprise Solutions with REST*

These books teach the programming and architecture behind Web-based service technology specifically within the context of SOA and service-orientation principles.

Alternatively, if you are already experienced with the use of Web-based service technologies, you can skip this chapter entirely.

---

## 5.1 SOAP-Based Web Services

SOAP is a messaging standard specifying how data is encoded "on the wire" when passing between services. Initially defined as an acronym for "Simple Object Access Protocol," the description failed to encompass the subject matter of the standard. Therefore,

"Simple Object Access Protocol" was dropped and SOAP was retained. SOAP defines the encoding of service requests and responses as XML documents.

SOAP-based Web services rely heavily on the use of the Web Services Description Language (WSDL), which provides the means of expressing the service contract as a collection of operations with associated request/response messages. Also relevant to SOAP-based Web services, especially from a historical perspective, is the Universal Description, Discovery, and Integration (UDDI) industry standard that was originally conceived as a "Universal Business Registry" that would support the dynamic discovery of e-commerce services. A public UDDI directory was maintained jointly by IBM, Microsoft, and SAP until 2005. For our purposes, UDDI can be considered as a standard for directories storing categorized descriptions of services that can be programmatically accessed.

A Web service's capabilities are described in a WSDL definition, which defines the contract for and utilizes the functionality exposed by the service. A WSDL definition describes a service as a collection of port types or interfaces, each of which comprised of as a number of operations.

Each operation has associated input and output messages that comprise one or more "parts" of different "types." Exceptions are handled by throwing faults also defined within the WSDL document. Faults provide an abstract definition, also known as an abstract WSDL, of the service interface independent of technology concerns, such as the protocol used to invoke the service. The content of messages is specified as types, which can either be defined within the WSDL document or in a separate XML schema referenced via the XML schema `import` element.

Required to call the service, the service endpoint and transport protocol exposing the service are specified in the concrete implementation section of the WSDL using the `service` and `binding` elements. The `service` element identifies a collection of endpoints (ports) exposed with a particular binding. The `binding` element binds the service to a physical implementation, specifying data type and protocol mapping.

The following code presented in Example 5.1 employs a single port type, port, and request/response operation with messages defined in a separate schema imported and referenced within the WSDL document. Specifically, it shows the WSDL document describing the Account Enquiry service, which returns a customer's balance and available funds using the account and branch number to identify the account. The data types are indicated as XML complex types, which are defined in a separate schema referenced within the WSDL document.

```xml
<?xml version="1.0" encoding="UTF-8"?>
<definitions name="AccountDetails" targetNamespace="http://com.
  example.services.personalbanking/AccountDetails/"
  xmlns=http://schemas.xmlsoap.org/wsdl/ xmlns:wsdl="http://schemas.
  xmlsoap.org/wsdl/" xmlns:xsd="http://www.w3.org/2001/XMLSchema"
  xmlns:soap="http://schemas.xmlsoap.org/wsdl/soap/"
  xmlns:tns="http://com.example.services.personalbanking/
  AccountDetails/" xmlns:ns1="http://com.example.services.
  personalbanking/AccountDetails">
  <types>
    <xsd:schema targetNamespace="http://com.example.services.
      personalbanking/AccountDetails/" xmlns:ns1="http://com.example.
      services.personalbanking/AccountDetails">
      <xsd:import namespace="http://com.example.services.
        personalbanking/AccountDetails"
        schemaLocation="AccountDetails.xsd"/>
      <xsd:element name="AccountId" type="ns1:AccountId" />
      <xsd:element name="AccountInformation"
        type="ns1:AccountInformation" />
    </xsd:schema>
  </types>
  <message name="GetAccountInformationRequest">
    <part name="AccountId" element="tns:AccountId"/>
  </message>
  <message name="GetAccountInformationReply">
    <part name="AccountInformation" element="tns:AccountInformation"/>
  </message>
  <portType name="AccountEnquiry">
    <operation name="GetAccountInformation">
      <input name="input1"
        message="tns:GetAccountInformationRequest"/>
      <output name="output1"
        message="tns:GetAccountInformationReply"/>
    </operation>
  </portType>
  <binding name="AccountDetailsBinding" type="tns:AccountEnquiry">
    <soap:binding style="document" transport="http://schemas.xmlsoap.
      org/soap/http"/>
    <operation name="GetAccountInformation">
      <soap:operation/>
        <input name="input1">
          <soap:body use="literal" namespace="http://com.example.
            services.personalbanking/AccountDetails/"/>
        </input>
        <output name="output1">
          <soap:body use="literal" namespace="http://com.example.
            services.personalbanking/AccountDetails/"/>
```

```
        </output>
      </operation>
    </binding>
  <service name="AccountDetailsService">
    <port name="AccountDetailsPort"
      binding="tns:AccountDetailsBinding">
      <soap:address location="http://localhost:18181/
        AccountDetailsService/AccountDetailsPort"/>
    </port>
  </service>
</definitions>
```

**Example 5.1**

The data types referenced in Example 5.1 are defined in Example 5.2, which provides the XML schema definition for the Account Details service.

```
AccountDetails.xsd
<?xml version="1.0" encoding="UTF-8"?>
<schema xmlns="http://www.w3.org/2001/XMLSchema"
  targetNamespace="http://com.example.services.personalbanking/
  AccountDetails" xmlns:tns="http://com.example.services.
  personalbanking/AccountDetails" elementFormDefault="qualified">
  <complexType name="AccountId">
    <sequence>
      <element name="AccountNumber" type="string" />
      <element name="BranchNumber" type="string" />
    </sequence>
  </complexType>
  <complexType name="AccountInformation">
    <sequence>
      <element name="AccountBalance" type="float" />
      <element name="AvailableFunds" type="float" />
    </sequence>
  </complexType>
</schema>
```

**Example 5.2**

All WSDL documents have the same basic structure and contents but the details can vary. Although Examples 5.1 and 5.2 show the interface, service, and binding together in a single WSDL document, splitting them into separate interdependent documents is also possible. Some implementation tools can handle the separation of WSDL files, although not all tools deal with separate WSDL files correctly. A single document is commonly used to aid interoperability.

Under the SOAP standard, a SOAP message consists of zero or more SOAP headers followed by one SOAP body. The body contains the message data intended for the service implementation. The headers provide a means of passing service metadata, such as processing directives, targeted at the Web services runtime rather than the service implementation. A broad variety of information related to the processing of SOAP messages can be carried by the header to facilitate interoperability between services.

A sample request/response message sent to the Account Enquiry service is shown in Examples 5.3 and 5.4. The `GetAccountInformation` request is a request/response operation that exchanges messages with the service consumer.

```
<?xml version="1.0" ?>
<SOAP-ENV:Envelope xmlns:SOAP-ENV="http://schemas.xmlsoap.org/soap/
envelope/">
  <SOAP-ENV:Body>
    <ns1:AccountId xmlns:ns1="http://com.example.services.pers
      onalbanking/AccountDetails/">
      <ns1:AccountNumberxmlns:ns1="http://com.example.services
        personalbanking/AccountDetails">101049</ns1:AccountNumber>
      <ns1:BranchNumberxmlns:ns1="http://com.example.services
        personalbanking/AccountDetails">2155</ns1:BranchNumber>
    </ns1:AccountId>
  </SOAP-ENV:Body>
</SOAP-ENV:Envelope>
```

**Example 5.3**

```
<?xml version="1.0" ?>
<soapenv:Envelope xmlns:soapenv="http://schemas.xmlsoap.org/
  soap/envelope/" xmlns:xsd="http://www.w3.org/2001/XMLSchema"
  xmlns:ns1="http://com.example.services.personalbanking/
  AccountDetails" xmlns:ns2="http://com.example.services.
  personalbanking/AccountDetails/">
  <soapenv:Body>
    <ns2:AccountInformation>
      <ns1:AccountBalance>100.0</ns1:AccountBalance>
      <ns1:AvailableFunds>100.0</ns1:AvailableFunds>
    </ns2:AccountInformation>
  </soapenv:Body>
</soapenv:Envelope>
```

**Example 5.4**

The SOAP over WSDL standards allow for two different styles of SOAP messaging, known as remote procedure calls (RPC) and literal style. RPC style is based on the premise that a SOAP message is a means of invoking a remote operation. In the case of the Account Details service, the root element of the SOAP body identifies the operation invoked and contains the request/response data. The root element of the SOAP body helps the Web services environment determine the operation invoked at runtime and dispatches the message to the appropriate method of the service implementation. Alternatively, the literal or "document" style is based on a view of services exchanging documents rather than invoking remote operations.

Traditionally, Java Web Service implementations favored RPC-style Web services, and Microsoft favored document style. Document-style SOAP messages further specify an operation name as the root element of the body in the same way as an RPC-style message. For wrapped document style, messages appear the same "on the wire" as those corresponding to an RPC-style service with matching operation names. Wrapped document-style services are preferred for being highly interoperable. The inclusion of the operation name simplifies the job of the Web services runtime, which includes marshaling/unmarshaling and passing of parameters to the correct service implementation.

The WSDL document from Example 5.1 is for a document-style Web service. The `soap:binding  style="document"` identifies the service as having document style, and data types used in the messages are defined using XML schema constructs either within the WSDL document or as a separate schema imported by the WSDL definition. Defining the data types in an imported schema is known as literal encoding that is specified by the `use` attribute of the `body` element, such as `soap:body use="literal"`.

SOAP encoding is another schema defining a generalized set of data types and a mechanism which maps the data to implementation that is used by Web service runtimes. The schema emerged as part of the WSDL standard in the early days of Web services, before XML schema usage became commonplace. SOAP encoding has become unnecessary with the advent of XML schemas.

Theoretically, there are four possible combinations of style and encoding, as seen in Table 5.1. RPC-style Web services were originally used with SOAP encoding before literal encoding. While document-style Web services are only used with literal encoding, document-style SOAP encoding is uncommon. The document/literal style is supported by most vendors.

| Encoding/Style | Document | RPC |
|---|---|---|
| **SOAP Encoding** | never used | early Java Web Services, no longer used |
| **Literal (or Wrapped Literal)** | preferred for interoperability by Microsoft, Java SE/EE 5 platforms | supported by J2EE 1.3/1.4 platform, can interoperate with equivalent wrapped document-style services |

**Table 5.1**
SOAP messages have four possible combinations of encoding and style.

### Extensibility of Web Services Standards (WS-*)

Standardization enables interoperability between vendors and technology platforms. For Web services, the standards that support communication between services are pivotal in supporting interoperability between services implemented using a variety of heterogeneous platforms and technologies. However, the SOAP, WSDL, and UDDI standards fail to address non-functional or QoS requirements common in implementing any SOA, such as transactionality, reliable message delivery, and security. The Web services standards manage these non-functional QoS requirements by adopting the approach of extensibility. Building on the core Web services standards are a number of WS-* standards that each define a way of extending Web services to provide additional capabilities. WS-* standards also define a contract between service consumers and services that often involves passing information between services in a SOAP header.

The WS-* standards stack addresses a number of areas including composition management, quality of service, service description, messaging, and transport protocol. Interoperable message exchange is provided by messaging standards, such as SOAP and XML, which rely on the use of existing transport protocols for communication between services.

WS-* standards are also composable, so that one standard can utilize another to provide required capabilities. For example, WS-Addressing provides a standard way of specifying a service's address in a SOAP message. WS-Notification and WS-Eventing standards that provide publish/subscribe capabilities for Web services use WS-Addressing to specify a service's address to which publications should be sent.

The following are common examples of WS-* standards that build upon the core SOAP and WSDL standards to provide various QoS features.

*WS-Addressing*

A common requirement of Web services is the ability to pass a reference to a Web service endpoint as part of a SOAP message. For example, a service consumer must provide the return address to a service when requiring an asynchronous response to an invocation via a callback. Another example is a publish/subscribe messaging paradigm used in conjunction with Web services standards. In this case, subscribers need a way of telling the broker where to send publications.

The WS-Addressing standard provides a way of passing reference to endpoints by defining an endpoint address syntax, standard SOAP headers, and Universal Unique Identifiers (UUIDs) without any dependency on what application-level protocol or API is used, such as HTTP over SMTP (HTTP/SMTP) or the JMS. A syntax specifies the address of a Web service in sufficient detail, such as the URI, service name, port type, and other required parameters. With the endpoint address syntax, a number of SOAP headers can specify where the replies and faults are sent. A standard header specifies a UUID that can be used within a response or fault to identify the related request.

The Account Enquiry service examples in this chapter are based on calling the service using a synchronous request/response message exchange pattern (MEP). The SOAP request is made over HTTP, and the service consumer waits for the SOAP response in an HTTP response. In many cases, using this synchronous request/response MEP is not possible because the service cannot produce the response quickly enough. Using an asynchronous request/response MEP can resolve delays in response caused by the need to take complex processing, manual steps, or temporary unavailability of one of the systems. The service can accept the request and return an acknowledgement before returning the response at some later point via a callback.

If an asynchronous response pattern is used to expose the Account Enquiry service, a sample WS-Addressing header generated by a service consumer is created, as shown in Example 5.5.

```
<SOAP:Envelope xmlns:SOAP="http://www.w3.org/2003/05/soap-envelope"
   xmlns:wsa="http://schemas.xmlsoap.org/ws/2004/08/ addressing">
   <SOAP:Header>
     <wsa:MessageID>uuid:9ef7732-0039-be1f-492a-0db152f8ee3f
     </wsa:MessageID>
     <wsa:ReplyTo>
       <wsa:Address>http://personalbanking.services.example.com/
         PersonalBankingService</wsa:Address>
     </wsa:ReplyTo>
```

```
        <wsa:To>http://personalbanking.services.example.com/
          Accoun tInformationService</wsa:To>
        <wsa:Action>http://com.example.services.personalbanking/
          Ac countDetails/AccountEnquiry/input1</wsa:Action>
      </SOAP:Header>
    </SOAP:Envelope>
```

**Example 5.5**

A service consumer generates a WS-Addressing header after the Account Enquiry service is exposed.

The `MessageID` identifies the request and is copied into the associated response by the service. The service consumer uses the response address to identify the corresponding request and specify the endpoints indicating the address the response should be sent to by the service.

In order to use WS-Addressing, an endpoint must be exposed that can be referenced by a URI. The service to which the request is addressed, and the operation being invoked, are identified by the `wsa:To` and `wsa:Action` elements. The action can either be explicitly defined within the service's WSDL definition by including `wsa:Action` elements or by using a default syntax involving a concatenation of the service namespace, port type, and message name.

### SOAP with Attachments (SwA)

Web services often require SOAP messages to carry some binary data, such as an image of a scanned document. Directly embedding binary data in a SOAP message is not possible because XML language is character data. Encoding the binary as character data, such as Base64 encoding, bypasses this limitation. However, Base64 encoding inflates the size by approximately one third, which results in a performance penalty and increased CPU processing due to parsing expenses.

The first set of standards to handle attachments was SOAP with Attachments (SwA). However, SwA specifications were not universally adopted. Microsoft pursued alternative approaches, first publishing the Direct Internet Message Encapsulation (DIME) specification and then the Message Transmission Optimization Mechanism. The MTOM is based on SOAP 1.2 and described in a W3C specification.

SwA, DIME, and the MTOM use multipart MIME messages in which the SOAP message is one of the parts and includes an XML reference to an attachment contained within another part. As MIME allows binary data to be directly included as part of a multipart message, the performance issues associated with Base64 encoding of binary data are avoided. The WS-I Attachments Profile is based on SwA although the support offered by the Java Web Services platform covers both the JAX-WS and AXIS2, which support SwA and the MTOM. Therefore, the interoperable implementation of SOAP attachments can be best achieved by using the MTOM.

### WS-ReliableMessaging

The core Web services standards are extensible to handle multiple transport mechanisms. In practice, HTTP is the most common choice in contemporary Web service implementations. While HTTP has advantages in terms of broad support and interoperability, it is inherently unreliable with no guarantee of message delivery. The HTTP protocol requires a synchronous response to be returned to the sender, and the receipt of a response provides confirmation that the request was received by the endpoint. However, the absence of a response leaves the sender in doubt about the status of the interaction. It is possible that either the request had failed to reach the destination, or that it was received but the response had failed to reach the sender.

Reliable messaging is generally inapplicable where the operation invoked is read-only. However, when driving an update to some entity or initiating a business process, the outcome of an invocation must not be left in doubt.

> **NOTE**
>
> Where SOAP over HTTP (SOAP/HTTP) is used as transport for a one-way Web service, a response is still returned to the sender in the form of an HTTP response, which does not contain a SOAP message.

Achieving reliable messaging with HTTP can be resolved through careful design of idempotent service interfaces. If a response is not received after an idempotent service is invoked, the message can be safely resent multiple times without deleterious effects until a response is received.

A transport mechanism can also offer reliable messaging, such as the many messaging engines that offer a JMS interface. However, the JMS is merely an API that can hide proprietary messaging protocols without ensuring interoperability between different messaging providers. While this can be acceptable in a homogeneous environment, the JMS does not provide reliable message exchange in a heterogeneous SOA where services are implemented on a variety of platforms using different messaging transports.

As the basis for the WS-I Reliable Secure Profile, WS-ReliableMessaging implements an additional layer in the Web services stack, which provides the guarantee of reliable message delivery when an unreliable transport mechanism is used. A number of QoS options for assured delivery and elimination of duplicates are offered through WS-ReliableMessaging, as follows:

- `AtLeastOnce` delivery

- `AtMostOnce` delivery

- `ExactlyOnce` delivery

- `InOrder` delivery

The first three modes of delivery are self-explanatory, and it can be further noted that `InOrder` delivery allows groups of messages to be delivered in strict sequence. In each case, quality of service is achieved using a reliable messaging layer that sits between the SOAP stack and the service implementation. The two ends of this reliable messaging layer are called the RM source (on the sender side) and RM destination (at the receiving end). Quality of service is achieved using unique identifiers carried in a SOAP header, with communication between the RM source and destination acknowledging receipt of messages and coordinating redelivery if required. The source and destination must be stateful to know the current state of each RM interaction.

Additional QoS considerations, such as the ability to resume an interaction following the failure or restart of a service, depend on implementation details, such as how state is managed by the RM layer. WS-ReliableMessaging focuses solely on the protocol and wire format and does not cover these considerations, which are left as implementation options.

### WS-Transaction

Service composability allows existing services to be reused for new purposes and composite applications to be built by assembling services in new ways through aggregation and orchestration. However, services built in this way must ensure systems and entities updated by the services are always left in a known, consistent state, regardless of any errors that might occur during the execution of one or more services included in the composition. Maintaining transactionality is common in distributed systems design, and familiar in the domain of relational databases and messaging systems. Standards for distributed transactions, such as the Open Group's XA protocol, provide a way for transaction managers to interact with multiple resource managers and guarantee the ACID properties of distributed transactions.

The three OASIS standards, which collectively make up WS-Transaction, address the issue of transactionality with WS-Coordination, WS-AtomicTransaction, and WS-BusinessActivity. Within the context of these specifications, a coordination is either a short-lived series of service invocations or a long-lived sequence of business activities. In each case, `coordination` must be performed as an atomic set.

WS-Coordination defines a standard way for services to participate in a composition by exposing a coordination service or coordinator. The coordination service must implement activation and registration methods defined within the WS-Coordination specification. Activation allows services to participate in a new coordination by creating a new coordination context, while registration allows services to participate in an existing coordination. In addition to the interactions between services, coordinators interact using a protocol specific to the `coordination` type not defined within the WS-Coordination specification.

WS-AtomicTransaction defines a coordination protocol for short-lived transactions and provides a distributed two-phase commit protocol conceptually similar to a Web service-enabled version of XA.

For long-lived coordination, WS-BusinessActivity is useful when the two-phase commit approach of locking resources for coordination is unreasonable by defining a relatively complex set of states with well-defined transitions. The basic approach to transaction management is compensation. Services must be able to compensate or undo operations if required to restore a consistent state following a failure in another service involved in a coordination.

### WS-Security

Often, the advantages of implementing Web-based services can render them particularly susceptible to attack, such as the firewall-friendly HTTP protocol. A common requirement is to restrict access to authenticated callers, which is addressed by the OASIS WS-Security standard.

The base WS-Security specification supports authentication by defining a message model for the transmission of security tokens within SOAP messages, and allows the use of different security models and systems by supporting the use of different types of security tokens. The tokens can be either unsigned or signed, such as a token containing a user id or password pair used for basic authentication or a digital certificate signed by a trusted certificate authority. Both scenarios are supported by the Web Services Security UserName Token Profile 1.0 and Web Services Security X-509 Certificate Token Profile 1.0, which form part of the WS-Security specification set.

By allowing SOAP messages to be signed with digital signatures and encrypted to ensure confidentiality when exchanged between services, WS-Security offers a means of ensuring message integrity and privacy. WS-Security supports different mechanisms for exchanging security tokens, which can be unsigned or signed by an authority with which the service has a trust association. Achieving interoperability between heterogeneous Web service implementations requires the use of security standards supported by all implementations.

X.509 certificates and Kerberos tickets are examples of commonly used signed tokens. The WS-Security specification allows for the use of binary security tokens, such as X.509 certificates, by defining a basic mechanism for inlining Base64-encoded tokens within the SOAP security header, and by extension the use of additional encoding schemes.

The WS-I Security Basic Profile establishes requirements to achieve interoperability with WS-Security-enabled services similar to what the WS-I Basic profile achieves for general interoperability. As with the other WS-* standards that provide enhanced QoS for Web services, WS-Security allows the decisions to be implemented through configuration, keeping the service implementation free of the details of how the services are secured.

### WS-Policy

WS-Policy is a W3C recommendation that allows the behavior, requirements, and characteristics of Web services to be specified as policies using an extensible syntax. A policy is defined as a set of policy alternatives, each consisting of a group of policy assertions that describe some requirement or characteristic of a service. Policies can cover a broad variety of concerns. Some policies describe technical aspects of the service's interaction, such as exchange of security and transaction context, while others are conceptual, such as description of the service's ownership or usage policy.

WS-Policy provides a means for WSDL-described Web services to express their requirements and characteristics in a standardized manner to potential service consumers. For example, the WSDL document describing a service is retrieved at development time and examined by a designer or developer who is considering using the service. This potential user can consider information included in WS-Policy expressions when evaluating the service's suitability, and is able to ensure that any stated requirements of the service are met when developing a service consumer. WS-Policy also supports negotiation between service consumers and services at runtime, such as when the service consumer and service both declare the security mechanisms they support and agree on a mutually acceptable option before invocation.

However, WS-Policy is not useful on its own and is often connected with a number of other specifications, such as the WS-Coordination and WS-Security specifications. Policies defined using WS-Policy assertions can be grouped as policy sets, which allow combinations of behaviors to be specified with a single definition. Grouped policy sets are useful when particular combinations of policies are frequently used.

### Web Services Distributed Management

The Web Services Distributed Management (WSDM) specification from OASIS provides a standard way of managing resources within a Web services landscape. The Management Using Web Services (MUWS) WSDM specification describes the use of Web services interfaces to manage resources, which allows resources to be discovered, controlled, and queried for operational status. The Management of Web Services (MOWS) specification builds on MUWS to describe the specific scenario where the resources being managed are themselves exposed as Web services. The two specifications provide a standard means of managing services, limiting their scope to services implemented based on Web services standards.

## Common Web Services Middleware

SOA infrastructure products can provide a range of extensions to Web services-based architectures, as explored in this section. This type of middleware provides various value-added features on top of the core SOAP and WS-* stack implementations, such as mediation, service composition, orchestration, management, and monitoring.

### Enterprise Service Bus (ESB)

ESBs provide connectivity between components, mapping between incompatible interfaces, and perform processing on messages en route through the middleware infrastructure. However, the ESB emphasizes support for WSDL, SOAP, and the mature WS-* standards not included in the integration broker or MOM technologies.

ESB products differ in implementation and terminology. The service bus is a logical entity, which can span multiple geographical locations. In order to provide connectivity to a service, the ESB must first be configured to connect to the service via some kind of off-ramp or outbound port. Once the ESB has been configured to connect to a service, the service can be made accessible to any other service with a connection to the bus by exposing an interface that acts as the corresponding on-ramp or inbound port.

For example, to expose a Web service via the ESB, the ESB must act as a service consumer. To make the Web service accessible to other service consumers, the ESB then exposes an interface and provides a WSDL description for consumption by other services.

In the simplest case, for example, the inbound and outbound interfaces match. The abstract WSDL definitions are the same, and the concrete WSDLs only differ by a different endpoint address being specified. The ESB must receive a message as a proxy service via the inbound interface and call the target service via the outbound interface. No mapping between interfaces is required.

Connecting services via an ESB, instead of connecting them directly, means that logic can be encapsulated within the bus and processing can be performed on messages en route between services. Mediations can be used for many different purposes, and some common use-case scenarios include:

- transforming the message in some way, such as mapping between different XML schemas

- performing protocol translation, such as SOAP/HTTP to SOAP over JMS (SOAP/JMS)

- dynamically routing the message to one of a number of endpoints, such as those based on the availability of target service instances

- throttling to restrict the load on target services, and prioritizing requests

- logging, auditing, and management of the service runtime environment

- providing security capabilities for incoming and outgoing messages, including authentication, authorization, encryption, and digital signing

Chapter 12 is dedicated to exploring the ESB as a means of adding middleware for Java-based service-oriented technology architectures.

*Orchestration*

Implementing a business process within an SOA involves modeling the process and then mapping the tasks within the process to services. For each task, the service inventory is examined to identify existing candidate services, and a new service is defined and implemented where no suitable service exists. As the service inventory grows, with careful design for reuse, an increasing number of business processes can be realized by orchestrating existing services from the service inventory.

Constructing coarse-grained composite services is possible by aggregating atomic services with finer-grained composite services. Business processes often consist of specific steps or tasks executed by an automated process or human interaction in a well-defined, predictable fashion.

Implementing a business process using the Java EE stack can be achieved by writing Java code to control the execution of steps. However, the process model is then encapsulated in complicated Java code. Realizing the model requires Java development skills beyond a typical business analyst's capabilities, and requires interpretation by the Java developer implementing the process. Instead, business processes can be specified in a declarative fashion to avoid Java development. The model can be interpreted by an orchestration engine and used to control the execution of the process. WS-BPEL provides a means of specifying the orchestration of WSDL-described Web services in long- and short-running processes. Executable models are fundamental to the WS-BPEL standard.

The Java EE specification does not include support for WS-BPEL or any comparable standard. However, the orchestration of services is a fundamental aspect of SOA, and WS-BPEL support is included as an option in most Java-based SOA infrastructure implementations and in the Microsoft platform.

Business processes commonly include a mixture of automated (machine) and manual (human) steps. In each case, the task can be modeled as a step that accepts one or more inputs and returns zero or more outputs. When implemented as an automated task, the process calls a service with a matching interface. In the case of a human task, the process pauses at this point and places an item on a work list, waiting for an appropriate person to claim and complete the task. Manual steps are completed via a user-interface, which displays the task's input parameters and waits for users to provide the required output parameters in order to complete the task and continue the process.

Processes can be constructed with a mixture of manual and automated tasks and even require the ability to change implementation between the two styles as part of process change and optimization. Most Java vendors provide extensions to WS-BPEL, which provide support for manual tasks within processes. Manual tasks in some vendor implementations are described with a WSDL interface in the same way as Web services included within a process.

Beyond a lack of support for manual tasks, WS-BPEL is unable to specify whether processes and subprocesses are short-lived or long-lived. In the case where processes are long-lived and steps within the process cannot be completed within seconds, having the process container hold the process state in-memory is unreasonable. The process container must instead persist the state of a process instance at the end of each step, such that it can be retrieved when some input is received to progress the process instance.

It is possible to treat all process instances as long-lived. However, holding process state in-memory can significantly impede performance. This limitation is again resolved with vendor-specific extensions to WS-BPEL, which allow process state in the process container to be specified by the designer as in-memory or persistent. Despite the challenges, WS-BPEL is the dominant standard for the orchestration of services in an SOA. Unlike other standards which allow the specification of processes in an abstract, high-level fashion, WS-BPEL processes include low-level implementation details, such as WSDL interface specifications, so that processes are executable.

WS-BPEL provides the following capabilities:

- composition of services into long and short-running processes, which can themselves be exposed as services

- specification of process logic in a model, which can be viewed graphically instead of as Java code

- management of process state, which includes the ability to record and monitor the state of process instances through deployment into a process engine

WS-BPEL plays an integral role in modern BPM, optimization, and reengineering, which involves a modeling approach to automating business processes using an orchestration engine. Through a combination of process execution simulation and monitoring, process logic and flows can be continuously adjusted to optimize process efficiency.

*Management and Monitoring*

Monitoring services in an SOA to ensure that they satisfy response time, availability, and other non-functional requirements can be more difficult than monitoring systems and components in a traditional distributed architecture. Service monitoring is relatively straightforward in the case of atomic services. However, other types of services, such as composite services and legacy wrapper services, have operational dependencies on other services, components, or systems.

In the case of a monolithic system running on a mainframe, monitoring the availability of the system is a question of monitoring the availability of the operating system and processes on which the system depends. In the case of a service in an SOA, the service might depend on other functionality implemented with a number of technologies and deployed across multiple servers. In operation, knowing which services are affected when a server crashes, or which component is responsible for the degraded response times achieved by a particular service, is necessary. Taking action when a fault has occurred can be required, perhaps by rerouting to another instance of the service in a different data center or by rejecting low-priority requests.

*Registries and Repositories*

During the early years, adoption of service registries proved more popular as a tool for use at design-time and development-time. One common example was for a registry to be shared between development teams, and for developers to search the directory's service inventory for services that might be reused as part of the development at hand. The WSDL definitions for any suitable services can then be imported and used to generate client or proxy classes.

The role of the service registry within an SOA has since expanded. If considering all of the aspects of the service lifecycle, information about a service is required for many different purposes, such as:

- during design-time to search for existing services suitable for reuse

- during development to retrieve service definitions (WSDLs)

- before deployment by providing input to reviews to satisfy governance requirements

- following deployment to support configuration of service monitoring and management infrastructure

- at runtime to support endpoint selection by an ESB or service consumer

- to track dependencies between services, for example to support impact analysis

Accessing information in any of these scenarios requires access to service metadata that can be stored on a single registry rather than distributed across multiple stores, which then require synchronization.

A number of vendors have adopted the expanded role of a registry, and responded by developing registry/repository products to satisfy a wide variety of use cases. Many of these products provide some level of UDDI support, with many proprietary and non-standards-based features. To support SOA governance, most of these vendor registries include a well-defined model of the service lifecycle. Workflow features support controlled transition between the states of the lifecycle by corresponding governance actions, such as moving a service from "ready for review" to "ready for release" by completing a review task.

*Service Construction and Assembly*

SOA aims to deliver services that can be utilized in the construction of composite applications. One example of composition is the orchestration of services within a business process. The tools and specifications of BPM allow processes to be modeled as a series of tasks, with each of the tasks bound to an underlying service implementation. Within early WS-BPEL implementations, the service binding is achieved with static configuration and the task is bound to a specified WSDL operation.

Vendors and analysts have gradually shifted their focus towards more dynamic styles of composition which support the agility demanded by rapidly changing business environments.

---

| NOTE |
| --- |
| More information about any of the aforementioned Web services industry standards and specifications can be found at www.servicetechspecs.com. |

---

**SUMMARY OF KEY POINTS**

---

- The first-generation Web services industry standards are SOAP, WSDL and, to a lesser extent, UDDI.

- WS-* standards build upon first-generation standards to add various QoS features that operate in different layers of a Web services architecture.

- Many WS-* standards rely on the use of SOAP headers to carry context between the two ends of a Web service interaction.

- Service infrastructure platforms span a wide range of capabilities, such as service mediation, orchestration, service assembly, runtime management, and monitoring.

---

## 5.2 REST Services

In this section, we briefly explore REST service design by highlighting some of the key technology and programming considerations.

---
**NOTE**

For an in-depth exploration of REST service design and the convergence of REST constraints and service-orientation principles, see the series title *SOA with REST: Principles, Patterns & Constraints for Building Enterprise Solutions with REST*. If you are building services for a service-oriented architecture using REST, it is highly recommended that you read this book. Note also that the REST design constraints referenced in this chapter are covered in this book and are also described at www.whatisrest.com.

---

A REST service is required to expose resources that include:

- one or more representations, either expected or provided

- an address to uniquely locate the resource

- a set of HTTP methods exposed at the interface level

- metadata carried in headers for requirements, such as security tokens or caching information

The service definition or service contract details the specific attributes for the service. For example, let's look at a REST service that retrieves a customer list and the details of an individual customer. In order to define the Customer Listing service using REST, we need to address the following questions:

- What is the root resource and address for accessing this service?

- Once the service consumer accesses this address, what attributes of a customer will be shown as part of the customer listing?

- How will service consumers retrieve details of an individual customer from a list of customers?

- What is the representation of the customer details?

- Will there be links to related resources, such as an account?

- Can the service consumer update or create new customers?

- What security credentials and other attributes are required by the service in order to provide the customer information to the service consumer?

### HTTP Response Codes

In a REST-based service interaction, standard HTTP methods (GET, PUT, POST, DELETE, HEAD, and OPTIONS) are used together with HTTP response codes to establish a communications framework based on a uniform contract that can invoke service capabilities and communicate success, failure, and error conditions.

A typical response code is captured in the first line of the HTTP response, with a number and corresponding self-explanatory description string. There can be additional details in the response body sent by the service. Most response codes have accompanying metadata in pre-defined HTTP headers essential for service consumers to make further decisions. For the discussion of this chapter and general industry use, service consumers often base their decisions on the response code along with the HTTP headers.

The key response codes based on the HTTP standard are as follows:

- *200 ("OK")* – The request was successful.

- *201 ("Created")* – The resource has been successfully created.

- *206 ("Partial Content")* – The server has fulfilled a partial GET request for the resource.

- *301 ("Moved Permanently")* – The requested resource has moved to a different location, and should include the updated location of the resource in the Location header field.

- *302 ("Found")* – The client must perform a temporary redirection (the Location header is used to point to the URI of the resource).

- *303 ("See Other")* – The response to the request can be found using another URI with a GET method (the 303 response must not be cached, but the response to the redirected request may be cacheable).

- *400 ("Bad Request")* – A service consumer-side error occurred in the invocation of the service request.

- *401 ("Unauthorized")* – The service consumer lacks the necessary authentication credential to make the request.

- *403 ("Forbidden")* – The service consumer has supplied all relevant information (well-formed request and any authentication credentials), but the server refuses to fulfill the request.

- *404 ("Not Found")* – The requested resource is not found.

- *409 ("Conflict")* – The request cannot be completed due to a conflict with the current state of the resource.

- *415 ("Unsupported Media Type")* – A representation of the request that is not supported by the service is sent.

- *500 ("Internal Server Error")* – The server encountered an unexpected condition and was unable to fulfill the request.

- *501 ("Not Implemented")* – The server does not support the functionality required to fulfill the request.

**Resources and Addresses**

A top-level address in the form of a URL is needed to expose the service. The concrete URL is of lesser importance than the context path to the service. With that in mind, a context for listing customers must be exposed. At the top level, the list of customers can be serviced by a choice of a resource, the collection of customers, and an associated URL, such as `http://server/services/customers`.

However, the individual details of a customer cannot be retrieved without navigation to a child resource of the collection of customers, an individual customer entity. In REST-based service design, containment relationships are represented by path parameters with a URL of the form, `/parent/{child-identifier}`. An individual customer resource can be retrieved at the URL `http://server/services/customers/1234`.

Assuming the resource representation is in XML (MIME type is `application/xml`), the service requests and responses are illustrated in Example 5.6.

*Service Request*

```
GET services/customers HTTP/1.1
Host: server
```

*Service Response*

```
HTTP/1.1 200 OK
Content-Type: application/xml;charset=UTF-8
<customers xmlns:atom="http://www.w3.org/2005/Atom">
  <atom:link rel="self" ref="http://server/services/customers/">
  <customer>
    <id>1234</id>
  <atom:linkrel="self" href="http://server/services/customers/12 34"/>
  <name>Jack Daniel</name>
  </customer>
  <customer>
    ...
  </customer>
</customers>
```

**Example 5.6**

The Customer Details service returns the request and response in Example 5.7.

*Service Request*

```
GET services/customers/1234 HTTP/1.1
Host: server
```

*Service Response*

```
HTTP/1.1 200 OK
Content-Type: application/xml;charset=UTF-8
<customer xmlns:atom="http://www.w3.org/2005/Atom">
```

```
     <id>1234</id>
     <atom:link rel="self"href=http://server/services/customers/123 4/>
     <first-name>Jack</first-name>
     <last-name>Daniels</last-name>
     <e-mail>jdaniels@jdaniels.org</e-mail>
     <phone>999-999-9999</phone>
        ...
</customer>
```

**Example 5.7**

Each of the resources, including the collection, has a `link` identifier element pointing to a `href` address attribute where this resource can be located. All of these elements and attributes are defined in the Atom Syndication Format specification, which is a standard method of describing Web feeds.

Retrieving a collection of resources, the details of an individual member resource in the collection, representation format, and resource content's carrying levels of details occur with a containment hierarchy via the customer id path parameter. Navigating to a related resource enforces the hypermedia constraint.

Example 5.8 shows how to retrieve account information for a customer.

```
<customer xmlns:atom="http://www.w3.org/2005/Atom">
   <id>1234</id>
   <atom:link rel="self"href=http://server/services/
   customers/1234/>
   ...
   <accounts>
     <account>
       <id>c1234-001</id>
       <atom:link rel="account"
         href=http://server/services/accounts/c1234-001/>
       <typecode>CHK</typecode>
       <currency>USD</currency>
       <balance>5000</balance>
       ...
     </account>
     <account>
       ...
     </account>
   </accounts>
</customer>
```

**Example 5.8**

The `<link>` element guides the service consumer of the root resource, such as the `customer`, to a related resource, such as an `account`, through an embedded hyperlink, such as `http://server/services/accounts/c1234-001`. The service consumer requires no extra information, as the application state is transitioned from representing a customer's information to related account information via hypermedia.

The semantics of the link relation are described by a link relation extension, such as the attribute value of `rel`, indicating that this relation describes an associated account. Other than the semantics shared beforehand, the service consumer does not need to know all the resources and their addresses, as these can be discovered through links embedded in resources.

Link relation is the basis of the hypermedia constraint. In a well-designed REST-based system, link relation can be a powerful technique that highlights the importance of exposing a well-known URL as a root resource to service consumers and letting them discover the related resources through embedded links. Decreased coupling accompanies this approach, as the service consumer needs to know less about the service.

Making the URLs informative and neutral is a design decision. Depending on the nature of the service consumer, keeping the URLs understandable to humans is always useful. Traditional Web URLs end in HTML or WML. Although it is good practice to denote the type or representation of the resource being accessed on the Web, doing so may not make sense in a REST-based service design. Therefore, if an XML and HTML representation of the same resource must be provided, the URI for a customer listing is morphed to two specific URLs with extensions, as shown in Example 5.9.

```
http://server/services/customers/xml
http://server/services/customers/html
```

**Example 5.9**

Although URLs convey the meaning, there are better ways of representing and requesting the different representations of the resources. For machine-processable REST services, URIs should be kept neutral, informative, and readable.

## HTTP Methods

Now with the service URLs defined, the HTTP methods needed to realize the requirement of viewing a customer listing can be explored. Let's first review the various HTTP methods and their intended use within a REST service. Each of these methods has valid responses based on various conditions.

This section will only highlight the most prominent HTTP methods as follows:

- GET is solely used to view and read resources. The service consumer can call the GET method any number of times on the resource using the URL and receive the same result in return. In other words, GET is side effect-free and idempotent. The response, such as 200 OK, to a GET request from a service consumer is well defined by the HTTP specification.

- DELETE is used to delete the resource, can be called once, and is idempotent but not side effect-free. Nothing happens when the caller invokes the DELETE method on an already deleted resource.

- HEAD is a lighter version of GET, which is used to check on the availability of a resource. The HTTP GET method returns only the response headers and not the actual content of the resource. The HEAD method can be invoked to see if a resource is found at a given URL. If the response is 200 OK, then a GET can be issued to access the resource. HEAD, like GET, is side effect-free and idempotent.

- PUT is traditionally used to update resources. Using this method, the service consumer sends in the entity representation to a known endpoint to update the resource. Repeating PUT simply updates the same resource with the same entity details, as it is idempotent but not side effect-free. In some rare situations, PUT can also be used to create resources when the client knows the URI of the resource to be created.

- POST is a versatile method that is causing some confusion in REST and Web discourse. Most developers are familiar with POST from HTML form submissions and SOAP/HTTP communications. In reality, this method can be used to create resources or perform operations that cannot be easily handled via the other verbs. The usage is based on the context of service and the desired functionality. POST is neither side effect-free nor idempotent.

- OPTIONS provide a mechanism for the caller or service consumer to perform simple access control checks.

The properties of idempotency and safety, as implied by side effect-free, are key design considerations for REST services determining reliability and other qualities of service, such as efficient performance. Two other auxiliary methods, known as TRACE and CONNECT, can be ignored in this discussion of REST services for simplicity.

The HTTP method can be used to identify what methods the service must support to realize the use case of listing customers. Listing the details of a particular customer using `services/customers/{id}` is a view operation exposing GET, HEAD, and OPTIONS methods. Sending a GET request to the URL will return the customer details, sending a HEAD request will return a valid response consisting of only the headers without the actual response body, and sending an OPTIONS request will show that only GET and HEAD are allowed for all users.

### Resource Representations

After defining resource methods, the representation of the request and response to the service can be reviewed. Using XML schemas is a standard approach for representing a resource. The REST service requests and responds to XML payloads that conform to a prescribed XML schema. However, for Web applications implemented in JavaScript via AJAX (JavaScript/AJAX), representing the resource in JavaScript Object Notation (JSON) can be considered an alternative. JSON describes the data in a name-value format.

```
{
  customer:
    {
      name:"John Smith",
      e-mail:"jsmith@example.org",
      phones: [
        {"home":"444-444-4444"},
        {"work":"555-555-5555"}
      ]
    }
}
```

**Example 5.10**

In Example 5.10, the `customer` is a container of various name-value pairs of attributes including an array of phone numbers. The content type is `application/json`, similar to `application/xml` or `text/xml` for the XML representation. When using HTTP functionality with a REST framework, the JSON format is also commonly supported. A Web application consuming this service from a browser can process the response with little overhead, as these are simply messages that happen to be another JavaScript object. JSON can yield a multitude of useful representations, such as an XHTML representation, for a more conventional Web-based service consumer.

An XML representation can be used with standardized Atom `<link>` elements to identify self-describing resources via the embedded URIs that facilitate navigability from one resource to another. JSON has no formal concept of hyperlinks, but a convention can be followed to embed a URI as a text value of a custom property. The service consumer must know about this `custom` element for resource navigation beforehand, which introduces a degree of coupling that is not applicable for a standards-based, Atomaware client.

The information requested can be encoded in a URL or URI. A design decision must be made as to when to use content representation as part of the request/response, and when to keep the information as part of the URI. In general, the HTTP methods and flexibility required by the service consumer will determine whether the information will be encoded in the URI or in the body of the request.

Recall the steps taken to request a specific customer by extending the initial service URI to have `cust_id` as a parameter. These were read-only resources (using the GET method) with no use in having a content body. Alternatively, SOAP-based services can use the request body to send the information with the POST method. The customer ID can be encoded in simple XML and used in the request to indicate which customer is requested.

## The ACCEPT Header

Some standard HTTP headers required by the HTTP specifications can be extended to provide custom HTTP headers. While maintaining standards for scalability and interoperability is preferable, specific cases can warrant extending and creating custom HTTP headers between services and service consumers to address non-functional requirements. This section introduces the `Accept` header, which connects the REST service design concepts with the service-orientation design principles.

The `Accept` header is used by the service consumer in the request to indicate the desired content expected in the response from the service. The value used in the `Accept` header is any one of the content type values from the HTTP specification. The `Accept` header can be set to the values seen in Example 5.11 if the service consumer requires a JSON or XML representation of the content, maintaining the simplicity of the URIs while locating metadata into the HTTP headers.

```
Accept: application/xml
Accept: application/json
```

**Example 5.11**

Example 5.11 can be applied to the Customer resource listing from Example 5.8. The first request is a GET request to the `/customers` URI, with the `Accept` header set to XML. The response the service consumer receives is a list of customers. The following request is a GET request for the customer with id `c1234` at the URI `/customers/c234`, with the `Accept` header set to XML. The information returned is an XML representation of the customer.

When the Customer resource is requested via a GET invocation with an `Accept` header indicating a JSON representation of the resource, the service must return a JSON representation of the customer information. When an attempt is made to DELETE the customer concerned, the server responds with response code 405, indicating the operation is not allowed in this context.

> **NOTE**
>
> For access to industry standards and specifications relevant to REST, visit www.servicetechspecs.com.

## SUMMARY OF KEY POINTS

- REST services can inherit a uniform contract with standard operational methods (such as GET, PUT, POST, HEAD, and DELETE).

- HTTP response codes are vital to maintaining a standard mechanism for informing service consumers about the nature of their requests.

- Custom and standard HTTP headers allow for the annotation of additional information, such as information that expresses security and content type characteristics.

# Chapter 6

# Building Web-Based Services with Java

JAX-WS and JAX-RS represent, by far, the most common implementation mediums for services as part of contemporary Java-based service-oriented technology architectures. This chapter is dedicated to exploring the technology behind these industry standards and further highlighting related and relevant Java-based technology advancements.

## 6.1 JAX-WS

SOAP-based Web services support in Java EE 5, 6, and 7 is based on the Java API for XML Web Services (JAX-WS) standard, which is an evolution of the Java API for XML-based RPC (JAX-RPC) standard from the previous versions of Java EE. In keeping with the contract-first service approach advocated by SOA, SOAP-based Web services are described by WSDL. Top-down service development starts from the WSDL to the generated service implementation. JAX-WS must process WSDL and generate Java artifacts that developers can work with. Conversely, bottom-up development creates a Web service and WSDL service description from an existing artifact, such as a Java class.

Bottom-up development is facilitated by many tools to enable the creation of Web services with a few clicks of a button, and early implementations emphasized this aspect of Web service development. However, the tools often provide insufficient control over the artifacts generated, and not all language-specific types map well to XML schema-type definitions. In such cases, bottom-up development can create an undesirable coupling between the service contract and an implementation technology. While many tools provide the option of working in either direction, top-down or bottom-up, using a contract-first service development approach can prevent any implementation technology-specific dependencies.

JAX-WS supports the following:

- SOAP 1.1, SOAP 1.2, WSDL 1.1, and WSDL 2.0

- compliance with WS-I Basic Profile 1.1, which precludes the use of any encoding other than literal (JAX-WS only supports literal encoding)

- asynchronous invocation provided by the service consumer programming model, which supports both polling and callback

- dynamic client- and dynamic server-side programming models

- MTOM, which has replaced SwA as the interoperable standard for handling attachments to SOAP messages

- use of JAXB for all type mapping, which is simpler than the mapping approach taken by JAX-RPC, with support for greater schema constructs

JAX-WS utilizes annotations to simplify the programming model, using an approach similar to EJB 3.0. Annotations remove the need for complex deployment descriptors. JAX-WS also simplifies XML-to-Java binding by delegating the data marshaling/ unmarshaling to JAXB. JAX-WS-based code generation maps WSDL portTypes to a Java interface called the service endpoint interface (SEI). Recall that portTypes are renamed interfaces in WSDL 2.0. SEI provides a Java abstraction of the service, which removes the need to manage the details of SOAP messages and leaves the service developer free to focus on service implementation.

Within SEI, WSDL operations are mapped to Java methods. Faults are mapped to Java exceptions, which inherit from `javax.xml.ws.soap.SOAPFaultException`. WSDL `service` elements are mapped to a service class. SEI is used in service implementations and service consumer implementations in JAX-WS. For service implementations, JAX-WS provides static and dynamic programming models.

With the static model, a SEI is generated at development time, which can be accomplished using a wsimport tool within many JAX-WS implementations. Using the top-down approach, the SEI is generated by specifying the location of a WSDL file as a parameter to wsimport. The service developer is left to provide the implementation of the SEI.

With the JAX-WS dynamic programming model, instead of implementing an SEI that relates to a specific WSDL, the service developer implements the generic `javax.xml. ws.Provider` interface. This requires greater development effort than the static implementation method. The developer must deal directly with the XML payload, including working out which operation has been called. However, dynamic programming allows the developer to avoid situations where the complexities of some XML schema constructs may not be satisfactorily handled by a data binding framework, such as JAXB. The developer can choose to handle the entire protocol message (the SOAP envelope) or just the message payload (the SOAP body).

The static and dynamic programming models offered by JAX-WS also benefit Web service consumers. With the static model, a proxy class is generated from the SEI. The service consumer calls Web service operations by invoking methods on the proxy. This has similar advantages to the static service model in providing a simple Java-centric abstraction of the service and shielding the developer from the details of the SOAP message. The proxy is created by calling the `getPort()` method of the `Service` class generated at build-time from the WSDL using wsimport or a similar tool.

The dynamic client or dispatch client model uses `javax.xml.ws.Dispatch`, which requires no SEI or WSDL. The invocation is performed by building the relevant objects dynamically using methods that accept qualified names as parameters. The generic `javax.xml.ws.Service` class acts as the factory for dispatch-based service consumers, and offers several overloaded `createDispatch` methods to return appropriate dispatch instances for the caller. The dispatch-based service consumer has a more labor-intensive programming model than the static alternative and exposes the developer to the details of SOAP messages. However, the dynamic model offers a more flexible, albeit complex, option of bypassing the XML-to-Java mapping, which is preferable in situations involving extremely complex mapping requirements that cannot be completely addressed by frameworks, such as JAXB.

Beyond service implementation and development, JAX-WS employs annotations to call Java Web services from a Java EE application. With JAX-RPC, calling a J2EE Web service from Java code running on the application server or in a client container is achieved via a resource reference or by performing a JNDI lookup. In the JAX-WS implementation of Java EE, resource injection uses a `@WebServiceRef` annotation within the Web service consumer. The annotation tells the container to look up the referenced resource and inject it into the annotated instance variable. The Java platform defines a rich set of annotations which allow a degree of control when developing Web services.

Annotations are covered by a number of Java Specification Requests (JSRs). JSR 181 (Web Services Metadata) defines annotations that allow control over the various elements defined in the WSDL, such as the names of portTypes, operations, and namespaces used. JSR 224 (JAX-WS) annotations are specific to JAX-WS, and allow control over artifacts generated for JAX-WS Web services, including specification of bindings, request/ response wrappers, faults, and handlers. JSR 222 (JAXB) annotations are specific to JAXB classes generated for data binding of Java Web Services. Finally, JSR 250 (Common Annotations) defines a number of annotations used to control resource injection, of which JAX-WS makes use for resource injection.

The Java Web Services platform keeps the implementation of services separate from the runtime requirements, such as security and transactionality, which are defined at deployment or assembly time through deployment descriptors without changing the code that provides the service implementation. JAX-WS is used to support top-down development, when a tool like wsimport is used to generate the SEI from the WSDL document. Wsimport also generates the JAXB implementation classes mapped from various WSDL constructs. A dynamic proxy or `javax.xml.ws.Dispatch`-based service consumer can use JAXB implementation classes or a raw XML payload-based message to invoke the service. On the server side, a statically generated SEI implementation or `javax.xml.ws.Provider`-based service implementation can handle JAXB implementation classes or a raw XML-based payload that represents the incoming message.

## SAAJ

The SOAP with Attachments API for Java (SAAJ) operates at a lower level than JAX-WS and offers APIs for managing SOAP messages with or without attachments. SAAJ uses a DOM-based model targeted specifically at SOAP, instead of generic XML messages. SAAJ has evolved from SOAP attachment management to be useful in scenarios where attachments are not involved, such as when a dynamic client is used and no stubs are available or when navigating the tree of a SOAP message directly is a requirement. The classes required to manipulate SOAP messages using SAAJ are included in the `javax.xml.soap` package.

SAAJ does allow SOAP messages to be sent to a service using the `SOAPConnection` class, but is more commonly used for the actual manipulation of SOAP messages themselves. Message transport is left to JAX-WS. The JAX-WS specification uses SAAJ 1.3, which has improved upon SAAJ 1.2 with added support for SOAP 1.2 messages. Example 6.1 illustrates the code required to implement an Account Enquiry service. The JAX-WS `@WebService` annotation allows the service name, port name, and other names for the service to be defined to match the names defined in the service WSDL. The service is implemented as a stateless session EJB, which requires the addition of the `@Stateless` annotation.

```
package com.novobank.services.personalbanking;

// imports required to allow use of @WebService and @Stateless
  annotations
import javax.ejb.Stateless;
import javax.jws.WebService;
// import JAXB binding classes (included in sample code for chapter)
import personalbanking.services.novobank.com.accountdetails.
  AccountEnquiry;
```

```
import personalbanking.services.novobank.com.accountdetails.
  AccountInformation;

@WebService(serviceName = "AccountDetailsService",
  portName = "AccountDetailsPort",
  endpointInterface = "personalbanking.services.novobank.com.
  accountdetails.AccountEnquiry",
  targetNamespace = "http://com.novobank.services.personalbanking/
  AccountDetails/", wsdlLocation = "META-INF/wsdl/AccountDetails/
  AccountDetails.wsdl")

// Deploy service endpoint as a stateless session EJB
@Stateless
public class AccountDetails implements AccountEnquiry {
  public AccountInformation getAccountInformation(AccountIdaccountId)
  {
    AccountInformation info = lookupAccount(accountId.
      getAccountNumber());
      return info;
  }

  public AccountInformationlookupAccount(String accNo){
    AccountInformation info = new AccountInformation();
    // placeholder for business logic to retrieve account info
    return info;
  }
}
```

**Example 6.1**

Implementing a JAX-WS service requires a few lines of code in the WSDL, as highlighted
in Example 6.1. Developing a service consumer using JAX-WS is just as straightforward.
Example 6.2 shows the code required to call the Account Enquiry service using a JAX-
WS dynamic proxy generated from the service WSDL with an IDE.

```
import com.novobank.services.personalbanking.client.AccountId;
...
AccountId id = new AccountId();
id.setAccountNumber(accId);
id.setBranchNumber(brNumber);
AccountDetailsService service = new AccountDetailsService();
AccountEnquiry port = service.getAccountDetailsPort();
AccountInformation result = port.getAccountInformation(id);
float balance = result.getAccountBalance();
```

```
float available = result.getAvailableFunds();
...
```

---

**Example 6.2**

Calling the service with a JAX-WS Dispatch service consumer, as seen in Example 6.3, requires greater development effort and more lines of code. The SAAJ API manipulates the SOAP request/response directly.

```
import javax.xml.namespace.QName;
import javax.xml.soap.MessageFactory;
import javax.xml.soap.SOAPBody;
import javax.xml.soap.SOAPBodyElement;
import javax.xml.soap.SOAPElement;
import javax.xml.soap.SOAPMessage;
import javax.xml.ws.BindingProvider;
import javax.xml.ws.Dispatch;
import javax.xml.ws.Service;
import javax.xml.ws.soap.SOAPBinding;
import org.w3c.dom.Node;
...
public static final String SERVICE_URI="http://com.novobank.services.
  personalbanking/AccountDetails";
public static final String SERVICE_NAME = "AccountDetailsService";

QNameserviceName = new QName(SERVICE_URI,SERVICE_NAME);

QNameportName = new QName(SERVICE_URI, "AccountEnquiry");

String  endpointAddress =  "http://localhost:8090/
  AccountDetailsService/AccountDetails";
Service service = Service.create(serviceName);
service.addPort(portName, SOAPBinding.SOAP11HTTP_BINDING,
  endpointAddress);
Dispatch<SOAPMessage> dispatch = service.createDispatch(portName,
  SOAPMessage.class, Service.Mode.MESSAGE);
BindingProviderbp = (BindingProvider) dispatch;
MessageFactory factory =((SOAPBinding) bp.getBinding()).
  getMessageFactory();

try{
  SOAPMessage request = factory.createMessage();
  SOAPBody body = request.getSOAPBody();
  SOAPElement operation = body.addChildElement("AccountId",
    "ns1","http://com.novobank.services.personalbanking/
    AccountDetails/");
```

```
    SOAPElementaccNo = operation.addChildElement("AccountNumber", "ns1",
      SERVICE_URI);
    accNo.addTextNode(accId);
    SOAPElementbranchNo = operation.addChildElement ("BranchNumber",
      "ns1", SERVICE_URI);
    branchNo.addTextNode(brNumber);
    request.saveChanges();
    SOAPMessage reply = null;
    reply = dispatch.invoke(request);
    body = reply.getSOAPBody();
    QNameresponseName = new QName(SERVICE_URI, "AccountInformatio n");
    QNamebalanceName = new QName(SERVICE_URI, "AccountBalance");
    QNameavailableFundsName = new QName(SERVICE_URI,"Available Funds");
    SOAPBodyElementbodyElement = (SOAPBodyElement) (body.
      getChildElements (responseName)).next();
    String balance = SOAPElement)bodyElement.getChildElements
      (balanceName).next()).getTextContent();
    String availableFunds = (SOAPElement)bodyElement.getChild
      Elements(availableFundsName).next()).getTextContent();
} catch(Exception ex){
  ex.printStackTrace();
}
...
```

**Example 6.3**

## Handlers

JAX-WS and JAX-RPC both provide a handler framework that allows processing to be performed on inbound and outbound messages. Handlers can access the contents of a message, perform processing based on the framework, and modify the contents of messages that are on the client side and server side or chained in a sequence.

JAX-WS includes protocol handlers and logical handlers. Protocol handlers allow access to protocol-specific aspects of service requests and responses and only protocol-specific parts. For example, a SOAP handler is a protocol handler that might be used to manipulate headers within a SOAP message. Logical handlers provide a means of accessing data within the body or payload of a service request or response without access to message headers, independent of the protocol and transport used for communication between the service consumer and invoked service. A logical handler can provide separation between protocol-agnostic handler logic that might be reused if an exposed service uses multiple protocols and protocol-specific logic.

Developing a JAX-WS handler involves extending `SOAPHandler` or `LogicalHandler` within the `javax.xml.ws.handler` package. In each case, a message context object is passed to the implementation providing access to the protocol-specific parts of the message or payload. To deploy handlers, a handler chain is defined to specify the order in which handlers are invoked. In JAX-RPC, the handler chain is defined in a deployment descriptor, while the `@HandlerChain` annotation can be used in JAX-WS with Java EE. Logical and protocol handlers can be mixed in a handler chain. For outbound messages, logical handlers are invoked before protocol handlers, while the reverse applies for inbound messages.

JAX-WS handler APIs make the development of custom handlers a viable option for meeting many requirements. In general, any processing that must be performed on messages that are sent or received by a Web service and not part of the core business or technical function of the service are candidates for implementation in a handler. Handlers can separate the functionality provided by the service and other peripheral functionality required to support the service. However, implementing business logic in a logical handler breaks the encapsulation of the service logic.

Common examples of handlers include logging messages for debugging/audit and generating events collated by a centralized end-to-end message tracking infrastructure. Handlers are also used within a number of Web service runtimes and commercial products for monitoring Web service infrastructures and to enforce WS-* standards compliance, such as the processing of WS-Security headers.

## Web Services Engines and Toolkits

The Java specifications and JSRs define a set of standard APIs for working with Web services in Java that include service development and deployment in a server and client environment. A suitable runtime is required to deploy services that are developed using these APIs, and tooling that can assist with development, such as wsimport, is useful.

Several Web services toolkits are available and commonly used to provide development and tooling capabilities. The Java SE Development Kit 7 includes an implementation of JAX-WS APIs. Oracle also provides a Web services runtime and development kit as part of their Java Web Services reference implementation codenamed Project Metro, which includes the implementations of several WS-* standards. The GlassFish Enterprise Server bundles the Metro libraries. Metro can also be bundled with other application servers, although this can sometimes require application configuration changes.

Several open-source Web services, runtimes, and toolkits, such as the Apache Web service projects, have also proven popular.

Apache Axis2 provides full support for JAX-WS and JAX-RPC APIs. Axis2 is a complete Web services runtime and toolkit extensible via pluggable modules that allow support for future standards. JAX-RPC and JAX-WS compliance is only one aspect of its functionality. Significant performance enhancements built on the previous Axis version can be attributed to the use of the Apache Axiom, which provides a DOM-like object model for manipulating XML structures in Java and uses the Streaming API for XML (StAX) to implement on-demand parsing. StAX parses XML documents only as data within the document is referenced in code, and only as far as required.

## JAXR

The Java API for XML Registries (JAXR) standard allows Java applications to access different types of XML registries using a standard API. Contemporary Java-based service implementations have emphasized proprietary registry technologies and specifications, such as UDDI, ebXML, and JAXR that have declined in practical relevance. This is reflected in how JAXR support has become an optional feature in Java EE 7.

The JAXR specification works in terms of registries and repositories. A repository is a storage space, such as a bank vault where money is stored. Alternatively, a registry is a place to store information about things. Reusing the bank vault example, a registry might be a ledger providing a record of the money stored within the vault. In the context of services and SOA, a registry is used to store metadata about repository items. The metadata could include information about the repository items, and be used for classification and categorization of services. Both registries and repositories can store schemas and WSDLs.

Although JAXR does not allow direct connection to a repository, it assumes that the repository always has an associated registry that enables access to repository items, in addition to holding item-related information. The JAXR model provides extensibility via a provider model that allows access to different types or classes of registries. The JAXR specification provides access to UDDI, ebXML, XML, and SPI registries. The Electronic Business using XML (ebXML) is a set of OASIS specifications defining common standards to facilitate business-to-business interactions via the Internet. The ebXML standards relating to registries are the ebXML Registry Services and Protocols (RS) and Registry Information Model (RIM).

The RS specification defines a set of interfaces used to access an ebXML registry implemented as SOAP/HTTP Web services, while RIM defines a standard metadata model used to describe the entities contained in the registry and their relationships. The UDDI specification similarly defines a different set of interfaces implemented as SOAP/HTTP Web services that provide access to a UDDI directory. The JAXR providers for ebXML registries and UDDI directories use the respective Web services to access the registry.

The ebXML RIM specification has greater relevance beyond the use of ebXML registries, since the JAXR information model is based on the model defined within the specification. The JAXR specification defines a detailed mapping between its own information model and those defined respectively by ebXML and UDDI. The JAXR information model classifies registry objects according to taxonomies defined either externally or as part of the JAXR provider.

The JAXR API follows a style that is consistent with other APIs used to access external enterprise systems from Java. Parameters defining the connection to the registry are encapsulated in a `ConnectionFactory` object that is typically retrieved via a JNDI lookup and used to establish a connection. Once a connection is established, JAXR provides methods for searching the registry (using a SQL-like syntax), navigating associations between objects, and managing the lifecycle of objects.

### SUMMARY OF KEY POINTS

- JAX-WS forms the basis of Web service support in Java EE 5, 6, and 7, and is an evolution of JAX-RPC/JSR 101/JSR 109 from J2EE 1.4.

- SAAJ is a lower-level API compared to JAX-WS and JAX-RPC that allows developers to deal directly with SOAP envelopes and their Java object counterparts in the `javax.xml.soap` package.

- Registries store metadata about various service artifacts, while repositories store the artifacts themselves. JAXR allows tools, vendors, and developers to use a standards-based Java API to access a wide variety of registries.

## 6.2  Java Implementations of WS-* Standards

Let's explore how the following basic WS-* extensions are handled within JAX-WS and other core Java Web Services specifications.

- *Addressing* – Project Metro is one of the most prominent Web services stacks in the Java platform, including a WS-Addressing implementation as part of the core technologies. The Metro Web services stack is bundled with the Java EE 5, 6, and 7 reference implementations and in the GlassFish application server.

- *MTOM* – Axis2 and JAX-WS reference implementations support the MTOM, which is used to achieve interoperable implementation of SOAP attachments well supported by non-Java Web Services implementations.

- *Reliable Messaging* – The WS-ReliableMessaging specification is supported in the WSIT project that provides support for reliability, security, and transactions. Apache also provides an open-source implementation of the 2005 pre-OASIS WS-ReliableMessaging specification with the Sandesha project. The Sandesha 2 project provides WS-ReliableMessaging support for Axis2 and for the OASIS WS-ReliableMessaging 1.1 specification.

- *Transactionality* – The WSIT project supports WS-Coordination and WS-Atomic-Transaction. Axis2 support for WS-Coordination and WS-AtomicTransaction is provided by Apache Kandula 2.

- *Security* – The XML and Web Services Security (XWSS) project, also part of Project Metro, supports various WS-Security standards, such as the Username Token Profile, X509 Token Profile, and SAML Token Profile. In addition, Project Metro implements WS-Trust, WS-SecureConversation, and WS-SecurityPolicy. Within the Apache Web services stack, Axis2 includes WS-Security support through a module provided by the Rampart project, which is based on the WSS4J implementation of WS-Security. The module provides support for Username tokens, X.509 certificates, and SAML tokens.

### Advanced Web Services Standards and Frameworks

The following sections briefly describe notable industry standards and frameworks relevant to Java support of WS-* standards.

**Service Component Architecture**

Service Component Architecture (SCA) and the associated Service Data Objects (SDO) specification were conceived and informally incubated by major software vendors including IBM, Oracle, and SAP, with a number of additional vendors joining as the specifications matured. Although subsequent attempts to drive standardization/adoption through OASIS have proven unsuccessful, SCA remains relevant with implementations included within vendor products such as IBM and BPM, and provided by Apache in the form of the Tuscany project.

SCA describes a model for the assembly of services implemented using different technologies, with an invocation framework providing support for locating and invoking services at runtime. SDO provides a standard means of manipulating language-agnostic data structures within service-based applications in a uniform manner.

The SCA model is based on the approach of assembling service components that can be implemented and exposed in a variety of different ways. The service components are exposed using logical interfaces that define input and output parameters without being tied to any particular implementation or transport mechanism. Where one service component must call another, a reference is created on the caller to the interface (described by a WSDL portType or Java interface) on the target service. The services and references are wired together, and the wiring model is captured in a Service Component Definition Language (SCDL) file. Services can be assembled in this way into modules exposed to the outside world via imports and exports that define the technology details of the interface, such as identifying SOAP or POX, and the transport mechanism used.

In addition to defining a model for the assembly/wiring of services, SCA provides an invocation framework used at runtime to determine the location of service endpoints invoked using the most appropriate mechanism, which is based on qualifiers defined at assembly time. If reliable, asynchronous qualifiers are specified at assembly time, the invocation framework will invoke the service endpoint using reliable JMS messaging at runtime. The invocation framework has awareness of the deployment topology of service components, and handles aspects, such as workload balancing, across multiple service endpoint instances where horizontal scaling is used.

The SDO specification provides a standard API and programming model for manipulating data within service components. SDO can be extended with Data Access Service (DAS) that binds to different data stores, such as relational databases and SOAP messages. The SDO specification provides static and dynamic programming models with similar advantages and disadvantages to JAX-WS and JAX-RPC static/dynamic proxies.

The dynamic API allows SDOs to be manipulated at runtime even if specifications of the data structure were unavailable at development time, although this involves more programming effort than the static model.

### Spring-WS

Spring-WS is based on the popular Spring framework, which led many of the innovations in enterprise Java computing formalized later in Java EE 5, 6, and 7. The Spring-WS framework supports top-down or contract-first development. Creating WSDLs from scratch is unnecessary, as WSDLs can be generated from schemas and other conventions.

Spring-WS provides a framework that runs in a Java SE or Java EE environment, and handles dispatching Web service messages to Web service endpoints by passing an XML message. Implementing a Web service with Spring-WS involves extending an abstract class defined by the framework. Directly coding to the JAX-RPC or JAX-WS APIs is unnecessary. A variety of different Object-to-XML mapping tools can be used to map XML messages to Objects, or directly navigate to the message tree using the SAAJ API.

**SUMMARY OF KEY POINTS**

- In the absence of standardized Java APIs for the implementation of WS-* extensions, each Web service vendor provides its own set of tools to facilitate building Web services with these additional qualities of service.

- Advanced standards, such as SCA and JBI, promote a simpler service construction, assembly, and integration model.

- Frameworks, such as Spring-WS, enforce SOA design practices, such as contract-first development and programming, with the raw XML payload by providing suitable abstractions.

## 6.3 JAX-RS

The JSR 311 for Java API for RESTful Web services (JAX-RS) 2.0 specification is HTTP-centric and aims to be Java EE container-independent. Like any JSR, a reference implementation of the specification under the codename Jersey is available. Jersey provides value-added features on top of the JAX-RS API to support Atom integration with the Spring framework and diverse resource representation formats, such as JSON and MIME Multipart. Like JAX-WS, the JAX-RS 2.0 specification relies on annotations to specify URI mappings, HTTP headers, content types, and resources.

The specific goals stated in the JAX-RS specifications are:

- *POJO-Based* – enabling use of simple Java objects through annotations and associated classes/interfaces

- *HTTP-Centric* – leveraging HTTP and the tenets introduced in Chapter 5, such as HTTP methods, headers, and URI

- *Format Independence* – supporting multiple content types or MIME types

- *Container Independence* – running JAX-RS artifacts in many different Web-tier containers

- *Inclusion in Java EE* – defining the environment for a Web resource class hosted in a Java EE container, to specify how to use Java EE features and components within the Web resource class

### Implementing JAX-RS

The JAX-RS API implements a Web resource class or annotated POJO with methods that respond to various HTTP operations. Based on the annotations, the JAX-RS runtime determines how to dispatch various HTTP operations to methods exposed on the class and how to choose appropriate format representations for both read and write operations on resources. The JAX-RS runtime leverages annotations to extract URL-related information, such as path information, query parameters, header values, and cookies, to populate method parameters or resource attributes with these values. The use of annotations eliminates the need for low-level HTTP plumbing code.

Let's consider a REST service that is exposing a list of customers as a resource and the details of an individual customer in Example 6.4.

```
import javax.ws.rs.*;
...
@Path("/customers/")
public class CustomerResource {
  @Get
  @Produces("application/xml")
  public String getCustomers()
```

```
    //return an empty list of customers, for now return "<customers/>";
    }
}
```

**Example 6.4**

The top-level JAX-RS package is `javax.ws.rs`, as highlighted in Example 6.4. To better understand the JAX-RS API implementation, annotations within the listing are defined as follows:

- The `javax.ws.rs.Path` annotation identifies the URL path for which the `Cus-tomerResource` class will serve requests. The URL path is in relation to the base URL of the server. The context root of the application and URL pattern to which the JAX-RS implementation servlet is mapped is `http://server/services/cus-tomers`. The `@Path` annotation can be applied at the resource class level or at an individual method level where it acts in relation to the base URL specified at the class level. The `getCustomers` method responds to the same `@Path` URL pattern specified at the class level.

- The `javax.ws.rs.GET` annotation is a request method designator indicating the getCustomer method will respond to HTTP GET requests. The JAX-RS runtime delegates an HTTP GET request for URL `http://server/services/customers` to the `getCustomers` method.

- The `javax.ws.rs.Produces` annotation indicates the MIME types of resource representation returned to the service consumer are an XML payload. The get-Customers method returns a string, so the `@Produces` annotation is necessary to tell JAX-RS what the content type of the returned HTTP response will be, such as `"application/xml"`.

An individual customer record often includes a unique identifier that can be used to retrieve further customer details, as seen in Example 6.5.

```
...
@GET
@Path("{id}")
@Produces("application/xml")
public String getCustomerById(
  @PathParam("id") Long id){
  return "<customer><name>" + "John Doe</name></customer>";
}
```

**Example 6.5**

The `javax.ws.rs.PathParam` annotation binds a URI template parameter to a resource method parameter, resource class field, or resource class bean property. In Example 6.5, a URI template parameter `/customers/{nnnn}` is bound to a resource method parameter `"id"` by the JAX-RS runtime. JAX-RS manages the type conversion between the string in the URI template parameter and the method parameter data type.

The `@Produces` annotation can be changed to return a JSON-based customer representation, as highlighted in Example 6.6.

```
@Produces("application/json")
 public String getCustomerById(
   @PathParam("id") Long id){
   return "{\"name\":\"John Doe\"}";
}
```

**Example 6.6**

Returning an XML or a JSON representation to the caller is the same through a change in the `@Produces("application/xml", "application/json")` annotation. The caller in Example 6.7 can indicate preference for one format over the other by specifying an appropriate accept parameter field in the request, such as a quality factor $q$.

```
GET services/customers/1234 HTTP/1.1
Accept: application/xml; q=0.8,application/json
```

**Example 6.7**

The $q$ factor value ranges from 0 to 1, with the default value set to 1 for highest priority. A value of 0.8 means the service consumer prefers `application/json` but will accept `application/xml` if `application/json` is not available. To restrict the search criteria for a collection of resources, the criteria can be specified in a query parameter. For example, to retrieve a list of customers whose last names match a certain value, the service consumers can issue the GET request `GET services/customers?lastname=perlman`.

Like URI path parameters, JAX-RS supports the extraction of query parameters from the URL, binding them to various resource attributes like method parameters, resource class fields, and resource bean properties. In Example 6.8, the parameter `lastname` would be populated with the value of the query parameter.

```
@Get
@Produces("application/xml")
public String getCustomersByLastName(
```

```
@QueryParam("lastname") String lastName) {
  ...
}
```

**Example 6.8**

JAX-RS facilitates the mapping of GET operations. The creation of new customers using the REST method, specifically the HTTP POST request, is shown in Example 6.9.

```
import javax.ws.rs.core.Response;
@POST
@Consumes("application/xml")
@Produces("application/xml")
public Response createCustomer(
  Customer cust) {
    // create customer in the system
    Customer customer = createCustomer(cust);
    return Response.ok(customer).build();
}
```

**Example 6.9**

The `javax.ws.rs.POSTannotation` is a request method designator indicating the `createCustomer` method will respond to HTTP POST requests. In Example 6.9, the JAX-RS runtime delegates an HTTP POST request for a URL, such as `http://server/ services/customers`, to the `createCustomer` method. Note the URL path for the creation is the same as the root resource path.

The `@Consumes` annotation indicates the MIME types of representation that the methods of a resource class can accept from the service consumer. An `@Consumes` annotation specified at the method level overrides one set at the class level. If a resource is unable to support the MIME type sent in the request data, the JAX-RS runtime returns an HTTP 415 Unsupported Media Type error.

The `javax.ws.rs.core.Response` class encapsulates any HTTP response metadata that the application chooses to provide. In this case, the `Customer` entity, a JAXB object, is returned in the response without any metadata. JAX-RS unmarshals HTTP request data into Java object types and Java objects to the appropriate HTTP response bodies. The operations for updating and deleting a customer can be mapped to HTTP PUT and DELETE methods, as seen in the code fragment in Example 6.10.

```
@Put
@Path("id")
@Consumes("application/xml")
public void updateCustomer(
  @PathParam("id") Long id, Customer cust){
  //...update customer
}
@DELETE
@Path("id")
public void removeCustomer(
  @PathParam("id") Long id){
    //...update customer
}
```

**Example 6.10**

Both PUT and DELETE methods can specify a URI template parameter to identify the customer for an update or delete operation. As with the GET operation, the URI template parameter is mapped to the resource method parameters. The `updateCustomer` method relies on the JAX-RS runtime to unmarshal the customer XML in the HTTP request body to the JAXB object in the resource method parameter.

## Implementing REST Services

Although no clear consensus about the need for a formalized REST service contract exists, WADL attempts to establish a format for formalized REST service contracts. The Customer Listing service presented in Example 6.5 can be described using WADL. For simplicity, assume that all representations from the service in Example 6.11 are described as XML.

```xml
<?xml version="1.0"?>
<application xmlns:xsi="http://www.w3.org/2001/XMLSchema-instance"
  xsi:schemaLocation="http://wadl.dev.java.net/2009/02 wadl.xsd"
  xmlns:tns="http://server/services/service1"
  xmlns:xsd="http:// www.w3.org/2001/XMLSchema"
  xmlns:cst="http://server/schemas/"
  xmlns:customer="http://www.mycompany.com/schema/customers"
  xmlns="http://wadl.dev.java.net/2009/02">
  <grammars>
    <include href="Customer.xsd"/>
  </grammars>
  <resources base="http://server/services/CustomerListing/v1">
    <resource path="all">
      <method href="#listing">
```

```
    </resource>
    <resource path="{id}">
      <method href="#customer">
    </resource>
  </resources>
  <method name="GET" id="listing">
    <request/>
    <response>
      <representation mediaType="application/xml"
        element="cst: customers"/>
    </response>
  </method>
  <method name="GET" id="customer">
    <request/>
    <response>
      <representation mediaType="application/xml"
        element="cst: customer"/>
      </response>
  </method>
</application>
```

**Example 6.11**

The WSDL document outlines the message template `Customer.xsd` using XML schema, sets up the base URI for the service, and describes the two resource paths `all` and `{id}`. The resource path `all` maps to the relative URI `/CustomerListing/v1/all`, which retrieves all customers and the resource path specified via a URI path template. The resource path `{id}` maps to `/CustomerListing/v1/{id}`, which responds with the customer's details and identifier id.

Code generation tools generate stubs from a WADL. Notable tools include the plain `wadl-cmdline`, the Ant-based `wadl-ant`, and Maven-based `wadl-maven-plugin` utilities. An XSL style sheet is available on the WADL site to create a more human-readable WADL document. The open-source community also offers tools that consume the WADL document and produce stubs or help visually inspect the WADL document.

## Scalability

REST offers scalability through simple abstraction and indirection, support for caching, addressability, statelessness, and replication of resources. Before looking at how these ideas can be applied to the sample Customer Listing service, this section introduces several Web features that contribute to scalability.

*Statelessness*

Individual HTTP requests are independent of one another and do not maintain conversational state information from any previous HTTP requests. HTTP is stateless by design, meaning REST services that are exposed over HTTP are also stateless by default unless specifically designed to be state-aware. Given any service consumer application, if the application state is maintained by the service consumer, the REST service deals only with the resource states and not the application state. Statelessness enables the REST service to be hosted on several different servers without replicating application state while still providing the same functionality to the service consumer. Resources can be replicated across a farm of servers. Web traffic interceptors, such as load balancers, can be used to distribute traffic to hosts without having to consider which server last served requests for the resource.

*Uniform Contract*

Supporting the HTTP methods GET, PUT, POST, HEAD, and DELETE and uniformly implementing the semantics for each of the methods across all of the REST services makes creating and supporting new types of service consumers possible. For example, a browser application accesses any Web site serving static HTML pages. Since all Web sites support the uniform interface of GET and POST in the same way, browsers do not have to change to render new Web sites that emerge daily. Similarly, new browsers can access Web pages through the exact same interface. As long as all new services (Webpages) satisfy the uniform interface with consistent semantics, such as how GET is idempotent and safe while PUT is idempotent, new types of services can be offered and additional service consumers can be introduced without changing either the services or the service consumers.

*Cacheability*

HTTP specification provides specific headers (`Expires`, `Cache-Control`, `Etag`, and `Last-Modified`) and guidance for caching resources at the service consumer end or in between the service and service consumer. The primary cacheable operations are GET and HEAD, since they are read-only. The intermediaries, such as proxy servers in use with traditional Web sites, can be used to support the caching on the server side for resources accessed using GET or HEAD. In addition, most of the standard HTTP library frameworks in various programming languages support caching on the service consumer side.

*Addressability*

The ability to have a unique address for each of the resources, and the inter-connections between resources, simplifies the partitioning of resources across hosts while maintaining a way to reach the resource. Partitioning is essential to scalability.

Due to the dynamic nature of customers, the main resource being added, the customer list is dynamic and cannot be cached. However, the customer profile can be cached as it seldom changes within a day. In addition, inter-connections exist between customers who are related or from same family. The design of the REST service is stateless and only supports GET and HEAD operations, since updates are not allowed. With these constraints, caching resources in an intermediary like a caching proxy server or at the service consumer end itself is possible.

Intermediaries are load balancers and caching proxies. Partitioning the primary entry point for the Customer Listing service `/customers` and subsequent calls to individual customers `/{id}` on to two sets of service farms with multiple hosts takes advantage of the statelessness and addressability characteristics. Depending on the anticipated load and frequency, the resulting layout can be expanded across data centers. The addressability and inter-connectedness facilitates seamless service operation in spite of the resources being physically spread across hosts.

For example, two service consumers can make calls at various times. A caching proxy determines if the resource must be cached, based on the `Cache-Control` field in the response header from the service. When the first caller makes a new request, the proxy checks its cache, finds no data in the cache, and forwards the request to the service. The response from the service has a directive to cache this resource for up to 10 hours or 36,000 seconds. When a second service consumer makes the request to the proxy server for the same customer profile, the proxy responds with the cached customer data.

Alternatively, the first service consumer accesses the list of all customers and the proxy forwards to the service. The service responds with the customer list and the `Cache-Control` field set to `no-cache` in the response header. Any subsequent calls on the customer list will be forwarded to the service by the proxy, as the service directive for caching was not to cache the customer list.

## Security

Authentication and encryption are primary considerations in the securing of services, which must ensure that the resource is inaccessible to unentitled service consumers and that the confidentiality of the data is not compromised. In order to satisfy a variety of service consumers, the service can support several types of user credential formats to perform authentication and support message and transport-level encryption.

In terms of authentication, the HTTP standard specifies basic access authorization and digest authorization as the primary schemes of using the Authorization request header to be sent when the service consumer invokes the service. Both schemes use the same request and response headers to carry information, whether it is the credential payload or an indication of what scheme to use.

When a service consumer requests a protected resource without proper credentials, the server responds with a 401 Unauthorized response code with an appropriate value in the WWW-Authenticate HTTP response header. The service consumer can then construct the appropriate credentials as desired by the service to gain access to the resource. The HTTP standard uses the status code 401 in situations where no credentials are sent with the request or the wrong credentials are sent.

A WWW-Authenticate response header sent to the service consumer can indicate that the basic authorization scheme is being used. Digest is another value that can be used in the WWW-Authenticate header, followed by the realm and additional information about the digest.

HTTP basic authentication is Base64-encoded and unencrypted. If the basic authentication scheme is used between the service consumer and service over HTTP, the credentials can be compromised if a malicious third party is monitoring traffic. A simple mechanism to overcome third-party monitoring is to use secure HTTP (HTTPS) and encrypt the communication channel between service consumer and service. Using the HTTP digest authentication scheme is another way to ensure data security.

The digest scheme uses a random string that changes on every request, in addition to a sequence number and the service consumer's username/password to authenticate the request. Due to the challenge mechanism of including a random string with a username/password known only to the service consumer, the service consumer's identity is preserved. However, the service consumer is then required to follow the HTTP specification in forming the proper digest token, along with necessary metadata to send to the service to be authenticated.

The HTTP standard allows extension of the standard authentication-related headers to accomplish specialized forms of authentication. By extending the standard, the service breaks the simplicity of REST principles and must provide additional information about the custom authentication scheme. The HTTP specification provides guidance on how to satisfy a requirement to use a custom scheme due to enterprise or other non-functional requirements.

Two means of achieving data confidentiality protection include encrypting the entire message content or portions of the message and the channel of communication between service and service consumer. Either Secure Sockets Layer (SSL) or Transport-Level Security (TSL) is used to encrypt the channel, such as HTTPS, but the message is susceptible once received at the endpoint.

Message-level encryption ensures security even after the message has been delivered to the recipient. The message payload, which is the request to the service or response from the service, can be encrypted either in full or in part. REST and SOAP-based Web services treat XML payloads similarly in that both use the XML Encryption specification. As the encryption mechanism grows in complexity, SOAP-based Web services have WS-Security and related specifications that address various aspects of how to deliver a robust message layer encryption implementation.

WS-Security specifications define how to associate security tokens with messages, reference encrypted XML elements, embed credentials used for decryption in the message headers, and embed other related metadata in the SOAP header. REST services have no clear guidelines or specifications available to provide a similar infrastructure. There are no standardized message-level encryption solutions for non-XML payloads. A JSON representation, for example, is left to the discretion of the developer building the service in terms of how to specify encryption parameters, encryption keys, and algorithms.

Security with REST services does not address the enterprise QoS concerns solved by WS-Security and its related standards.

## REST Service Support

Three other aspects of significance to the discussion on REST-related quality of service include reliable messaging, transaction, and asynchronous messaging support.

Reliable messaging transport ensures parties involved in the communication can send and receive messages with a degree of confidence which can be quantified as the number of times and order in which the messages will be delivered. Messages can be delivered at most once, at least once, and only once. An additional delivery guarantee can require messages to be delivered to the receiver in exactly the order they were sent from the sender.

The concept of reliable messaging was introduced in message queuing systems with no equivalent available in the REST-style architecture. Message guarantees can be satisfied by building additional infrastructure on top of the standard HTTP frameworks to accommodate retry, sequencing, and failure-handling logic. However, doing so would require maintaining application state. Relaxation of the statelessness constraint violates REST-style architecture principles and negates the advantages provided by this architecture. Transaction support illustrates what can be achieved by leveraging standard HTTP.

Transaction support in REST services is achieved with HTTP methods. If the REST service is designed following HTTP standards, then most of the HTTP methods, excluding POST, are idempotent. The GET, PUT, DELETE, and HEAD methods can be used more than once and obtain the same result as the first time. If PUT is used to update a customer, the service consumer can call multiple PUT operations and be updated with the same information.

Idempotent REST service invocations alleviate the need for guaranteed delivery with a retry mechanism. An eventually successful method invocation retry will ensure that messages are delivered without any unintended side effects. The retry mechanism does not ensure the ordering of messages, which must still be implemented at the application level if necessary as REST does not provide any solutions for maintaining message order. Reliable HTTP (HTTP-R) is another standard used to address transaction support, although its coverage is beyond the scope of this book.

Since transaction support requires the maintenance of session state and adherence to a set of standard protocols to ensure that the properties of atomicity, consistency, isolation, and durability (ACID) are not violated, there is no viable way to accomplish transaction support in REST services without violating the REST statelessness and cache constraints. Interesting examples of how to use an overloaded POST method to handle the coordination of transactions for REST services can be found online, although they are largely exploratory in nature. Utilizing SOAP-based Web services and the WS-AtomicTransaction or WS-BusinessActivity standards is preferable if there is a need to support distributed transactions spanning multiple systems within the enterprise.

Supporting asynchronous communications is challenging because of the synchronous nature of HEAD, GET, and PUT can be used to create new resources, such as an invocation status and polling the resource, to simulate publish/subscribe, broadcast, and one-way message exchange scenarios. These message exchange scenarios can still be accomplished using the synchronous HTTP protocol. Additional constraints must be placed on the MEPs and associated status codes to accomplish asynchronous communication over HTTP, which require custom engineering effort and a deviation from the standards.

### SUMMARY OF KEY POINTS

- JAX-RS is the standards-based Java API for building and consuming REST services. There are several popular open-source implementations of JAX-RS, such as Jersey and RESTEasy.

- JAX-RS allows Web resources to be modeled as annotated POJOs with methods that respond to standard HTTP operations.

- JAX-RS provides a range of annotations that control how various URI attributes, such as template parameters and query parameters, can be extracted from the URI and automatically mapped to resource attributes, such as resource variables and method parameters.

# Part II

# Services

# Chapter 7

# Service-Orientation Principles with Java Web-Based Services

Building services for service-oriented solutions requires the application of the service-orientation paradigm whose established design principles drive many Java service contract and implementation decisions. In certain cases, the programming language and runtime environment used for services can also be influenced by these guiding principles. This chapter visits each of the eight service-orientation principles in depth to highlight considerations specific to design and development with Java.

> **NOTE**
>
> The service-orientation principles are formally documented in the series title *SOA Principles of Service Design*. Concise profiles of the principles are also available in Appendix B and at www.serviceorientation.com.

## 7.1 Service Reusability

The following are common design characteristics associated with reusable services:

- The service is defined by an agnostic functional context.

- The service logic is highly generic.

- The service has a generic and extensible contract.

- The service logic can be accessed concurrently.

Let's take a closer look at each of these characteristics in relation to Java.

### Agnostic Functional Contexts

Ensuring that the logic encapsulated by a service is agnostic to any particular functional context allows for the building of service interfaces independent of one particular business process or functional domain. The term "context" refers to the service's functional scope. An agnostic functional context is not specific to any one purpose and is therefore considered multi-purpose. A non-agnostic functional context, on the other hand, is intentionally single-purpose.

A checkpoint that can be part of a regular code review or service interface quality gate is to look at the imports in a Java interface or implementation class for a service. Java interfaces and classes are often structured according to the applicable business domain, and focusing on the list of imported packages can help identify dependencies in the code. Returning to the simplified order management example, the Java service interface for the Credit Check service is seen in Example 7.1.

```
import com.acme.businessobjects.om.Order;
public interface CreditCheck {
  public boolean hasGoodCredit(Order order);
}
```

**Example 7.1**

The `import` statement indicates that the service logic depends on the functional context of order management. Such a dependency cannot always be avoided if a service is developed specifically for a particular business domain at the cost of its reusability. Utility services are generally agnostic and reusable, as explained in Chapter 8.

## Highly Generic Service Logic

Generic Java service logic refers to logic independent of its service contract. In the Java world, this means that a Java service interface is created with no mapping for the data types referenced in the service contract.

The `javax.xml.ws.Provider` interface avoids dependency on the service contract when using the JAX-WS programming model for SOAP-based Web services. An incoming message can be received by the service as a SAAJ `javax.xml.soap.SOAPMessage` with the `Provider` interface, which allows the entire message to be parsed or navigated as a DOM tree, as seen in Example 7.2.

```
@ServiceMode(value=Service.Mode.MESSAGE)
@WebServiceProvider()
public class GenericProviderImpl implements
  Provider<javax.xml.soap.SOAPMessage> {
  public SOAPMessage invoke(SOAPMessage message) {
    // read and process SOAPMessage...
  }
}
```

**Example 7.2**

For the same SOAP-based Web service, the request message can be alternatively read as a `javax.xml.transform.Source`. As shown in Example 7.3, the message can be treated as a plain XML document with no relationship to SOAP. Only the payload of the request message can be retrieved. Developers can ignore the SOAP envelope or SOAP header to focus on the content in the body of the message.

```
@ServiceMode(value=Service.Mode.PAYLOAD)
@WebServiceProvider()
public class GenericProviderImpl implements
  Provider<javax.xml.transform.Source> {
  public Source invoke(Source source) {
    // read and process SOAPMessage...
  }
}
```

**Example 7.3**

In both Examples 7.2 and 7.3, the response data returns in the same way the request data was received. If the request is received in an object of type SOAPMessage, then a new SOAPMessage object must be built for the response. Correspondingly, a new Source object must be returned if Source is used.

Generic Java types can capture the appropriate MIME media type or resource representation format produced or consumed by a target resource when building a REST service. For text-based request/response entities, Java String, char[], and the character-based java.io.Reader or Writer interfaces can be used in the resource methods. For completely generic entity representations, which can include binary content, a java.io.InputStream, OutputStream, or a raw stream of bytes can be used as byte[]. For XML-based resource representations, the javax.xml.transform.Source type can be used to handle XML documents at a higher level than a raw stream.

As seen in Example 7.4, a slightly reworked customer resource example of the REST service from the Chapter 6 uses an InputStream. The contents of an entity are extracted in the incoming request to keep the service contract generic.

```
@Post
@Consumes("application/xml")
public void createCustomer(
  InputStream in){
  //extract customer from request
  Customer customer = extractCustomer(in);
  //create customer in system;
}
```

**Example 7.4**

Similarly, `javax.xml.transform.Source` can extract the customer information from the incoming request. JAX-RS relies on a bottom-up service design philosophy for building REST APIs except when using WADL. Using generic types, such as `java.lang.Object` or `byte[]`, on a JAX-RS resource interface should be sufficient to keep the service contract generic. However, consider what corresponding data types will be used in the WSDL for SOAP-based Web services.

Avoid the use of concrete data types on the Java service interface. The payload of a message is cast into a Java object, such as a `byte` array or `string`. The service contract, such as the WSDL for a Web service, must match the generic type, such as `java.lang.Object` maps to `xsd:anyType`, `byte[]`, which maps to `xsd:hexBinary`, and `java.lang.String` maps to `xsd:string`. The matching generic types require specific code to be developed in both the service consumer and service for the data to be inserted into the request/response messages.

In Example 7.5, the public class employs a `byte` array on its interface to hide the details of the data processed by the service.

```
@WebService
public class OrderProcessing {
  public void processOrder( Order order,
    byte[] additionalData) {
    // process request...
  }
}
```

**Example 7.5**

Supertypes in the service interface can aid in generalizing a service contract. For example, a service returns detailed account information for a bank's customer. When creating a data model for the different types of information provided by the different types of accounts, take advantage of inheritance in XML Schema. A superclass called `Account` can be created in Java, with a number of subclasses defined for each type of account, such as checking, savings, loans, and mortgages. A return type of `Account` which includes all of the different types of accounts can be specified in the service interface.

The considerations for supertypes are the same for both SOAP and REST services. As in both cases, the XML Java marshaling/unmarshaling is handled by JAXB for XML and MOXy or JSON-P for JSON. MOXy is a framework for marshaling/unmarshaling between JSON and Java objects. JSON-P (Java API for JSON Processing) supports low-level JSON parsing in Java EE 7.

A generic service implementation can serve multiple types of request/response messages, which generally increases reuse opportunities. However, the service logic must be implemented to handle different types of messages. Type-specific code uses language-specific data types. Tooling can generate code that automatically parses messages into the right Java objects, although at the cost of increased coupling. If generic types are used, the processing of incoming and outgoing messages is left to the service implementer. However, generic types offer greater flexibility in terms of type-independence and loose coupling.

Generalizing service logic also applies to the service consumer. For example, JAX-WS defines a generic service invocation API using the `javax.xml.ws Dispatch` interface. Services can be invoked with unknown interfaces when the service consumer code is developed. Similar to how the use of the `Provider` interface supports handling requests from different types of service consumers, the use of the Dispatch API allows a service consumer to interact with different types of services. For REST service clients, if a JAX-RS implementation is used, all the generic Java types the JAX-RS implementation supports can be used to build requests and consume responses. However, generic service logic requires the client code to handle different types of messages and have some knowledge about the message formats expected.

### Generic and Extensible Service Contracts

Service logic can be made generic for reuse across a wide range of scenarios and adapted to changes in its environment, such as by changing and evolving services or service consumers. A service contract can be made generic by restricting the dependencies on data types referred to in the service contract and limiting the services composed inside the service logic to a minimum. When translated into Java-specific terms, reduce or eliminate the number of business-domain-specific classes in the service implementation.

Creating a generic service contract means applying generic types like `string`, `hexBinary`, or `anyType` in the schema type definitions for a Web service. Alternatively, message formats can be defined in a service contract with schema inheritance to use common supertypes, and the runtime allowed to determine which concrete subtype is used. Generic types are not only true for the top-level elements in a message but can also be used within a type definition. In Example 7.6, the schema describes a `Customer` type with a number of well-defined fields and a generic part.

```
<xs:complexType name="Customer">
  <xs:sequence>
    <xs:element name="accounts" type="ns:Account"
      nillable="true" maxOccurs="unbounded"
      minOccurs="0"/>
    <xs:element name="address" type="ns:Address"
      minOccurs="0"/>
    <xs:element name="customerId" type="xs:string"
      minOccurs="0"/>
    <xs:element name="name" type="ns:Name" minOccurs="0"/>
    <xs:element name="orderHistory" type="ns:OrderArray"
      nillable="true" maxOccurs="unbounded"
      minOccurs="0"/>
    <xs:any/>
  </xs:sequence>
</xs:complexType>
```

**Example 7.6**

When used in a service contract, the schema in Example 7.6 allows the service to process messages that have a fixed part at the beginning and a variable part at the end, which is represented by the `<xs:any>` element. SOAP-based Web services can use the Dispatch APIs in the service logic and Provider APIs in the service consumer logic without affecting how the service contract is built.

Service consumer logic can be implemented generically even if a detailed and specific service contract is provided. For REST services, the same considerations hold true for resource representations. XML-based representations can use highly specific types while the JAX-RS resource class can leverage generic Java types. The programmer then becomes responsible for performing the type mapping between XML and Java in the service logic.

## Concurrent Access to Service Logic

A particular instance of a shared service will almost always be used by multiple service consumers simultaneously at runtime. How the service is deployed and the characteristics of the service's runtime environment as influences on service reuse are significant design considerations.

For example, each service request starts a new process that executes the service logic for the request, which ensures that the processing of one request does not affect the processing of another request. Each execution is completely independent of other executions and creates a new thread in the process. However, starting a new process is a relatively expensive operation in terms of system resources and execution time in most runtime environments. Sharing services in this way is inefficient.

All service requests executed within the same process share all the resources assigned to that process, which provides a lightweight method of serving multiple concurrent requests to the same service. Starting a new thread is an inexpensive operation on most systems. Most, if not all, Web service engines work this way. Implementing services in a multithreaded environment requires adherence to the basic rules of concurrent Java programming.

## CASE STUDY EXAMPLE

As part of an initiative to comply with recently introduced legal obligations, the NovoBank IT team decides to create a Document Manager service that stores documents for auditing purposes. The service supports storing and retrieving XML documents. To maximize the reusability of this service, the NovoBank IT team creates a generic service contract and flexible service implementation to handle different types of documents, which can be extended over time.

Initially, the service will have the operations of `store` and `retrieve`. The service contract does not imply any structure of the documents stored, as shown in Example 7.7.

```
<definitions targetNamespace="http://utility.services.novobank.com/"
  name="DocumentManagerService" xmlns:tns="http://utility.services.
  novobank.com/" xmlns:xsd="http://www.w3.org/2001/XMLSchema"
  xmlns:soap="http://schemas.xmlsoap.org/wsdl/soap/"
  xmlns="http://schemas.xmlsoap.org/wsdl/">
  <types>
    <xs:schema version="1.0" targetNamespace="http://utility.
      services.novobank.com/" xmlns:xs="http://www.w3.org/2001/
      XMLSchema">
      <xs:element name="retrieve" type="ns1:retrieve"
        xmlns:ns1="http://utility.services.novobank.com/"/>
      <xs:complexType name="retrieve">
        <xs:sequence>
          <xs:element name="arg0" type="xs:string" minOccurs="0"/>
        </xs:sequence>
      </xs:complexType>
      <xs:element name="retrieveResponse" type="ns2:retrieveResponse"
        xmlns:ns2="http://utility.services.novobank.com/"/>
```

```
      <xs:complexType name="retrieveResponse">
        <xs:sequence>
          <xs:any processContents="skip"/>
        </xs:sequence>
      </xs:complexType>
      <xs:element name="store" type="ns3:store"
        xmlns:ns3="http://utility.services.novobank.com/"/>
      <xs:complexType name="store">
        <xs:sequence>
          <xs:any processContents="skip"/>
        </xs:sequence>
      </xs:complexType>
      <xs:element name="storeResponse" type="ns4:storeResponse"
        xmlns:ns4="http://utility.services.novobank.com/"/>
      <xs:complexType name="storeResponse"/>
    </xs:schema>
  </types>
  <message name="store">
    <part name="parameters" element="tns:store"/>
  </message>
  <message name="storeResponse">
    <part name="parameters" element="tns:storeResponse"/>
  </message>
  <message name="retrieve">
    <part name="parameters" element="tns:retrieve"/>
  </message>
  <message name="retrieveResponse">
    <part name="parameters" element="tns:retrieveResponse"/>
  </message>
  <portType name="DocumentManager">
    <operation name="store">
      <input message="tns:store"/>
      <output message="tns:storeResponse"/>
    </operation>
    <operation name="retrieve">
      <input message="tns:retrieve"/>
      <output message="tns:retrieveResponse"/>
    </operation>
  </portType>
  <binding name="DocumentManagerPortBinding"
    type="tns:DocumentManager">
    ...
  </binding>
  <service name="DocumentManagerService">
    ...
```

```
    </service>
</definitions>
```

**Example 7.7**
NovoBank's service contract for the Document Manager service is deliberately generic.

Example 7.7 shows that the content of the stored messages is represented by an `<xs:any/>` element, which means that any well-formed XML can be inserted in the content. The `<xs: any/>` element allows the Document Manager service to be reused across many different types of messages and documents.

The development team decides to create a flexible implementation of the service which is independent of the specific type of document being sent or retrieved. The service must extend without affecting the existing implementation, preparing support for more specific processing of specific document types. A flexible implementation is achieved with a handler and factory. The implementation leverages the `javax.xml.ws.Provider` interface and delegates the processing of each message to a handler. The handler instance is then retrieved via a factory.

Example 7.8 shows the implementation class for the Document Manager service in the detailed source code.

```
package com.novobank.services.utility;
import javax.xml.transform.Source;
import javax.xml.ws.Provider;
import javax.xml.ws.Service;
import javax.xml.ws.ServiceMode;
import javax.xml.ws.WebServiceProvider;

@ServiceMode(value=Service.Mode.PAYLOAD)
@WebServiceProvider
public class DocumentManager implements Provider<Source> {
  public Source invoke(Source source) {
    DocumentHandler handler =
      DocumentHandlerFactory.instance().getHandler(source);
    handler.process(source);
    return null;
  }
}
```

**Example 7.8**
The implementation of the Document Manager service utilizes a factory to retrieve a handler.

This class implements the `Provider` interface, so that any invocation of the service is directed to the `invoke()` method. The `@ServiceMode` annotation indicates that only the actual content of the SOAP body should be passed into the implementation.

In the implementation of the `invoke()` method, a single instance of a class called `DocumentHandlerFactory` is used to retrieve a `DocumentHandler` for this message. Example 7.9 shows the source code for the `DocumentHandler` interface.

```
package com.novobank.services.utility;
import javax.xml.transform.Source;
public interface DocumentHandler {
   public void process(Source source);
}
```

**Example 7.9**

The source code for the `DocumentHandler` interface

The `DocumentHandler` interface only defines the `process()` method, which processes the message. Different implementations of the interface that process messages in different ways can exist. The message content is passed into the `process()` method as a stream of type `javax.xml.transform.Source`. When revisiting the source code for the Document Manager service in Example 7.2, the message returned by the factory can be seen to be passed to the handler.

A part of the source code for the factory is presented in Example 7.10.

```
package com.novobank.services.utility;
import javax.xml.transform.Source;
public class DocumentHandlerFactory {
   protected static DocumentHandlerFactory theInstance = new
     DocumentHandlerFactory();
   public static DocumentHandlerFactory instance() {
     return theInstance;
   }
   protected DocumentHandlerFactory() {}
   public DocumentHandler getHandler(Source source) {
     DocumentHandler handler = null;
     // the code where the message is parsed and
     // the appropriate handler is retrieved would be here.
     return handler;
```

```
    }
}
```

**Example 7.10**

The DocumentHandlerFactory source code

The message is parsed to the point where an appropriate handler can be found. Handlers are registered via several mechanisms that can include hardcoding into the factory class, retrieval from a file, or lookup in a registry. The concrete `DocumentHandler` implementation chosen for a particular message is often based on the root element of the passed message. The root element typically provides adequate indication of the nature of the message.

Using the factory mechanism, where the service implementation class calls a factory to retrieve a handler to process the message, allows new handlers to be later added without affecting the existing code. The combination of a generic service definition using the `<xs:any/>` element, a flexible service implementation using the `Provider` interface, and a factory to delegate the processing of the message ensures maximum reusability of the service across a variety of environments and domains.

## SUMMARY OF KEY POINTS

- For SOAP-based Web services, the JAX-WS standard offers ways of implementing service logic as generic and therefore capable of handling different types of messages.

- For REST services, Java generic types can be used in JAX-RS-based resource implementations. The request/response entities are treated as a raw sequence of bytes or characters.

- Using generic data types for domain entities or resource representations allows the service to be reused across a greater number of potential service consumers.

## 7.2  **Standardized Service Contract**

A foundational criterion in service-orientation is that a service have a well-defined and standardized contract. When building Web services with SOAP and WS-*, portable machine-readable service contracts are mandatory between different platforms as WSDL documents and associated XML schema artifacts describing the service data model. The finite set of widely used HTTP verbs for REST services form an implicit service contract. However, describing the entity representations for capture in a portable and machine-independent format is the same as SOAP and WS-*.

For REST services, capturing and communicating various aspects of resources can be necessary, such as the set of resources, relationships between resources, HTTP verbs allowed on resources, and supported resource representation formats. Standards, such as WADL, can be used to satisfy the mandatory requirements. Having a standards-based service contract exist separate from the service logic, with service data entities described in a platform-neutral and technology-neutral format, constitutes a service by common definition. Even the self-describing contract of HTTP verbs for a REST service establishes a standards-based service contract. Recall the standards used for service contracts, such as WSDL/WADL and XML Schema, from Chapter 5.

### **Top-Down vs. Bottom-Up**

Ensuring that services are business-aligned and not strictly IT-driven is necessary when identifying services for a service portfolio in an SOA. Services are derived from a decomposition of a company's core business processes and a collection of key business entities. For a top-down approach, services are identified and interfaces are designed by creating appropriate schema artifacts to model either the operating data and WSDL-based service contracts, or model REST resources and resource methods. The completed service interface is implemented in code.

However, enterprises can have irreplaceable mission-critical applications in place. Therefore, another aspect of finding services is assessing existing applications and components to be refactored as services for a bottom-up approach. This includes creating standard service contracts, such as WSDL definitions or REST resource models, for the existing components.

Tooling provides support for both approaches in a Java world. For SOAP-based Web services, tools play a more prominent role than in Java-based REST services. JAX-WS defines the wsimport tool, which takes an existing WSDL definition as input to generate Java skeletons. These skeletons can be used as the starting point for implementing the actual service logic. Similarly, the wsgen tool generates WSDL from existing Java code. The mapping between WSDL/XML schema and Java is an important function associated with the wsimport tool.

Machine-readable contracts are also necessary for REST services. JAX-RS, if WADL is not used, starts with a resource model to implement the resources in Java. Consider the contract as a logical collection of the resource model, with the supported resource methods, resource representations, and any hyperlinks embedded in the representations allowing navigability between resources. If WADL is used, tools like wadl2java can generate code artifacts. Initiatives exist to help generate WADL from annotated JAX-RS classes for a bottom-up approach, although these recent developments can have limited usefulness.

Some SOA projects will employ both a bottom-up and a top-down approach to identify and design services and service contracts, which often results in a meet-in-the-middle approach. Service definitions and Java interfaces are tuned and adjusted until a good match is found.

Sometimes an XML schema definition developed as part of the service design cannot map well into Java code. Conversely, existing Java code may not easily map into an XML schema. Java code that does not precisely map to a service interface designed as part of a top-down approach can exist. In this case, the Service Façade pattern can be applied to insert a thin service wrapper to satisfy the service interface and adapt incoming and outgoing data to the format supported by the existing Java code.

## Mapping Between Java and WSDL

WSDL is the dominant method of expressing the contract of a Java component. While typically related to Web services, the language can also be utilized for other types of services. Formalization and standardization of the relationship between Java and WSDL has made this possible, such as the work completed on the JAX-RPC standard.

The JAX-RPC standard initially defined basic tasks, such as "a service portType is mapped to a Java interface" and "an operation is mapped to a method." However, formalizing allows the definitions described in the JAX-RPC standard to define how an existing Java component (a class or interface) can generate a WSDL definition, and vice versa. Consequently, most contemporary Java IDEs support generating one from the other without requiring any manual work.

JAX-WS, the successor standard for JAX-RPC, builds on top of its predecessor's definitions and delegates all the issues of mapping between Java and XML to the JAXB specification (as discussed in Chapter 6). These sections serve to highlight some of the issues raised when creating standard service contracts from Java or creating Java skeletons from existing service contracts. The majority of the details explained in the next section apply specifically to Web services.

### Wrapped Document/Literal Contracts

The WSDL standard identifies a variety of styles for transmitting information between a service consumer and service. Most of the styles are specific for the chosen message and network protocol, and specified in a section of the WSDL definition called the binding. A common binding found in a WSDL definition uses SOAP as the message protocol and HTTP as the network transport. Assume that SOAP/HTTP is the protocol used for the services presented as examples.

The portType is a binding-neutral part of a service definition in WSDL that describes the messages that travel in and out of a service. Reusable across multiple protocols, the portType is not bound to the use of a Web service. Any service, even if invoked locally, can be described by a WSDL portType, which allows service interfaces to be defined in a language-neutral fashion regardless of whether the service logic will be implemented in Java or another language.

As discussed in Chapter 5, the WSDL binding information defines the message format and protocol details for Web services. For SOAP-based bindings, two key attributes known as the encoding style and the invocation style determine how messages are encoded and how services are invoked.

The wrapped document/literal style supported by default in all Java environments for services dictates that an exchange should be literal. Literal means that no encoding happens in the message, so the payload of the message is a literal instantiation of the schema descriptions in the `<types>` element of the WSDL. The invocation style is document. Document means that the runtime environment should generate a direct copy of the input and output messages as defined in the portType and not just an arbitrary part of the message. Wrapped means that the payload of the message includes a wrapper element with the same name as the operation invoked.

In order to understand how the WSDL standard relates to Java, let's review Example 7.11 to expose the following class as a service and create a standardized contract.

```
package pack;
import javax.jws.*;
@WebService
public class Echo {
  public String echo(String msg) {
    return msg;
  }
}
```

**Example 7.11**

Using the wrapped document/literal style implements a wrapper element called `"echo"` after the `echo()` method in the public class. Echo is included in the XML schema associated with this service. An excerpt in the resulting schema is provided in Example 7.12.

```
...
  <xs:element name="echo">
  <xs:complexType>
    <xs:sequence>
      <xs:element name="arg0" type="xs:string" minOccurs="0"/>
    </xs:sequence>
  </xs:complexType>
  </xs:element>
...
```

**Example 7.12**

Wrapping a message in one additional element named after the operation is prevalent and the default in any commonly used tool. Note that naming the global element after the operation is common practice and not required by the specification.

## Implicit and Explicit Headers

Transferring information as part of the `<Header>` portion of the SOAP message, to be added to the WSDL definition, is another important part of the binding information for SOAP. This section discusses how to bind the information with explicit, implicit, or no headers.

### Explicit Headers

Header data is part of the messages referenced in the portType of the service, which is often called an explicit header. The header definition in the SOAP binding refers to a message part either included in the input message or the output message of an operation.

In Example 7.13, assume an Echo service takes a `string` as input and returns that `string` as the response. A `timestamp` must also be added into the header of the SOAP request message, indicating the time at which the request was sent.

```
<definitions targetNamespace="http://pack/" name="EchoService"
  xmlns:tns="http://pack/" xmlns:xs="http://www.w3.org/2001/
  XMLSchema" xmlns:soap="http://schemas.xmlsoap.org/wsdl/soap/"
  xmlns="http://schemas.xmlsoap.org/wsdl/">
  <types>
    <xs:schema targetNamespace="http://pack/">
      <xs:element name="echo">
        <xs:complexType>
          <xs:sequence>
            <xs:element name="arg0" type="xs:string" minOccurs="0"/>
          </xs:sequence>
        </xs:complexType>
      </xs:element>
      <xs:element name="echoResponse">
        <xs:complexType>
          <xs:sequence>
            <xs:element name="return" type="xs:string" minOccurs="0"/>
          </xs:sequence>
        </xs:complexType>
      </xs:element>
      <xs:element name="timestamp" type="xs:dateTime"/>
    </xs:schema>
  </types>
  <message name="echo">
    <part name="parameters" element="tns:echo"/>
    <part name="timestamp" element="tns:timestamp"/>
  </message>
  <message name="echoResponse">
    <part name="parameters" element="tns:echoResponse"/>
  </message>
  <portType name="Echo">
    <operation name="echo">
      <input message="tns:echo"/>
      <output message="tns:echoResponse"/>
    </operation>
  </portType>
  <binding name="EchoPortBinding" type="tns:Echo">
    <soap:binding transport="http://schemas.xmlsoap.org/ soap/http"
      style="document"/>
    <operation name="echo">
      <soap:operation soapAction=""/>
      <input>
        <soap:body parts="parameters" use="literal"/>
```

```
          <soap:header message="tns:echo" part="timestamp"
            use="literal"/>
        </input>
        <output>
          <soap:body use="literal"/>
        </output>
      </operation>
    </binding>
  ...
  </definitions>
```

**Example 7.13**

The Echo service WSDL definition with an explicit header contains a timestamp.

Example 7.13 contains an extract of the respective WSDL definition for an Echo service that shows:

- an additional element in the schema, called "timestamp" of type xs:dateTime

- an additional part in the input message definition, which refers to the timestamp element

- an additional definition for the header in the SOAP binding, which indicates that the timestamp element should be carried in the SOAP header of the request message

The header binding shown in Example 7.14 refers to a part also included in the portType of the service, the input message, and the Java service interface generated by the JAX-WS wsimport tool. Note that the import statements are left out.

```
@WebService(name = "Echo", targetNamespace = "http://pack/")
@SOAPBinding(parameterStyle = ParameterStyle.BARE)
public interface Echo {
  @WebMethod
  @WebResult(name = "echoResponse", targetNamespace = "http://pack/",
    partName = "parameters")
  public EchoResponse echo(
    @WebParam(name = "echo", targetNamespace = "http://pack/",
      partName = "parameters")
    Echo_Type parameters,
      @WebParam(name = "timestamp", targetNamespace = "http://pack/",
      header = true, partName = "timestamp")
    XMLGregorianCalendar timestamp);
}
```

**Example 7.14**

The service interface includes a parameter for the explicit header and indicates two parameters: one that contains the string wrapped into the Echo_Type class and another that carries the timestamp element. Note that nothing in the interface indicates that the timestamp will go into the SOAP header, as this information is only contained in the WSDL definition.

*Implicit Headers*

Assume that the header data is not part of the portType but instead uses a message part unused in any input or output message, known as an implicit header. The header information is not included in the portType of the service or in the Java interface. Example 7.15 shows that the WSDL for the Echo service has been changed to include an explicit header.

```
<definitions targetNamespace="http://pack/" name="EchoService"
  xmlns:tns="http://pack/" xmlns:xs="http://www.w3.org/2001/
  XMLSchema" xmlns:soap="http://schemas.xmlsoap.org/wsdl/soap/"
  xmlns="http://schemas.xmlsoap.org/wsdl/">
  ... (this part is as before) ...
  <message name="echo">
    <part name="parameters" element="tns:echo"/>
  </message>
  <message name="echoResponse">
    <part name="parameters" element="tns:echoResponse"/>
  </message>
  <message name="header">
    <part name="timestamp" element="tns:timestamp"/>
  </message>
  <portType name="Echo">
    <operation name="echo">
      <input message="tns:echo"/>
      <output message="tns:echoResponse"/>
    </operation>
  </portType>
  <binding name="EchoPortBinding" type="tns:Echo">
    <soap:binding transport="http://schemas.xmlsoap.org/ soap/http"
      style="document"/>
    <operation name="echo">
      <soap:operation soapAction=""/>
      <input>
        <soap:body parts="parameters" use="literal"/>
        <soap:header message="tns:header" part="timestamp"
          use="literal"/>
      </input>
```

```
    <output>
      <soap:body use="literal"/>
    </output>
  </operation>
</binding>
 ...
</definitions>
```

**Example 7.15**

A WSDL definition contains an implicit header for an Echo service.

The WSDL definition presented in Example 7.15 is not that much different from Example 7.13, with a separate message defined for the header. The separate message has a significant impact on the Java interface seen in Example 7.16, where the import statements have been omitted again.

```
@WebService(name = "Echo", targetNamespace = "http://pack/")
public interface Echo {
  @WebMethod
  @WebResult(targetNamespace = "")
  @RequestWrapper(localName = "echo",
    targetNamespace = "http://pack/", className = "pack.Echo_Type")
  @ResponseWrapper(localName = "echoResponse",
    targetNamespace = "http://pack/", className = "pack.EchoResponse")
    public String echo(
      @WebParam(name = "arg0", targetNamespace = "")
      String arg0);
}
```

**Example 7.16**

The service interface does not include the implicit header.

The interface in Example 7.16 takes a simple `string` parameter, and does not refer to the `timestamp` element or use the `Echo_Type` class to wrap the input message. The implicit header definition requires extra work on the service implementer by the service client developer to ensure the appropriate header information is inserted into the message. The implicit header definition cannot simply be passed to the service proxy as a parameter. In both cases, JAX-WS handlers can be leveraged to process the SOAP header, or intermediaries inserted between service consumer and service can manage all header information, such as part of an ESB.

The header portion of a service message should only contain contextual information, omitting any business connotation. The implementations of the service consumer and the service should only deal with business logic and not with infrastructure-level information. The use of implicit headers is common, although extra code to generate and process the headers must be written.

*No Headers*

A final option is to put no header information in the WSDL definition, which can appear to leave the contract incomplete but is actually preferable. Headers typically contain information independent from the business payload being exchanged between services. Recall a timestamp that had been inserted into the SOAP message presented in Examples 7.13 and 7.15. Inserting a timestamp might be a defined company policy across all services, and a common method for doing so can be established. Adding this detail to each WSDL definition is not required and creates an unnecessary dependency between the business-relevant service contract and technical cross-service policy.

## Data Mapping with REST

XML schemas can be used to represent service data elements, with JAXB and JAX-WS generating the mapped Java classes and Web service artifacts for SOAP-style Web service implementations. For REST services, the JAX-RS service implementations are similar. When the convenience of code generation is needed, JAXB annotated POJOs can be used as the service entities in JAX-RS resource classes. Behind the scenes, the JAX-RS runtime will marshal the Java objects to the appropriate MIME-type representations for the entities, such as `application/xml`. A `customer` object annotated with JAXB annotations is shown in Example 7.17.

```
@XmlRootElement(name="customer")
@XmlAccessorType(XmlAccessType.FIELD)
public class Customer {
  private int id;
  private String name;

  public Customer() {}
  //...other attributes omitted
  //...getters and setters for id and name
  //...
}
```

**Example 7.17**

The resource methods in the JAX-RS implementation that produce or consume customer information in the form of XML can be seen in Example 7.18.

```
//...retrieve customer and return xml representation
@Get
@Path("id")
@Produces("application/xml")
public Customer getCustomer(
  @PathParam("id") Long id){
  Customer cust = findCustomer(id);
  return cust;
}
//...create customer with an xml input
@POST
@Consumes("application/xml")
public void createCustomer(
  Customer cust){
  //...create customer in the system
  Customer customer = createCustomer(cust);
  //...
}
```

**Example 7.18**

The JAX-RS implementation automatically handles the marshaling and unmarshaling of the XML-based resource representation to and from JAXB objects. Generic types, such as a `javax.xml.transform.Source`, can be handled in the resource class to keep the resource class independent of any specific types defined in the domain, such as a `customer` type. However, extra work is required to handle the extraction of the customer information from the `Source` object seen in Example 7.19.

```
@PUT
@Path("id")
@Consumes("application/xml")
public void updateCustomer(@PathParam("id") Long id,
  javax.xml.transform.Source cust) {
  // do all the hard work to
  // extract customer info in
  // extractCustomer()
  updateCustomer(id, extractCustomer(cust));
}
```

**Example 7.19**

JAX-RS supports alternate MIME types, such as JSON. Just as JAXB handles the binding of XML to and from Java objects, numerous frameworks exist that handle mapping JSON representations to Java objects and vice versa. Some commonly used frameworks for mapping between JSON and Java are MOXy, Jackson, and Jettison.

In the Jersey implementation of JAX-RS 2.0, the default mechanism for binding JSON data to Java objects leverages the MOXy framework. When the Jersey runtime is configured to use MOXy, the runtime will automatically perform binding between Java objects (POJOs or JAXB-based) and a JSON representation. Jackson or Jettison can also perform similar binding with appropriate runtime configuration. A low-level JSON parsing approach can be achieved with the newly introduced JSON-P API (Java API for JSON Processing) in Java EE 7. JSON-P should not be confused with JSONP (JSON with Padding), which is a JavaScript communication technique used to avoid certain types of browser restrictions.

### Conversion Between JSON and POJOs

Given the same customer representation as illustrated in Example 7.20, no special code is required to handle an incoming JSON document or return a JSON-based representation.

```
//...
@GET
@Path("id")
@Produces("application/json")
public Customer getCustomer(
@PathParam("id") Long id){
  return findCustomer(id);
}
```

**Example 7.20**

The returned customer representation would be a JSON string, such as `{"name":"John Doe","id":"1234" ... }`.

The same JAXB objects can be used for handling JSON media types that would normally be used for XML representation. The addition of another MIME type in the @Produces can be seen in Example 7.21.

```
@GET
@Path("id")
@Produces("application/json", "application/xml")
```

```
public Customer getCustomer(
//...
```

**Example 7.21**

The JAX-RS runtime returns an appropriate representation (XML or JSON) that is determined by the client's preference. In spite of the convenience offered by JSON binding frameworks like MOXy or Jackson, greater control over the processing of the JSON input and output can be a requirement, as opposed to letting the JAX-RS runtime perform an automatic binding between JSON and Java objects.

For example, REST service operations must consume or produce only selective parts of large JSON documents, as converting the whole JSON document to a complete Java object graph can cause significant resource overheads. In such cases, a JSON parsing mechanism based on a streaming approach can be more suitable. JSON-P APIs allow a developer complete control over how JSON documents are processed. JSON-P supports two programming models, the JSON-P object model and the JSON-P streaming model.

The JSON-P object model creates a tree of Java objects representing a JSON document. The `JsonObject` class offers methods to add objects, arrays, and other primitive attributes to build a JSON document, while a `JsonValue` class allows attributes to be extracted from the Java object representing the JSON document. Despite the advantage of convenience, processing large documents with the object model can create substantial memory overheads, as maintaining a large tree of Java objects imposes significant demands on the Java heap memory. This API is similar to the Java DOM API for XML parsing (`javax.xml.parsers.DocumentBuilder`).

In comparison, the JSON-P streaming model uses an event parser that reads or writes JSON data one element at a time. The `JsonParser` can read a JSON document as a stream containing a sequence of events, offer hooks for intercepting events, and perform appropriate actions. The streaming model helps avoid reading the entire document into memory and offers substantial performance benefits. The API is similar to the StAX Iterator APIs for processing XML documents in a streaming fashion (`javax.xml.stream.XMLEventReader`). The `JsonGenerator` class is used to write JSON documents in a streaming fashion similar to `javax.xml.stream.XMLEventWriter` in StAX API.

JSON-P does not offer binding between JSON and Java. Frameworks, such as MOXy or Jackson, are similar to JAXB in how they will need to be leveraged to perform conversion between Java objects and JSON.

**CASE STUDY EXAMPLE**

SmartCredit launches an aggressive expansion campaign with the intention of offering premium credit cards with cashback offers to high-value customer prospects across a retail chain's locations. After signing an agreement with the retail chain, SmartCredit obtains prospect data from all the retail stores containing prospect names, e-mail addresses, and net transaction values at the end of every month. An internal Prospect Analyzer application will process the data to target prospects with high monthly transaction values and send out e-mails with new premium credit card offers.

The retail chain's IT department sends customer data to SmartCredit in large JSON documents containing prospect information. However, the SmartCredit Prospect Analyzer service is only interested in prospects that spend in excess of 2,000 dollars during the month. A fragment of a typical monthly JSON extract from the retail stores is provided in Example 7.22.

```
"txnsummary":{
"date":"2014-01-31T23:30:00-0800",
"store":"Fashion Trends #132",
"txn": [
  {
    "type":"cash",
    "amount":235.50,
    "e-mail":null
  },
  {
    "type":"credit",
    "amount":3565.00,
    "e-mail":"jane@doe.com"
  }
]}
```

**Example 7.22**

SmartCredit IT accepts the prospect and transaction data through an HTTP POST from the retail stores at the end of every month. A REST API that consumes this JSON data and extracts the prospects for marketing campaigns is built. After reviewing the size of the monthly feed, a SmartCredit architect quickly realizes that memory limitations will prevent a typical JSON-Java binding approach from working for such large payloads. In addition, SmartCredit is only interested in processing selective parts of the payload, such as credit card transactions with amounts greater than 2,000 dollars.

Converting the entire JSON data into Java objects is a waste of time, memory, and resources. The JSON-P streaming API is a suitable option for allowing selective processing of only the data sections meeting the given criteria. A simplified version of the final resource class is illustrated in Example 7.23.

```java
import javax.ws.rs.Consumes;
import javax.ws.rs.Path;
import javax.ws.rs.POST;
import javax.ws.rs.core.MediaType;
import java.io.Reader;
import javax.json.Json;
import javax.json.streaming.JsonParser;
import javax.json.streaming.JsonParser.Event
@Path("upload")
@Consumes(MediaType.APPLICATION_JSON)
public class ProspectFilteringResource {
  private final double THRESHOLD = 2000.00;
  @POST
  public void filter(final Reader transactions) {
    JsonParser parser = Json.createParser(transactions);
    Event event = null;
    while(parser.hasNext()) {
      event = parser.next();
      if(event == Event.KEY_NAME&&"type".equals(parser.getString()))
      {
        event = parser.next(); //advance to Event.VALUE_STRING for
          the actual value of "type"
        if("credit".equals(parser.getString()) {
          parser.next(); //Event.KEY_NAME for "amount"
          event = parser.next(); //Event.VALUE_NUMBER for amount
          value
          if(parser.getBigDecimal().doubleValue() > THRESHOLD) {
            parser.next(); //advance to Event.KEY_NAME for "e-mail"
            parser.next(); //advance to Event.VALUE_STRING for
            e-mail info
            String e-mail = parser.getString();
            addToCampaignList(e-mail);
          }
        }
      }
    }
}
```

```
      }
    }
  private void addToCampaignList(String e-mail) {
    // actual logic of adding e-mail to campaign list
  }
}
```

**Example 7.23**
The JSON-P streaming API can parse a large JSON document selectively.

The code uses the streaming API to advance the parser to consume only specific events and avoids reading the entire JSON data structure into memory, which would have been the case using the standard JSON-Java binding approach. One drawback to the JSON-P approach is the cumbersome maneuvering of the event stream in the application code, although such trade-offs are often necessary in real-world usage.

*Binary Data in Web Services*

Candidates looking to utilize a service-oriented solution often require the transfer of large amounts of data kept in some binary format, such as a JPEG image file. The Java language offers support for handling binary data in its JavaBeans Activation Framework (JAF) as well as classes and interfaces in other packages, which depend on the format. For example, the `java.awt.Image` class hierarchy supports image formats, such as JPEG. The JAXB specification defines how to map certain Java types to XML schema, such as the mapping of a `java.awt.Image` type to `base64Binary`.

Binary formats without a special Java type associated can use the `javax.activation.DataHandler` class defined in JAF. However, `byte[]` is the most generic way of representing binary data in Java. JAXB defines that a `byte[]` is mapped to `base64Binary` and `hexBinary`.

When generating a WSDL contract from a Java interface, binary data types are mapped using JAXB mapping rules. Generating the reverse is not as straightforward. An XML schema element of type `base64Binary` can map into multiple different Java types. By default, `byte[]` is used. Indicating that an element declared as `base64Binary` in the schema should be mapped to `java.awt.Image` in the Java service implementation can be performed in a number of ways. Binary data can be transferred in a SOAP message or inline, which means binary data is encoded into text and sent like any other data in the message.

Transferring the data inline maintains interoperability between different vendor environments, but is ineffective when dealing with large pieces of binary data, such as a CAD drawing of an airplane. The text encoding increases the size of the message by an average of 25%. The MTOM is an alternative to text encoding, which describes how parts of a message can be transferred in separate parts of a MIME-encoded multipart message. The binary content is removed from the SOAP payload, given a MIME type, and transferred separately.

JAXB provides support for MTOM, which must be explicitly enabled for the JAX-WS runtime. JAX-WS plugs into this support when building and parsing messages with attachments. An element definition can be annotated in an XML schema document with two specific attributes indicating which MIME type to give the element. When using MTOM, the `contentType` and `expectedContentTypes` attributes demonstrate how to MIME-encode the element and determine which Java type the element is mapped to in the Java service interface.

Nothing in the schema or in any of the Java code indicates whether the binary data is transferred as an attachment using MTOM or inserted directly into the SOAP envelope. In JAX-WS, distinguishing the difference is defined either by a setting on the service configuration file or programmatically. The following case study example illustrates a SOAP-based Web service managing attachments via MTOM.

## CASE STUDY EXAMPLE

NovoBank offers a remote method of opening an account from its Web site for customers to download a form, fill it out, and mail or fax it to a branch office. Alternatively, customers can fill out the form in branch and provide the completed form to a bank employee. The forms are scanned in at the branch office for further processing by NovoBank's back-end system before being archived.

To reduce processing time, the bank wants to offer customers and employees a Web application that accepts an uploaded binary image of the form to send to the bank. Internally, the Open Account service uses a Web service that takes the binary image as a parameter. To simplify the implementation of the associated service logic in Java, the service contract uses the `expectedContentType` attribute in its schema to indicate that the scanned image is formatted as a JPEG document. The resulting WSDL definition is shown in Example 7.24 with parts of the WSDL document omitted for brevity.

```
<definitions targetNamespace= "http://personalbanking.services.
  novobank.com/" name="AccountService"
  xmlns:tns="http://personal banking.services.novobank.com/"
  xmlns:xsd="http://www.w3.org/ 2001/XMLSchema"
  xmlns:soap="http://schemas.xmlsoap.org/wsdl/soap/"
  xmlns=http://schemas.xmlsoap.org/wsdl/
  xmlns:xmime="http://www.w3.org/2005/05/xmlmime">
  <types>
    <xsd:schema>
      <xs:element name="openAccount" type="ns1:openAccount"
        xmlns:ns1="http://personalbanking.services.novobank.com/"/>
      <xsd:complexType name="openAccount">
        <xsd:sequence>
          <xsd:element name="arg0" type="xsd:base64Binary"
            xmime:expectedContetTypes="image/jpeg" minOccurs="0"/>
        </xsd:sequence>
      </xsd:complexType>
      ...
    </xsd:schema>
  </types>
  <message name="openAccount">
    <part name="parameters" element="tns:openAccount"/>
  </message>
  <message name="openAccountResponse">
    <part name="parameters" element="tns:openAccountResponse"/>
  </message>
  <portType name="Account">
    <operation name="openAccount">
      <input message="tns:openAccount"/>
      <output message="tns:openAccountResponse"/>
    </operation>
  </portType>
</definitions>
```

**Example 7.24**

The WSDL for NovoBank's Open Account service with an MTOM content type definition will now accept the JPEG format.

An element of type `base64Binary` will be mapped to a `byte[]` in the Java interface. However, the additional annotation of the `parameter` element, using the `expectedContentTypes` attribute, leads to the following Java interface presented in Example 7.25.

```
package com.novobank.services.personalbanking;
import java.awt.Image;
// other imports omitted
@WebService(name = "Account", targetNamespace = "http://
  personalbanking.services.novobank.com/")
public interface Account {

  @WebMethod
  @WebResult(targetNamespace = "")
  @RequestWrapper(localName = "openAccount",
    targetNamespace = "http://personalbanking.services.novobank.
    com/", className = "com.novobank.services.personalbanking.
    OpenAccount")
  @ResponseWrapper(localName = "openAccountResponse",
    targetNamespace = "http://personalbanking.services.novobank.
    com/", className = "com.novobank.services.personal banking.
    OpenAccountResponse")
  public String openAccount(
  @WebParam(name = "arg0", targetNamespace = "")
    Image arg0);
}
```

**Example 7.25**

The content type is mapped to the appropriate Java type in the service interface.

Note how the `parameter` passed to the service implementation is mapped to the `java.awt.Image` type. Defining whether MTOM is used to transfer the form image as an attachment can be performed programmatically using JAX-WS, or in the client or the endpoint configuration for the service endpoint. A sample client for the new Open Account service is shown in Example 7.26.

```
package com.novobank.services.personalbanking.client;
import java.awt.Image;
import java.awt.Toolkit;
import javax.xml.ws.BindingProvider;
import javax.xml.ws.soap.SOAPBinding;

public class AccountServiceClient {
  public static void main(String[] args) {
    Image image = Toolkit.getDefaultToolkit().getImage("c:\\temp\\
      java.jpg");
    Account serviceProxy = new AccountService(). getAccountPort();
    SOAPBinding binding = (SOAPBinding)((BindingProvider)
      serviceProxy).getBinding();
```

```
    binding.setMTOMEnabled(true);
    String accountNumber = serviceProxy.openAccount(image);
    System.out.println("returned account number is
      "+accountNumber);
  }
}
```

**Example 7.26**
A Java client enables MTOM transport.

After deploying the service and running the test client listed in Example 7.26, the
SOAP message sent can be reviewed by executing the client in Example 7.27.

```
POST /attachment/account HTTP/1.1
Content-Length: 13897
SOAPAction: ""
Content-Type: Multipart/Related; type="application/xop+xml";
boundary="----=_Part_0_14949315.1177991007796"; start-info="text/
xml"
Accept: text/xml, application/xop+xml, text/html, image/gif, image/
jpeg, *; q=.2, */*; q=.2
User-Agent: Java/1.5.0_11
Host: 127.0.0.1:8081
Connection: keep-alive

------=_Part_0_14949315.1177991007796
Content-Type: application/xop+xml; type="text/xml"; charset=utf-8

<?xml version="1.0" ?><soapenv:Envelope xmlns:soapenv=http://
schemas.xmlsoap.org/soap/envelope/ xmlns:xsd=http://www.w3.org/2001/
XMLSchema xmlns:ns1="http://personalbanking.services.novobank.
com/">/"><soapenv:Body><ns1:openAccount><arg0><xop:Include
xmlns:xop="http://www.w3.org/2004/08/xop/include" href="cid:f17b4f2b-
db2c-4bc5-96d1-2d4857aaa5b8@example.jaxws.sun.com"></xop:Include></
arg0></ns1:openAccount></soapenv:Body></soapenv:Envelope>

------=_Part_0_14949315.1177991007796
Content-Type: application/octet-stream
Content-ID: <f17b4f2b-db2c-4bc5-96d1-2d4857aaa5b8@example.jaxws.sun.
com>
Content-transfer-encoding: binary_KýÝ_ÔF-¡úÞr*îÉu1_)Š1áñ}K²£•Ñ\
êKQZ_Ý4Ï¡É)*G'~ªohBïýfÙÈï¦zùìf_Ö(Ö & Èõmâoå¨\Ó\( ò¹åq€°Ê _W¶èÁh";_
ÐÚ´z0"ç5WÃ"_üv|DÜî7IÚù_é6³ÈÚ1•lëÉäl›BîöWÈ"ý|›i"ì™Åä]ÓÉÝ9ƒ_"7Üý¶j9{
ßáÉ?w(_"86‹ü£Ã_´?_:Ž§òÔŠvM¦éÈë4_ŸÊ"=ƒÑ]™EýÕ×Ès˜Hýå÷©?7‹â""¨r{‹â³‾
```

```
Rè<...R×©Ô]z_íµÙ4_ÿBîùš_?ÿPé3ê
... the rest of the data omitted ...
------=_Part_0_14949315.1177991007796--
```

**Example 7.27**
A SOAP message with an MTOM-compliant binary part

The request message is divided into the SOAP message, including reference to the binary data, and the binary data sent as an attachment. The message can be handled more efficiently and does not impact the processing of the remaining XML information. Again, whether the data is sent as an attachment or not is not defined in the service contract (the WSDL definition).

*Binary Data in REST Services*

JAX-RS supports the conversion of resource representations into Java types, such as `byte[]` or `java.io.InputStream`, in resource methods. To produce or consume binary data from resource methods, JAX-RS runtime handles the conversion through a number of built-in content handlers that map MIME-type representations to `byte[]`, `java.io.InputStream`, and `java.io.File`. If binary content must be handled as a raw stream of bytes in a resource method, the corresponding resource method is seen in Example 7.28.

```
@Get
@Produces("image/jpg")
public byte[] getPhoto() {
  java.io.Image img = getImage();
  return new java.io.File(img);
}

@Post
@Consumes("application/octet-stream")
public void processFile(byte[] bytes) {
  //...process raw bytes
}
```

**Example 7.28**

> **NOTE**
>
> Indicate the MIME type through an appropriate `@Produces` annotation, such as a JPG image, so that the runtime can set the right content-type for the returned resource representation.

The `java.io.File` type can help process large binary content in a resource method, such as an attachment containing medical images, as seen in Example 7.29.

```
@POST
@Consumes("image/*")
public void processImage(File file) {
  //...process image file
}
```

**Example 7.29**

The JAX-RS runtime streams the contents to a temporary file on the disk to avoid storing the entire content in memory. For complete control over content handling, JAX-RS offers several low-level utilities which can be useful for custom marshaling/unmarshaling of various content types. The `javax.ws.rs.ext.MessageBodyReader` and `javax.ws.rs.ext.MessageBodyWriter` interfaces can be implemented by developers to convert streams to Java types and vice versa.

Back-and-forth conversion is useful when mapping custom MIME types to the domain-specific Java types. The classes that handle the mapping are annotated with the `@Provider` annotation and generically referred to as JAX-RS entity providers. Entity providers are used by the JAX-RS runtime to perform custom mapping.

A special case of `javax.ws.rs.ext.MessageBodyWriter` is the `javax.ws.rs.core.StreamingOutput` callback interface, which is a wrapper around a `java.io.OutputStream`. JAX-RS does not allow direct writes to an `OutputStream`. The callback interface exposes a `write` method allowing developers to customize the streaming of the response entity. Example 7.30 demonstrates the `gzip` format used to compress a response entity.

```
import javax.ws.rs.core.StreamingOutput;
...
@GET
@Produces("application/gzip-compressed")
public StreamingOutput getCompressedEntity() {
```

```
return new StreamingOutput() {
  public void write(OutputStream out)
    throws IOException, WebApplicationException {
      try {
        ...
        GZipOutputStream gz =
          new GZipOutputStream(out);
          //...get array of bytes
          //   to write to zipped stream
          byte[] buf = getBytes();
          gz.write(buf, 0, buf.length);
          gz.finish();
          gz.close();
          ...
          } catch(Exception e) { ... }
      }
  };
}
```

**Example 7.30**

For mixed content containing both text and binary payload, entity providers can be used to perform custom marshaling, while multipart MIME representations are suitable for dealing with mixed payloads. JAX-RS standards do not mandate support for handling mixed MIME multipart content types apart from multipart FORM data (multipart/form-data), which is useful for HTML FORM posts but has limited use in a system-to-system interaction context. Various JAX-RS implementations, such as Jersey and RESTEasy, provide support for mixed multipart data. Handling mixed content with binary data is common, as seen in the following case study example for SmartCredit's Submit Credit Application service.

## CASE STUDY EXAMPLE

SmartCredit is building a REST service known as the Submit Credit Application service that is intended for service consumers to submit credit card applications. Apart from basic information such as customer details, the supporting information in the form of various collaterals, such as mortgage papers and loan approvals, must be scanned as images and attached to the application.

The SmartCredit application development team considered using Base64 encoding, but moved onto other alternatives after realizing a substantial size bloat would result. The development team decides on the mixed multipart representation for the application data. The multipart application data will have the customer information in an XML format as the first part, and a series of images in the subsequent parts.

A sample multipart application request over HTTP is shown in Example 7.31.

```
POST /creditapps/ HTTP/1.1
Host: smartcredit.com
Content-Type: multipart/mixed; boundary=xyzw

--xyzw
Content-Id: <abcdefgh-1>
Content-Type: application/xml
<customer>
  <name>John Doe</name>
  <Address>...</Address>
  ...

--xyzw
Content-Id: <abcdefgh-2>
Content-Type: image/jpg
...
&_Èõmâoå¨\Ó\( ò¹åq °Ê _W¶èÁh";_ÐÚ´z0"ç5WÃ"_üv|DÜî7IÚù_
é6³ÈÚ1•1ëÉäl›BîöWÈ"ý|›ì"ì™Åã]ÓÉÝ9ƒ_"7Üý¶j9{ßáÉ?w(_"86‹ü£Ã_´?_:ŽŞòÔŠv
M¦éÈë4_ŸÊ"=ƒÑ]™EýÕ×Ès˜Hý...rest of the binary data goes here
--xyzw—
```

---

**Example 7.31**

The SmartCredit service development team considered using a custom JAX-RS Entity Provider to handle the mixed multipart data, but realized the reference JAX-RS implementation Jersey already provides support for mixed multipart data through an add-on called `jersey-media-multipart`. The key classes leveraged in this implementation include:

- The `org.glassfish.jersey.media.multipart.BodyPartEntity` represents the entity of a part when a MIME Multipart entity is received and parsed.

- The `org.glassfish.jersey.media.multipart.BodyPart` is a mutable model representing a body part nested inside a MIME Multipart entity.

The resource class method that handles the submitted application can be seen in Example 7.32.

```java
import org.glassfish.jersey.media.multipart.MultiPart;
import org.glassfish.jersey.media.multipart.BodyPart;
import org.glassfish.jersey.media.multipart.BodyPartEntity;
import javax.ws.rs.core.Response;
...

import com.smartcredit.domain.Customer;
...

@Path("/creditapps")
public class CreditAppResource {

    @POST
    @Consumes("multipart/mixed")
    public Response post(MultiPart multiPart) {
      // First part contains a Customer object
      Customer customer =
        multiPart.getBodyParts().get(0).
          getEntityAs(Customer.class);

      // process customer information
      processCustomer(customer);

      // get the second part which is a scanned image
      BodyPartEntity bpe =
        (BodyPartEntity) multiPart.getBodyParts().
        get(1).getEntity();
      try {
        InputStream source = bpe.getInputStream();
        //process scanned image
      }

      // Similarly, process other images in the multipart
      // content, if any...

      //If everything was fine, return Response 200
      return Response.status(Response.Status.OK).build();

      //else if there were errors...
      return Response.status(Response.Status.BAD_REQUEST).
      build();
}
```

**Example 7.32**

In the code fragment, the `@Consumes` annotation indicates that a resource representation of multipart/mixed is expected. In this case, the payload contains customer data in XML and one or more scanned images. The following Jersey utilities perform different steps in managing the mixed multipart data:

- `com.sun.jersey.multipart.MultiPart.getBodyParts()` returns a list of `com.sun.jersey.multipart.BodyParts`.

- `BodyPart.getEntityAs(Class<T> cls)` returns the entity converted to the passed-in class type.

- `com.smartcredit.domain.Customer` is a regular JAXB-annotated Java class. Since the first entity in the multipart message is known to be the customer entity, the `BodyPart.getEntityAs(Customer.class)` method is used to unmarshal the XML entity body into a JAXB `customer` object.

- `BodyPart.getEntity()` returns the entity object to be unmarshaled from a request. The entity object is known to be a `BodyPartEntity` and is cast accordingly.

- `BodyPartEntity.getInputStream()` returns the raw contents, which in this case are the contents of the scanned image.

Note that by using the MIME multipart utilities in Jersey, the development team is able to avoid writing much of the plumbing code that would otherwise be necessary to deal with multipart MIME messages.

### Use of Industry Standards

The use of industry standards in developing service contracts builds on the IT-specific standards and seldom offers challenges when using Java as the language and runtime environment. Many industries have established data formats that ensure interoperability between business partners, suppliers, and between systems within an enterprise, such as the ACORD standard for insurance, HL7 for the healthcare industry, or SWIFT for banking.

Used primarily to exchange information between companies or independent units within an enterprise, industry standards are prime candidates for use as part of the service contract. Industry standards are generally expressed as XML schema definitions, which can be directly referenced in a service contract or serve as the basis for a specific schema.

Before the advent of JAXB 2.0 which supports the full set of XML schema constructs, a common issue was the inability to map all of the elements used in an industry schema into Java because such mapping was not defined. JAXB 2.x nearly resolves this issue, but cases still occur where a large and complex industry standard schema cannot be handled by a data binding tool like JAXB. Using an industry standard unchanged in a service contract can be tedious and lead to the generation of hundreds of Java classes mapping all of the complex types defined in the schema.

### SUMMARY OF KEY POINTS

- SOAP-based Web services can be developed top-down, bottom-up, or meet-in-the-middle.

- For REST services, a resource implementation artifact is used to model a Web resource that responds to HTTP operations. Apart from XML, support for resource representations can encompass a wide range of other media types. REST services can also use MIME features, such as multipart messages, to deal with binary content. JAX-RS implementations provide content handlers which can be customized for dealing with different representations.

- Standards-based service contracts can map the relevant XML schema constructs to and from Java. For both SOAP and REST services, the JAXB 2.0 standard offers support for the entire set of XML schema features. Industry standards are widely used in service contracts and do not introduce particular challenges when using Java.

- For SOAP-based Web services, special considerations apply when leveraging specific WSDL features, such as header fields, attachments with binary data, or the use of wrapper elements.

## 7.3 Service Loose Coupling

In a service-oriented environment, components can be coupled at a number of different levels. Coupling can occur at the level of the service contract, the service implementation logic, or the underlying technology platform the service is running on if a service consumer is coupled with a particular service. In general, SOA promotes the notion of decoupled systems by which the parts of a service-oriented solution are as decoupled as possible. Reducing the dependency of one part on another allows one area, such as a service or an aggregation, to be changed without requiring changes to other areas.

The following design characteristics are helpful in the creation of decoupled systems:

- separation of contract and implementation
- functional service context with no dependency on outside logic
- minimal requirements for the service consumer

When service logic is implemented in Java and executed in a JRE, a coupling is created between the logic and the underlying technology platform, Java. Additional dependencies arise when Java EE is used as the hosting platform. For an in-depth explanation of the variations of positive and negative coupling, see Chapter 7 in *SOA Principles of Service Design*.

## Separation of Contract and Implementation

The separation of a service contract from its implementation is a key characteristic of service-oriented design that was first established as part of the definition of remote procedure calls and then in object-oriented programming. The interface of a component is exposed to a point that allows other logic to invoke this component, but no details about the implementation are added. Changes to the implementation can then be made without affecting the client. SOA took this concept further by establishing the notion of a standards-based contract. For example, the service interface can be expressed in a programming language-neutral way to allow for the integration of logic written in different languages and running on different platforms.

The choice of programming language can be exposed in the service contract. In the context of a SOAP Web service from the *Top-Down vs. Bottom-Up* section, a common approach is to generate the service contract from existing Java logic. In JAX-WS, the wsgen tool can be used to generate a complete WSDL document, including the XML schema definition from an existing JavaBean or Java interface. However, the existing Java code may not be easily mapped into XML schema.

For example, assume that the `public java.util.Hashtable<String, String> getTable(int i);` method is part of an interface to be turned into a service. Using the wsgen tool to generate both the WSDL and XML schema definition from this interface creates the type definitions presented in Example 7.33.

```
<xs:element name="getTableResponse" type="ns2:getTableResponse"
  xmlns:ns2="http://the.package/"/>
<xs:complexType name="getTableResponse">
  <xs:sequence>
    <xs:element name="return" type="ns3:hashtable" minOccurs="0"
      xmlns:ns3="http://the.package/"/>
  </xs:sequence>
</xs:complexType>
<xs:complexType name="hashtable">
  <xs:complexContent>
    <xs:extension base="ns4:dictionary"
      xmlns:ns4= "http://the.package/">
      <xs:sequence/>
    </xs:extension>
  </xs:complexContent>
</xs:complexType>
<xs:complexType name="dictionary" abstract="true"/>
```

**Example 7.33**

The result is a valid XML schema definition, although a Java `Hashtable` is exposed in the service interface which renders the schema not useful or usable outside of Java. The same is true for many other classes and interfaces in Java, which, while useful as part of the implementation, do not map well into XML schema and non-Java environments. Many of the more technically-oriented classes, including the members of the `java.io` package, fall into this category.

The use of internal, platform-specific information carried in a generic type is another aspect of decoupling the contract and implementation. For example, the name of a file usually stored as a string can be mapped into XML schema and added to a service contract. However, exposing file names on a service contract is considered poor practice, and revealing details of the service implementation to the service consumer should be avoided. The same holds true for names of databases, database tables, machine names, and addresses.

Using the reverse approach is another way of creating this coupling, particularly when generating a service logic skeleton directly from a service contract. In JAX-WS, the wsimport tool is used to create Java code skeletons representing a given WSDL definition. Despite being the recommended approach, be aware that the generated Java code is now tightly coupled to its contract, which prevents the code from being easily reused to serve other types of service contracts or updated versions of the current contract. In most cases, the tight coupling is acceptable because the logic is created for a particular contract and nothing else.

However, instances occur where service logic must be created for reuse despite changes to the underlying contract changes or the need to concurrently serve multiple versions of the same contract. The JAX-WS `Provider` API is equipped for such instances. In this model, the service logic parses the incoming message at runtime for dynamic processing with no direct dependency on the types and elements defined in the WSDL contract. Use of the JAX-WS `Provider` API is detailed in Chapter 8.

For a REST service, coupling the code to the service contract is inconsequential because generating implementation artifacts from a machine-readable contract, unless WADL is being used, is uncommon. Implementing a Web resource for a platform, such as JAX-RS, out of the box supports only a finite subset of Java classes that can be automatically mapped to appropriate content-types. For custom types not mapped automatically by the built-in content handlers, developers must provide implementations of `javax.ws.rs.core.MessageBodyReader/MessageBodyWriter` interfaces to map such types to a known set of resource representations or media types.

### Independent Functional Contexts

Besides the direct compile-time of coupling services, consider the coupling of a service to its outside functional context. Service invocations happen as part of a business transaction or process to establish a context that effectively binds the services, which are invoked downstream, into an aggregated set. Having a set of services as part of the same process establishes a type of coupling between the services, a coupling that should always be top-down. Particularly when leveraging other services to fulfill functionality, a service implementation can be coupled with or have dependency on those services. However, the service should not have a dependency on any services at a higher level of the process hierarchy, or be coupled with the invoking service or with peer services.

For example, assume that a service offers Credit Check functionality. The service is implemented as a business process that invokes a number of other finer-grained services, such as Credit Lookup, Credit Eligibility, Update Profile, and Notification. All four downstream services are peers within the Credit Check business process. Service peers should have no dependency on each other, or be aware of or coupled with their upstream Credit Check service.

Services representing business processes, such as Credit Check and Maintain Customer Information, are decomposed into a set of fine-grained services to create a downstream dependency. A service should not introduce a dependency on another service that is higher level. For example, the implementation of the Update Profile entity service should not introduce any dependency on the Maintain Customer Information task service.

In Java, the same principles of downstream dependency hold true. Unwanted dependencies can be detected by examining the classes that are used by a piece of Java logic. Organizing classes into packages directly identifying the service and/or affiliated business process and ensuring that logically decoupled functions are not packaged together is recommended. A package name should be selected with consideration for possible reuse opportunities. For Web services, the same requirements for namespaces are used in the service contract.

## Service Consumer Coupling

For SOAP-based Web services, a service consumer will often be tightly coupled with the service contract and not the implementation of the service being invoked. However, a looser coupling lessens the impact when the service contract changes.

Using the JAX-WS Dispatch API, service consumer logic can dynamically assemble a request message at runtime and manage any response messages. Additional effort is required to build service consumer logic that can build request messages that the intended service can process.

### CASE STUDY EXAMPLE

After using the Account service in production for some time, a new operation is added to enhance account services. NovoBank wants to allow all required information about new accounts to be sent to the service as XML on top of the binary image that the initial version supported. Different branch offices use different systems to capture the data required to open a new account, such as traditional "fat client" or browser-based solutions. Additionally, the details of the information stored with new accounts change consistently.

The development team will design the new operation to process different types of input XML formats, and deliver a generic piece of service consumer code that shows how to invoke the new operation from within a JAX-WS supported client. Example 7.34 illustrates the updated WSDL definition for the enhanced Account service to accept the input of XML formats.

```
<definitions targetNamespace="http://personalbanking.services.
  novobank.com/" ...>
  <types>
    <xsd:schema>
      <xsd:element name="openAccount" type="ns1:openAccount"
        xmlns:ns1="http://personalbanking.services.novobank.com/"/>
      <xsd:complexType name="openAccount">
        <xsd:sequence>
          <xsd:element name="arg0" type="xs:base64Binary"
            xmime:expectedContentTypes="image/jpeg" minOccurs="0"/>
        </xsd:sequence>
      </xsd:complexType>
      <xsd:element name="openAccountXML" type="ns1:openAccountXML"
        xmlns:ns1="http://personalbanking.services.novobank.com/"/>
      <xsd:complexType name="openAccountXML">
        <xsd:sequence>
          <xsd:any/>
        </xsd:sequence>
      </xsd:complexType>
      <xsd:element name="openAccountResponse"
        type="ns2:openAccountResponse"
        xmlns:ns2="http://personalbanking. services.novobank.com/"/>
      <xsd:complexType name="openAccountResponse">
        <xsd:sequence>
          <xsd:element name="return" type="xsd:string" inOccurs="0"/>
        </xsd:sequence>
      </xsd:complexType>
    </xsd:schema>
  </types>
  <message name="openAccount">
    <part name="parameters" element="tns:openAccount"/>
  </message>
  <message name="openAccountResponse">
    <part name="parameters" element="tns:openAccountResponse"/>
  </message>
  <message name="openAccountXML">
    <part name="parameters" element="tns:openAccountXML"/>
  </message>
  <portType name="Account">
    <operation name="openAccount">
      <input message="tns:openAccount"/>
      <output message="tns:openAccountResponse"/>
    </operation>
    <operation name="openAccountXML">
      <input message="tns:openAccountXML"/>
```

```
      </operation>
   </portType>
...
</definitions>
```

**Example 7.34**

The updated WSDL definition for the enhanced Account service accommodates the new operation, `openAccountXML`.

Note how the element named `openAccountXML`, which acts as the wrapper element for the `openAccountXML` operation, contains only one `<xsd:any/>` element. The contract indicates that any kind of XML content can be sent to the service without providing any further details, which allows for decoupling of the service logic from the contract.

Use of the `<xsd:any/>` element minimizes the requirements for service consumers of this service. Any XML document can be passed to the service, allowing the development of generic service consumer logic. As an example of completely decoupling the service consumer from the service, the NovoBank development team delivers the following piece of client code to the users of the Account service in Example 7.35.

```java
package com.novobank.services.personalbanking.client;

import java.io.StringReader;
import java.net.URL;
import javax.xml.namespace.QName;
import javax.xml.transform.Source;
import javax.xml.transform.stream.StreamSource;
import javax.xml.ws.Dispatch;
import javax.xml.ws.Service;

public class Account2Client {
  public static String testMessage =
    "<ns1:openAccountXML xmlns:ns1=\"http://personalbanking.
    services.novobank.com/\"><someDocument><personalData>Here goes
    the information</personalData></someDocument> </
    ns1:openAccountXML>";

  public static void main(String[] args) throws Exception {
    QName serviceName =
      new QName("http://personalbanking.services.novobank.com/",
        "AccountService");
```

```
QName portName = new QName("http://personalbanking.services.
  novobank.com/","AccountPort");

Service service = Service.create(
  new URL("http://localhost:8080/account2/account2?wsdl"),
  serviceName);
Dispatch<Source> dispatch = service.createDispatch(
  portName, Source.class, Service.Mode.PAYLOAD);
  dispatch.invoke(new StreamSource(new StringReader(testMessage)));
  }
}
```

**Example 7.35**

Java client code decouples the service consumer from the service for the Account service.

First, an instance of the `Service` class providing the location of the appropriate WSDL file and the name of the targeted service is created. A `Dispatch` object is then created from the `Service` class, and the `Service.Mode.PAYLOAD` is defined to indicate that only the content within the SOAP `<body>` element and not the entire message will be passed. Finally, the service can be invoked dynamically via the `Dispatch` object. The service consumer has no compile-time dependency on the service or its contract.

The payload XML document has one root element called `openAccountXML`. Given that the service definition used the wrapped document/literal style described in the *Mapping Between Java and WSDL* section, this `openAccountXML` element indicates which operation of the service is being invoked. Similarly, the service code can be developed in a flexible way with regard to any kind of input message being sent, of which a detailed case study can be found in Chapter 8. Even though any XML content can be sent to the service, the implementation logic will always have constraints on what can be processed. The message must contain data meaningful in the context of the invoked operation.

Another way of further decoupling a service consumer from the service is to insert an intermediary between the two. The intermediary, generally deployed as part of an ESB, can mediate the differences in message format and network protocol to further decouple the service consumer and service. Chapter 12 explores this further as part of its coverage of ESBs.

## SUMMARY OF KEY POINTS

- For SOAP-based Web services, coupling between service contract and implementation can also occur. Generating service contracts directly from existing Java logic often exposes language-specific details and creates an unwanted tight coupling between the logic and the contract. However, service consumers can be developed in a generic way independent of a particular service contract using the JAX-WS `Dispatch` API.

- With REST services, the service contract is tightly constrained by a known set of media types and a handful of HTTP operations.

- Namespaces and Java package names can help structure code to control and minimize the dependencies among service implementation pieces.

## 7.4  Service Abstraction

The appropriate level of abstraction at which services are described achieves additional agility and alignment between business and IT areas of an enterprise. Abstracting information means taking technical details out of a problem to be solved on a higher level. Since the beginning of computer technology, information has been abstracted into higher levels in a number of ways, for example:

- Assembler constructs, which are instructions for a processor, are translated into a series of 1 and 0.

- Operating systems offer access to system resources and APIs that encapsulate lower-level constructs.

- Programming languages, such as Java, introduce a more abstract way of describing logic, which is then compiled into a format that the operating system can understand.

Service-orientation continues the evolution of higher-level abstraction use to make creating and changing solutions easier. For example, a business process defined with WS-BPEL describes a sequence of service invocations and the data flows between them by expressing this sequence in XML form without writing any actual code. A side effect of this increased abstraction is the ability to utilize visual programming tools that support the creation of process definitions via drag-and-drop-style interfaces. The Service Abstraction principle advocates that the technical details of the technology platform underlying a service contract are hidden from the service consumer. It also promotes hiding non-essential details about the service itself.

### Abstracting Technology Details

The service contract represents an abstraction of the functionality implemented in the service logic. Included in this notion is the abstraction of technical resources utilized to fulfill a service's functionality.

Filenames, database tables, machine names, and network addresses should be omitted from the service contract and completely hidden from service consumers. Given that a service contract should always be designed with a particular business purpose in mind, this should never be a problem.

Concerns arise when services are generated straight out of existing code, because technology details which should have otherwise been abstracted away will often be exposed. For example, whether or not a service is implemented in Java or running in a Java environment such as Java EE should be completely irrelevant to the service consumer.

### Hiding Service Details

Maximum flexibility is achieved when the technology used to implement a service and additional details about that service are hidden, which can be divided into information about the input or output message format and contextual information.

Hiding the information about the input or output message format may seem counterintuitive. If a service's input and output messages are hidden, what is left to put into the service contract? Message formats can be abstracted to a generic level without surrendering the message definition altogether.

For example, assume a Credit Check service receives customer information as input. The customer information can be defined and represented by a Customer complex type in the XML schema definition to a detailed level, adding constraint information to each attribute and element of that schema. The length of the `lastName` character field is limited to 35 characters in Example 7.36.

```
<complexType name="Customer">
  <sequence>
    <element name="firstName" type="string"/>
    <element name="lastName">
      <simpleType>
        <restriction base="string">
          <length value="35"/>
        </restriction>
      </simpleType>
    </element>
    <element name="customerNumber" type="string"/>
  </sequence>
</complexType>
```

**Example 7.36**

XML schema definition with added constraint inheritance can limit the `lastName` field to a set number of characters.

The XML schema definition in Example 7.36 maps to a Java class, `Customer.java`, as seen in Example 7.37. (The generated Javadoc comments are omitted.)

```
public class Customer {
  @XmlElement(required = true)
  protected String firstName;
  @XmlElement(required = true)
  protected String lastName;
  @XmlElement(required = true)
  protected String customerNumber;

  public String getFirstName() {
    return firstName;
  }
  public void setFirstName(String value) {
    this.firstName = value;
  }
  public String getLastName() {
    return lastName;
  }
  public void setLastName(String value) {
    this.lastName = value;
  }
  public String getCustomerNumber() {
    return customerNumber;
  }
  public void setCustomerNumber(String value) {
```

```
    this.customerNumber = value;
  }
}
```

**Example 7.37**
The generated Java type does not include the schema type restriction.

> **NOTE**
>
> The limit on the length of the `lastName` element was not carried over into Java because Java has no concept of a fixed-length string.

On the opposite end of the abstraction spectrum would be a message definition stating that the incoming message is an XML document with a root `Customer` element. No information is given about individual attributes or elements contained in the document, as seen in Example 7.38.

```
<complexType name="Customer">
  <sequence>
    <any/>
  </sequence>
</complexType>
```

**Example 7.38**
An XML schema definition using the `<any/>` element

The generic type definition leads to a generic Java class, as shown in Example 7.39.

```
public class Customer {
  @XmlAnyElement(lax = true)
  protected Object any;
  public Object getAny() {
    return any;
  }
  public void setAny(Object value) {
    this.any = value;
  }
}
```

**Example 7.39**
The `<any/>` element is mapped to `java.lang.Object`.

Hiding service details and increasing what is abstracted about a service may always appear to be a prudent step. However, the service consumer is sometimes not provided with all of the necessary information on what exactly the service expects and what will be returned in response. Details of an interaction on both sides are left to be resolved at design-time or runtime (outside of the service contract).

In Example 7.38, the generic version states that a `Customer` object contains a `java.lang.Object`, which must be defined at runtime to allow for processing. Generally, more Java code must be written for errors that can occur at runtime. For XML payloads, this consideration is equally valid for SOAP and REST services, as the mechanics perform the same role for both in mapping XML to Java via a binding tool such as JAXB. An abstract service contract can be appropriate in some instances, such as utility services.

Contextual data can also be hidden, as this type of data is commonly about an interaction which does not contain any business-relevant payload information. When using SOAP-based Web services, SOAP header fields store contextual data, such as unique message identifiers, timestamps, and service consumer identity. For greater abstraction, detailed information about contextual header fields can be left out of the service contract altogether. This contextual information can be added or removed depending on the environment in which a service runs, is not relevant for its business purpose, and can often be left out of the contract.

For REST services, in the absence of any kind of a payload envelope, contextual information must be part of a resource representation. Such resource metadata can still be packaged inside specially designated header elements. The technical details of a service that are not part of the service interface, such as a WSDL or service-level information about response times and availability, can be abstracted. The technical details can be important to know, but often change and depend on a particular runtime environment and deployment of a service. For REST services, such service-level agreement characteristics can be described in a separate document.

## Document Constraints

Non-technical information about a service cannot be articulated in a standard format. A generic example of this is a service-level agreement, but may also include other constraints about the usage of a service, valid ranges of input data beyond what can be expressed in WSDL and XML schema, and any additional applicable documentation.

A service can be implemented and deployed in different ways throughout an enterprise. As such, this documentation should not be directly linked with a service. Java, for example, is well suited for deployment on multiple platforms and operating systems. A Unix-based environment has different performance, scalability, and availability characteristics than a Windows-based system. Additionally, a Java EE application server can be leveraged to host the Java logic. A service instance can run on just one server instance on a small machine. As reuse of the service increases, the service instance can be moved to a clustered environment with greater computing power.

As per the Dual Protocols pattern, a Web service offered over HTTP can be later exposed via JMS for additional reliability requirements by particular service consumers. Abstract service contracts provide the freedom to make changes throughout the lifetime of the service, without breaking or violating previous versions. REST service implementations are synonymous with HTTP, making transport mechanism abstraction a non-issue. As the information about a service grows in abstraction, the service implementation and service consumer logic must become more flexible to anticipate future changes.

### SUMMARY OF KEY POINTS

- Details about a specific technology used to implement and/or host a service should be abstracted out of a service contract, which is achieved by REST services over HTTP by default.

- Services can be built in a more abstract fashion by using abstract and generic message specifications and leaving contextual information out of the service contract altogether.

- Non-technical information about a service often assumes a separate life-cycle from the service contract and its implementation.

## 7.5 Service Composability

The composability of a service is an implicit byproduct of the extent to which the other service-orientation design principles have been successfully applied. The ability to compose services into new, higher-level services is an inherent, logical consequence if the other design principles outlined in this chapter are followed. For example, a service contract that is standardized allows interaction and composition between services implemented in different languages using different runtime environments. Decoupling a service implementation from its contract allows the same logic to be reused in other compositions.

With regards to the implications that service composability has for the service contract, this section highlights some of the issues and requirements for the runtime environment in which the services run. See Chapter 11 for further exploration of service composition with Java.

### Runtime Environment Efficiency

A highly efficient and robust runtime environment is required for service compositions. The ability for services to participate in multiple compositions places severe challenges on runtime environments and must be taken into account when designing a service inventory.

If a service is used by multiple compositions, applying different non-functional characteristics can be necessary. One composition rarely invokes a service with no particular requirement for fast response times, whereas another composition using the same service can require support for high transaction loads with short response times. Similarly, one composition can require a reliable connection between the composition controller and its members, whereas another can be tolerant of lost messages. Applying different QoS definitions to the same service, depending on the composition, must be possible without requiring code changes in the service logic itself.

Java, as a programming language, has no built-in features that help or hinder the runtime environment. In most cases, Java-based services are hosted in a Java EE-compliant application server or an alleged Web server environment, which is Java SE-compliant. In either case, the runtime environments provide advantages over other traditional server platforms in terms of composability.

> **NOTE**
>
> Depending on how a given service or service consumer participates in a service composition at runtime, it may assume one or more roles during the service composition's lifespan. For example, when a service is being composed, it acts as a composition member. When a service composes other services, it acts as a composition controller. To learn more about these roles, visit www.serviceorientation.com or read Chapter 13 of *SOA Principles of Service Design*.

Java EE defines the management of solution logic according to the roles people perform, such as component provider, deployer, and assembler. As a result, much of the information on the execution of solution logic at runtime is not hardcoded into the logic itself but is instead stored in declarative configuration files, called deployment descriptors. The same piece of Java code can be used differently with different deployment descriptors and changed at runtime without requiring recompilation of the code. Despite being undefined by the Java EE standard, most Java EE application servers support defining individual server instances with specific runtime definitions. One instance usually runs in one process with its own configuration for elements like thread pools or memory heap sizes. In many cases, instances can be clustered to provide one logical application server across multiple physical processes or machines.

Separating runtime information about a component from its actual logic is possible because the Java EE application server runs as a container. This means that all incoming and outgoing data is intercepted and processed by the application server based on the current configuration. For example, if a certain piece of Java logic can only run within the scope of a transaction, the container can be configured to ensure a transaction is present whenever this piece of logic is invoked.

The same approaches to the runtime environment apply to Web services on two levels:

1. The runtime environment that processes an incoming message, such as a SOAP or REST request message, can perform several tasks before forwarding the request to the actual service. These tasks include the ability to decrypt data sent in an encrypted form, establish handshaking between service consumer and service by returning acknowledgement that the message has been received, interpret information in the request message header indicating that the invocation of the service must be part of a distributed transaction, and convert incoming XML data into Java objects.

2. For SOAP-based Web services, JAX-RPC and JAX-WS provide a mechanism and an API that allow the insertion of custom logic to parse, interpret, or change incoming and outgoing messages. The custom logic runs inside a handler. For JAX-RS-based implementations of REST services, such interception logic can be implemented by developers in special entity handlers known as entity providers. The JAX-RS 2.0 release provides added filters and interceptors otherwise not included in previous versions.

Both approaches are similar regardless of the Web services used. One is controlled by the user of the system, whereas the other is implicitly included with the runtime. Reading and manipulating incoming and outgoing messages separate from the service logic is crucial to supporting the Service Composability principle. Composing hosted services, including both composition members and composition controllers, is supported by the concept of containers and deployment descriptors and enhanced by SOAP-based Web services, such as handlers.

Ultimately, implementing a highly efficient runtime allows the developer to focus on the business logic of the actual service implementation, leaving everything else to the underlying Java platform. More advanced technologies, such as the SCA, expand on this concept by separating core business logic implementation further away from aspects of a service component, such as the protocol bindings used to interact with service consumers and other services used to fulfill functionality.

### Service Contract Flexibility

Service contracts can be designed to increase the ability of a service for multiple compositions. Generally, multiple compositions are only applicable to the composition members for increasing the reusability of a service in different business contexts or business tasks. A service contract can be rewritten to enable reuse of a service without changing the core functionality of the service.

To write a flexible service contract that is reusable, recall the following approaches:

- Use generic data types or supertypes instead of concrete subtypes. If an enterprise deals with both commercial customers (`CommercialCustomer`) and personal customers (`PersonalCustomer`), evaluate whether a common supertype can be established for both (`Customer`) to be used in the service contract. JAXB supports polymorphism to ensure that the appropriate Java object is created when a message containing a subtype is received.

- Decouple the service contract from its underlying runtime platform by hiding details about QoS characteristics, which can change over time and will vary depending on service consumer requirements and how a service is deployed.

- Decouple the service implementation from its contract by utilizing generic APIs, such as the JAX-WS Provider API for SOAP-based Web services. For REST services, deal with generic Java types in resource methods, such as `String`, `byte[]`, and `InputStream`. Note that generated generic service consumer or service logic results in additional code that must be developed and tested.

## Standards-Based Runtime

Composition members and controllers benefit from a runtime environment that supports a wide range of accepted standards. Composing services means the services interact and interoperate. Interoperability of services is supported by a runtime environment upheld by relevant standards, such as the WS-I. Java's APIs for SOAP-based Web services, JAX-RPC and JAX-WS, require support for the WS-I Basic Profile, which allow services to be designed with a high degree of interoperability. REST services achieve full interoperability inherently through HTTP.

Advanced standards relevant in a composition of services include the WS-Security standards for which a WS-I profile also exists, the WS-Transaction and related standards, WS-Addressing, and WS-ReliableMessaging, which supports the reliable exchange of messages between services. These advanced standards are combined in another WS-I profile known as the Reliable Secure profile.

## SUMMARY OF KEY POINTS

- Composability is supported in utilizing a runtime environment that allows hosting both composition members and composition controllers efficiently and flexibly, such as Java EE-compliant application servers.

- Creating flexible service contracts can facilitate the use of services as composition members.

- Platforms that support accepted and established standards can be utilized to improve service interoperability and composability.

## 7.6 Service Autonomy

Service-orientation revolves around building flexible systems. Flexibility is, to a large degree, achieved through making services decoupled and autonomous to enable them to be composed, aggregated, and changed without affecting other parts of the system. For a service to be autonomous, the service must be as independent as possible from other services with which it interacts, both functionally and from a runtime environment perspective. Java and Java EE provide a highly efficient runtime environment that supports service composition. For example, a Java EE application server supports concurrent access to its hosted components, making each access to such a component autonomous from the others.

### Well-Defined Functional Boundary

Occasionally, the functional boundary is defined by a certain business domain that a service lives within, as is the case if a service implements a particular business process or task within that domain. Alternatively, the functional boundary of a service can be described by the type of data the service operates on, such as entity services.

Translating this requirement into Java and XML schema utilizes namespaces and Java packages as structuring elements. Checking the list of imported classes and packages for a particular service implementation will help identify dependencies throughout the system and provide an indication of whether the functional boundary of the service is maintained in its implementation.

For example, an entity service called Customer delivers customer data retrieved from a variety of data sources for reuse across many business processes. The service is defined in the `http://entity.services.acme.com/Customer` namespace and uses `com.acme.services.entity` as the Java package for its implementation. The Customer service imports a package called `com.acme.services.accounting`, which immediately identifies that the Java service implementation contains a potentially undesired dependency on a business domain-specific piece of code. This warrants further investigation of the underlying logic and removal of the dependency.

The Customer service has a well-defined functional boundary in delivering relevant customer data to its service consumer. However, a dependency on logic specific to the Accounting service business domain naturally reduces the autonomy of the Customer service.

**Runtime Environment Control**

The underlying runtime influences the degree of autonomy a service can achieve. For each service to have control over its runtime environment, the environment must be partitioned to allocate dedicated resources accordingly. The JVM offers all internal code a degree of autonomy by isolating the executed code from the operating system and providing controlled access to physical resources, such as files or communication ports. Java EE application servers leverage the concept of a container in which components run.

For SOAP-based Web services, runtime control in Java can be achieved (while maintaining a high degree of autonomy) by exposing plain JavaBeans as Web services or utilizing Stateless Session EJBs. The service implementation and all other relevant artifacts, such as WSDL files, are packaged in a module, such as a JAR or WAR file, which can then be installed on an application server independent of other code running on that server.

The same is true for non-Web services or services implemented as regular EJBs. The components related to the service have individual private deployment descriptors that can be configured on the application server as independent entities.

Java EE allows for the packaging of multiple modules and multiple services in one Enterprise ARchive file. This EAR file is deployed and installed on the application server as an independent enterprise application. To increase a service's autonomy, use of only one service packaged per EAR file is recommended. This allows each service to be treated as a completely independent unit to configure, start, stop, or replace without affecting any other services running on the same system.

To decrease the number of moving parts in the environment, however, multiple services can be packaged into one enterprise application. Co-locating services is suitable when the services interact frequently with each other in a performance-critical manner.

In JAX-RS, POJOs are more commonly used to model Web resources, although stateless and single session beans can be designated as root resource classes. The JAX-RS runtime packages the resource artifacts into a WAR or EAR file which can be deployed as a standalone module in an application server. Some JAX-RS implementations support embeddable containers, in which a JAX-RS runtime is bootstrapped from inside a driver program for testing purposes.

## High Concurrency

Developing services for reuse across multiple service consumers is a benefit of implementing service-oriented design. The considerations presented in the *Agnostic Functional Contexts* and *Concurrent Access to Service Logic* sections help illustrate the benefits of providing each service consumer exclusive access to a certain instance of the service implementation, which is true regardless of whether the service implementation is located in a JavaBean or is a stateless session EJB.

For REST services, the default lifecycle of root resource classes is per-request. A new instance of a root resource class is created every time the request URL path matches the `@Path` annotation of the root resource. With this model, resource class fields can be utilized without concern for multiple concurrent requests to the same resource. However, a resource class can also be annotated with the `javax.inject.Singleton` annotation, creating only one instance per Web application. Using the default lifecycle model for resources is recommended, unless compelling reasons arise to do otherwise.

In general, each Java component that implements a service is accessible concurrently by definition via the application server. However, installing the same service separately on different machines is also acceptable. The ultimate autonomy of a service is achieved if one instance of a service, running in its own process and controlling all of its underlying resources, serves only one specific service consumer. While inefficient from a resource utilization and maintenance perspective, requirements can dictate a service as part of a mission-critical business process which requires high performance and high transaction loads that force a dedicated instance of the service to be deployed for that specific purpose.

---

**NOTE**

Establishing environments that support high levels of concurrent access introduces scalability considerations that some IT enterprises may not be equipped to handle, relational directly to the amount of service compositions a given service participates in and the amount of access within each composition the service is subjected to.

Cloud computing platforms provide infrastructure with IT resources that can dramatically improve the extent to which the Service Autonomy principle can be applied to a service implementation, by reducing or eliminating the need for the service implementation to share or compete for resources within the enterprise boundary. For more information about scalability and elasticity as part of cloud computing environments, see the series title *Cloud Computing: Concepts, Technology & Architecture*.

## SUMMARY OF KEY POINTS

- A well-defined functional boundary of a service, reflected in its contract, ensures a high degree of autonomy. However, this boundary must also be maintained in the service implementation by avoiding any dependencies on other services outside of that functional boundary.

- A service can increase autonomy by having complete control over its runtime. Java and Java EE support control over the runtime with the concept of containers, which depict virtual runtime boundaries that can be controlled individually and independently.

- Despite being accessed concurrently by multiple service consumers, services running in a Java application server can run autonomously on behalf of each service consumer. The JAX-WS and JAX-RS programming models automatically ensure that a new thread is started for each new service request.

- Highly critical services can have total autonomy by being deployed on a server for exclusive access by one particular service consumer.

## 7.7 Service Statelessness

Each invocation of a service operation is completely independent from any other invocation, whether by the same service consumer or any other service consumer. The Service Statelessness principle offers various benefits centered around improved scalability by which additional stateless service instances can be easily provisioned on available environments. With the advent of cloud computing, on-demand scaling out of services is considered as a natural evolutionary step for stateless services.

Many real-life business scenarios can be expressed as business processes that include automated steps, which can require manual intervention. Designing and implementing such a process requires some state to be maintained for the duration of the process. Executing an instance of the process definition forms the notion of a session or transaction across multiple service invocations. Therefore, a service implementing the execution of a business process cannot be stateless and may need to even maintain context information over extended periods.

## Orchestration Infrastructure

An orchestration infrastructure, such as a WS-BPEL execution environment, will support state maintenance either by storing state in the local stack of the thread executing the process or in a permanent relational data store. A permanent relational data store ensures that a process instance can be continued after a system crash or other interruption. This style of statefulness is built into WS-BPEL and its execution environment, so there is little to be aware of when designing such a service. Designing a service that aggregates other service invocations in its implementation without utilizing WS-BPEL will require the developer to decide whether to store temporary data in a relational data store for later recovery in case of failure.

## Session State

Another aspect of achieving service statelessness occurs when a service must establish some form of session with a service consumer, such as when the state is not kept in the calling logic but in the called service itself. Compare this to the shopping cart scenario in which a service consumer uses a service repeatedly to collect a set of data, which is then committed all in one final step. Java Servlets, which at the core also offer a stateless programming model, leverage the `HTTPSession` information and the concept of cookies to enable data to be stored on behalf of a certain client.

For REST services, using cookies as handles to store client state violates the stateless constraint of a REST-style architecture. Any maintenance of server-side session state is not recommended, and REST limits application state to be held on the client and not on the server.

Using cookies breaks the statelessness model as the server is expected to maintain a reference to a session and use the information in the incoming cookie for discovery. Each invocation is expected to carry the complete contextual information without any references to any previous interaction, promoting scalability where any available service instance can process this request. For idempotent requests, the failed request can be redirected to another functioning stateless service. Note that the convenience of server-side session maintenance and the associated personalization benefits are sacrificed for superior scalability and optimum resource usage.

REST services can read or write state information for various domain entities from or to databases or other persistent stores, but storing client state violates the statelessness constraint with implications for scalability and resilience. SOAP-based Web services have no such constraints and the servlet model is leveraged by JAX-WS to handle stateful interactions.

## Storing State

Two methods are available for clients to store state as part of a repeated interaction with a servlet. The first allows the data to be sent back and forth with each request, and the amount of data grows with each invocation. The second method enables the servlet to maintain the state, and the servlet sends back a key to this data (the cookie). The client sends the same key along for a subsequent request, which allows the servlet to retrieve the appropriate state for this particular client. The interface used to store the data is called `javax.servlet.http.HTTPSession`.

The behavior described in maintaining a key is a well-defined part of the standard servlet programming model, and APIs are available to enable its use. The `javax.servlet.http.HTTPSession` interface offers methods for storing simple key-value pairs. JAX-WS describes a mechanism to pass a reference of the `HTTPSession` instance into the service implementation class.

A Web service implementation can be made stateful by leveraging HTTP sessions and the JAX-WS support for the sessions. This requires that the service consumer receives and reuses the cookie sent back with the response to the original HTTP POST request.

### CASE STUDY EXAMPLE

Several of NovoBank's business processes require that certain forms and brochures be mailed to customers. The need for mailing each form is established in a separate part of the process, but in each case, the same back-end system is called via a Web service interface offering an `addOrderForm` operation. To reduce mailing costs, the design team makes the service establish a session with each process instance so that all orders can be bundled together. This requires the service to keep track of all forms requested. All orders are confirmed at once with the invocation of the `confirm` operation.

Example 7.40 shows an excerpt of the WSDL definition for the Order Form service.

```
<definitions targetNamespace="http://utility.services.novobank.com/"
  name="OrderFormService"
  xmlns:tns= "http://utility.services.novobank.com/"
  xmlns:xsd= "http://www.w3.org/2001/XMLSchema"
  xmlns:soap= "http://schemas.xmlsoap.org/wsdl/soap/"
  xmlns= "http://schemas.xmlsoap.org/wsdl/">
  ...
  <xs:element name="addOrderForm" type="ns1:addOrderForm"
    xmlns:ns1="http://utility.services.novobank.com/"/>
  <xs:complexType name="addOrderForm">
    <xs:sequence>
      <xs:element name="arg0" type="xs:string" minOccurs="0"/>
    </xs:sequence>
  </xs:complexType>
  <xs:element name="addOrderFormResponse" type="ns2:
    addOrderFormResponse" xmlns:ns2="http://utility.services.
    novobank.com/"/>

  <xs:complexType name="addOrderFormResponse"/>
  <xs:element name="confirm" type="ns3:confirm" xmlns:ns3= "http://
    utility.services.novobank.com/"/>

  <xs:complexType name="confirm">
    <xs:sequence>
      <xs:element name="arg0" type="xs:string" minOccurs="0"/>
    </xs:sequence>
  </xs:complexType>
  ...
  <xs:element name="confirmResponse" type="ns4:confirmResponse"
    xmlns:ns4="http://utility.services.novobank.com/"/>
  <xs:complexType name="confirmResponse"/>
  <portType name="OrderForm">
    <operation name="addOrderForm">
      <input message="tns:addOrderForm"/>
      <output message="tns:addOrderFormResponse"/>
    </operation>
    <operation name="confirm">
      <input message="tns:confirm"/>
      <output message="tns:confirmResponse"/>
    </operation>
  </portType>
</definitions>
```

**Example 7.40**
The WSDL definition for the Order Form service

Nothing in the contract indicates that the `addOrderForm()` operation keeps state from previous invocations by the same client in its `HTTPSession`, meaning this information must be documented elsewhere.

Example 7.41 identifies the implementation class for the Order Form service with the `addOrderForm()` operation in Java.

```java
package com.novobank.services.utility;

import java.util.Vector;
import java.util.Iterator;
import javax.annotation.Resource;
import javax.jws.WebService;
import javax.servlet.http.HttpServletRequest;
import javax.servlet.http.HttpSession;
import javax.xml.ws.WebServiceContext;
import javax.xml.ws.handler.MessageContext;

@WebService
public class OrderForm {

  @Resource
  private WebServiceContext webServiceContext;

  public void addOrderForm(String formNumber) {
    System.out.println("Form with number "+formNumber+" was
      ordered.");
    HttpSession session = retrieveSession();
    Vector<String> formList = (Vector<String>)session.
      getAttribute("formList");
    if (formList==null) {
      formList = new Vector<String>();
    }
    formList.add(formNumber);
    session.setAttribute("formList", formList);
  }

  private HttpSession retrieveSession() {
    MessageContext messageContext = webServiceContext.
      getMessageContext();
    HttpServletRequest servletRequest =
      (HttpServletRequest)messageContext.get(MessageContext.
        SERVLET_REQUEST);
    return servletRequest.getSession();
```

```
    }
...
}
```

**Example 7.41**
The implementation class for the Order Form service

Each invocation of the `addOrderForm()` method retrieves the `HTTPSession` instance by using the `WebServiceContext` attribute injected via the `@Resource` annotation. This attribute provides access to the `MessageContext` for the request, which in turn stores a pointer to the servlet request object. Finally, the servlet request allows the session to be retrieved. These steps are all encapsulated in the private `retrieveSession()` method.

The list of ordered form numbers is stored in a `Vector`, which is kept in the `HTTPSession` under the name `formList`. Each time the `addOrderForm()` method is called, the new form number is added to that `Vector`.

What is missing from Example 7.41 is the implementation for the `confirm()` operation. This is where the accumulated information from previous invocations is used, as seen in Example 7.42.

```
public void confirm(String customerNumber) {
  HttpSession session = retrieveSession();
  List<String> formList =      (Vector<String>)session.
getAttribute("formList");
  if (formList==null) {
    System.out.println("No orders found.");
  } else {
    System.out.println("Confirming "+formList.size()+" orders.");
    for (String s : formList) {
     System.out.println("Order for Form " + s + ".");
    }
    session.removeAttribute("formList");
  }
}
```

**Example 7.42**

Access to the `HTTPSession` is provided using the same private method called `retrieveSession()` which provides the complete list of ordered forms. Note how the list is reset by setting the `formList` attribute in the `Vector` to `null` after processing.

The service consumer of this Web service must store the cookie returned from the first invocation to send along with any subsequent invocations, which JAX-WS is equipped to manage. The NovoBank team decides to provide a sample client along with their service for service consumer reuse, as shown in Example 7.43.

```
package com.novobank.services.utility.client;

import java.util.Map;
import javax.xml.ws.BindingProvider;

public class OrderFormClient {

  public static void main(String[] args) {
    OrderForm orderForm =
      new OrderFormService().getOrderFormPort();

    Map<String, Object> requestContext =
      ((BindingProvider)orderForm).getRequestContext();

    requestContext.put(BindingProvider.SESSION_MAINTAIN_PROPERTY,
      true);

    orderForm.addOrderForm("123");
    orderForm.addOrderForm("456");
    orderForm.confirm("any customer");
  }
}
```

**Example 7.43**
Sample client code for the Order Form service

Note that the local service proxy is cast to the `javax.xml.ws.BindingProvider` interface so that the request context can be retrieved and the `SESSION_MAINTAIN_PROPERTY` value can be set to `true`.

HTTP sessions and JAX-WS are only applicable for services with SOAP/HTTP bindings, although similar behavior in a service not accessed over HTTP can be created using the same principles. At invocation by a specific service consumer, the service can return a unique identifier to the service consumer, such as in the SOAP response header, and expect that identifier to be returned with every subsequent request. The service uses the identifier as a key into a table where the data is stored.

How the data is physically stored depends on the developer's requirements. The data stored on behalf of specific service consumers must be recoverable across a server restart persistently in a relational database, which can be accessed using JDBC or a similar mechanism.

Note that state as discussed in this section is usually transient and only exists for the duration of the interaction with the relevant service consumer. Business-relevant data, which needs to be persisted permanently, would not be stored using the mechanisms described. Business data should be stored using data access APIs, such as JDBC, or persistence frameworks, such as JPA or Hibernate.

### SUMMARY OF KEY POINTS

- Many scenarios require data to be stored beyond a single invocation of a service in the calling service, such as from either within a WS-BPEL process or in the called service. Data is often stored for long durations.

- JAX-WS provides a mechanism to utilize the `HTTPSession` object to store temporary state on behalf of a specific service consumer.

- Business-relevant data that must be stored permanently should be handled through entity services that explicitly wrap the handling of such data.

## 7.8 Service Discoverability

The two primary aspects of the Service Discoverability principle are discovery at design-time (which promotes service reuse in a newly developed solution), and discovery at runtime (which involves resolving the appropriate endpoint address for a given service or retrieving other metadata). Even though the information can be physically stored in one place, the way in which the information is accessed in each scenario varies.

### Design-Time Discoverability

At design-time, it is important for project teams to be able to effective identify the existence of services that contain logic relevant to the solution they plan to build. This way they can either discover services that they can reuse or confirm that new service logic they plan to build does not already exist. For example, a service is designed to address an Order Management business process for which customer information is required. The service designer must investigate whether a `Customer` data type already exists, and if so, determine whether it meets the requirements for the Order Management Process service. If the data sent into the newly designed service is missing information, the designer can also check whether an entity service encapsulating all data access to this type of data exists. Additional customer information required can be built or retrieved via a Customer entity service.

During the design of a new service, several types of artifacts must be evaluated for reuse directly on the new service's interface and within the service via some kind of aggregation. This includes non-functional aspects, which may not be expressed in machine-readable form. Meta information, such as performance and reliability of existing services, can influence whether a service is reusable in a new context.

Code can exist for existing data type definitions. JAXB, for example, defines a mapping between XML schema and Java. Java code can be directly generated from a schema definition and reused wherever that particular data type is used.

All of the relevant information must be available to the designer during design-time, ideally via the development environment directly. This relevant information includes the artifacts themselves, such as the WSDL, XML schema, and Java source code as well as relationships and dependencies between them. These dependencies must be documented thoroughly, as part of the service profile so that a complete metamodel of the service exists once the design is complete.

Since the design of a service is manually performed by a service designer, this information must be accessible and searchable by humans. How this feature is enabled depends on the registry type used and the access mechanisms offered, without depending on the programming language used to implement services or on the runtime platform that the service will run on. The underlying mechanism should offer a way to control access to the information and support versioning of artifacts.

## Runtime Discoverability

Runtime service discovery refers to the ability of software programs to programmatically search for services using APIs exposed by the service registry. Doing so allows for the retrieval of the physical location or address of services on the network. Because services may need to be moved from one machine to another or perhaps redundantly deployed on multiple machines, it may be advisable for service addresses not to be hardcoded into the service consumer logic.

For SOAP services using JAX-WS, the location of the target service is included in the `<port>` element of the WSDL definition by default. In turn, the location of the WSDL file is automatically added to the generated `...Service` class and passed to the tooling, or wsimport, that generates the appropriate service consumer artifacts. Pointing to the local WSDL file in the `filesystem` will result in a service consumer that cannot be moved to a different environment, because functionality depends on that particular location for the WSDL file and the endpoint address contained by the WSDL file.

Using the URL and appending `"?wsdl"` to the service is a more flexible approach. For example, a service can be located at `myhost.acme.com:8080/account/account`, in which case the WSDL definition can be retrieved via the URL `http://myhost.acme.com:8080/account/account?wsdl`. During the installation and deployment of a service, the endpoint information in this WSDL file is updated to reflect the real address of the hosting system.

The address points to a fixed location for the WSDL file despite now residing on the network, meaning the address of any target services should always be resolved separately from the generated service consumer code. JAX-WS provides a way to set a target endpoint address on a proxy instance at runtime that utilizes the `javax.xml.ws.BindingProvider` interface. Each proxy implements this interface and allows properties to be dynamically set on an exchange between a service consumer and service, with the endpoint address being one of the pre-defined properties. The code in Example 7.44 illustrates how a service consumer sets a new endpoint address on a service proxy before invocation.

```
String endpointAddress = ...; //retrieve address somehow
OrderForm orderForm =
  new OrderFormService().getOrderFormPort();
  java.util.Map<String, Object> requestContext = (javax.xml.
    ws.BindingProvider)orderForm).getRequestContext();
  requestContext.put(BindingProvider.ENDPOINT_ADDRESS_PROPERTY,
    endpointAddress);
orderForm.addOrderForm("123");
```

**Example 7.44**

The WSDL location can alternatively be set for a service at runtime instead of the endpoint address, to maintain the address of the service together with the rest of the service contract in its WSDL file and not in multiple locations, as shown in Example 7.45.

```
URL wsdlLocation = ...; //retrieve WSDL location
OrderFormService orderFormService =
  new OrderFormService(wsdlLocation, new QName("http://utility.
  services.novobank.com/", "OrderFormService"));
OrderForm orderForm = orderFormService.getOrderFormPort();
orderForm.addOrderForm("123");
```

**Example 7.45**

In addition to the lookup of a service endpoint address, other artifacts can be used by service consumers at runtime to identify an appropriate service and build the applicable request message. The JAX-WS `Dispatch` API allows a service request to be completely built at runtime. Theoretically, a service consumer could look up a WSDL definition at runtime, read its portType and XML schema definitions, and build the right messages from scratch. However, building a service request completely at runtime is impractical in a real-life scenario, as the service will likely perform poorly and require plenty of tedious coding.

Non-functional characteristics of a service are other examples of information that a service consumer can discover at runtime. For example, assume that two physical instances of a service exist on both a slower machine and a faster machine. The service consumer can retrieve this information and select the appropriate service to be used, depending on the business context of the call. For instance, a silver customer is routed to the slower machine, whereas a gold customer is routed to the faster machine. The service is still implemented in both invocations, as the differentiation in routing is a non-functional characteristic.

API endpoints are unnecessary in a REST-based system because no RPC-style invocation is involved. Recall that URI-based addressability, like statelessness, is a formal REST constraint. Resources that offer services are the fundamental entities and must be discoverable through URIs before clients can invoke operations on them. The hypermedia constraint, if followed accurately, requires only the URI of the root resource to be provided to the service consumer.

Various operations on the root resource will publish URIs of related resources, which can then be used by the service consumers to reduce the amount of foreknowledge required. However, service consumers would still require knowledge of the semantics associated with the URIs to be able to make meaningful use of them, which makes this approach impractical in real-life application.

## Service Registries

Information can be retrieved by a service consumer at runtime with the service registry. As the following methods are inapplicable to REST services, the remainder of this discussion will only apply to SOAP-based Web services. Storing information about WSDL locations and endpoint addresses in a file accessible through a proprietary API at runtime is a retrieval mechanism appropriate for small environments. However, the format in which the information is stored, such as XML or a character-delimited format, must be defined, and the location of this file must always be maintained throughout the enterprise for easy accessibility.

Alternatively, storing the information in a relational database allows for remote access and query using a standard language, such as SQL, although a proprietary relational model for this information must still be invented. Other options include leveraging the JNDI or LDAP to serve the same purpose.

In the early days of Web services, a platform-independent standard describing how to uniformly store, find, and retrieve business and technical information about services was developed as the UDDI registry, which offers a query and publish interface. As a Web service, the UDDI registry allows the API to be described by the WSDL so that any Web service-capable service consumer can access a UDDI registry by generating a proxy from the standard WSDL. For accessing registries at runtime, many IDEs such as Eclipse's Web Tools Platform have built-in support for existing UDDI registries.

> **NOTE**
>
> Discoverability processing can be delegated into the ESB, where tasks such as service lookup can be handled centrally and uniformly. The service lookup logic does not then clutter the service consumer, which can instead focus on the business purpose.

## SUMMARY OF KEY POINTS

- For Web services, JAX-WS provides runtime APIs to set the endpoint address of a target service. UDDI defines a standardized way for storing service meta information, which includes access via a Web service-based API.

- REST services use embedding-related resource links in resource representations to leverage the hypermedia constraint and lead the client through a discovery of networked resources.

# Chapter 8

# Utility Services with Java

Utility services provide highly generic functionality that is separate from any domain-specific business processes and usually applicable across a range of business. This chapter explores the design and implementation of utility services with Java.

## 8.1 Inside the Java Utility Service

The following sections raise generation design considerations distinct to utility service architectures, and further provide a list of common utility service types.

### Architectural Considerations

Utility-centric generic functionality is identified by looking for candidate services repeated in many business processes with no inherent affinity to a specific business process or business domain. In a multi-layered architecture of services wherein each layer represents an architecturally significant area of concern, the utility service layer contains services focused on providing reusable functions that address intersecting concerns of existing applications and their technical infrastructure.

Typical characteristics of utility-centric logic include:

- *Business Domain-Agnosticism* – Utility logic has no direct dependency on business domains or processes and is generally applicable across multiple domains.

- *High Reusability* – Utility logic tends to be naturally reusable because of its generic functional context.

- *Low-Level Processing* – Utility logic typically provides the type of processing used by other higher-level business-centric services and processes.

Because utility services work across multiple business domains, they may need to follow a separate development and governance lifecycle potentially implemented and maintained by a separate custodian within the enterprise. The characteristics of utility logic can affect the underlying funding model of utility services, as well as the way new requirements are addressed and managed overall.

Utility services are delegated and not typically coupled with services in higher layers of the architecture directly. Decoupling service components facilitates the management of different concerns or aspects in separate locations of the architecture and independently of each other.

Utility services are not identified as part of the business process or business domain decomposition, and are instead found later in the development process. Addressing non-functional requirements (NFR) and integrating existing application logic into a new architecture can trigger the identification of utility services. NFR describes technical characteristics of the targeted solution which often require the functionality afforded through utility services. Many of the requirements, such as the need for data encryption of messages, are similar between different business domains.

For example, assume that the interaction between two business services must be reliable and offer assured delivery of messages. The standard HTTP protocol does not offer this level of support without application-level programming, so a utility service that enables the application of a reliable messaging standard, such as JMS, to the services' communication is required. Another example is a need for a common method of logging messages and monitoring a service inventory's health as part of an overall management solution.

Existing systems are generally considered for reuse and often cannot be easily replaced without integration into the SOA landscape. Utility services help bridge the technology gap between legacy systems and a service inventory by exposing legacy logic and functions via service contracts that comply with the service inventory's contract standards. Wrapper utility services are one method of this form of integration.

The Java language has a standard set of APIs well suited as utility services. Java, and Java EE in particular, offers interfaces for persistence and data access, security, transactions, and XML document handling. Therefore, an initial set of utility service candidates in Java can be collected through examining the base set of standard Java APIs and evaluating each against the needs of the problem at hand.

Another way of compiling a list of utility services is to start categorizing common application areas, with each area requiring support from a set of utility services. Note that whether or not support for these areas is required by a given solution is often driven by the non-functional requirements presented in Figure 8.1.

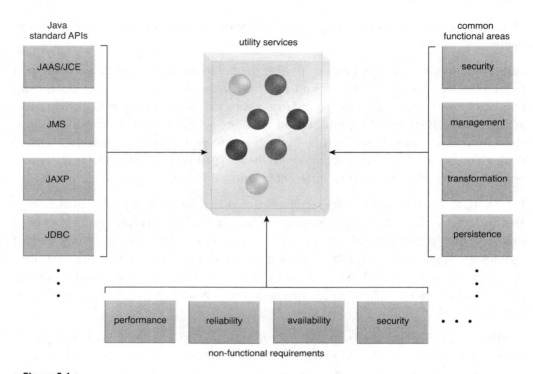

**Figure 8.1**
The set of required utility services can be identified by evaluating the Java language, various aspects of existing services, and non-functional requirements.

The areas of utility services can be partially derived from existing standard Java APIs and then complemented by other common function groups, such as:

- *Security* – Common utility services can address aspects of functionality, such as authentication, encryption, credential mapping, and authorization. An example is a utility service that encrypts an arbitrary XML document using public key cryptography.

- *Management* – The ability to track messages and services and monitor their overall health is part of a service-based management framework that can be implemented via utility services. Services can be managed through other services, such as a utility service that returns the operational state of a given business service.

- *Message Transport and Message Exchange Patterns* – Data that flows between services may require transport over a variety of protocols. Multiple MEP message exchange patterns (MEPs) such as request/response, one-way, and publish/subscribe must be supported. This functionality is delegated to a set of utility services that are often positioned with an ESB. An example is a Publish Message service that allows an XML message to be sent to multiple subscribers asynchronously.

• *Message Manipulation* – Integration of multiple services into a single solution often requires conversion of messages from one format into another. For example, documents may have to follow industry standard formats before they can be sent to an external partner. Data transformation services complement the utility service portfolio with this functionality, for example by supporting XML-to-XML mapping with XSLT or XQuery. This group also includes services for mapping Java objects to XML and vice versa, such as the commonly used Transform service that converts XML documents.

• *Tracing and Logging* – Tracing and logging of information can be considered part of the management framework, although these functions can exist independently and often have high priority. Examples include various forms of logger services.

• *Persistence and Transactions* – Java EE offers a full set of APIs for persistence (the Java Persistence API) and transactions (the Java Transaction API). The Java APIs are appropriate in their original forms for Java-only solutions. However, if non-Java components are required, establishing access to the APIs via a utility service layer may be a viable option. An example for this function is a generic Query service that returns business object data based on passed query parameters.

• *Registry* – The decoupled nature of SOA manifests in levels of indirection between service consumers and services. For a SOAP-based Web service, a service consumer will never contain the hardcoded location or endpoint URL of the service used and instead will delegate the lookup of that address to a well-known location. The lookup of service locations and other metadata is typically contained in a set of common utility services.

For example, a Lookup Endpoint service would return the URL of a SOAP/HTTP service endpoint. REST services have not yet established the need for a centralized registry. The URI of the root resource(s) may be stored in a centralized location. A Resource Lookup service could be created for REST services to support various GET operations that retrieve the URIs of relevant resources. Alternatively, a handful of key resource URIs, or ideally one root resource URI, can be communicated to service consumers out-of-band through informal documentation that allows the hypermedia constraint to guide the REST service consumers through the network of connected resources.

Besides identifying the list of required utility services, positioning utility services in the overall architecture of the system is important because of their broad applicability and ability to be invoked in-process or out-of-process. The main approaches of making utility services available to service consumers include:

- *Local Java Class* – Certain fine-grained performance-critical functionality is well suited to in-process invocation via a local Java invocation. For example, assume that a utility service is built to generate a unique identifier for each message sent across the system. When building an environment with a high volume of messages, the generation of the unique identifier can be placed as close to the origin of a message as possible to prevent a potential performance bottleneck.

- *Remote Java Component* – Services that become part of a highly distributed topology with less performance-critical function and volume can be deployed as a remotely invoked Java component. Generally, the service is hosted in a Java EE-compliant application server and invoked over a communication protocol such as RMI/IIOP. Note that the standard Java RMI communication is omitted from this category, because the limitations related to the lack of a defined application server and container environment make this technology unfit for enterprise-level production environments.

- *Event-Driven Remote Java Component* – An event-driven remote Java component is invoked asynchronously. JMS is the API used for event-driven logic. A client sends a JMS message to a queue without waiting for the message to be processed by its destination or for any response message that may be returned. JMS can be used for request/response messaging, although this method of communication is discouraged in an event-driven architecture. Request/response messaging is commonly implemented in Java EE by use of a MDB method called `onMessage()`, which is invoked on the corresponding queue as soon as a message arrives. The asynchronous nature of MDBs is useful for utility services.

- *Web Service/API* – Web services are accessed across process boundaries. A SOAP or REST service can be accessed by non-Java service consumers, which make Web-based services and APIs integral to any SOA.

Figure 8.2 illustrates the different ways in which a utility service can be deployed using the four approaches discussed.

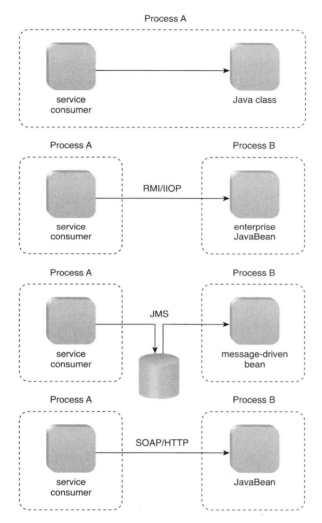

**Figure 8.2**
Utility services can be deployed in a variety of ways to exist in the same process as the service consumer or in a separate process altogether.

Several concerns for consideration include whether a service is invoked locally or across process boundaries. Note that despite this discussion being true for Java services in general, the methods apply particularly to utility services because of their technical nature and close relationship to standard Java APIs. Cross-process invocations indicate pass-by-value semantics because object references are JVM-specific, which renders one JVM's reference to an object meaningless to another JVM. Parameters passed into a remote method call are copied, and changing this data in the invoked method has no effect on the data inside the invoker.

The aforementioned semantics do not also apply to in-process invocations of services. For local Java invocations, if an object is passed to a method instead of a primitive, a copy of the value of the object's reference is passed into a method. If the method uses the object's reference to modify the object, the original object's content will also be modified. In many cases, modifying the original object is a negative side effect. To address the modification of the invoker's object state, copy any parameter objects inside the service implementation to guarantee that the caller's object is not modified by local, in-process invocations.

## CASE STUDY EXAMPLE

NovoBank creates a utility service named Transfer Logger that logs Funds Transfer messages. The messages can originate in a number of locations and contain the amount of the transferred sum as a non-formatted string, such as 1234. For legibility, the utility service formats the amount string into US currency before logging the message, in the form of $1,234.00. Initially, the Transfer Logger service is only available via the Web with the implementation shown in Example 8.1.

```
@WebService
public class TransferLogger {
  @WebMethod
  public void log(FundsTransfer fundsTransfer) {
    try {
      NumberFormat format =
        NumberFormat.getCurrencyInstance(Locale.US);
      String updatedAmount =
        format.format(new Double(fundsTransfer. getAmount()));
      fundsTransfer.setAmount(updatedAmount);
    } catch (Exception x) {...}
    // logging the message to a file goes here...
  }
}
```

**Example 8.1**

After some time, a new solution built entirely in Java is deployed into NovoBank's IT environment, which is architected to take advantage of the Transfer Logger service in-process through a local Java call. However, a copy of the `fundsTransfer` object's reference is passed into the method. The current implementation modifies the `fundsTransfer` object via its reference `fundsTransfer.setAmount`, which updates the originally passed-in `fundsTransfer` object. To avoid this, the implementation must be updated, as seen in Example 8.2.

```
@WebService
public class TransferLogger {
  @WebMethod
  public void log(FundsTransfer fundsTransfer) {
    try {
      fundsTransfer =
        (FundsTransfer)fundsTransfer.clone();
      NumberFormat format =
        NumberFormat.getCurrencyInstance(Locale.US);
      String updatedAmount = format.format(
        new Double(fundsTransfer.getAmount());
        fundsTransfer.setAmount(updatedAmount);
    } catch (Exception x) {...}
      // logging the message to a file goes here...
  }
}
```

**Example 8.2**

In the updated code, the passed object is copied before being updated. The code sample requires the `fundsTransfer` class to implement the `clone()` method and invoke the `Cloneable<FundsTransfer>` interface.

SOAP-based Web services are invoked across process boundaries and use an interoperable message format, such as XML. The data transported to and from a service must be mapped from Java to XML and vice versa. Certain restrictions apply contingent on the standard used for the Web service. For example, the JAX-RPC standard requires that parameters on a service method implement `java.io.Serializable`, since this standard does not support all XML schema constructs. JAX-WS 2.x utilizes JAXB for Java-to-XML mapping, which introduces a different set of constraints. More information on how JAX-WS leverages JAXB to map data between Java and XML was introduced in Chapter 6.

REST services are also invoked across process boundaries and use various interoperable messaging formats, such as XML, JSON, HTML FORM data, and MIME multipart messages. Data binding frameworks, such as JAXB (XML-Java) and MOXy (JSON-Java), manage the mapping between the language-neutral data types and the Java programming language types, and knowledge of the constraints imposed by these mapping technologies is imperative.

A utility service exposed as a Web-based service can be invoked by multiple service clients simultaneously, which introduces concerns about concurrency and thread-safety. For use across a wide range of service clients, utility services should be built for concurrent invocation to run within multiple threads.

For utility services built with Web-based service technologies, the JAX-WS service or JAX-RS-based resource implementations by default ensure that different requests are handled by different object instances with no special programmatic measures necessary to guarantee thread safety.

However, situations occur where the service/resource lifecycle model must change to have a single service/resource manage multiple concurrent requests. Developers must use appropriate concurrency constructs in the Java programming language to ensure correct program behavior.

## Utility Service Taxonomy

The utility service model can be decomposed into further sub-categories of service models that each addresses a specific type of utility-centric functionality, as follows:

- *Omni Utility Services* – Utility services that deliver common functionality needed across a variety of applications and solutions, such as security, logging, or auditing, are called omni utility services.

- *Resource Utility Services* – Resource utility services encapsulate physical system resources, such as data stores and messaging resources, and are not related to REST resources.

- *Micro-Utility Services* – Micro-utility services are fine-grained and highly specialized services that perform technical tasks, such as a service offering XML encryption.

- *Wrapper Utility Services* – Existing legacy systems offer useful functionality that cannot be rewritten, such as mainframe applications developed in COBOL that are often not directly accessible as services. Wrapper utility services are based on the Legacy Wrapper pattern and provide access to legacy logic via standardized service contracts.

These sub-categories will be further referenced in subsequent sections.

### SUMMARY OF KEY POINTS

- Utility services provide a basic service model for generic, cross-domain functionality existing in the utility service layer.
- Utility services are technical in nature and highly reusable.
- Standard Java APIs can aid in identifying functional areas for utility services.
- Utility services can be used in-process and across process boundaries.

## 8.2 Utility Service Design and Implementation

The following section explores design and implementation considerations for utility services.

### Utility Service Design

Having an independent lifecycle means that utility services can often be designed, developed, and maintained on their own timeline. This is true both for the implementation of a service and for its interface. As per the Canonical Schema pattern, it is important to establish canonical data models across a service inventory, especially for business-centric services such as entity and task services. However, relationships between utility services and the canonical schemas are less common.

In the previous case study example, a Transfer Logger service is created to log a message every time money is transferred from one account to another. The instances of transferred money are represented by an object of type `fundsTransfer`, which contains information on the amount of money transferred and references to the account, such as pertinent customer information. Every time the types are updated as part of their natural evolution within the overall enterprise information model, the Transfer Logger service must also be updated, which creates an unwanted dependency with the utility service. Recall that utility services should be agnostic to any business process or domain and a particular set of business object types.

To resolve unwanted dependency on the utility services, the service interface can be designed to have no dependencies on the business objects it handles. Utility services often handle business-relevant data, but rarely contain logic specific to the nature of this data. A service that logs, persists, or transforms messages from one schema to another can be designed so that the structure of the payload of the message does not appear on its interface. Whether exposed as a Web-based service, a remote Java component, or a locally invoked Java class, the interface takes different shapes depending on how the service is deployed:

- *Web Service/API* – Service data is captured in XML schema definitions describing the input and output parameters. A generic utility service interface has no reference to any namespace that is business domain-specific and instead uses generic types, such as `<xsd:string>`, `<xsd:anyType>`, or `<xsd:hexBinary>`.

- *Remote Java Component* – The service interface is a Java interface that wraps an EJB. Each parameter of the remote interface must be serializable as per Java serialization rules, such as `java.lang.String`, `byte[]`, or any other of the basic Java types that implement `java.io.Serializable`. The following interface definition:

```
public interface Logger extends java.rmi.Remote {
  public void log(java.lang.String message) throws RemoteException;
}
```

...illustrates an example of implementing Java serialization rules. Note that the Transfer Logger interface has no reference to an account transfer, but simply logs whatever string is passed. A real logging interface would contain additional parameters, such as indicating log levels, but will never reference business classes.

- *Local Java Class* – The service interface is a Java interface with parameters passed to the service that do not have to be serializable, because they are passed by reference. A service invocation through a local Java invocation creates tight coupling between the service consumer and the service that should be avoided. However, the interface can now define parameters of type `java.lang.Object`. The service implementation logic can incorporate Java reflection to further use the passed objects.

The `LocalJavaLogger` class takes any arbitrary Java object as input and logs it using a standard Java Logger. The content logged is retrieved by invoking the `toString()` method on the object or alternatively using reflection. To identify unwanted and unnecessary dependencies of utility services upon higher-level, business domain-specific schemas and types, structure the data model into complex types that belong to different XML namespaces or Java packages.

A utility service has the highest potential of all service model types for reuse across a large number of service compositions, which results in greater need for scalability and concurrency. Most JREs support the execution of concurrent service invocations in multiple threads, requiring the service logic to be implemented in a thread-safe fashion. Detailing all of the aspects of multithreading in Java is beyond the scope of this book, but in short, multithreading affects how data is treated on the local heap and whether certain blocks of code are wrapped with the `synchronized` keyword. Java 5.0 introduced a package of more advanced classes and interfaces related to concurrency called `java.util.concurrent`, which helps developers build sophisticated concurrent applications without using low-level synchronization constructs.

If a service stores data on behalf of a particular service consumer that is establishing a form of session with another service consumer, subsequent requests from the same service consumer must run in a thread with exclusive access to this temporary information. Generally, the same rules that apply to Java servlet programming from the *Service Statelessness* section apply to the storage of local temporary data, because servlets are also stateless and highly concurrent with similar constraints. Minimize the temporary state held by the service implementation class and use synchronized methods where necessary, especially in mutator methods that change data.

## CASE STUDY EXAMPLE

The SOA architects at NovoBank determined the need for a service that returns a list of company holidays for a specific month. In its first iteration, the service is only required by Java-based service consumers and is consequently built as a Java class that can be locally embedded into any Java application. The designer of the new Holiday Calendar service decides that returning a list of `java.util.Calendar` objects is most valuable to the service's clients, and defines the following interface as:

```
public List<Calendar> getCompanyHolidays(int month);
```

The service requires an input parameter or index of the month as defined in the `java.util.Calendar` interface, such as `Calendar.JULY`. The implementation for the service uses a static table containing the list of holidays. The service operation is achieved in Example 8.3.

```
public List<Calendar> getCompanyHolidays(int month) {
  List<Calendar> list = new ArrayList<Calendar>();
  for (int i=0;i<holidays.size();i++) {
    Calendar c = holidays.get(i);
    if (c.get(Calendar.MONTH)== month) {
      list.add(c);
    }
  }
  return list;
}
```

**Example 8.3**

After deployment, the team at NovoBank discovers that the Holiday Calendar service introduces numerous interoperability problems.

The implementation assumes that the months are represented from 0 to 11 for January to December respectively, which is not obvious from the interface definition. Conventionally, service consumers might assume that 1 represents holidays during the month of January as the first month of the year. To resolve confusion, a comment to the XML schema definition indicating how the months are indexed can be added. Alternatively, the parameter can be made more self-explanatory by using a string like:

```
public List<Calendar> getCompanyHolidays(String month);
```

...that allows the service implementation logic to be written to support the different ways of specifying months, such as `"jan,"` `"Jan,"` or `"January."`

Even though the service uses standard Java, it leverages the `java.util.List` interface with generics only available in Java 5.0. Older Java environments cannot directly include this class and require a Web services invocation layer. Assuming that this service is offered as a Web service, the JAXB standard defines that the return parameter must comply with the XML schema definition, as seen in Example 8.4.

```
<xs:complexType name="getCompanyHolidaysResponse">
  <xs:sequence>
    <xs:element name="return" type="xs:dateTime"
      maxOccurs="unbounded" minOccurs="0"/>
  </xs:sequence>
</xs:complexType>
```

**Example 8.4**

The `List<Calendar>` return type is converted into an unbounded array of elements of type `dateTime` in the schema. Note that this is the only interoperable method of transferring a collection of objects across a Web service interface. However, the semantics of the Java collection class are lost. Each collection class has its own way of storing and sorting elements. What is transferred across the SOAP interface is a plain array with no advanced algorithms available.

Some organizations at NovoBank still use the older JAX-RPC standard, in which mapping of the `List<Calendar>` type is not defined. Depending on the SOAP engine and tools used, the Holiday Calendar service may not work at all. A more compatible version of the interface:

```
public Calendar[] getCompanyHolidays(int month);
```

...is created to interoperate with NovoBank's older JAX-RPC standards and ensure accessibility across the organization.

## Utility Services and Java Editions

Let's explore some of the relevant criteria for building utility services on each of the Java platforms introduced in Chapter 4.

### Utility Services in Java SE

Utility services are business process-agnostic in nature and cover a wide range of technical functional areas. Some of these areas are considered enterprise-level by the Java community and are only addressed in the Java EE platform.

Many of the APIs defined and supported in Java SE are relevant to the design of utility services:

- *Security* – The Java Authentication and Authorization Service (JAAS) and the Java Cryptography Extension (JCE) provide core functionality for security in a Java environment and are both included in Java SE.

- *Management* – The Java Management Extensions API is included in Java SE, beginning with version 5.

- *Transformation* – Parsing and transforming of XML documents are addressed in the Java API for XML Processing and related APIs, such as Streaming API for XML Processing and Transformation API for XML (TrAX). Mapping Java objects into XML documents and vice versa via APIs, such as JAXB, is also considered transformation.

- *Tracing and Logging* – Support for tracing and logging are included in standard Java in the `java.util.logging package`. The open-source Jakarta Commons Logging (JCL) package, which works with any standard Java application, is currently a popular alternative.

- *Persistence* – Java SE includes the Java Database Connectivity API, which is used to access relational databases.

Besides identifying functional areas supported by pre-defined Java APIs and implemented by standard Java packages within JRE, the way in which these are offered to potential service consumers is important. Java SE does not provide the concept of an application server, nor does it support remote communication with Java components hosted in a separate process. Consequently, if the utility services are restricted to a single Java Virtual Machine, they must be deployed as local Java components.

### Utility Services in Java EE

Java EE further encompasses the notion of a secure, scalable, transactional, and distributed container that hosts Java components as part of an application server. The platform allows service capabilities to be offered across processes, instead of solely as local Java components.

In conjunction with the container runtime and associated deployment model for installing Java components into this runtime, Java EE is an umbrella for a number of additional Java technologies relevant to the identification, definition, and design of utility services:

- *Messaging* – The Java Message Service describes a protocol and API for the reliable exchange of messages between applications. Between Web services over HTTP, JMS serves as an alternative network protocol for the exchange of messages. For SOAP-based Web services, JMS can be used as an underlying transport that is separate from the abstract service contract and specified as a binding detail in the concrete WSDL definition.

  Acting as a provider of services and not just a transport protocol, the JMS includes classes and interfaces offering functionality that can add to the collection of utility services.

- *Transformation* – To be interoperable, Web services offer an interface that receives and returns data in form of XML documents, which require back-and-forth conversion between XML documents and Java objects. Java EE defines the Java Architecture for XML Binding.

- *Transactions* – A Java EE-compliant application server contains the logic required to include a series of executions on Java components into the same physical transaction with JTA. Transaction-related services are common utility services required within a number of automated business processes using a service inventory.

  SOAP-based Web services can use certain WS-* standards to complement the JTA functionality included in Java EE by utilizing support for long-running transactions via compensation features found in specifications, such as the WS-BusinessActivity.

- *Registry* – A naming server typically stores information about the Java components and other artifacts supported by the application server exposed via JNDI.

However, JNDI is highly Java-centric and does not satisfy requirements for storing information about services. JAXR stores information about SOAP-based Web services as part of Java EE.

- *Legacy Integration* – The standard defines the J2EE Connector Architecture to allow embedding non-Java applications into a Java EE solution. Within JCA, connectors can be created to run in the application server process and provide seamless access to legacy environments. This architecture is most important in the context of wrapper utility services.

> **NOTE**
>
> For REST services that manage multitudes of resource representations apart from the customary XML, the Java EE platform does not provide support for binding tools between Java and such representation formats. Common JAX-RS implementations, such as Jersey, manage the formats by bundling other open-source libraries, such as EclipseLink, MOXy, and Jackson or Jettison for JSON.

When designing utility services, we need to examine the available APIs and determine which require augmentation for use as part of an enterprise service inventory. Some service functionality can require wrapping in a Web service layer for use across a network by non-Java service consumers. For example, a requirement for a generic XML-to-XML transformation service is identified for redesign as a Web service wrapped around the JAXP `javax.xml.transform.Transformer` class.

Java EE defines the programming model for distributed Java components as EJBs and describes how they can be accessible as Web-based services. EJBs offer scalability and built-in support for concurrent access. Services can be deployed across a number of application server instances without affecting the service logic, and grow with increased usage over time.

> **NOTE**
>
> However, Java EE 6 offers greater flexibility where special types of annotated POJOs known as managed beans offer the same level of concurrency and scalability support as EJBs. An EJB in Java EE 6 is a type of managed bean.

The lifecycle of a managed bean is handled by the container with support for additional features, such as resource injection, interceptors, and lifecycle callback methods. Unlike EJBs, managed beans do not support declarative transactions or security. Building REST utility services with managed beans can take advantage of the container features, such as automatic support for concurrency and scalability, without the need to use less useful features, such as transactions or role-based authorization checks.

**Utility Services and Open-Source Frameworks**

Enhancements to building Java applications once came in the form of tools and frameworks, which were commonly run as open-source efforts through simplifying the use of the underlying Java APIs and packages, or creating new ways of performing tasks unsupported by the standard set of Java specifications. Some enhancements have since become obsolete as support for the target problem was introduced to the standard platform, but other frameworks are still widely popular and undergo their own evolution and innovation.

The open-source frameworks relate to utility service design and implementation as much as the standard Java libraries within the constraints of the design principles, such as Service Reusability and Service Abstraction. Utilizing additional frameworks to fulfill the functional requirements for utility services is likely the type of reuse intended. Three popular complementary framework examples are introduced in the following sections to explore the different types of functionality relevant to the creation of utility services for an enterprise.

*Spring Framework*

The Spring framework provides a comprehensive set of interfaces and classes that assist in creating Java solutions. Logic coded in POJOs is configured into the Spring framework via XML-based configuration files or annotated Java objects, known as Spring beans. The framework provides a base for the presentation layer of an application through its implementation of the Spring Web model-view-controller (MVC). The Spring framework supports the following functionality relevant to utility services:

*Transaction Management*

Spring provides an abstraction layer on top of the existing JTAs for higher-level access to transactional functionality. Since Spring promotes the JavaBean-based approach, the abstraction layer can be added to a utility service inventory for local and remote access. For Web services, a standard, such as WS-AtomicTransaction, is required to create transactions across multiple service invocations.

### Data Access Objects

Data access objects (DAOs) represent a way to group a dataset into large-grained objects, which can be transferred between layers of an application. DAOs can be mapped to messages exchanged between services, and used within a service interface as input and output messages.

### Object-Relational Mapping

Accessing relational data through mapping into Java objects is another use of the Spring framework. Core standards in this context are JDBC and JPA, and alternative methods of accessing data supported by the same layer include Spring-Hibernate, JDO, and Oracle TopLink.

Creating a Spring-based utility service layer for data access allows for interfaces to be defined independent of the underlying technology used, which supports service abstraction. The object-relational data access set of interfaces are a prime candidate for becoming part of a utility service inventory.

### JMS

JMS is considered the protocol binding layer of services and not necessarily as a source for services. Spring supports JMS as a transport mechanism for simple invocation of methods on JavaBeans, which provides a method of service invocation for services that are not Web services.

When using the Spring method of exposing functionality as Web services, JMS can be leveraged as a protocol for Web service invocations. Alternative APIs for reuse as utility services beyond the use of JMS include classes for retrieving the JMS destination names from JNDI, which can be exposed to find appropriate resources to which to send messages as enterprise-wide services.

### JMX

JMX allows for active management and monitoring of Java applications, which encompasses its potential as a utility service. Correspondingly, Spring provides wrapper classes around JMX that enable management to Java solutions.

*JCA*

Similar to how other APIs within the Java platform are wrapped in a more abstract, user-friendly interface by Spring, the CCI is encapsulated to allow Spring-style access to the back-end system supported by the connector via JavaBeans defined in Spring XML configuration files.

*Spring MVC*

Spring MVC is a model-view, controller-based HTTP request dispatcher framework. REST services can be built by leveraging features that support the standard HTTP operations and extraction of URI template values.

*Hibernate*

Hibernate, which is part of the JBoss Enterprise Middleware System (JEMS) suite, is an effective framework for implementing object-relational mapping in Java and allows access to persistent, relational data by manipulating standard Java objects. Focused solely on how to write data to persistent data stores and read it back, Hibernate uses a POJO-based model augmented with XML configuration files and/or Java annotations. Just as with the Spring DAO support, the Hibernate framework offers a means of mapping relational data into objects for transfer between services, and includes helper classes more suitable for definition as utility services. These helper classes generally involve querying persistent data stores.

*Commons Logging and Log4J*

The Commons Logging package is part of the Apache Jakarta project and provides generic support for the logging of data within Java code. The main interface Log provides access to different logging implementations, such as the standard Java logging support. Another open-source package offering logging support is Log4J, which was also developed within an Apache project. Log4J can serve as a logging implementation in Commons Logging, because the two can be used simultaneously.

While the Log4J package has more recent widespread use, both open-source packages offer convenience classes and methods to fulfill the logging function. Logging of interactions between services is a common example of utility-centric service logic.

## Utility Services as Web-Based Services

Various considerations critical to building utility services with SOAP/WSDL and REST utility services are discussed in the following sections.

*Sending XML Data as a String*

The interface definition must first be considered when sending XML data as a string. Since business object-specific schemas must not be referred to in the service contract to avoid dependencies between utility services and higher layers of services, generic XML schema types can be used in the WSDL definition.

Consider interpreting any incoming XML message as a string in light of the Transfer Logger service defined in the previous case study example. A `fundsTransfer` object was used as the payload. Together with the appropriate wrapper element, the object in schema could resemble Example 8.5.

```
<xs:complexType name="log">
  <xs:sequence>
    <xs:element name="arg0" type="ns2:fundsTransfer"
      minOccurs="0"
      xmlns:ns2="http://utility.services.novobank.com/"/>
  </xs:sequence>
</xs:complexType>

<xs:complexType name="fundsTransfer">
  <xs:sequence>
    <xs:element name="amount" type="xs:string" minOccurs="0"/>
    <xs:element name="fromAccount" type="xs:string"
      minOccurs="0"/>
    <xs:element name="toAccount" type="xs:string"
      minOccurs="0"/>
  </xs:sequence>
</xs:complexType>
```

**Example 8.5**

A more generic version of the schema that does not introduce dependency on the `fundsTransfer` object is shown in Example 8.6.

```
<xs:complexType name="log">
  <xs:sequence>
    <xs:element name="arg0" type="xs:string" minOccurs="0"/>
  </xs:sequence>
</xs:complexType>
```

**Example 8.6**

The interface definition declares to the service consumer that the message logged should be transferred as a string. However, the service consumer must create an appropriate string from the business object, which can require further coding.

Despite assuming the message is XML, declaring it as a string results in encoding by the SOAP engine. The encoded SOAP body is presented in Example 8.7.

```
<soapenv:Body>
  <ns1:log>
    <arg0>&lt;?xml version=&quot;1.0&quot;&gt;&lt;ns1:log
      xmlns:ns1=&quot;http://utility.services.novobank.com/&quot;&
      gt;&lt;arg0&gt;&lt;amount&gt;1234&lt;/amount&gt;&lt;/
      arg0&gt;&lt;/ns1:log&gt;</arg0>
  </ns1:log>
</soapenv:Body>
```

**Example 8.7**

To the Web service engine, the message is a string of characters. The engine goes through the encoding effort to prevent confusion with XML. Each angle bracket, such as < and >, is replaced with an escape sequence. The encoding makes the message bigger, the execution slower, and the transferred message harder to read and debug. Even though this method provides a somewhat generic interface with no dependency on the business object, it is not a recommended way of handling XML information.

*Utilizing* <xsd:any/>

An alternative to the string-approach is to change the schema in the service contract to include the <xsd:any/> element, as shown in Example 8.8.

```
<xsd:complexType name="log">
  <xsd:sequence>
    <xsd:any processContents="skip"/>
  </xsd:sequence>
</xsd:complexType>
```

**Example 8.8**

While similar to the string definition, the changes in the service contract acknowledge that the payload of the message will contain XML data. The <xsd:any/> element serves as a wildcard indicating XML is sent without specifying the exact structure. The resulting message is smaller and easier to debug than as seen in the string method.

However, this mechanism of preventing any dependencies on the business object has disadvantages. The XML data cannot be serialized into Java helper classes. As per the JAXB specification, an `<xsd:any/>` element discovered in a schema is mapped to a `java.lang.Object`, because no information about the kind of object being transferred is available. Extra work in the JAXB binding configuration is required to allow the JAX-WS engine to serialize and deserialize the data properly. To avoid this extra effort, an alternative technique is described in the following section.

### *Provider-Style Web Service Logic in JAX-WS*

Typically, a utility service implemented as a Web service has no prior knowledge about the data received or what data it will return to its service consumers at design-time. The only knowledge the service has is that the data handled is exchanged in XML. Converting the data into a graph of Java objects may be unnecessary if it is only received for routing to a different endpoint address or transformed from one XML format to another using an XSLT style sheet. The JAX-WS specification defines a way to create a service interface that routes the XML data directly into the service logic without any parsing or serialization.

### CASE STUDY EXAMPLE

After NovoBank's Transfer Logger service has successfully been in production for some time, the team receives requirements for a more generic version of the service functionality independent of the Transfer Account schema. The Generic Logger service interface is created to log messages without reviewing the included data. An extract from the service implementation class is provided in Example 8.9.

```
package com.novobank.services.utility;
import javax.xml.ws.Provider;
import javax.xml.ws.Service;
import javax.xml.ws.ServiceMode;
import javax.xml.soap.SOAPMessage;
import javax.xml.transform.Transformer;
import javax.xml.transform.TransformerFactory;
import javax.xml.transform.dom.DOMSource;
import javax.xml.transform.stream.StreamResult;
import javax.xml.ws.WebServiceProvider;
@ServiceMode(value=Service.Mode.MESSAGE)
@WebServiceProvider()
```

```
public class GenericLoggerImpl
  implements Provider<SOAPMessage> {
  public SOAPMessage invoke(SOAPMessage source) {
    printRequest(source);
    return null;
  }
  private void printRequest(SOAPMessage request) {
    try {
      Transformer transformer = TransformerFactory.newInstance().
        newTransformer();
      transformer.transform(
        new DOMSource(request.getSOAPPart()),
        new StreamResult(System.out));
      System.out.println();
    } catch (Exception e) {
      System.out.println(e);
    }
  }
}
```

**Example 8.9**

Note that the underlying schema uses the `<xsd:any/>` element, as seen in
Example 8.10.

```
<xsd:complexType name="log">
  <xsd:sequence>
    <xsd:any processContents="skip"/>
  </xsd:sequence>
</xsd:complexType>
```

**Example 8.10**

A generic service can implement the `javax.xml.ws.Provider` interface. The
class retrieves the content of the message as an instance of `javax.xml.trans-`
`form.Source` or as an instance of `javax.xml.soap.SOAPMessage`. Configuring the
`@ServiceMode` annotation can indicate whether the entire SOAP envelope or just its
payload, such as the content of the SOAP body, is passed into the implementation class.

In the previous NovoBank Generic Logger service case study example, `Service.Mode.`
`MESSAGE` is specified and indicates that the entire SOAP message is passed, which is the

only option unless a `SOAPMessage` parameter is defined. The `invoke()` method must be implemented within the implementation class and is called when a request to the associated service endpoint is sent. The entire received message is printed to the screen.

Another example could also log the message content to a file or database. Note that the method body returns `null` at the end to indicate that this class represents a one-way operation with no response message defined. In the associated WSDL document, the operation definition is illustrated in Example 8.11.

```
<portType name="GenericLogger">
  <operation name="log">
    <input message="tns:log"/>
  </operation>
</portType>
```

**Example 8.11**

There is no `<output>` element in the operation, which directly relates to the statement `return null;` in the service logic.

*Building REST Utility Services*

When building utility services with REST, the challenge is in identifying an appropriate resource that may not always be obvious.

For example, a Postal Code Validation service determines the validity of a postal code when given a country and code. Identifying a Web resource is necessary to model this as a REST service. Assuming the postal code entity is the resource itself, mapping the validate operation to any of the standard set of HTTP verbs, such as GET to return the postal code entity itself, POST to create a new postal code, PUT to update a postal code, and DELETE to remove the entity in question, is not possible.

To solve this problem, consider which HTTP method best fulfills this functionality. The operation is idempotent, making the GET method suitable. An HTTP request for validating the postal code is illustrated in Example 8.12.

```
#Request to validate a postal code
GET /validatepostalcode?country=CA&code=M4B1B4
Host: www.postalservices.org
```

```
#Response
HTTP/1.1 200 OK
Content-Type: text/plain
Valid
```

**Example 8.12**

The results of the invocation can be cached because postal code validation results are unlikely to change often. JAX-RS supports injecting the query parameter values into method parameters annotated with @QueryParam. The implementation of a JAX-RS resource class to perform postal code validation should be straightforward. Example 8.13 illustrates another way of extracting the query parameter values which can be useful when the prior query parameters passed in are unknown.

```
import javax.ws.rs.GET;
import javax.ws.rs.Path;
import javax.ws.rs.Produces;
import javax.ws.rs.core.Context;
import javax.ws.rs.QueryParam;
import javax.ws.rs.core.Response;
import javax.ws.rs.core.UriInfo;

public class PostalCodeValidationResource {
  @GET
  @Path("/validatepostalcode")
  @Produces("text/plain")
  public boolean validate(@Context UriInfo info) {
    String country = info.getQueryParameters().getFirst("country");
    String code = info.getQueryParameters().getFirst("code");
    checkPostalCode(country, code);
  }
  private boolean checkPostalCode(String country, String code) {
    boolean result = false;
    //actual logic to check postal code...
    return result;
  }
}
```

**Example 8.13**

The query parameters can be programmatically obtained via calls to the `Uri-Info` object. To retrieve a list of all query parameters passed in the URI, the `UriInfo.getQueryParameters()` method can be used to obtain a `javax.ws.rs.core.MultiValuedMap` containing the query parameters in the form of key-value pairs.

For building REST utility services with a generic JAX-RS resource implementation, `java.io.InputStream` or `java.io.Reader` can be used in the input methods and the corresponding types, such as `java.io.OutputStream` or `java.io.Writer`, are used in the output.

For complete control over input and output types, JAX-RS also provides developers with use of the custom entity providers for arbitrary representation formats or any arbitrary Java types.

For deserializing arbitrary representation formats to any Java type, JAX-RS extension APIs provides the `javax.ws.rs.ext.MessageBodyReader` class. The `javax.ws.rs.ext.MessageBodyWriter` class allows for the serializing of any arbitrary Java type to an appropriate resource representation.

### Testing Considerations

All the regular service testing considerations also apply to utility services. Functional testing are often conducted via JUnit, which is directly supported by many of the available JDEs. It is often easier to write unit test cases for utility services than for other types of services, because they are technical, fine-grained, and agnostic to business processes.

Integration and system testing is more difficult, because utility services are widely reused and have a lifecycle independent from their service consumers. For example, it is not always possible to determine non-functional requirements, because the kind of load a particular service must satisfy cannot be estimated.

Determining and documenting the service levels supported in the service profile will help with testing. If the target deployment environment is known, a system test can help measure data such as the response time and throughput of a given utility service, which can be taken into consideration if the service is to be later reused by additional service consumers.

**Packaging Considerations**

Utility services implemented in Java are packaged according to Java packaging technology. Java components are packaged in a variety of archive formats:

- *JAR* – The Java archive format allows multiple classes and interfaces to be bundled in one file and added to the classpath of a JVM. These classes and interfaces are then available to any code executing in that JVM's process. A JAR file cannot expose its contents as Web-based services, so it is restricted to offering functionality for local Java invocations.

- *WAR* – On top of regular Java classes and interfaces, the Web archive format includes deployment descriptors and artifacts that allow the file to run in the Web container of an application server. In Java EE 6, the deployment descriptor is optional.

  For example, servlet logic and UI artifacts (JSPs) can be invoked from within a Web browser. A WAR file includes one or more JAR files with content available to the resulting Web application. With EJB 3.1, simplified WAR packaging allows for EJB artifacts to be bundled. Web-based services can be packaged in a WAR file, because they contain the necessary infrastructure code on top of any service logic required.

- *EAR* – The enterprise archive file contains all of the artifacts necessary for an enterprise application to run in the Java EE container of an application server, such as Web functionality and EJBs. An EAR file can include one or more JAR files, one or more WAR files, and Web-based services.

  An EAR file can offer all three types of service components relevant to Java-based utility services: local components (through embedded JAR files), remote Java components (through the remote EJB layer), and Web-based services.

Utility services can be packaged as JAR, WAR, or EAR formats depending on their design and functional requirements. Service logic contained in JAR files will be duplicated many times, since a single JAR file may be embedded into a number of WAR and EAR files.

A Java class containing service logic is usually only available on the classpath of a Web or enterprise application if it is bundled with the corresponding WAR or EAR file. A Java class or JAR file cannot be easily deployed and maintained in a central location.

---

**SUMMARY OF KEY POINTS**

---

- Utility services can be designed as local Java components, remote Java components, or Web-based services. Java SE or Java EE can design utility services depending on the required functionality.

- Open-source frameworks, such as Spring or Hibernate, offer a viable alternative for identifying and collecting utility-centric functionality.

- For SOAP-based Web services, Java supports many different programming models. However, the Provider-style programming model in JAX-WS is the most applicable for utility services.

---

## 8.3 Utility Service Types

This section describes a set of specialized variations of the utility service model.

### Omni Utility Services

Omni utility services provide generic, cross-cutting functions, such as security, logging, eventing, and notification.

Common uses for omni utility services include:

- *Security* – Basic functionality to secure a service-oriented environment provides the following: authentication to test the supplied credentials, such as a user id/password combination, against a list of know users; authorization to verify whether or not an authenticated user has access rights to a certain resource; digital signatures for a given document; encryption for documents/messages to only be read after being decrypted with an appropriate key; and identity federation to map credentials that represent a user's identity between different security domains.

- *Logging* – A Logging service should provide a context within which a certain piece of data is logged. This context can be either functional, such as aspects within the service, or transactional, such as actions executed by or on the service.

- *Eventing* – The term "eventing" represents the ability of service components to emit, receive, and exchange information about events. Logging can be considered a special instance of eventing. The events can be highly technical in nature, such as "Could not connect to server at address x.x.x.x," and business-oriented, such as "Item #1234 was replenished in warehouse." Given the strong affinity of any service-oriented solution with concrete business goals, a set of omni utility services should be available and allow for the communication of business events consistently across the enterprise. This requires a well-designed interface that can address the breadth of business situations that occur and a distributed infrastructure to manage events occurring across a network, which ideally stores data relevant to these events in a central location.

- *Notification* – For SOAP-based Web services, the OASIS Web Services Notification workgroup has published three specifications that describe the interfaces required for the exchange of event data between Web services. Utilizing a standard format and standard interfaces increases the interoperability and reusability of any service. The interfaces defined in the WS-Notification family of standards can be mapped into Java and become the base of a Java implementation.

> **NOTE**
>
> Organizations do not typically build a complete framework for Web services-based event handling from scratch, and instead utilize support in existing middleware packages.

### Design Considerations

Omni utility services are broadly applicable, which emphasizes the importance of the relevant service-orientation design principles of Service Abstraction, Service Autonomy, and Service Reusability. Given that these services are reused across many service consumers, they will often be designed as Web-based services with generic, loosely typed interfaces.

### Service Implementation

Omni utility services handle a large variety of payloads, and are often created using the JAX-WS Provider programming model for SOAP-based Web services or the custom entity providers, leveraging `MessageBodyReader` and `MessageBodyWriter` in JAX-RS for REST services.

### Service Consumption

Omni utility services are consumed just like any other services via a generated Java proxy. Since they are typically used more than once by any given service consumer, it is recommended to instantiate proxy objects only once and cache them for later reuse.

## CASE STUDY EXAMPLE

Many of the messages in NovoBank's service inventory pass through a number of intermediaries. The increasing number of moving parts prompts the SOA architect team to create a set of services for notification. NovoBank's Notification service is a Web service that collects information across the enterprise on messages processed, with the option to correlate the individual events to help identify bottlenecks.

The team recognizes that the WS-Notification standard addresses this type of event notification between services, and is not yet implemented in the middleware used by NovoBank. They decide to create their own temporary solution by designing the Notification Consumer service. The WS-Notification standard includes a WSDL file that defines such a service consumer. Therefore, NovoBank decides to reuse the same WSDL file for their implementation and, in particular, the portType from Example 8.14.

```
<wsdl:portType name="NotificationConsumer">
  <wsdl:operation name="Notify">
    <wsdl:input message="wsntw:Notify" />
  </wsdl:operation>
</wsdl:portType>
```

The `Notify` message refers back to the following XML schema definition:

```
<xsd:complexType name="NotificationMessageHolderType" >
  <xsd:sequence>
    <xsd:element ref="wsnt:SubscriptionReference" minOccurs="0"
      maxOccurs="1" />
    <xsd:element ref="wsnt:Topic" minOccurs="0" maxOccurs="1" />
    <xsd:element ref="wsnt:ProducerReference"  minOccurs="0"
      maxOccurs="1" />
    <xsd:element name="Message">
      <xsd:complexType>
        <xsd:sequence>
          <xsd:any namespace="##any" processContents="lax"
            minOccurs="1" maxOccurs="1"/>
        </xsd:sequence>
      </xsd:complexType>
    </xsd:element>
  </xsd:sequence>
</xsd:complexType>
<xsd:element name="NotificationMessage"
  type="wsnt:NotificationMessageHolderType"/>
```

```
<xsd:element name="Notify" >
  <xsd:complexType>
    <xsd:sequence>
      <xsd:element ref="wsnt:NotificationMessage" minOccurs="1"
        maxOccurs="unbounded" />
      <xsd:any namespace="##other" processContents="lax"
        minOccurs="0" maxOccurs="unbounded"/>
    </xsd:sequence>
  </xsd:complexType>
</xsd:element>
```

**Example 8.14**

The schema is not complete, but the main parts of the service are illustrated. The `Notify` element contains a `NotificationMessage` element, followed by an optional `any` element indicated by the `minOccurs="0"` attribute. This leaves room for additional XML content to be added to the event message after the standardized portion. The `NotificationMessage` element is of the `NotificationHolderType` type, which defines some optional standard elements and a mandatory `Message` element containing yet another `any`. The content of the actual event message is undefined beyond the fact that it must be well-formed XML.

This structure is reusable as a template for other purposes, since it makes parts and elements either mandatory or optional. Using wsimport or any other tool that generates Java from WSDL, Java classes that correspond to the XML schema definition can be created. However, the NovoBank team decides to create the service implementation class based on the JAX-WS Provider programming model seen in Example 8.15.

```
package com.novobank.services.utility;

import javax.xml.ws.Provider;
import javax.xml.ws.Service;
import javax.xml.ws.ServiceMode;
import javax.xml.soap.SOAPMessage;
import javax.xml.ws.WebServiceProvider;

@ServiceMode(value=Service.Mode.MESSAGE)
@WebServiceProvider()
public class NotificationConsumerImpl implements
  Provider<SOAPMessage> {
    public SOAPMessage invoke(SOAPMessage source) {
      logEvent(source);
```

```
      return null;
    }
  private void logEvent(SOAPMessage request) {
    try {
      // do something with the event...
    } catch (Exception e) {
      System.out.println(e);
    }
  }
}
```

**Example 8.15**

The code looks similar to the GenericLogger code used in another NovoBank service, which illustrates the fact that JAX-WS creates generic service logic with almost no dependency on its surroundings.

**CASE STUDY EXAMPLE**

The retail chain has requested that SmartCredit offer a utility for downloading customers' monthly credit card charges in a PDF format. SmartCredit plans to build a Document Processor service to allow for the retrieval of monthly charges, but it must use a utility service that can consume an XML document and transform it to a specified output format. The IT team decides to build a REST utility service that can generate PDF and potentially other formats from an XML document.

SmartCredit already uses developed custom Java classes that represent PDF documents, which can be leveraged in the utility service. A skeletal representation of the custom Java type is provided in Example 8.16. Note that the detailed implementation of the logic for converting to and from PDF formats is omitted to highlight the usage of custom entity providers and not different types of document formatting logic.

```
package com.smartcredit.documentprocessing;
public class PDFDocument implements java.io.Serializable{
    ...//methods for reading and writing PDFs
}
```

**Example 8.16**

The resource class for the utility service is shown in Example 8.17.

```
@Path("documentprocessor")
public class DocumentProcessorResource {

  @GET
  @Produces("application/pdf")
  public PDFDocument getPDFDocument(InputStream in) {
    PDFDocument doc = convertXMLToPDF(in);
    return doc;
  }
  private PDFDocument converXMLToPDF(InsputStream in) {
    //logic for converting XML to PDF...
  }
}
```

**Example 8.17**

Since the output response format is a custom Java type that must be serialized into the application/pdf media type, the built-in mapping facilities in JAX-RS cannot be leveraged to perform the Java type-to-media type conversion. The JAX-RS custom entity providers, based on `MessageBodyReader` and `MessageBodyWriter` classes, can handle conversion between arbitrary Java types and other media types, which can be leveraged for the utility service. In this case, a custom entity provider must be built to serialize the `PDFDocument` type. The JAX-RS runtime requires an implementation of the `MessageBodyWriter` class to allow for serialization of the message body.

Creating a JAX-RS custom entity provider involves implementing a JAX-RS Provider. The SmartCredit custom entity provider must also produce PDF formats from XML input, which creates a class that can be seen in Example 8.18.

```java
import javax.ws.rs.ext.MessageBodyWriter;
//...other imports
import com.smartcredit.documentprocessing.PDFDocument;

@Produces("application/pdf")
public class DocumentEntityProvider implements
MessageBodyWriter<PDFDocument>{

  @Override
  public long getSize(PDFDocument doc,
    Class<?> type,
    Type genericType,
    Annotation[] annotations,
    MediaType mediaType) {
    /* return -1 if the content length cannot be determined */

    return -1;
  }

  @Override
  public boolean isWriteable(Class<?> type,
    Type genericType,
    Annotation[] annotations,
    MediaType mediaType) {
    return PDFDocument.class.isAssignableFrom(type);
  }

  @Override
  public void writeTo(PDFDocument doc,
    Class<?> type,
    Type genericType,
    Annotation[] annotations,
```

```
    MediaType mediaType,
    MultivaluedMap<String, Object> headers,
    OutputStream stream) throws IOException,
    WebApplicationException {
    ObjectOutputStream oos = new ObjectOutputStream(stream);
      oos.writeObject(doc);
  }
}
```

**Example 8.18**

Note the following characteristics of the custom entity provider implementation:

- The `DocumentEntityProvider` is called by the JAX-RS runtime before the serialization of the returned resource representation, which in this case is a `PDFDocument`.

- Since the `@Produces` annotation on the custom provider matches the value of the `@Produces` on the resource class, the `writeTo` method is called.

- The `writeTo` method determines how the custom Java type `PDFDocument` is serialized to an `application/pdf` media type as the outbound response.

The custom entity provider is discovered by the JAX-RS runtime automatically because the provider class is annotated with the `@Provider` annotation.

## Resource Utility Services

Resource utility services offer functionality related to the use of common distributed IT resources, such as data, network, and messaging resources. Much of this type of processing is provided by existing Java technologies that allow APIs to be wrapped as part of the utility service layer. The following sections describe resource utility services further.

### Persistence/Data Access Resources

The Service Statelessness design principle refers to the delegation of state data kept by a service implementation when being used by its service consumers. In the context of resource utility services for data, the state data is persistent business data kept in a database (as per the State Repository pattern) and only accessed within a transaction. The services in this category are directly related to database access technologies, with the goal of abstracting the details of these technologies away from the service consumer.

Hibernate is an example of an open-source framework that encapsulates access to relational database tables and handles the mapping between relational data and Java objects, which includes support for collections and inheritance. With Java EE, the JPA has standardized data access to persistent relational data. Hibernate and TopLink are examples of JPA implementations. Data access services provide data. If invoked over a network and exposed as Web services, this data must be serializable into XML for network transfer in an interoperable manner, which is usually handled by a JAXB implementation. However, the SDO specification defines an alternative generic data access model that includes serialization to and from XML.

### Messaging Resources

Interactions between services require support for the transfer of messages between services running in different processes. Support is offered by messaging artifacts for different types of protocols and different types of message exchange patterns.

If HTTP is utilized as the transport mechanism, as is the case for most Web-based services, a layer of HTTP-specific resource services is used to transport messages. The resource services are usually embedded within the Web service engine and are transparent to the service consumer and the service logic. Many of these engines expose lower-level APIs related to the transport of messages across HTTP, allowing direct programming against this level. Another significant transport mechanism for service interactions is JMS, which is often preferred over HTTP because it supports transactional, reliable transfer of messages. JMS also provides asynchronous message transfer and a publish/subscribe model.

*Transaction Resources*

This service type includes transaction resources include transactional resources and the management capabilities needed to coordinate between the resources. Coordination means that a certain protocol is executed to synchronize the transactional behavior of resources that are included in a transaction, an example of which is the two-phase commit protocol. JTA is significant for transaction resources. Spring provides wrapper APIs for handling transactions in Java, and can be a good starting point for Java-based resource utility services for transactions. If transactions are run across Web services, however, a system that can coordinate non-Java resources into a transaction is needed. Significant work has been done in the WS-* world to support both short-lived ACID transactions and long-running compensation-based transactions.

The WS-AtomicTransaction standard addresses the short-running ACID transaction scenario, which transfers a two-phase commit type of protocol into the Web services and SOAP space. Similarly, the WS-BusinessActivity standard covers a different kind of coordination protocol, addressing longer running transactions where each invoked operation can be compensated in case the transaction was not completed successfully. The two standards describe the interfaces and schemas needed for resource utility Web services engaging in transactional behavior. The underlying design patterns that the standards support are called Atomic Service Transaction and Compensating Service Transaction. Many Java implementations offer intrinsic support for these patterns.

Modeling two-phase commit transactions or recording in-flight transaction information for subsequent compensation or rollbacks in REST is not supported because it would require storing transactional state information.

*Design Considerations*

Resource utility services are at a relatively low level in the overall services stack. While encapsulating physical resources that all solutions must handle eventually, resource utility services should limit their exposure to areas of service logic that map business-style interfaces and capabilities into the reality of the environment in which they are running. Resource utility services often change over time and must be replaced or adjusted in the consuming service logic without affecting higher-level service contracts. For example, an entity service utilizing a persistent data store to load data offered to its service consumers will never expose the fact that the data comes from a relational database to its service consumers.

Resource utility services are deployed as Web services used over a network that affects how fine-grained their interfaces should be. When a large number of transactions are expected for a particular service, design patterns like the Service Façade pattern are leveraged to create coarse-grained interfaces and delegate "chatty" interactions into the same process, as illustrated in Figure 8.3.

**Figure 8.3**

The resource utility service acts as a façade, encapsulating fine-grained interactions with the resource database.

service consumer        resource utility service        resource database

For example, assume that a higher-level entity service requires customer data retrieved from a relational table. Hibernate is selected to create a mapping between the relational information and a hierarchy of Java classes. At the top of the hierarchy is a `Customer` class, as shown in Example 8.19.

```
public class Customer {
   private Name name;
   private String customerId;
   private Address address;
   private Account[] accounts;
   private Order[] orderHistory;
   public Name getName() {
      return name;
   }
   public void setName(Name name) {
      this.name = name;
   }
   public String getCustomerId() {
      return customerId;
   }
   public void setCustomerId(String customerId) {
      this.customerId = customerId;
   }
   public Account[] getAccounts() {
      return accounts;
   }
   public void setAccounts(Account[] accounts) {
      this.accounts = accounts;
   }
   public Address getAddress() {
      return address;
   }
```

```
  public void setAddress(Address address) {
    this.address = address;
  }
  public Order[] getOrderHistory() {
    return orderHistory;
  }
  public void setOrderHistory(Order[] orderHistory) {
    this.orderHistory = orderHistory;
  }
}
```

**Example 8.19**

Despite appearances, the `Customer` class is not a resource utility service candidate. To obtain customer information, any service consumer of the service must make repeated calls to the getter methods of the service to obtain all of the attributes relevant to the customer. Being too fine-grained will result in substandard performance, especially if the information is obtained via a Web service interface.

Instead, a service that retrieves and returns the customer object as a whole (in one step) can be designed. The `Customer` object is the payload of the service response message and is returned to the client as one object. If the data is accessed via a Web service interface, ensure that the objects, including complex object graphs and large collections, can be serialized into XML.

### Service Implementation

Resource utility services are rarely created from scratch, and the Java EE set of standards and/or a higher-level framework (Spring or Hibernate) are often leveraged. In the implementation, be careful not to introduce any dependencies on data types that are defined in the business layer. For example, when implementing services for persistence, ensure the business objects retrievable from within your code are not directly referenced.

### Service Consumption

Service consumers of resource utility services often use several in concert to retrieve data or gain access to other physical resources, which means they should be aware of potential transactional boundaries within their logic. Such service consumers must also be aware of the transactional capabilities of any resource utility service used, such as whether it supports participating in a distributed transaction or supports compensation, or whether the results of an invocation of an operation can be undone.

Since many of the services in NovoBank's inventory require some form of access to relational data, a study is conducted to determine how to best deal with this data in Java. The study concludes that JPA, coupled with the Hibernate framework, is the best option for NovoBank's services.

The Data Session service modeled after Hibernate's `org.hibernate.Session` interface is added to the resource utility service inventory. It will not be exposed as a Web service because of tight coupling with the logic that uses it for performance and efficiency purposes. Moreover, many of the required methods cannot be easily mapped into WSDL operations and the exchanged parameters cannot be mapped into XML schema.

A new Java class is created with an inner variable of type `org.hibernate.Session` and a number of additional convenience methods, as seen in Example 8.20.

```
package com.novobank.services.utility;
import java.util.Map;
import java.util.HashMap;
import java.util.UUID;
import org.hibernate.Session;
import org.hibernate.SessionFactory;
import org.hibernate.cfg.Configuration;
public class DataSessionHandler {
  private static Map<String, Session> sessionTable =
    new HashMap<String, Session>();
  private static SessionFactory sf =
    new Configuration().configure().buildSession Factory();
  public static String createSession() {
    Session session = sf.openSession();
    String sessionID = UUID.randomUUID().toString();
    sessionTable.put(sessionID, session);
    return sessionID;
  }
  public static Session getSession(String sessionID) {
    return sessionTable.get(sessionID);
  }
  // additional static convenience methods...
}
```

**Example 8.20**

## Micro-Utility Services

At the finest level of granularity of all services, micro-utility services are not usually exposed as Web services because they are invoked frequently and are performance-critical. Instead, they are usually called in-process. It still makes sense to view this functionality as services, and their reuse potential is high despite being highly specialized. If certain functionality can be executed with such efficiency in an external process, the benefits outweigh the disadvantages of higher network transfer costs.

Examples of micro-utility services are encryption and decryption, digital signatures, data transformation, and mathematical calculations. Many of these functions are already supported by standard Java libraries or open-source frameworks. The creation of XML digital signatures in Java is standardized under JSR 105, for which an implementation exists as the Apache XML Security project. Given that XML digital signatures and XML encryption are included in the WS-Security standard, however, any open-source or commercial package that supports it will include support for this functionality.

Transformation, encryption, and decryption of XML documents are relatively expensive and performance-critical functions. Appliances have recently emerged on the marketplace offering XML encryption in hardware, with better performance than Java-based software solutions. The services associated with this functionality run in a separate process and are invoked via a Web service interface. The performance benefit of hardware-based XML document manipulation may justify paying a performance penalty for the transfer of the information to and from an appliance.

### Design Considerations

A micro-utility service inventory is similar to a collection of class libraries. These services offer fine-grained, highly specialized functionality usually invoked locally and generally performance-critical. Therefore, the most important design principle to apply here is Service Statelessness. In other words, ensure no state persists between service invocations and implement the service logic accordingly, which makes this as much a service implementation consideration as a service design consideration.

### Service Implementation

Micro-utility services are expected to be concurrently utilized by a large number of service consumers, meaning their implementation must be thread-safe. Avoid handling temporary state where possible, and be aware of regular Java performance best practices by unit testing the service early to ensure that required service levels can be met.

*Service Consumption*

Micro-utility services are typically invoked locally as part of utility JAR files that package the service consumer logic. This creates a close coupling between the service consumer and the service logic, meaning that maintenance updates to the implementation of a micro-utility service cannot be easily deployed to an existing production environment. The services do not typically exist in one location, but are duplicated and distributed to each service consumer as well.

---

**CASE STUDY EXAMPLE**

Many interactions between services at NovoBank utilize XML documents. Even though the SOA architect team strives to establish a canonical message model across all services, some transformations between different schemas are still required to allow for communication with legacy systems and external business partner applications.

The team defines a micro-utility service called XMLTransform to deal with transformations in a consistent manner. The service is also exposed as a Web service for service consumers that are not performance-critical and can afford the overhead associated with the network transport.

Example 8.21 is an extract of the WSDL file representing this service.

```
<?xml version="1.0" encoding="UTF-8" standalone="yes"?>
<definitions
  targetNamespace="http://utility.services.novobank.com/"
  name="XMLTransformService"
  xmlns:tns="http://utility.services.novobank.com/"
  xmlns:xsd="http://www.w3.org/2001/XMLSchema"
  xmlns:soap="http://schemas.xmlsoap.org/wsdl/soap/"
  xmlns="http://schemas.xmlsoap.org/wsdl/">
  <types>
    <xsd:schema>
      <xsd:element name="transform" type="tns:transform"/>

      <xsd:complexType name="transform">
        <xsd:sequence>
          <xsd:any processContents="skip"/>
          <xsd:element name="transformName" type="xsd:string"/>
        </xsd:sequence>
```

```
          </xsd:complexType>

          <xsd:element name="transformResponse"
            type="tns:transformResponse"/>

          <xsd:complexType name="transformResponse">
            <xsd:sequence>
              <xsd:any processContents="skip"/>
            </xsd:sequence>
          </xsd:complexType>
       </xsd:schema>
    </types>

    <message name="transform">
       <part name="parameters" element="tns:transform"/>
    </message>
    <message name="transformResponse">
       <part name="parameters" element="tns:transformResponse"/>
    </message>
    <portType name="XMLTransform">
       <operation name="transform">
         <input message="tns:transfrm"/>
         <output message="tns:transformResponse"/>
       </operation>
    </portType>
    ...
</definitions>
```

**Example 8.21**

Note that both the input and the output messages refer to `any` elements, meaning any arbitrary XML content can be sent in this message and some XML content will be returned. The input message includes a string that indicates the name of the transforming style sheet to be used.

Next is the Java code associated with the WSDL definition. In this case, the team uses the `Provider<Source>` model to define that only the payload of the message is passed into the implementation. Since the standard Java APIs for XML transformations are used, an input of type `javax.xml.transform.Source` is applied in Example 8.22.

```java
package com.novobank.services.utility;

import javax.xml.ws.Provider;
import javax.xml.ws.Service;
import javax.xml.ws.ServiceMode;
import javax.xml.transform.Source;
import javax.xml.ws.WebServiceProvider;

@ServiceMode(value=Service.Mode.PAYLOAD)
@WebServiceProvider()
public class XMLTransformImpl implements Provider<Source> {
  public Source invoke(Source source) {
    String transform = parseRequest(source);
    return prepareResponse(source, transform);
  }

  private String parseRequest(Source request) {
    String transform=null;
    // parse the input XML document to retrieve the name
    // of the stylesheet to be used
    // ...
    return transform;
  }
  private Source prepareResponse(Source source,String transform) {
    Source response=null;
    // build a new XML document and store it
    // in the response message
    // ...
    return response;
  }
}
```

**Example 8.22**

### Wrapper Utility Services

This type of utility service is primarily based on the application of the Legacy Wrapper pattern, whereby existing legacy logic is encapsulated by a wrapper service that exposes a standardized service contract. A wrapper utility service can be considered as an intermediary between the service consumer and the actual back-end logic. This intermediary can be located close to the service consumer, close to the back end, or in the middle between the two, such as part of an ESB as shown in Figure 8.4.

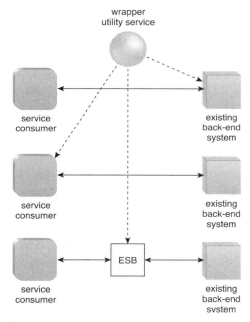

**Figure 8.4**
Wrapper utility services can be placed close to either the service consumer or service, and be delegated into the ESB.

While the location of the actual service affects its runtime behavior, its overall design does not change significantly. Even though they encapsulate or wrap business logic in many cases, wrapper utility services are still utility services and have no dependency on the business service layer of the overall architecture. There is usually some transformation required between the data formats supported by a back end and the schemas supported by higher-level services, creating a level of indirection between business and wrapper utility services.

*Design Considerations*

Contrary to how services are usually identified and designed, wrapper utility service design is not focused on any identified business process activities or requirements of higher layer services, such as entity services or task services. Instead, design is solely based on the existing logic and approached bottom-up, and then mapped to any functional requirements that are raised through the regular design process.

An important design decision for a wrapper utility service is whether to support canonical data and message models, or to allow the service consumer to handle any necessary transformations. Typically, the wrapper utility service should be lightweight and not contain excessive extra logic since its only job is to make the back-end function available as a service. Instead of becoming burdened with any additional transformation or logic, its interface can be classified as one that does not conform to enterprise standards that may be in place. This also avoids any unwanted dependencies on the business object schema layer. The burden is on the service consumer to correct the returned information.

Cases occur where this method of designing wrapper utility services is unsuitable. Let's assume, for example, that an existing back-end function is required by many components throughout a solution but does not return data whose format follows enterprise guidelines. If this function is now exposed as a service via a wrapper utility service, each service consumer must handle the transformation of the data sent to and received from this service, which can lead to unnecessary duplication of effort. In this case, the wrapper utility service should handle the transformation.

The J2EE Connector Architecture is one example of a technology that allows access to an existing back-end application, making it available as if it were a regular Java component living safely within the boundaries of the Java EE container. The native functionality is mapped to a Java interface, and all handling of non-Java data, and the required means to communicate with a back end, are delegated to the inner workings of the connector.

A JCA connector runs in the same process as the Java EE container and takes advantage of the container's connection pooling, authentication, and transaction capabilities. However, it is only directly available to other components running in the same container, such as EJBs and servlets. The client interface is either proprietary for each particular connector or uses the record-based CCI. Therefore, a J2EE connector is usually only used locally and in pure Java solutions. The Spring framework offers a set of convenience classes around JCA that can easily be classified as wrapper utility services.

Wrapper utility services can also be designed to run tightly coupled with the back-end function they encapsulate. A commercial example is Web service interfaces that allow SOAP-based access to SAP BAPI programming interfaces. The wrapper utility services in this case are bundled directly with the SAP system via the SAP application server in NetWeaver.

Because of this tight coupling, the Service Abstraction design principle and, similarly, the Service Loose Coupling design principle are not as important for wrapper utility services as for other utility service types. Moreover, the application of the Service Autonomy design principle is limited by the characteristics of the wrapped environment. The main reason for the existence of wrapper utility services is so that a standardized contract for an existing piece of functionality can be created. With the standardized contract comes support for standardized data formats, such as Java classes in the case of JCA connector, XML schema in the case of Web-based services, and protocols (CCI for JCA connectors or SOAP or REST for Web-based services).

### Service Implementation

The service logic for a wrapper utility service is highly dependent on the native API and protocol that it encapsulates. Some existing functionality may expose an external interface that can be invoked over a network. Some applications have a clearly supported documented data format, which is XML-based in some cases. The implementation of a wrapper utility service follows the existing back end and adapts to the service interface that is communicated to its service consumers.

### Service Consumption

The design and runtime characteristics of wrapper utility services are heavily influenced by the existing encapsulated back end. Consumers of these services must be aware of any associated restrictions, as the services automatically inherit the service-level attributes of the existing application environment. If the wrapped system has a scheduled regular downtime for maintenance, not all of the associated wrapper utility services will be available at the same time.

Wrapper utility services are closely related to resource utility services in how they often encapsulate back-end applications with physical resources. Similar considerations regarding the transactional scope within which the service is invoked also apply. For example, whether or not a function that is wrapped by a wrapper utility service can be listed as part of a distributed transaction involving multiple resources directly depends on whether the existing back end supports this type of transaction. Note that JCA connectors implicitly support the Java EE transactional model, but are limited to what level of support is offered by the back end.

---

### CASE STUDY EXAMPLE

NovoBank uses an existing mainframe system for handling personal accounts and customer information. The mainframe application is running on CICS. Various service implementations must access the functionality offered by this application, and the service design team decides to channel all access to the mainframe through a consistent set of wrapper utility services. After evaluating a number of technologies to implement and deploy these services, the use of a JCA connector is deemed to be appropriate for NovoBank. This connector allows access to the mainframe application directly from within the Java EE container, utilizing the CCI.

The services utilize the CCI convenience classes in the Spring framework, and apply Spring's bean-based programming model to use the connector and expose the connector's functionality as a Web service.

---

### SUMMARY OF KEY POINTS

- Omni utility services provide cross-cutting functionality focused on areas like security, logging, eventing, and notification.
- Resource utility services are used for persistence, and the processing of messaging and transaction resources.
- Wrapper utility services expose a standardized service contract for legacy functions and back-end logic.

# Chapter 9

# Entity Services with Java

Existing data architectures can be problematic for businesses, as they pose a number of inherent challenges. For example:

- *Multiple Versions of the Truth* – Data concerning the same business entity contains different values in different systems. For example, an enterprise can store customer information on several databases, which have little to no inter-database integration or synchronization.

- *Inconsistent Information* – Applications that can return varying results when asked for the same information apply different business rules to the data, because of application-specific methods to retrieve and process data or the applicable data formats supported.

- *Difficulty in Managing Geographically Distributed Supply Chains* – Information cannot be properly propagated along a supply chain consisting of internal and external partners in different geographical locations, which creates the need for manual intervention.

Addressing these issues to establish a consistent method of accessing and processing business data is a fundamental objective of the entity service model. Entity services represent data that is not limited to one business domain, and are instead supported by canonical data models across the entire service inventory. Being highly reusable, entity services are generally utilized by higher-level task services.

Unlike utility services, entity services are business-centric and have correspondingly business-based functional contexts. Entity services are also data-centric, and traditional create-read-update-delete (CRUD) interfaces are substituted for useful capabilities that fall within the services' functional boundaries. Therefore, entity services provide a level of indirection between higher-level process services and the underlying data sources, as shown in Figure 9.1.

## 9.1 Inside the Java Entity Service

Entity service architecture is substantially independent of the programming platform used for its implementation. Let's explore the design and implementation considerations associated with building entity services in Java.

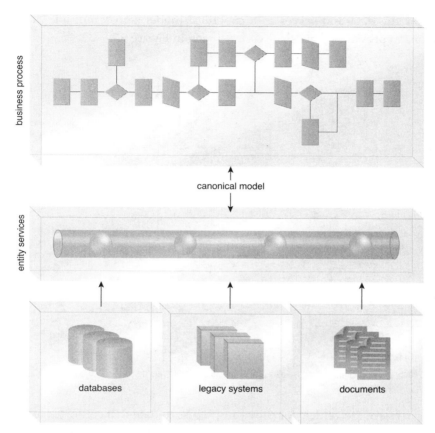

**Figure 9.1**

Entity services provide higher-level services with uniform access to data.

## Architectural Considerations

A typical enterprise has formal data models to describe core data elements and their formats exactly, with some elements of the model limited to a certain domain. Entities like Customer, Order, or Product occur in applications across a number of domains. Many companies use multiple disparate systems to store their own versions of data in their own formats. The data must be transformed manually for every interaction between these systems and any other internal or external system.

For example, many companies have several customer databases that store details relevant to the particular application that uses the data. The enterprise data model attempts to consolidate these different formats by defining a structure that satisfies all potential requests for the data and serves as a canonical model across multiple domains and applications to provide a consistent view, as seen in Figure 9.2.

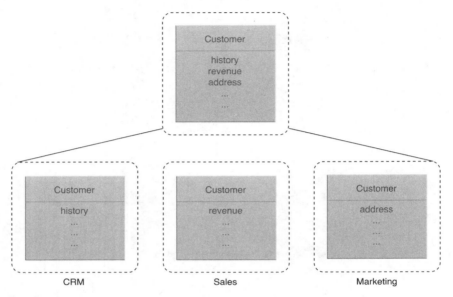

**Figure 9.2**
The canonical form of the enterprise data model consolidates different domain-specific views on data.

Entity services are the vehicle for providing access to data that conforms to the canonical model, which is reflected in the messages travelling in and out of the services. The entity service implementation manages differences between how data is stored in the data source and the canonical model. The way in which data can be retrieved from data stores is also encapsulated in the implementation, which is transparent to the service consumer.

Some data can be retrieved by directly accessing a relational database, instead of a JDBC-based API or employing resource utility services. Other data must be accessed via a particular application interface, such as a mainframe transaction. Entity services are responsible for transforming data into a canonical form supported by the enterprise data model, which is typically described in XML Schema.

### Domain Entities vs. Message Entities

An entity service can act as an access point to a potentially large set of data sources. This level of indirection supports both a canonical data view and specialized interfaces that serve the requirements of certain service consumers. To help distinguish these views, we'll refer to canonical data models within a service inventory as a *domain entities* and the data models specific to an entity service contract as *message entities*.

Specialized interfaces are created because data models instantiated into Java objects in memory can consist of large graphs of objects, which are expensive to serialize into messages for transfer over a network and/or between process boundaries. Figure 9.3 illustrates the relationship between domain and message entities.

Consider, for example, an order entity. Each order typically references the customer that initiated the order and includes individual line items that refer to products. The combined relevant information about an order creates a potentially large amount of data for retrieval from persistent storage. Java or JPA entities implicitly support lazy instantiation mechanisms that only load the required data.

Typical JPA implementations allow for the interception of client requests and additional data to be loaded from its source when needed. However, this approach cannot be applied for services, because a service must always return a complete message that supports call-by-copy semantics. Exposing the full data model is often inefficient in a service context.

If services are identified and specified with a view of the business and its processes, they will include a definition of the messages that flow into and out of each service operation to facilitate the creation of message entity definitions. At the same time, domain entities are created via the definition of a canonical data model. Subsequently, the entity service in its implementation maps existing data from a variety of sources into canonical domain objects (unless already supported by the existing environment) and transforms data into a variety of message objects exposed via the service interface.

Domain entities often follow a different lifecycle than message entities. The definition of domain objects does not change as frequently as the definition of message entities, which are subject to new or constantly changing service consumer requirements. Different design approaches exist to address a dynamic definition in relation to Java, examples of which are explored in the following sections.

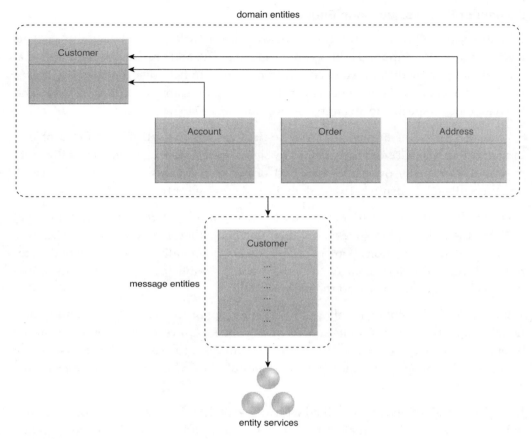

**Figure 9.3**

Message entities provide an abstract view of data based on the domain entity model.

## Data Aggregation

Frequently, the data exposed through an entity service must be aggregated from a variety of sources. One-to-one relationships between the domain and message entities the service uses and the data sources that exist in the enterprise are often absent.

For example, a customer domain entity may consist of attributes for retrieval from multiple databases, such as from a relational database table, third-party Web service, or mainframe transaction invoked using an adapter. The entity service shields its service consumers from these details. The way in which the data is collected and aggregated can be changed at any time without affecting clients.

Data aggregation can be problematic if data is kept at more than one location, which differs between systems. Some business data can be replicated across several data sources at specific points in time, such as an overnight batch load. The data may not be the same for some time. An explicit decision must be made about which version of data represents the master copy, so that the entity service can use the appropriate data source.

Data ownership is directly related to data aggregation. Whenever data is changed via an entity service, it must be ensured that the service can update the data without conflicting with other existing applications. Some applications are built to assume exclusive access to the underlying database. Being tightly coupled to the database creates unwanted side effects when changing data without going through the owning application.

In situations where data is owned by an existing application, the entity service implementation should go through the owning application to make updates to the data. Additional considerations can arise when combining multiple entity services to provide an aggregated view of data, which are explored in Chapter 11.

### Data Access Modes

Entity services do not need to support a plain CRUD interface. Many business processes will never need to update a given domain object or require any service operation that supports writing data.

The need to create and update data immediately raises questions about the transactional characteristics of a service. Should the appropriate table and/or row be locked from access by other service consumers in case a service consumer retrieves data stored in a relational database with the intention of performing updates later? If an update to the data is made, should the system check whether the data has been updated since being read by the service consumer? In a traditionally built application, these issues would be addressed by leveraging support for transactions. A piece of logic that needs exclusive write access to a piece of data would set the boundary of an atomic transaction to prevent concurrent updates. The appropriate database locks are usually put in place.

The Java EE standard and EJBs support a variety of access modes for data without requiring Java coding. Instead, declarative attributes can be set on EJB classes that let the system determine which transactional behavior is desired. Moreover, most Java EE-compliant application servers offer support for declaring data access or locking modes for a persistent entity EJB. For example, a mechanism to read a persistent entity with a pessimistic write lock indicates that other clients cannot update the same data until the owning transaction has completed.

However, these implementation details are not exposed on the entity service interface. Therefore, transactional characteristics and data access modes will not appear on a service interface. A series of invocations on a given service should not be related to each other. Allowing a service consumer to invoke tasks, such as "start a transaction" or "put a lock on this row of data," violates the Service Statelessness design principle.

A common method of accessing and changing data in a service-oriented architecture is called the disconnected or optimistic approach. A service consumer using this approach will obtain a copy of the data by invoking a service, which does not place any locks on the underlying physical resources. Other service consumers interested in the same data are automatically allowed full access. After the service consumer has finished updating, the data is sent back to the service for permanent storage.

The optimistic approach assumes that, in a large majority of cases, no other service consumer will have made an update to the same data while the first service consumer was in the middle of a transaction. In cases where a conflict is detected, the behavior depends on the specific requirements of the application. In some cases, overwriting the updated data is acceptable, while in other cases an error is reported back to the service consumer. A high-level overview of the steps involved in disconnected data access is shown in Figure 9.4.

SDO is based on a disconnected data access approach. The disconnected mode does not support the defining of transactional boundaries. Applications can require the ability to define transactional boundaries for a series of services invocations, such as being able to specify that either all invocations or none are made permanent within a given boundary. For such instances, the WS-AtomicTransaction standard defines how to turn a service into a transactional resource that is then coordinated as part of a two-phase commit-style scenario.

## Change Notifications

During the time in which a service consumer is working with data, that data is not physically locked or otherwise prevented from being updated by other service consumers. Data can become stale and other users may not receive the actual state. Preventing stale data from being altered requires clients to be notified of changes made to the data offered by an entity service. However, some Web-based services are incapable of actively sending out notifications about certain events that have occurred.

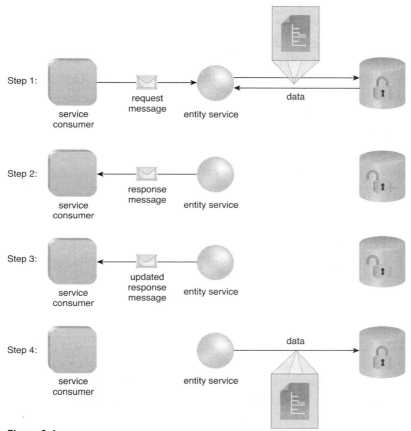

**Figure 9.4**
Disconnected data access leaves no locks on the data source while the data is being worked on by the service consumer.

---

**SUMMARY OF KEY POINTS**

---

- Special considerations apply when aggregating data from multiple sources for exposure by an entity service. The way in which the data is collected and aggregated can be changed at any time without affecting clients.

- Entity services often support a disconnected or optimistic data access mode, by which a copy of the data obtained via service invocation does not place any locks on the underlying physical resources.

- Preventing stale data from being changed requires notifications, which are typically not possible with Web services.

---

## 9.2 Java Entity Service Design and Implementation

Entity services are highly reusable, based on their lack of affinity to a particular business domain. At the same time, design challenges are raised because the services must satisfy service consumers with different specific needs.

An entity service can be performance-critical with a focus on short response times, while other times the service can be run in batch mode with a high throughput of messages.

Service consumers can retrieve large amounts of data with a single invocation, which requires the service implementation to aggregate data from several sources for more fine-grained access with small message sizes. The varying functional and non-functional requirements will affect the design and implementation of an entity service in Java in different ways that are explored in the following sections.

### Entity Service Design

The entity service acts as a level of indirection and isolation between service consumers of data and their source. An existing physical data model is translated into a view relevant to business service consumers, which makes the exposed data structures more useful in higher-level service models.

Entity services tend to be stateless and avoid storing information that is pertinent to any one particular service consumer. An interface relevant and meaningful to higher-level service consumers and services is offered, which means technical terms in the naming of operations and messages are avoided. Entity services can be designed in a strongly typed or weakly typed manner.

*Designing Domain Entities and Message Entities*

When designing Java entity services, Java classes are typically mapped to the physical data model and exist in their own specific Java package for reuse in other entity services.

As an example, an enterprise has customer data stored across a variety of physical databases with a core `Customer` table. The `Customer` table can be mapped into a Java class using a variety of tools and mechanisms.

Each attribute in the `Customer` class represents a column in the relational table. Other tables referred to by the `Customer` table are traversed, mapping the entire relational model into a set of Java classes. The result is a set of domain entity classes available to the entity service implementation.

To identify and indicate that classes are domain entities, classes can be packaged as, for instance, `com.acme.data.customer`. This example of a naming convention isolates the created classes from any service-related classes and interfaces. The domain classes are created based on an existing relational data model, and can be based on other methods of storing data persistently.

---

**NOTE**

Domain entities can also exist only as a reference model with no Java representation of this model being created. Data structures that already exist may be transformed to support the defined service interface, such as utilizing the message entity design, with no intermediate form that follows the domain entity design.

---

The service interface is created separately from the set of domain entity classes and exists in its own package. A set of message entity classes that represent the data transfer objects the service will expose to its service consumers is then defined. In select cases, the data transfer objects will be simple wrappers around the domain entity classes, but in most cases the objects will only contain a relatively shallow version of the original domain object.

For example, a Customer entity service is being built to offer a consolidated view of customer data. The operations of the service are identified through a top-down analysis, identification, and design process that results in a set of different criteria used to select and retrieve the desired customer information. All the operations define, as their response message, a customer message entity that only includes a set of attributes.

This version of the `Customer` class goes into the same package as the service interface to which it belongs. Following the Customer entity service example, this package can be called `com.acme.services.entity.customer`, although `...Domain` and `...Message` can be appended to their class names to make the distinction between the domain entity and message entity more explicit. Keeping the domain entity and message entity in separate packages often helps prevent naming collisions.

The set of classes representing the physical data model and the messages exposed by the new service share no technical dependencies, as they exist in separate Java packages shown in Figure 9.5. The implementation of the service ties these two sets of classes together.

### Designing Stateless Entity Services

The access modes that exist for technical interfaces and influence transactional characteristics of data manipulation are typically not exposed at the entity service interface level. Entity services promote a disconnected data access mechanism and generally do not store any information about individual service consumers between service invocations. They are ideally stateless with respect to individual service consumers, and do not offer any operations that would require storage of state.

For example, it may be undesirable for entity services to offer a `load` or `save` operation because those operations would imply that a service consumer could start conversational interactions with the service.

com.acme.services.entity.customer        com.acme.data.customer

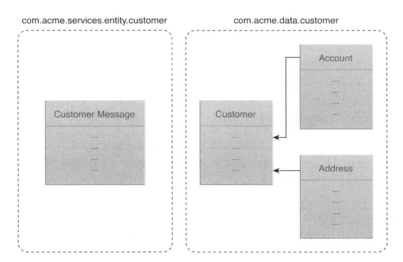

**Figure 9.5**

Message entities and domain entities have no direct technical dependency on each other.

## Designing Business-Relevant Entity Services

An important consideration of entity service design that can relate to the design of any service type is ensuring that the capabilities or exposed operations carry a certain level of business semantics.

The business semantics can be seen in the naming of operations, as these names should not expose any of the technical details of the underlying implementation. Ensuring business-relevant entity services means that, for example, they should not include operations named `executeCustomerQuery` or `loadCustomerTable`, and instead should have operations named `getCustomerAddress` or `findCustomerByAccountNumber`.

## Designing Generic Entity Services

Using concrete types is generally recommended on a service interface to ensure that the service contract is not ambiguous with respect to the types of messages supported. The same is true for entity services. However, certain situations require a more generic interface, such as when a service has many different service consumers with many different requirements for the messages they expect to exchange with the service.

For example, assume that an insurance company uses the Association for Cooperative Operations Research and Development (ACORD) industry standard to build a part of its enterprise data model. This standard defines large and complex data types, which in many cases provide much more information than any single service consumer requires.

The insurance company designs a service that offers vehicle information across the enterprise. The vehicle domain entity is modeled after the standard ACORD definition. Many service consumers may require vehicle information, but each of them requires a different subset of the attributes available in the domain entity.

In order to avoid defining a specific message entity for each service consumer, a single message entity can be defined to hold different sets of attributes, which depend on the attributes retrieved by a particular service consumer. The names of the attributes requested are encoded in the request message, and the entity service implementation collects the appropriate array of attributes accordingly. The message entity stores generic arrays of attributes instead of concrete attributes.

A strongly typed `Vehicle` message entity class is seen in Example 9.1.

```
package com.acme.services.entity.vehicle;
public class Vehicle {
  public String VIN;
  public java.util.Calendar year;
  public String make;
  public String model;
  public String cylinders;
  ...
}
```

**Example 9.1**

A more generic version of the `Vehicle` class is provided in Example 9.2.

```
package com.acme.services.entity.vehicle;
public class Vehicle {
  public String VIN;
  public java.util.Calendar year;
  public String[] furtherInfo;
  ...
}
```

**Example 9.2**

The service consumer and the entity service must agree on what kind of data is exchanged without exposing the method in the service interface. Messages parsed and evaluated at runtime run the risk of unpredictable errors, and circumventing Java's type safety has consequences. Another example scenario that utilizes generic message entities includes a frequently changing structure of data offered by an entity service. The effect of constant changes in the data model can be minimized by making the interface more generic, although generalizing the interface delegates the change in the data model to the implementation.

*Designing Aggregating Entity Services*

The data exposed by an entity service can stem from a variety of sources. Message entities are shallow, or flattened, representations of this distributed domain data. Some data elements can be stored redundantly across multiple sources, requiring the entity service to maintain the appropriate relationships between the data and the data source. Datasets from different sources will likely carry different identifiers or primary keys, and the entity service must create the necessary correlation between keys for the data elements aggregated.

During the design of the entity service, establish which primary keys are required to obtain the data for the service interface, as well as how these keys relate to each other and to any foreign keys that may exist. For example, a bank's `Customer` table can include an array of `Account` identifiers to indicate the accounts this customer has with a bank. However, these identifiers may not be usable directly as primary keys for retrieving account data from the `Accounts` table, and a translation can be necessary. Therefore, a correlation set shows the relationship between identifiers for accounts as contained in the `Customer` table. The identifiers used in the `Accounts` table must be designed.

## CASE STUDY EXAMPLE

Customer information is commonly required by business applications across Novo-Bank, and customer data has been modeled as part of the enterprise data model. A customer record contains one or more addresses for that customer stored in a separate table in the database, which refer to the associated customers and addresses that form a one-to-many relationship.

An SQL statement illustrates the relational model for both the `customer` and `Address` tables in Example 9.3.

```
CREATE TABLE  Customer (
  customer_id int NOT NULL,
  first_name varchar(32) NOT NULL,
  last_name varchar(32) NOT NULL,
  date_of_birth date DEFAULT NULL,
  ssn varchar(11) DEFAULT NULL,
  sex varchar(12) DEFAULT NULL,
  PRIMARY KEY (customer_id)
);

CREATE TABLE  Address (
  address_id int not null,
  name varchar(32) NOT NULL,
  street1 varchar(32) DEFAULT NULL,
  street2 varchar(32) DEFAULT NULL,
  city varchar(32) NOT NULL,
  state char(2) NOT NULL,
  zipCode varchar(10) NOT NULL,
  phone varchar(12) DEFAULT NULL,
  phone varchar(12) DEFAULT NULL,
  m_phone varchar(12) DEFAULT NULL,
  customer_id int not null,
  primary key(address_id),
  foreign key (customer_id) references customer (customer_id)
);
```

**Example 9.3**

The NovoBank design team decides to build an entity service that offers customer data. However, the Customer service does not directly expose the data as stored in the underlying relational model, and a new message entity that fits the needs of an already known service consumer is designed instead. The schema for the new message entity is seen in Example 9.4.

```
<xs:schema version="1.0" targetNamespace="http://customer.entity.
  services.novobank.com/" xmlns:tns="http://customer.entity.
  services.novobank.com/" xmlns:xs="http://www.w3.org/2001/
  XMLSchema">

  <xs:complexType name="customer">
    <xs:sequence>
      <xs:element name="customerId" type="xs:string" minOccurs="0"/>
      <xs:element name="firstName" type="xs:string" minOccurs="0"/>
```

```
      <xs:element name="lastName" type="xs:string" minOccurs="0"/>
      <xs:element name="streetAddresses" type="xs:string"
        nillable="true" maxOccurs="unbounded" minOccurs="0"/>
  </xs:sequence>
</xs:complexType>
```

**Example 9.4**

The message entity includes simplified address information, which is stored as a string and not as a separate complex type. The service implementation logic handles the conversion between the domain entity and the message entity. The target namespace of the schema also indicates that this definition is meant to be used on a service interface, as opposed to being part of the enterprise data model.

The service interface is designed to obtain all customer records and search for a particular customer by name. The resulting WSDL file, with binding information omitted for simplicity, is seen in Example 9.5.

```
<?xml version="1.0" encoding="UTF-8"?>
<definitions xmlns="http://schemas.xmlsoap.org/wsdl/"
  xmlns:tns="http://customer.entity.services.novobank.com/"
  xmlns:xsd="http://www.w3.org/2001/XMLSchema"
  xmlns:soap="http://schemas.xmlsoap.org/wsdl/soap/"
  targetNamespace="http://customer.entity.services.novobank.com/"
  name="CustomerServiceService">

<types>
  <xsd:schema>
    <xsd:import namespace="http://customer.entity.services.
      novobank.com/" schemaLocation="..."
      xmlns:wsdl="http://schemas.xmlsoap.org/wsdl/"
      xmlns:soap12="http://schemas.xmlsoap.org/wsdl/soap12/"/>
  </xsd:schema>
</types>

<message name="getAllCustomers">
  <part name="parameters" element="tns:getAllCustomers"/>
</message>
<message name="getAllCustomersResponse">
  <part name="parameters" element="tns:getAllCustomersResponse"/>
</message>
<message name="getCustomerByName">
  <part name="parameters" element="tns:getCustomerByName"/>
```

```
    </message>
    <message name="getCustomerByNameResponse">
      <part name="parameters"
        element="tns:getCustomerByNameResponse"/>
    </message>

    <portType name="CustomerService">
      <operation name="getAllCustomers">
        <input message="tns:getAllCustomers"/>
        <output mesage="tns:getAllCustomersResponse"/>
      </operation>
      <operation name="getCustomerByName">
        <input message="tns:getCustomerByName"/>
        <output message="tns:getCustomerByNameResponse"/>
      </operation>
    </portType>

    ...
</definitions>
```

**Example 9.5**

## Entity Service Implementation

One aspect of designing the relevant Java interfaces for an entity service is the separation between domain entities and message entities, each of which are represented by their own interfaces in their own packages. Specific and generic types used on the service interface must be business-relevant. The following section will explore the ways in which the interfaces are implemented in Java, which are dependent on the Java edition used.

### Java Editions

There are two main approaches to accessing and handling data when using standard Java APIs that depend on whether or not a Java EE environment is utilized.

Java SE implements the Java Database Connectivity (JDBC) standard, which consists of two levels of API for applications and database drivers. The API for applications provides a set of classes and interfaces for manipulating and querying data from a relational database.

The `java.sql.Statement` interface offers a number of `execute...` methods allowing SQL statements to execute on the target database. With the `executeQuery` method, the resulting data is returned in the form of a `java.sql.ResultSet` with rows of data that can then be retrieved individually.

An entity service with an implementation based on the JDBC can utilize the Java API application classes to retrieve and copy relevant data from a database into the appropriate domain and message entity objects. The mapping from a relational table into a Java object must be done manually. The code must ensure that an attribute in the Java class exists for each column of the table and that the Java attribute types are consistent with their respective database column types.

Before data can be retrieved from a database using the JDBC, a connection to that database must be made. The `java.sql.Connection` interface, which has specific implementations for each JDBC driver, can create a connection and specify the methods responsible for committing or rolling back any transactions against the database.

Despite the seeming simplicity of the Connection API, the code must handle a wide variety of conditions and situations, including partial loading and scrolling of data, caching of both database connections and data, maintaining relationships between objects, and mapping between relational and Java types.

Complicating the implementation can hinder testing and maintenance over time. The JPA has many features evolved as part of popular open-source frameworks to resolve the code conditions for implementation. While this API was originally intended for Java EE, its reference implementation also functions in Java SE. Persistent objects are POJOs provided by the JPA that expose persistent objects via the interface of the entity service, without creating unwanted dependency on other interfaces and classes. The `@Entity` annotation is the only requirement to designate the classes as persistent. Additional annotations are available for storing more information in a persistent class, such as the correspondence between attributes and keys or columns in a relational table.

The JPA provides a standard for object-relational mapping, including the definition of relationships between objects. For example, assume that a `Customer` object has an `Address` object and one or more `Account` objects. The underlying relational model can be defined via the appropriate annotations, including the foreign key relationships between the tables for `Customer`, `Address`, and `Account`. Ownership relationships can be described to, for example, remove the `Address` object automatically whenever its owning `Customer` object is deleted.

In the JPA, the `javax.persistence.EntityManager` interface is used to read and/or write data to and from a database. The interface contains methods for finding entities, which are persistent objects in the JPA, and managing their lifecycle during transactions. Each persistent object is associated with a persistence context, and through this context the `EntityManager` instance manages the individual entities. The `EntityManager` also allows queries to be run against the database.

Queries can either be pre-defined via annotations in the entity class or dynamically built at runtime. The supported query language is an extension of the old EJB Query Language. Dealing with persistent entities in the JPA is similar to calling methods on any Java object. All aspects of persistence, such as loading and storing of data from database tables, are handled implicitly under the covers or by calling the appropriate method on the `EntityManager`.

Apart from managed entities which are managed by persistence context, the JPA also supports detached entities, which are not managed but tracked for changes by the persistence context. Any changes made to a detached entity would not be persisted to the database until the detached entity is brought back under the control of a persistence context or turned into a managed entity. Reintegrating a detached entity back into a persistence context is known as merging.

Versions of J2EE predating Java EE 5 (and JPA) did not support detached entities, and so developers created DTOs that wrap persistent entity EJBs so that repeated fine-grained remote calls to the entity EJBs are avoided. The introduction of detached entities in the JPA has negated the prior need to create DTOs, although use of DTOs as wrappers around the domain entities is recommended to avoid exposing the domain entities to the service consumers. DTOs help insulate the service consumers from underlying data schema changes a nd, if needed, can expose only a certain subset of the domain data to the end user.

A persistent entity can be accessed from multiple concurrent transactions, which creates the possibility of concurrent updates to the same entity that result in lost or conflicting data updates. The JPA offers various locking modes to mitigate such risks. With optimistic locking, a persistent entity can be accessed from concurrently running transactions. When changes are written back to the database, any collision is detected by the runtime and an `OptimisticLockException` is thrown to roll back the attempted update. A simple version field-based annotation on the entity is sufficient to detect conflicting updates.

Optimistic locking is a useful technique to reduce the risks of stale updates when detached entities are modified outside of a transaction and subsequently merged back into a managed entity. JPA 2.0 also supports pessimistic locking, which implements a write lock while reading an entity in the middle of a transaction and ensures that no other concurrent transactions can update the same entity simultaneously. However, maintaining a transactional session during a potentially long entity update is a questionable design decision. Employing pessimistic locking in such situations can result in poor scalability because of the possibility of bottlenecks or deadlocks. Pessimistic locking is useful for certain high-frequency, concurrent update scenarios in which the cost of recovering from numerous failed optimistic concurrency conflicts can outweigh the locking delays incurred in pessimistic locking.

The JPA is the core persistence API underneath the latest standards for EJBs, such as EJB 3.x. Entity beans are based on POJOs with the `@Entity` annotation, as per the JPA. However, no deployment descriptor forces descriptions of attributes and relationships in XML. Also, home interfaces are not required to obtain access to a persistent instance or to run a query. Finally, no JNDI lookup is needed, as all access goes through the local `EntityManager` instance.

In previous versions of J2EE, accessing persistent entity beans directly from a client was not recommended even though persistent entity EJBs were accessible over the network. Access directly from a client often led to excessive network traffic, because the object remained on the server and each call to a method, such as GET, had to go across the network. The recommended approach was to utilize a stateless session bean as a façade to return complete transfer objects to the client. The same practice applies when using EJB 3.x and the JPA. The persistent entity objects are accessed exclusively via a façade session bean that will send data transfer objects to its clients.

As a result, the service implementation class becomes a stateless session bean that obtains an instance of `EntityManager` to retrieve data when needed in support of its interface. The interface of the stateless session bean matches the service interface. Figure 9.6 illustrates how the entity service is implemented as a stateless session bean that leverages the JPA `EntityManager` to manage persistent data instantiated in the form of entity EJBs.

The stateless session EJB façade can be exposed over several protocols, such as RMI/IIOP or via SOAP or REST services using a Web services adapter. Beginning with Java EE 6, REST entity services implementing resources as stateless session beans should take advantage of the transactional facilities offered by the container, as opposed to a non-EJB JAX-RS resource where transactions are handled by the developers themselves.

The implementation of an entity service should take advantage of the JPA and avoid accessing the database directly or using the JDBC API. Any JPA service implementation is offered support for caching and transactions that avoid manual implementation. If utilizing Java EE, the implementation class will often be a stateless session bean that acts as a façade on top of the persistent entities managed by the JPA.

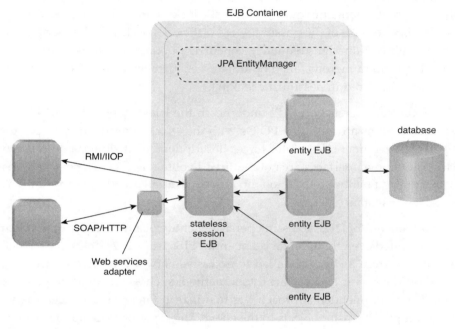

**Figure 9.6**
A stateless session EJB acts as a façade in front of a persistent entity EJB.

## Entity Services as Web-Based Services

Regardless of whether SOAP or REST is used to build Web-based entity services, certain design considerations concerning message entities and domain entities remain applicable.

The difference between domain entities and message entities becomes even more significant when Web services are used, because the service consumer and service exist in different processes and messages must travel via a network. Pass-by-value semantics apply, and data is copied from one participant to another instead of being passed by reference.

Creating message entities that are shallow and contain only a subset of the attributes and relationships of the respective domain entities ensures superior service performance.

The entity service interface should be as coarse-grained as possible, especially when the service is deployed as a Web service. Creating these services as wrappers around each defined domain entity, or defining them for each business object used in an existing application, is not a recommended approach. Instead, service interfaces should be identified and specified beginning with a decomposition of core business processes top-down, which facilitates defining them in a coarse-grained way that offers improved performance when implemented.

## Entity Web Services Using SOAP

When a data model only exists as a relational model, Java classes can be generated from the relational model using the JPA. The appropriate XML schema can then be created from those Java classes. The design of the entity service can start with Java so that the XML schema is generated depending on how the data model is developed, as seen in Figure 9.7.

When the data model is based on industry standards, which are almost exclusively developed in XML schema language, JAXB and its tools can be used. For example, the ACORD standard defines common data types for the insurance industry. In cases where the ACORD schema is the basis for an enterprise-wide data model, the xjc tool included with any JAXB implementation can be used to generate Java classes for use in the respective entity services.

There is a direct relationship between Java package names and XML namespaces. Even though the exact JAXB mapping between the package name and the XML schema namespace can be individually configured, the default is acceptable in most cases. Consider the message entity package example where message entities would go into the `com.acme.services.entity.customer` package. This name maps to a namespace of `http://customer.entity.services.acme.com` in the XML schema.

A namespace definition of `http://entity.services.acme.com/customer` maps to the same Java package. When using an industry standard schema, defining a different mapping from the default can allow for adherence to the specific conventions of Java package names.

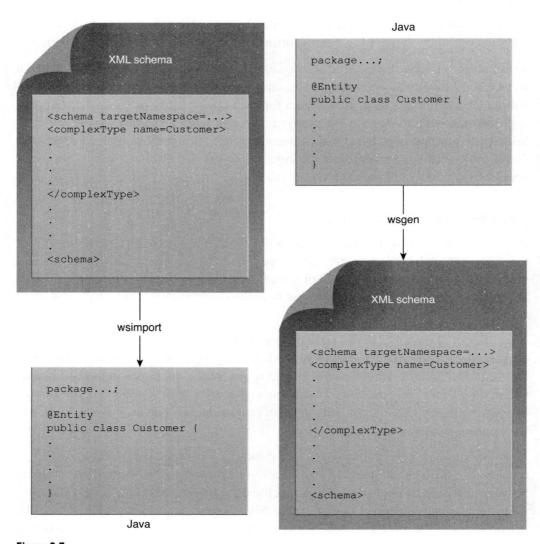

**Figure 9.7**
Entity Web services can be developed with XML schema definitions or Java code.

Entity services based on the JPA can be implemented by either a JavaBean or stateless session EJB. Exposing a JavaBean as a Web service is addressed by the JAX-WS standard API, and exposing the stateless session EJB is defined in JSR 109 Web Services for Java EE. The JSR 109 positioned on top of the JAX-WS adds definitions that are required if the service implementation runs in a Java EE container.

There is no difference in using a JavaBean over a stateless session EJB for the service consumer. For services, a stateless session bean requires a Java EE-compliant runtime environment, which offers many additional features that are not available in a standard Java environment. Service implementations based on stateless session beans can take full advantage of those features. Significant to entity services are the transactional capabilities of EJBs, which allow implicit definition of the transactional characteristics of each instance.

Stateless session EJB instances that are automatically pooled undergo a defined lifecycle, which allows for the reuse of instances across multiple clients. The use of stateless session beans offers advantages over plain JavaBeans, because they exist in a functionally richer environment that allows the developer to focus more on the service logic. Alternatively, a standard Java environment requires less support from the underlying runtime and is generally more lightweight. However, the advent of Java EE 5 promotes a lightweight EJB model.

Stateless session beans are ideal for use as the implementation type for a Web service because service implementations also typically need to be stateless. The same is true when using JavaBeans to implement a service, as the JavaBean is created within a Web container at runtime and each service consumer invocation of the service is executed in its own thread.

Maintaining data in a service instance across invocations is at times unavoidable. Techniques to maintain data without creating unwanted side effects include storing data for individual threads only, exchanging keys to session-oriented data with a service consumer for resolution each time a new message arrives, and synchronizing access to state within the service implementation class.

Reducing the cached state in an entity service implementation class to a minimum is recommended, because the great reuse potential of these services might lead to a rather large number of concurrently active instances. The same is true for any other resources used by a service implementation, such as database connections.

NovoBank's Customer entity service is implemented using the Java Persistence API with Java EE Enterprise JavaBeans. Creating the Java classes that map to the relational tables is the IT team's first step. Both `customer` and `address` tables are mapped to a Java class in Example 9.6.

```
package com.novobank.data.customer;

// imports omitted here...
@Entity
@Table(name = "customer")
@NamedQueries({
  @NamedQuery(name = "Customer.findByName",
    query = "SELECT c FROM Customer c LEFT JOIN FETCH
    c.addressesWHERE c.firstName = ?1 AND c.lastName = ?2"),
  @NamedQuery(name = "Customer.findBySsn",
    query = "SELECT c FROM Customer c LEFT JOIN FETCH
    c.addressesWHERE c.ssn = :ssn"),
    @NamedQuery(name="Customer.findAll",
    query = "SELECT c FROM Customer c LEFT JOIN FETCH c.addresses")
})

public class Customer implements Serializable {
  private static final long serialVersionUID = 1L;
  @Id
  @Column(name = "customer_id", nullable = false)
  private Integer customerId;
  @Version
  @Column(name="version")
  private int version;

  @Column(name = "first_name", nullable = false)
  private String firstName;

  @Column(name = "last_name", nullable = false)
  private String lastName;

  @Column(name = "date_of_birth")
  @Temporal(TemporalType.DATE)
  private Date dateOfBirth;

  @Column(name = "ssn")
  private String ssn;
```

```
  @Column(name = "sex")
  private String sex;

  @OneToMany(cascade = CascadeType.ALL,mappedBy = "customerId")
  private Collection<Address> addresses = new ArrayList<Address>();

  public Customer() {}
  // getters and setters omitted...
}
```

---

**Example 9.6**

Note how the class has a `Collection` attribute of type `Address`, even though the `customer` table has no column of that type. The `@OneToMany` annotation indicates the relationship between the two. The `Address` class is listed in Example 9.7.

```
package com.novobank.data.customer;

// imports omitted here...
@Entity
@Table(name = "address")
@NamedQueries({})
@XmlAccessorType(XmlAccessType.FIELD)
public class Address implements Serializable {
  private static final long serialVersionUID = 1L;
  @Id
  @Column(name = "address_id", nullable = false)
  private Integer addressId;
  @Version
  @Column(name="version")
  private int version;
  @Column(name = "name", nullable = false)
  private String name;

  @Column(name = "street1")
  private String street1;

  @Column(name = "street2")
  private String street2;

  @Column(name = "city", nullable = false)
  private String city;

  @Column(name = "state", nullable = false)
  private String state;
```

```
@Column(name = "zipCode", nullable = false)
private String zipCode;

@Column(name = "phone")
private String phone;

@Column(name = "m_phone")
private String mPhone;

@JoinColumn(name = "customer_id",
  referencedColumnName = "customer_id")
  @ManyToOne
  @XmlTransient
  private Customer customerId;
  public Address() { }

// getters and setters omitted here...
}
```

**Example 9.7**

The `@Version` annotation indicates that the corresponding persistent fields and database columns will be used by the JPA runtime to track updates from concurrent transactions. The JPA implementation reads in the value of this column at the beginning of a transaction. An `OptimisticLockException` is thrown to allow the transaction to roll back if the value changes during the intervening period at write time by another transaction. However, the application should not attempt to update the version information, as this will interfere with the operation of the runtime.

The `@JoinColumn` and `@ManyToOne` annotations indicate the relationship with the customer table. The `@Entity` annotation indicates that both classes are deployed as persistent entity EJBs. Following the Service Façade design pattern with Example 9.8, a stateless session bean that allows access to the entity EJB via two methods named `getAllCustomers()` and `getCustomerByName()` are created.

```
package com.novobank.data.customer.ejb;

// imports omitted here...
@Stateless
public class CustomerBean implements CustomerRemote {
  @PersistenceContext
  private EntityManager em;
```

```
  public void persist(Object object) {
    em.persist(object);
  }

  public List<Customer> getAllCustomers() {
    return em.createNamedQuery("Customer.findAll")
      .getResultList();
  }

  public Customer getCustomerByName(String firstName,
    String lastName) {
      return (Customer)em.createNamedQuery("Customer.findByName")
        .setParameter(1, firstName)
        .setParameter(2, lastName)
        .getSingleResult();
  }
}
```

**Example 9.8**

The session bean takes advantage of the JPA `EntityManager` to gain access to the entity beans. All database access is handled under the covers by the JPA implementation in the application server. The stateless session bean is exposed as a Web service to allow access to customer information for non-Java service consumers in Example 9.9.

```
package com.novobank.services.entity.customer;
import com.novobank.data.customer.Customer;
@WebService()
public class CustomerService {
  @EJB
  private CustomerRemote ejbRef;

  private CustomerConverter converter = new CustomerConverter();

  @WebMethod(operationName = "getAllCustomers")
  public List<Customer> getAllCustomers() {
    List<com.novobank.data.customer.Customer> list =
      ejbRef.getAllCustomers();
    List<Customer> newList =
      new LinkedList<Customer>();
    Iterator<Customer> iterator = list.iterator();
    while (iterator.hasNext()) {
      newList.add(converter.convert(iterator.next()));
```

```
    }
    return newList;
  }

  @WebMethod(operationName = "getCustomerByName")
  public Customer getCustomerByName(String firstName,
    String lastName) {
      Customer domainCustomer =
      ejbRef.getCustomerByName(firstName, lastName);
      return converter.convert(domainCustomer);
  }
}
```

**Example 9.9**

The session bean directly exposes the entity EJB on its interface. The Customer entity service exposes a message entity version of customer information, and a `converter` class that transforms one into the other is required. Therefore, the last line in the source listing illustrates how a `convert()` method is called to perform this transformation. The `converter` class converts the domain entity class `com.novobank.data.ustomer.Customer` into the message entity `class com.novobank.services.entity.customer.Customer` in Example 9.10.

```
package com.novobank.services.entity.customer;
import com.novobank.data.customer.CustomerDTO;
public class CustomerConverter {
  public Customer convert(CustomerDTO domainCustomer) {
    Customer c = new Customer();
    c.setCustomerId(domainCustomer.getCustomerId(). toString());
    c.setFirstName(domainCustomer.getFirstName());
    c.setLastName(domainCustomer.getLastName());
    List<String> newAddressList = new LinkedList<String>();
    Collection<Address> addressList = domainCustomer.getAddresses();
    for (Address a : addressList) {
      StringBuilder sb = new StringBuilder();
      sb.append(a.getStreet1())
        .append("\n")
        .append(a.getStreet2())
        .append(a.getCity())
        .append(", ")
        .append(a.getState())
        .append(" ")
        .append(a.getZipCode();
```

```
        newAddressList.add(sb.toString());
      }
    c.setStreetAddresses(newAddressList);
    return c;
  }
}
```

**Example 9.10**

## REST Entity Services

REST entity services require identifying the right resources on which the HTTP operations will be invoked. Modeling the domain entities as resources is insufficient and overlooks the following considerations:

- Do the domain entities require read-only or read-write permission? If the same domain entity must offer both views, should they be modeled as different resources?

- How is varying granularity of the same domain entity handled? For service consumers interested in different subsets of the same domain entity information, should the same domain entity be modeled as different resources?

- How are new domain entities created? How does a service consumer of an entity service locate a newly created resource, possibly with a view of updating the same resource later on?

- How are service consumers expected to discover related domain entities? Can all the related entities or URI addresses be discovered dynamically, or are they required beforehand?

- How are collections of domain entities managed? Should the entire collection be modeled as a resource? How is a subset of a collection of domain entities returned to a service consumer?

- How are entity services that retrieve information from multiple domain entities in a single operation handled? What resources can be used to represent the aggregate information?

The remainder of this section provides design guidance when establishing REST entity services and concludes with a SmartCredit case study example to illustrate the design strategies applied and implemented using the JAX-RS API.

### Read-Only and Read-Write Resources

Certain domain entities often only have read-only access as the entities themselves are rarely updated. An example is the category of data known as reference data, such as product codes and currency codes. For read-only entities, REST services can be built by modeling resources that only support a subset of the HTTP interface, such as GET and HEAD. Domain entities that support reads and writes can be modeled as typical resources supporting all the HTTP methods.

However, a domain entity may be scattered across multiple systems, such as databases, legacy systems, and ERP systems. Up-to-date entity information can only be obtained by performing potentially expensive queries against all source systems, which is undesirable and often unnecessary. In such situations, the complete domain entity may be assembled and refreshed only once during a 24-hour cycle, such as during a batch run at night.

A read-only view of information can be offered out of an operational data store (ODS) to requesting service consumers who do not necessarily need the most up-to-date entity information. The same domain entity can be modeled as a read-only variant supporting only GET, and as a read-write variant supporting PUT and POST.

### Resource Granularity

The same domain entity may need to offer different subsets of information to different service consumers. The entity can be modeled as a single resource, and return the complete set of information for service consumers to pick the attributes of interest. However, for large datasets that can contain numerous connected resources, a more flexible, albeit complex, option can be used to model the same entity as multiple resources offering different views in different use cases.

### Resource Creation and Location

All entity services that create new resources must return the URI of the newly created resources so that entity service consumers can use this information for subsequent operations. All resources must be addressable, so the address of a newly created resource must be communicated. Example 9.11 illustrates the creation of a resource.

### Request Message

```
POST /customers HTTP/1.1
Content-Type: application/xml
```

```
<customer>
  <first-name>John</first-name>
  <last-name>Doe</last-name>
  ...
</customer>
```

*Response Message*

```
HTTP/1.1 201 Created
Content-Type: application/xml
Location:http://server/services/customers/1234

<customer id="1234">
  ...
</customer>
```

**Example 9.11**

A John Doe request/response example of entity services for a newly created resource

In Example 9.11, the entity service for creating a customer accepts a POST request and returns a response with an HTTP `Location` header, which indicates the URI address of the newly created `customer` resource. Example 9.12 revisits the example from Chapter 6 where a customer was created from a `CustomerResource` class within a JAX-RS resource.

```
import javax.ws.rs.core.*;
...
@POST
@Consumes("application/xml")
public Response createCustomer(Customer cust) {
  //...create customer in the system
  String baseURI = ...;
  Customer c = createCustomer(cust);
  return Response.created(java.net.URI.create(
    baseURI+c.getCustomerId()).entity(c).build();
}
```

**Example 9.12**

The JAX-RS `javax.ws.rs.core.Response.created` method returns an HTTP 201 response `Created` with a `Location` header carrying the URI of the newly created resource. The `Response.created` method returns a `javax.ws.rs.core.Response-Builder` object, which can be chained with the `ResponseBuilder.entity` method passing in any `java.lang.Object` as the returned entity. Apart from the 201 status code with a `Location` header, a resource representation is returned to the newly created customer. The mapping of the JAXB object to the XML resource representation is handled by the JAX-RS runtime.

*Resource Relationships*

Most domain entities participate in a web of relationships, such as "an order entry may have multiple order items," and "an order item may have a number of suppliers associated with it." If the creation of an order is to be modeled as an entity service, the service consumer must be able to discover information about the order items. The relationship between resources in a resource representation is best described through links.

A link has an associated URI address that service consumers can use to navigate to a related resource. Describing a link in a way that non-human service consumers can interpret and act upon is important for the service consumer to be able to understand the semantics of the link. Embedding a custom element, such as <uri>, in a resource representation can be intuitive enough for human service consumers, but an application must know what <uri> signifies.

The Atom syndication format provides standardized link elements and a relation attribute that can take on a range of well-known values for interpretation by an Atom link-aware service consumer application, as seen in Example 9.13.

*Request Message*

```
POST /orders HTTP/1.1
Content-Type: application/xml
<Order>
  ...
</Order>
```

*Response Message*

```
HTTP/1.1 201 Created
Content-Type: application/xml
Location:http://server/services/orders/333
<order id="1234">
  ...
  <orderitem id="456">
    <atom:link rel="self" href=http://server/services/orderitems/456
      type="application/xml"/>
    ...
  </orderitem>
</order>
```

*Request Message*

```
GET orderitems/456 HTTP/1.1
Content-Type: application/xml
...
```

**Example 9.13**

The Atom `link` element's `href` attribute in Example 9.13 specifies the URI and indicates the location of the order item resource. The value of the `relation` attribute indicates the `link` represents the preferred address of the resource, and the `type` attribute describes the resource representation format.

The hypermedia constraint enables service consumers to discover and navigate to linked resources via standardized means, such as Atom links. In resource representations, such types of links are known as structural links that encapsulate other aggregate entities. Structural links are embedded in the same location as the aggregating entity.

*Resource Collections*

Entity services must often return a collection of domain entities based on set criteria. To find all orders priced over 1,000 dollars, the collection of orders can be modeled as a resource and issue a GET operation to filter the results, as seen in Example 9.14.

*Request Message*

```
GET /orders?minimum=1000 HTTP/1.1
Content-Type: application/xml
...
```

*Response Message*

```
HTTP/1.1 200 ok
Content-Type: application/xml

<orders>
  ...
  <order id="444">...</order>
  <order id="666">...</order>
  <!- more orders, possibly thousands... -->
</orders>
```

**Example 9.14**

The result of the GET operation produced orders with unnecessary information. To navigate through the list ten orders at a time, adding the additional query parameters:

```
GET /orders?minimum=1000&start=1&size=10
```

...increases the coupling between the service consumer and service by requiring the service consumer to know and pass in additional information beyond what is part of the service interface, such as the start and size information as opposed to the minimum order value. Transitional links, which are based on RFC 5988 that leverage HTTP headers with the link header fields, can be used to resolve the increased coupling. A new HTTP link header field in the response can point to the next allowed state transition of the resource, as in Example 9.15.

```
HTTP/1.1 200 ok
Content-Type: application/xml
Link: <http://server/services/orders?minimum=1000&start=1&size=10>;
rel=next
<orders>
  <order id="444">...</order>
  <order id="666">...</order>
  <!- ...8 more orders in the current batch of 10... -->
</orders>
```

**Example 9.15**

The client follows the `link` in the link header to request the next set of resources and the response changes, as highlighted in Example 9.16.

```
HTTP/1.1 200 ok
Content-Type: application/xml
Link: <http://server/services/orders?minimum=1000&start=11&size=10>;
rel=next

<orders>
  <order id="4444">...</order>
  <order id="6666">...</order>
  <!- ...8 more orders in the current batch of 10... -->
</orders>
```

**Example 9.16**

The RFC 5988 link relation attribute `rel=next` refers to the next resource in an ordered set of resources. A transitional link-aware client can correctly interpret the relation attribute value and discover the URI pointing to the next resource set, which reinforces the hypermedia-driven navigation constraint.

The JAX-RS 2.0 APIs support transitional links through the `javax.ws.rs.core.Link` class, and a `Link` header can be embedded along with the response via the call listed in Example 9.17.

```
List<Order> orders = getNextOrders();
//getNextOrders returns a batch of orders
Response resp = Response.ok(orders).link("http://server/services/orde
rs?minimum=1000&start=1&size=10", "next").build();
```

**Example 9.17**

Instead of moving the query parameters inside the attribute of an Atom `link` element, the value of the relation attribute of the `link` element `next` points to the next set of resources in an ordered collection of resources. An Atom-aware client can correctly interpret the relation attribute value and discover the URI of the next set of resources in the collection without requiring any additional information beforehand.

## Aggregate Entities

Domain entities often participate in complex relationships, and use cases often demand aggregating information from multiple domain entities. The level of details in the aggregate entity may not capture all of the fine-grained attributes of all the related entities, but rather present summary-level information spanning the entities. For example, a Customer Account Summary service retrieves customer account balances from all of the account holdings. The summary information is an aggregate of various disparate attributes, such as `customer id`, `name`, `account type`, `description`, and `account balances` that span multiple entities, such as `customer` and `account`.

Modeling a REST service for retrieving the summary information must capture both `customer` and `account` resource states. If the client is left to retrieve individual bits of information from multiple entities, such as `customer` and `account` information, not only is traffic increased over the network, but internal implementation details of how the customer account summary information is obtained are also exposed to the service consumer.

An alternative is to offer an aggregate entity, such as a Customer Summary, that can provide the requested information via an HTTP GET operation and avoid multiple network trips while hiding the internal implementation details of how individual account attributes are retrieved, as seen in Example 9.18.

*Request Message*

```
GET /customersummary/5678 HTTP/1.1
```

*Response Message*

```
HTTP/1.1 200 ok
Content-Type: application/xml
<customersummary xmlns:atom="http://www.w3.org/Atom/2005">
  <customer id="5678">
  <atom:link rel="self"
    href="http://server/services/customer/5678"/>
  <name>John Doe</name>
    ...
  </customer>
  <accounts>
    <atom:link rel="http://server/services/custaccts"
      href="http://server/services/accounts?customerid=5678"/>
    <account id="666" type="chk">
      <balance>500</balance>
    ...
    </account>
    <account>
      ...
    </account>
    ...
  </accounts>
</customersummary>
```

**Example 9.18**

An aggregate entity provides the Customer Summary service information via an HTTP GET operation.

Structural links are embedded to enable discovery of related resources, such as a collection of related accounts. The value of the `rel` attribute for the `accounts` resource points to a URI. Instead of referring to another resource location, the URI is an Atom link relation extension identifying the purpose of the link via a URI without any guarantee that this URI resolves to a locatable resource.

The Collection of Accounts resource can be located at the URI indicated by the `atom:link` `href` attribute. A link relation extension is used with a custom value for the `rel` attribute because the standard values of the `rel` attribute, such as `"self"` and `"alternate,"` are inapplicable in this case. In terms of updates to an aggregate resource, the service consumers should not be allowed to update a customer summary, transfer the balance from the checking account to a savings account, or deactivate the checking account, as seen in Example 9.19.

```
PUT /customersummary/5678 HTTP/1.1
Content-Type:application/xml
<customersummary>
<!- ...transfer checking account balance,
  cancel checking...-->
</customersummary>
```

**Example 9.19**

Aggregate resources assemble information from various resources but should not be the vehicle to update or create any of their constituent resources, as the update operations should be handled by the individual resources. The response to the request to alter the `customersummary` from Example 9.19 is presented in Example 9.20.

```
HTTP/1.1 405 Method Not Allowed
Allow: GET, HEAD
```

**Example 9.20**

The response indicates the invoked operation is `Not Allowed` on this resource, and the `Allow` header indicates that the only allowed operations are GET and HEAD.

---

**CASE STUDY EXAMPLE**

Internal applications at SmartCredit often require a customer profile for different marketing use cases, such as marketing campaigns and promotional offers. A customer profile is a combination of various attributes that include customer details, existing accounts, revolving credit amounts, and any outstanding credit applications.

Gathering this aggregated information is an expensive operation that requires querying numerous back-end systems, filtering, and assembling the results. The customer relationship management (CRM) division wants to use this information repeatedly throughout the day, and going through an expensive computation for such high-frequency operations does not make sense.

The IT team builds an operational data store to hold the customer profile information for the Credit Application service. A nightly batch job performs the synchronization between various data sources and the ODS, which the marketing department can use to obtain the customer profile information. The SmartCredit development team builds a REST service to obtain this information and models the customer profile information as an aggregate resource, as seen in Example 9.21. The `CustomerProfileResource` class only responds to a GET operation.

```
package com.smartcredit.credit.services;
import javax.ws.rs.core.*;
import com.smartcredit.domain.Customer;
import com.smartcredit.domain.Account;
import com.smartcredit.domain.Application;
import javax.xml.stream.*;
...

@Path("/customerprofile")
public class CustomerProfileResource {
  @Get
  @Path("{id}")
  @Produces("application/xml")
  public String getCustomerProfile(@Context UriInfo uri,
    @PathParam("id") int id) {
    //Get base request uri
      URI baseUri = uri.getBaseURI();
      // Get aggregate profile information from ODS
      Customer customer = getCustomerData(id);
      List<Account> accts = getAccountsSummary(id);
      List<Application> apps = getApplicationSummary(id);
      //Start writing a raw xml with aggregate information
      StringWriter sw = new StringWriter();
      XMLStreamWriter wr = XMLOutputFactory.newInstance()
        .createXMLStreamWriter(sw);
      wr.writeStartDocument();
      wr.writeStartElement("CustomerProfile");
      wr.writeStartElement("Customer");
      //Write out an Atom link for customer resource
      wr.writeStartElement("Atom",
        "link","http://www.w3.org/Atom/2005");
      wr.writeAttribute("rel", "self");
      wr.writeAttribute("href",
        baseUri.toString()+"/customer/"+id);
      wr.writeEndElement();
```

```
        //Write out customer information
        wr.writeStartElement("Name");
        wr.writeCharacters(customer.getName());
        wr.writeEndElement();
        //...write other customer information
        wr.writeStartElement("Accounts");
        //...write out Accounts
        wr.writeEndElement();
        //...write out Applications
        wr.writeEndElement();
        //End writing CustomerProfile information
        wr.writeEndDocument();
        //return the accumulated string as xml... JAX-RS
        //will do the appropriate Content-Type conversion
        return sw.toString();
    }
}
```

**Example 9.21**

Key points from the resulting definition in Example 9.21 include:

- The resource class is returning an XML-based resource representation.

- The individual domain entities, such as `Customer`, `Account`, and `Application`, are queried from the ODS via internal APIs and returned as JAXB objects.

- The resource method implementation uses the StAX parsing API to create a raw XML document, combining attributes from various constituent resource objects.

- The implementation adds in appropriate Atom links for related resources in the resource representation returned.

- The resource class uses the JAX-RS `@Context` annotation to inject request URI information into a method parameter. This information is used later to form the appropriate Atom link relations for embedded resources.

- The return type from the resource method, a String, is mapped to the `application/xml` media type by the JAX-RS runtime.

Using a low-level XML streaming API such as StAX gives the implementation complete control over how the resource representation is written out, and may be a more appropriate choice for populating aggregate resource information over using a binding framework like JAXB.

*Open-Source Frameworks*

Many Java developers preferred to utilize persistence frameworks built on top of the standard Java support. These frameworks leverage existing APIs such as the JDBC, but offer more convenient methods of handling persistent data that include mapping to Java classes and objects.

In the open-source space, a common framework for persistence is Hibernate. Many of its features heavily influenced the design of the Java Persistence API. Hibernate implements the Java Persistence API and can act as a persistence service in any Java EE-compliant application server.

## Testing Considerations

Entity services can introduce special considerations for testing. For example, service consumers can utilize an entity service in a synchronous online fashion, which requires fast response times and high availability. Other service consumers could use an entity service in a more batch-oriented asynchronous manner, in which many transactions requiring high throughput with less stringent response time requirements are handled.

These different usage profiles all require testing, both individually and in concert. For example, the response time of a particular entity service should function normally if heavy streams of requests by a batch service consumer are received. Heavy batch processing can result in multiple instances of the service being deployed to isolate certain service consumers from affecting each other. Such deployment needs are identified through frequent and early testing of the performance characteristics of any given entity service.

High service reuse accompanies a high degree of concurrency for consideration. An entity service accessed simultaneously by many different service consumers requires thorough testing for side effects that may hinder or impede functionality, such as data changed by a service consumer and whether optimistic locking is used. Each service must implement a specific optimistic strategy for situations where the same data is updated by different service consumers at the same time. Simultaneous saved changes to the data can nevertheless be written to a persistent data store, or result in an error signaled back to the servi ce consumer. Testing will ensure functionality regardless of the implemented strategy.

When data is aggregated from multiple sources, the performance of the overall service is defined by the combined performance characteristics of every accessed data source.

In many cases, aggregated entity services are more susceptible to performance problems that require appropriate testing.

## Java Packaging Considerations

Code artifacts related to domain entities and message entities should be packaged separately with no direct dependency on each other. Sometimes domain entities have no code artifacts to begin with. Classes and interfaces for message entities should be packaged with the entity service implementation classes, as they are tightly coupled and not reused across several service implementations.

For deployment into a Java EE runtime environment, the service implementation classes and the message entity classes go into the same enterprise archive (EAR) application module. Message entities can be packaged as a utility jar file or be directly included in the EJB module containing the EJB classes for the service. Domain entity classes and interfaces are packaged in a separate utility jar file for reuse across multiple services if they are leveraged in the service implementation.

Note that packaging entity services separately can result in a large number of enterprise applications in cases where many entity services are defined. Having a Java EE environment handle large numbers of applications can result in maintenance challenges if certain procedures and process steps must be applied to each enterprise application. For example, grouping several entity services into one enterprise application to install updated applications can be reasonable under time constraints. The enterprise application can group entity services based on their associated business domains.

### SUMMARY OF KEY POINTS

- The Java Persistence API facilitates access to data stored in relational databases, which make it possible to focus on business logic in the entity service implementation. For XML data exchange, the JAXB standard defines a common tool-supported method of converting between Java objects and XML documents.

- REST entity services must consider special design details about how domain entities can be mapped to appropriate resources, such as structural or transitional links. Structural links guide clients to related aggregate resources via embedded links, such as Atom links. Resource state transitions are guided via transitional links captured via HTTP link headers, such as the RFC 5988.

# Part III

# Service Composition and Infrastructure

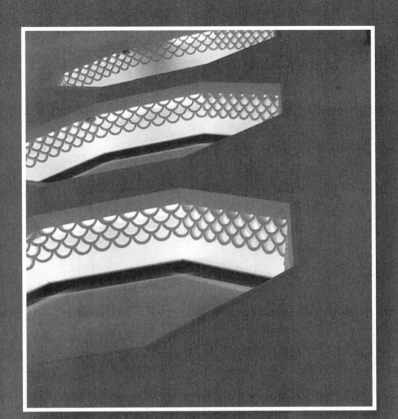

# Task Services with Java

Task services encapsulate the non-agnostic automation logic of business processes and have a scope of execution that often corresponds to that of a business process instance. This chapter explores the design and implementation of task services with Java.

## 10.1 Inside a Task Service

The service logic of a task service will often consist of controller logic, which composes entity and utility services as needed to fulfill functionality (Figure 10.1). Unlike agnostic services, which are generally built as standalone, shared IT resources, task services are modeled according to business process logic and designed around the execution of that logic via the composition of other services. The following case study demonstrates a simplified business process automated by a task service.

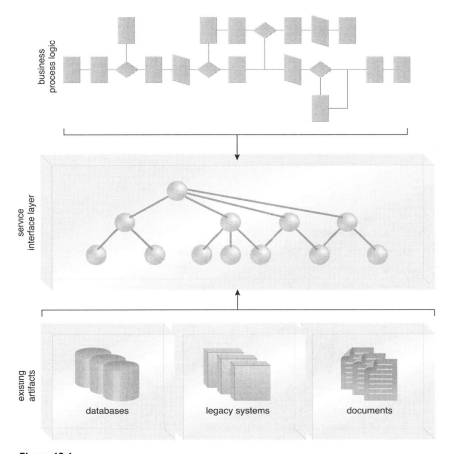

**Figure 10.1**

Task service design is focused on implementing non-agnostic logic that is, to a significant extent, comprised of composition logic.

---

## CASE STUDY EXAMPLE

During the service identification phase, the Credit Approval process is decomposed into a set of individual tasks, resulting in the Process Customer Account service candidate with the capability candidates retrieveCustomerAccountInfo and sendCustomerNotification.

**Figure 10.2**

The Process Customer Account service candidate with two candidate capabilities: retrieveCustomerAccountInfo and sendCustomerNotification.

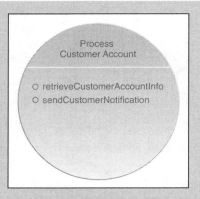

Part of the required customer information needed for credit approval includes data about all of the accounts that a particular customer has with NovoBank. The data is retrieved from within the `retrieveCustomerAccountInfo` operation by leveraging the Customer entity service and an additional Account entity service. The new Account entity service uses a message entity type that represents a summary of account data presented in Example 10.1.

```xml
<?xml version="1.0" encoding="UTF-8" standalone="yes"?>
<xs:schema version="1.0" targetNamespace="http://account.entity.
  services.novobank.com/" xmlns:tns="http://account.entity.services.
  novobank.com/" xmlns:xs="http://www.w3.org/ 2001/XMLSchema">
  <xs:element name="findAccountByCustomer"
    type="tns:findAccountByCustomer"/>
  <xs:element name="findAccountByCustomerResponse"
    type="tns:findAccountByCustomerResponse"/>

  <xs:complexType name="findAccountByCustomer">
    <xs:sequence>
      <xs:element name="arg0" type="xs:string" minOccurs="0"/>
    </xs:sequence>
  </xs:complexType>

  <xs:complexType name="findAccountByCustomerResponse">
    <xs:sequence>
      <xs:element name="return"
        type="tns:account" maxOccurs="unbounded" minOccurs="0"/>
    </xs:sequence>
  </xs:complexType>

  <xs:complexType name="account">
```

```
    <xs:sequence>
      <xs:element name="accountId" type="xs:string" minOccurs="0"/>
      <xs:element name="accountType" type="xs:string" minOccurs="0"/>
      <xs:element name="balance" type="xs:double"/>
    </xs:sequence>
  </xs:complexType>
</xs:schema>
```

**Example 10.1**

An entity service returns data found in a database, and returns message entities that reflect the needs of the calling business service consumer. For the NovoBank credit approval process, only the current balance of each of a customer's accounts is taken into consideration. Therefore, the Account entity service returns a list of `Account` message entity objects, which only contain information about the type of account and its current balance. A customer can have one or more accounts, all of which are relevant when considering an issued credit request.

Both entity services are composed by the Process Customer Account service. The Customer entity service returns the appropriate customer ID for a given name, which is then used to retrieve detailed account data by calling the Account entity service. Figure 10.3 shows the dependencies between the Process Customer Account task service and the Customer and Account entity services.

**Figure 10.3**

The Process Customer Account service composes the Customer and Account entity services.

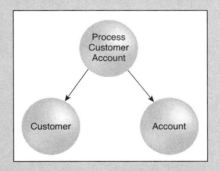

The input parameters to the `retrieveCustomerAccountInfo` operation are the customer's first and last names. The returned data is a combination of customer and account information, and the response message is a new message entity modeled on the needs of the credit approval process. The schema definition of the `CustomerAccountInfo` message entity in Example 10.2 contains element definitions for the `retrieveCustomerAccountInfo` operation of the Process Customer Account service.

```xml
<xs:schema version="1.0" targetNamespace="http://creditapproval.
  task.services.novobank.com/" xmlns:tns="http://creditapproval.
  task.services.novobank.com/" xmlns:ns1="http://account.entity.
  services.novobank.com/" xmlns:xs="http://www.w3.org/2001/
  XMLSchema" xmlns:ns2="http://customer.entity.services.
  novobank.com/">

  <xs:import namespace="http://account.entity.services.novobank.
    com/" schemaLocation="CustomerAccountService
    Service_schema3.xsd"/>
  <xs:import namespace="http://customer.entity.services. novobank.
    com/" schemaLocation="CustomerAccountService
    Service_schema1.xsd"/>

  <xs:element name="retrieveCustomerAccountInfo"
    type="tns:retrieveCustomerAccountInfo"/>

  <xs:element name="retrieveCustomerAccountInfoResponse"
    type="tns:retrieveCustomerAccountInfoResponse"/>
  <xs:complexType name="retrieveCustomerAccountInfo">
    <xs:sequence>
      <xs:element name="arg0" type="xs:string" minOccurs="0"/>
      <xs:element name="arg1" type="xs:string" minOccurs="0"/>
    </xs:sequence>
  </xs:complexType>

  <xs:complexType name="retrieveCustomerAccountInfoResponse">
   <xs:sequence>
      <xs:element name="return" type="tns:customerAccount Info"
        minOccurs="0"/>
   </xs:sequence>
  </xs:complexType>

  <xs:complexType name="customerAccountInfo">
    <xs:sequence>
      <xs:element name="accounts" type="ns1:account" nillable="true"
        maxOccurs="unbounded" minOccurs="0"/>
      <xs:element name="customer" type="ns2:customer" minOccurs="0"/>
    </xs:sequence>
  </xs:complexType>
</xs:schema>
```

**Example 10.2**

In Example 10.2, the `Customer` message entity and the `Account` message entity schemas are imported from separate XML schema files because they are defined in different namespaces. The resulting WSDL definition is shown in Example 10.3.

```
<definitions xmlns="http://schemas.xmlsoap.org/wsdl/"
  xmlns:tns="http://creditapproval.task.services.novobank.com/"
  xmlns:xsd="http://www.w3.org/2001/XMLSchema"
  xmlns:soap="http://schemas.xmlsoap.org/wsdl/soap/"
  targetNamespace="http://creditapproval.task.services.novobank.
  com/" name="ProcessCustomerAccountServiceService">
 <types>
  <xsd:schema>
    <xsd:import namespace="http://customer.entity.services.
      novobank.com/" schemaLocation="http://192.168.1.100:8080/
      ProcessCustomerAccountServiceService/ProcessCustomerAccount
      Service/__container$publishing$subctx/META-INF/ wsdl/
      ProcessCustomerAccountServiceService_schema1.xsd"
      xmlns:wsdl="http://schemas.xmlsoap.org/wsdl/" xmlns: soap12=
      "http://schemas.xmlsoap.org/wsdl/soap12/"/>
  </xsd:schema>
  <xsd:schema>
    <xsd:import namespace="http://creditapproval.task.
    services.novobank.com/" schemaLocation="http://192.168.
    1.100:8080/ProcessCustomerAccountServiceService/
    ProcessCustomerAccountService/__container$publishing$subctx/
    META-INF/wsdl/ProcessCustomerAccountServiceService_schema2.xsd"
    xmlns:wsdl= "http://schemas.xmlsoap.org/wsdl/"
    xmlns:soap12= "http://schemas.xmlsoap.org/wsdl/soap12/"/>
  </xsd:schema>
  <xsd:schema>
    <xsd:import namespace="http://account.entity.services.
      novobank.com/" schemaLocation="http://192.168.
      1.100:8080/ProcessCustomerAccountServiceService/Process
      CustomerAccountService/__container$publishing$subctx/META-INF/
      wsdl/ProcessCustomerAccountServiceService_schema3.xsd"
      xmlns:wsdl="http://schemas.xmlsoap.org/wsdl/"
      xmlns:soap12= "http://schemas.xmlsoap.org/wsdl/soap12/"/>
  </xsd:schema>
 </types>

 <message name="retrieveCustomerAccountInfo">
   <part name="parameters"
     element="tns:retrieveCustomer AccountInfo"/>
 </message>
 <message name="retrieveCustomerAccountInfoResponse">
```

```xml
  <part name="parameters"
    element="tns:retrieveCustomer AccountInfoResponse"/>
</message>
<message name="sendCustomerNotification">
  <part name="parameters" element="tns:sendCustomer Notification"/>
</message>

<message name="sendCustomerNotificationResponse">
  <part name="parameters"
    element="tns:sendCustomer NotificationResponse"/>
</message>

<portType name="ProcessCustomerAccountService">
  <operation name="retrieveCustomerAccountInfo">
    <input message="tns:retrieveCustomerAccountInfo"/>
    <output message="tns:retrieveCustomerAccountInfo Response"/>
  </operation>
  <operation name="sendCustomerNotification">
    <input message="tns:sendCustomerNotification"/>
    <output message="tns:sendCustomerNotification Response"/>
  </operation>
</portType>

<binding name="ProcessCustomerAccountServicePortBinding"
  type="tns:ProcessCustomerAccountService">
  <soap:binding transport="http://schemas.xmlsoap.org/soap/http"
    style="document"/>
  <operation name="retrieveCustomerAccountInfo">
    <soap:operation soapAction=""/>
    <input>
      <soap:body use="literal"/>
    </input>
    <output>
      <soap:body use="literal"/>
    </output>
  </operation>
  <operation name="sendCustomerNotification">
    <soap:operation soapAction=""/>
    <input>
      <soap:body use="literal"/>
    </input>
    <output>
      <soap:body use="literal"/>
    </output>
  </operation>
</binding>
```

```
<service name="ProcessCustomerAccountServiceService">
  <port name="ProcessCustomerAccountServicePort"
    binding="tns:ProcessCustomerAccountServicePortBinding">
    <soap:address location="http://192.168.1.100:8080/
      ProcessCustomerAccountServiceService/
      ProcessCustomerAccountService"
      xmlns:wsdl="http://schemas.xmlsoap.org/wsdl/"
      xmlns: soap12="http://schemas.xmlsoap.org/wsdl/soap12/"/>
  </port>
</service>
</definitions>
```

**Example 10.3**

Note that the included `element` and `message` definitions for the `sendCustomerNoti-fication` operation are revisited in Chapter 11.

The messages defined for a task service are ideally derived from a canonical data model, although non-standard message structures can also be defined since task services are often used in and designed for one business process. A task service that needs to compose entity services that support canonical messages should utilize or map them appropriately in the implementation logic.

The service definition and message entity schema are generally defined in the same namespace.

## Performance Considerations

The interaction between the task service and the underlying entity and utility services can be resource-intensive. An invocation of a task service can result in a large number of invocations on the underlying composed set of services. Simplifying the communication path between services can help maintain performance.

For optimal performance, task services should be hosted in a location close to where the composed services reside. However, because the types of services composed by task services are generally agnostic, they are used across business domains and may be part of multiple service compositions. Options for redundant implementations of shared agnostic services can be explored to support performance requirements, as per the Redundant Implementation pattern.

Task services need to retain the state data required for their task-centric processing across service invocations. State data can be represented by local, thread-specific variables in the code if the service is implemented in Java.

Additional mechanisms can be required to allow the service to store state information temporarily in a persistent store (as per the State Repository pattern) or a dedicated state management utility service (as per the Stateful Services pattern) if the handled state becomes too large.

**SUMMARY OF KEY POINTS**

- Task services are ideally located close to the services they compose for performance reasons.

- Task services often need to maintain state data. Common options include storing state data locally via thread-specific variables, using a state repository, or deferring to a stateful service.

## 10.2 Building Task Services

The upcoming sections delve deeper into the architectural and programming details of task service implementations.

### Implementation Considerations

The implementation logic for Java task services should be independent of the underlying technologies and code that use low-level Java APIs. This can be accomplished by abstracting lower level API functions into the utility service layer.

As an example, assume that an e-mail should be sent as part of a task service's execution. The JavaMail API offers e-mail functionality that the service logic can utilize directly.

Alternatively, the service logic can delegate e-mail processing to an E-Mail utility service, further decoupling the task service from any dependency on underlying runtime features. The utility service can handle the details of accessing mail servers and the formatting and parsing of e-mail content.

Building task service logic can require the generation of code skeletons from service logic can require the generation of code skeletons from the interface, using the wsgen tool in the JAX-WS or implementing the logic for REST task services in a POJO with the JAX-RS annotations. Similarly, all services composed by the task service are available in WSDL format for Web services or as POJOs. When starting from WSDL, the appropriate Java interfaces and proxy classes can be generated using the same tool.

Sometimes the designed WSDL service interface document or resource representation format, such as the XML schema, is inappropriate for implementation in Java. For example, many Java classes will be generated using a data binding tool, such as the JAXB, from an interface or representation using schemas with large numbers of defined complex types.

The generation of too many classes can often be resolved by adjusting the schemas, but in many cases, the schemas are reused across many services and cannot easily be modified. Certain process automation environments can dictate the structure of schemas in a way that results in the same inflation of generated Java classes.

Task services compose entity services to retrieve business-centric data required for business task processing. The result of an invocation of one entity service operation may be used for the invocation of another, so that data from various sources can be aggregated. To avoid large data caches during invocation, ensure entity services are used to limit the amount of returned data. Efforts should be made to restrict query parameters to prevent excessively generic queries.

Data can be cached in the local heap. Ensure the data is stored in local variables so that it is scoped to only the current thread, although the multithreaded nature of Web service deployments already reinforces data storage in local variables. Data that cannot be stored in the local heap, such as amounts of data beyond the size of memory available, must be outsourced by storing it directly in a local file or database.

Simultaneously, ensure outdated data is cleared. Just as with other low-level APIs in a task service implementation, delegating the handling of local temporary caches to a utility service is advised. This type of cache service can be invoked locally as a Java class and exist in the same process as the actual service implementation, because of the potential performance impact of moving large amounts of data between processes.

The behavior of a task service often depends on the identity of the invoking caller, which needs to be transferred from the service consumer to the service if such behavior must be implemented in the service logic. If the service logic is implemented in an EJB, the caller's identity can be discovered using the `getCallerPrincipal()` method on the EJB context. If the service is implemented in a JAX-RS resource class, the `javax.ws.rs.core.SecurityContext` interface can be used to obtain security-related information, such as user principals and user role information.

Incoming requests carry user credentials that are carried within the scope of the application server or container, translated into the Java security context `java.security.Principal`. Explicitly passing user identity information along with a request is often unnecessary if a proper security model has been established.

If a full Java EE environment is one of the deployment options for the task service, implementing the service logic inside a stateless session EJB is recommended. EJBs are stateless and offer a set of features and characteristics useful for task services without requiring any special coding, such as concurrent access, instance pooling, and transactional settings.

Implementing a task service as a stateless session bean allows for accessibility as a Web service via RMI/IIOP as a remote EJB, and locally via its local interface. A stateless session bean that has a Web service interface as well as a remote and local EJB interface can be deployed once and accessed in all three ways.

Multiple deployment options offer potential service consumers various choices based on performance requirements, available platforms, and other considerations. However, using local EJB interfaces requires that both service consumer and service are bundled together in a single deployment artifact and deployed on the same application server. Tight coupling between the service consumer and services should be avoided wherever possible.

For example, both service consumer and service must be redeployed together with the service consumer code if maintenance must be carried out on the service logic. The coupling is not as tight when using remote EJB interfaces, but the service consumer must still use a number of Java artifacts to provide access to the EJB. Using a Web-based service interface offers the loosest degree of coupling between service consumer and service. Figure 10.4 summarizes the different access options for service consumers with a service implemented as a stateless session EJB.

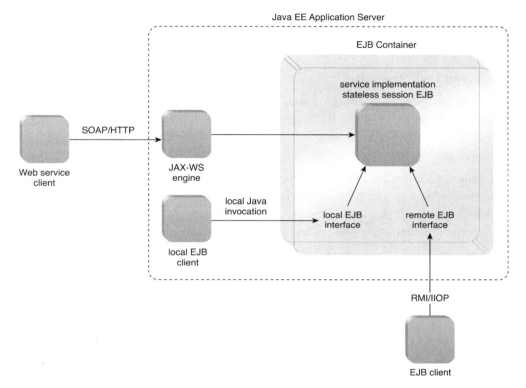

**Figure 10.4**

Stateless session EJBs can be accessed over a variety of interfaces with varying degrees of coupling.

Since Java EE 6 and EJB 3.1, REST services that are stateless session beans or singleton beans can be marked as JAX-RS resources that can leverage the features of the EJB container. If a service is deployed in a pre-Java EE 6 container, a regular JAX-RS annotated POJO can be used to model a REST resource and the transaction handling delegated to a session EJB. When deploying services in a servlet or Java EE 6 or 7 Web Profile containers, the degree of support for transaction handling can vary from one implementation to another. Therefore, investigate the extent of support to determine whether any special application-level transaction handling is required.

A task service often composes one or more entity services to retrieve required data stored in a persistent and transactional data store. Changes to data must be made within the scope of a transaction, and multiple changes to data stored in different data stores must be made within the same transaction to avoid leaving the data stores in an inconsistent state. The task service implementation often determines the boundaries of transactions.

## Web-Based Task Services

The following sections highlight issues pertaining to the creation of task services as SOAP-based Web services and REST services.

### Task Services with SOAP and WSDL

Deploying a task service as a remote Java component, such as an EJB, tightly couples the service consumer and service. The process execution environment can be based on non-Java technology, if required, as Web services can be problematic in cases where a non-functional context must be preserved across service invocations.

The RMI/IIOP protocol used between Java EE application server processes automatically promotes context information about transactions or identity. This is not the case when using Web services, unless advanced WS-* standards (such as WS-Security and WS-AtomicTransaction) are used. Support for these standards is required on both the service consumer and service sides.

The following NovoBank case study example demonstrates the use of JAX-WS APIs for the creation of a SOAP-based task Web service.

### CASE STUDY EXAMPLE

After the design of the Process Customer Account service is complete, the NovoBank team advances to the implementation of the service logic. The service implementation will be created in Java, and the service will be exposed as a stateless session bean. They use a JAX-WS-compliant runtime and deploy the service on a Java EE application server.

The service aggregates the existing Customer and Account entity services, which are both deployed as Web services. Even though these entity services are implemented in Java and could be invoked directly without going across the network or creating XML messages, the NovoBank team concludes that a Web service invocation will be more appropriate.

To increase the level of isolation between the task service and the aggregated entity services, both are deployed in physically different locations. The entity services interact directly with and are located close to underlying data sources, whereas the task service runs closely to its associated business process.

A JAX-WS service endpoint interface is generated for each service and imported into the project for the new task service. The JAX-WS wsimport tool is used to take the services' WSDL definition files as input. In Example 10.4, the `CustomerAccountInfo` message entity returned by the `retrieveCustomerAccountInfo` operation is a POJO.

```java
package com.novobank.services.task.creditapproval;

import java.util.List;
import com.novobank.services.entity.account.Account;
import com.novobank.services.entity.customer.Customer;

public class CustomerAccountInfo {
  private Customer customer;
  private List<Account> accounts;

  public Customer getCustomer() {
    return customer;
  }

  public void setCustomer(Customer customer) {
    this.customer = customer;
  }

  public List<Account> getAccounts() {
    return accounts;
  }

  public void setAccounts(List<Account> accounts) {
    this.accounts = accounts;
  }
}
```

**Example 10.4**

Since the service is implemented as a stateless session EJB, the team defines the remote interface in Example 10.5.

```java
package com.novobank.services.task.creditapproval;
import javax.ejb.Remote;
@Remote
```

```
public interface ProcessCustomerAccountRemote {
  public CustomerAccountInfo retrieveCustomerAccountInfo(
    String firstName, String lastName);
  public void sendCustomerNotification(String firstName,
    String lastName, String content);
}
```

**Example 10.5**

The service implementation class shows how the two entity services for customer and account information and a utility service for sending e-mails to customers are reused. The implementation logic only contains business logic and delegates all other logic to the aggregated services that do not exhibit any dependencies on the underlying infrastructure, existing applications, data models, or low-level Java APIs.

Two annotations, @WebService and @Stateless, are added to make this class available as a stateless session EJB and Web service. The implementation in Example 10.6 is handled automatically upon deployment of the resulting EAR file on the application server.

```
package com.novobank.services.task.creditapproval;

import java.util.List;
import javax.ejb.Stateless;
import javax.jws.WebService;

import com.novobank.services.entity.account.Account;
import com.novobank.services.entity.account.AccountService;
import
  com.novobank.services.entity.account.AccountServiceService;
import com.novobank.services.entity.customer.Customer;
import com.novobank.services.entity.customer.CustomerService;
import
  com.novobank.services.entity.customer.CustomerServiceService;
import com.novobank.services.utility.e-mail.E-mailService;
import
  com.novobank.services.utility.e-mail.E-mailServiceService;

@WebService
@Stateless
public class ProcessCustomerAccountService
  implements ProcessCustomerAccountRemote {
  public CustomerAccountInfo retrieveCustomerAccountInfo(
    String firstName, String lastName) {
```

```
    CustomerAccountInfo info = new CustomerAccountInfo();

    // retrieve customer info
    CustomerService cs =
      new CustomerServiceService()
      .getCustomerServicePort();
    Customer customer =
      cs.getCustomerByName(firstName, lastName);
    info.setCustomer(customer);

    // retrieve account info
    AccountService as =
      new AccountServiceService()
      .getAccountServicePort();
    List<Account> accounts =
      as.findAccountByCustomer(
    customer.getCustomerId());
    info.setAccounts(accounts);

    return info;
}

public void sendCustomerNotification(String firstName,
  String lastName, String content) {
  // covered in Chapter 11
  }
}
```

**Example 10.6**

Some of the class names used end with `ServiceService`, which is the naming convention used in this particular service definition. The preceding examples used names ending in `Service` in the WSDL `portType` element. For example, the `portType` name in the Customer entity service is `CustomerService`. The associated WSDL `service` element containing the endpoint address for the service is therefore called `CustomerServiceService`.

The generated JAX-WS classes are named accordingly, such as the service interface as `CustomerService` and the client proxy implementation as `CustomerServiceService`. The resulting name in the service interface can be changed by naming the `portType` and `service` elements in the WSDL definition differently.

*Task Services with REST*

Modeling any one of the entity services composed by a task service as a resource may not useful. As discussed in Chapter 9, an aggregate resource can be unsuitable for handling updates across multiple entities. In this case, the solution is to model the action itself as a controller resource. The controller hides the complex coordination details of the task service, gathers the response from multiple actions, and returns the results of the execution to the caller. However, two issues arise when modeling the action as a REST controller resource:

- Multiple entities could be created or updated from a task service. How can the results be communicated in a REST-based way back to the service consumer?

- Depending on the results of the processing, a number of different subsequent actions may be performed by the service consumer. How can the service consumer be guided through the appropriate sequence of subsequent actions?

The following case study example for SmartCredit's Credit Application Processing service illustrates methods to resolve the issues involved in modeling the action itself as a controller resource.

### CASE STUDY EXAMPLE

SmartCredit wants to offer its partners and customers the ability to submit credit applications for different products, such as credit cards and lines of credit. Once an application for credit is submitted, a complex business process that can take days to complete is executed. From the applicant's standpoint, the following functionalities must be supported:

- The caller of the service should be able to check the status of the application at any time.

- The service consumer should have the flexibility to cancel the application until a certain stage in the application process has been reached.

- Once a credit application has been approved, the process must return information about the resulting accounts.

SmartCredit has already built a number of REST services that are mostly entity services. SmartCredit now wants to build a REST service for the credit application process that must coordinate various activities between entities, such as

Customers, Credit Applications, and Accounts. Designed as a task service, the Credit Application service must compose utility services to perform generic processing, such as checking the credit scores of applicants. However, not all of the complex coordination details of the business process can be exposed to the service caller.

The team decides to model the controller as a resource for this task service, which will carry out the necessary sequence of steps and hide the complex back-end service invocation sequence from the service consumer. Since this is a complex operation involving creation and updates to multiple resources that are neither safe nor idempotent, the team decides to model the service as a POST operation on a `submitcreditapp` controller resource, as seen in Example 10.7.

```
POST /submitcreditapp HTTP/1.1
Content-Type: application/xml

<submitcreditapp>
  <customer>
    <ssn>xxx-xxx-xxxx</ssn>
    <name>John Doe</name>
    <dob>12121979</dob>
    <address>...</address>
    <!-- other customer details like assets, loans etc....-->
  </customer>
  <application>
    <productcode>CC</productcode>
    <credit>5000</credit>
    <!-- other application details ...-->
  </application>
  <!--misc...-->
</submitcreditapp>
```

**Example 10.7**

The amount of information needed for a typical credit application is much more than what is presented, and modeling the response resources presents further challenges. An application entity must be created in the system once an application is submitted, which means that the application itself must be modeled as a resource. The service consumers must also be able to enquire about the status of the application and have a way to cancel a pending application.

The SmartCredit team determines that the application not only has resource state, such as customers, credit application, and accounts, but moves through a state life-cycle. The application moves from a state of not-created to pending to approved or canceled, depending on the actions taken at various points. To handle the transition management, the SmartCredit team considers modeling these services as resources at the beginning, and captures the resource addresses, operations, and representation formats in an informal service contract handed to the service consumers beforehand.

Such a contract would include:

- `POST` – `http://smartcredit.com/submitcreditapp`
  POST to the `submitcreditapp` resource to submit a new credit application

- `GET` – `http://smartcredit.com/creditapp/{id}`
  the `creditapp` is a resource, check for status information

- `PUT` – `http://smartcredit.com/creditapp/{id}`
  PUT to the `creditapp` resource with a canceled status

The resource design requires up-front knowledge that must be communicated to the clients. Mid-step changes in the application, such as canceling a pending application, would change the resource URI, break the client, and result in the need to modify the service consumer to coordinate with the new cancelation service interface. Modeling the design on the Web resolves many of these issues.

On the Web, users start with a hyperlink and navigate through other linked hyper-media content to carry out additional functions, such as checking on or canceling an order status. Knowledge about the links becomes available as the user navigates through different application states. The SmartCredit team realizes that the hyper-media constraint can help model the necessary system-system interaction.

Satisfying the hypermedia constraint is vital to maintaining loose coupling between the service consumer and service so that they can evolve independently. Embedding links that the service consumer can discover and use reduces the up-front informa-tion the service consumer requires and helps transition the application through dif-ferent stages in its lifecycle. A response to the POST request for the `submitcreditapp` resource in accordance with the hypermedia constraint is provided in Example 10.8.

*Response Message*

```
HTTP/1.1 201 Created
Location: http://smartcredit.com/creditapp/xw5f45892
Content-Length: 0
```

**Example 10.8**

Example 10.8 indicates a credit application was created on behalf of the customer, and the newly created credit application resource can be accessed at the URI pointed to by the HTTP `Location` header. In Example 10.9, the service consumer can access the URI to retrieve a representation of the credit application.

*Request Message*

```
GET /creditapp/xw5f45892 HTTP/1.1
Host: smartcredit.com
```

*Response Message*

```
HTTP/1.1 200 OK
Content-Type:application/xml
```

*Link*

```
http://smartcredit.com/creditapp/xw5f45892/cancel";rel=cancel
<application id="xw5f45892"
  xmlns:atom="http://www.w3.org/Atom/2005">
  <atom:link rel="self" type="application/xml"
    href="smartcredit.com/creditapp/xw5f45892"/>
  <status>
    <code>01</code>
    <message>Pending</message>
  </status>
    . . .
</application>
```

**Example 10.9**

Example 10.9 includes a structural link for the application itself (described via the standard `self` atom link relation) and a transitional link for canceling an application (described via an HTTP link header with the value `cancel`). As long as the service consumer is aware of the semantics of the `cancel` link relation, the appropriate resource can be discovered for further actions, such as cancelation of the credit application.

The information that service consumers require about operations supported by the resource at the indicated URI can be part of the documented semantics associated with the atom link. Alternatively, the service consumer can submit an OPTIONS operation to the URI to discover that the supported resource operations are PUT and POST.

As opposed to pre-publishing the resources and their associated URIs, modeling on the Web allows for dynamic discovery of the resource address. The associated operations reduced the coupling between the service and service consumer to ensure that the service can evolve the service without adversely affecting the service consumer. If an application is approved, a response containing the application resource representation could look like Example 10.10.

*Response Message*

```
HTTP/1.1 200 OK
Content-Type:application/xml

<application id="xw5f45892"
  xmlns:atom="http://www.w3.org/Atom/2005">
  ...
  <status>
    <code>00</code>
    <message>Approved</message>
    <atom:link rel="related" type="application/xml"
      href=http://smartcredit.com/accounts/zk367/>
  </status>
  ...
</application>
```

**Example 10.10**

The response indicates the application was approved, and the application resource embeds an atom link pointing to a related account resource created. The service consumer can submit a GET request to the account resource URI and obtain details about the new account as seen in Example 10.11. Note that the atom link relation type has a value of `related`, which is a standardized atom link relation that indicates the linked resource is related to the containing resource.

*Request Message*

```
GET /accounts/zk367 HTTP/1.1
Host:smartcredit.com
```

*Response Message*
```
HTTP/1.1 200 OK
Content-Type:application/xml

<account id="zk367" xmlns:atom="http://www.w3.org/Atom/2005">
  <type>CC</type>
  <limit>2000</limit>
  ...
</account>
```

**Example 10.11**

When canceling an application, the service consumer can perform an empty POST at the `href` URI associated with the `cancel` link relation. The server returns a new representation of the `creditapplication` resource, now canceled in Example 10.12.

*Request Message*
```
POST creditapp/xw5f45892/cancel HTTP/1.1
Host: smartcredit.com
Response Message
HTTP/1.1 200 OK
Content-Type: application/xml
<application id="xw5f45892" xmlns:atom="http://www.w3.org/
  Atom/2005">
  ...
  <status>
    <code>03</code>
    <message>Canceled</message>
  </status>
  ...
</application>
```

**Example 10.12**

Properly applying the hypermedia constraint can allow the service consumer to drive an application through various resource state transitions by pointing to new resources and associated URIs through embedded links. In Java, a combination of the structural link and transitional link constructs can implement the hypermedia constraint with JAX-RS.

The controller resource, `SubmitCreditAppResource` class, accepts a credit application and returns an HTTP 201 response with the HTTP `Location` header pointing to the newly created `creditapp` resource. Example 10.13 captures the `SubmitCreditAppResource` class implementation.

```
package com.smartcredit.credit.services;
  ...
@Path("/submitcreditapp)
public class SubmitCreditAppResource {

  @POST
  @Consumes("application/xml")
  public Response submitCreditApp(@Context UriInfo uri, String
    creditapp) {
    CreditApp app = createCredtitApp(creditapp);
    URI baseURI = uri.getBaseURI();
    return Response.created( URI.create(baseURI+app.getID()).
      build();
  }
}
```

*Response Message*

```
HTTP/1.1 201 Created
Location:http://smartcredit.com/creditapp/xw5f45892
```

**Example 10.13**

When the client makes a GET request to the URI for the new `creditapp`, the request is handled by the `CreditAppResource` class as seen in Example 10.14.

```
package com.smartcredit.credit.services;
   ...
@Path("/creditapp")
public class CreditAppResource {

  @GET
  @Path("{id}")
  @Produces("application/xml")
  public Response getCreditApp(@Context UriInfo uri,
    @PathParam("id") int id) {

    //Get base request uri
    URI baseUri = uri.getBaseURI();
    URI requestUri = uri.getRequestURI();
```

```
  // Get application information
  CreditApp capp = getCreditApp(id);

  //Start writing a raw xml
  StringWriter sw = new StringWriter();
  XMLStreamWriter wr =
    XMLOutputFactory.newInstance()
    .createXMLStreamWriter(sw);
  wr.writeStartDocument();
  wr.writeStartElement("application");

  //Write out an Atom link for self
  wr.writeStartElement("Atom", "link",
    "http://www.w3.org/Atom/2005");
  wr.writeAttribute("rel", "self");
  wr.writeAttribute("href", requestURI.toASCIIString());
  wr.writeEndElement();

  //...write out rest of the core application data
  writeElementBody(capp);
  wr.writeEndElement();
  //End writing application information
  wr.writeEndDocument();

  // If application can be canceled write out an HTTP
  // relation link for the cancel resource

  if(canCancelApp(capp))
    return Response.ok(sw.toString()).link(requestURI.
    toASCIIString()+"/cancel", "cancel").build();
//otherwise, return the accumulated string as xml
// without any HTTP links...
return Response.ok(sw.toString()).build();
}
}
```

**Example 10.14**

The CreditAppResource class performs a check to determine if the application can be canceled, and if so, embeds an HTTP link relation for the application cancelation.

## Testing Considerations

Unit testing for task services is challenging because of the number of dependencies they have on other services. As a result, testing the task service implementation can require a relatively large environment. To reduce task service dependency on other services which may or may not be available at the time of implementation, consider generating local or remote stubs used in place of the actual services invoked.

The service interface definition can be a WSDL document tooled to generate a Java interface for stubs. A simple Java class that implements this interface and returns some meaningful hardcoded data can be developed. In the service logic, an instance of a proxy to the target service is often retrieved via the standard JAX-WS mechanisms by utilizing the generated `javax.xml.ws.Service` instance class.

For unit testing purposes, the call can be temporarily removed to the `getPort()` method to retrieve a reference to the service proxy. The local implementation that can be locally invoked can instead be used to prevent creation and parsing of XML and cross-process invocations. This allows developers to focus on the actual business logic within the service implementation for testing purposes.

### CASE STUDY EXAMPLE

To test the Process Customer Account service without affecting the Customer and Account services, locally invoked stubs are created to implement the appropriate service interface and return meaningful, hardcoded data. Example 10.15 is a listing of a test stub version of the `AccountService`.

```
package com.novobank.services.entity.account.test;

import java.util.LinkedList;
import java.util.List;
import com.novobank.services.entity.account.Account;
import com.novobank.services.entity.account.AccountService;

public class AccountServiceTest implements AccountService {

  public List<Account> findAccountByCustomer(String arg0) {
    Account a1 = new Account();
    a1.setAccountId("12345-0");
    a1.setAccountType("Savings");
```

```
    a1.setBalance(2500.0);

    Account a2 = new Account();
    a2.setAccountId("12345-1");
    a2.setAccountType("Checking");
    a2.setBalance(894.30);

    List<Account> list = new LinkedList<Account>();
    list.add(a1);
    list.add(a2);

    return list;
  }
}
```

**Example 10.15**

The implementation of the Process Customer Account service is temporarily changed. In Example 10.16, the retrieval of the proxy instance is replaced with an instance of the test stub `AccountServiceTest` to reduce dependencies on other services during testing.

```
...
// retrieve account info
// AccountService as = new AccountServiceService().
  getAccountServicePort();
AccountService as = new AccountServiceTest();
// all other code remains unchanged
List<Account> accounts =
  as.findAccountByCustomer(customer.getCustomerId());
info.setAccounts(accounts);
...
```

**Example 10.16**

The implementations of composed services can be wrapped into a Web service layer but deployed on a server similar to the one where the task service logic is tested. The JAX-WS code can be reinstated for retrieving a reference to the service proxy class but set to a URL of the locally deployed service, thereby avoiding dependencies on existing deployments of target services and allowing the code to be tested for remote invocation of the composed services through the JAX-WS layer.

In the integration testing phase, all instances of invoking test stub services can be replaced by invocations of the target services. Chapter 11 details how to manage endpoint addresses of composed services across development phases. For testing a REST task service, as with any other REST service, any HTTP library can be used for making the appropriate HTTP requests. For example, the `curl` utility can be used to issue a GET request for a credit application, as seen in Example 10.17.

```
curl -H "Accept: application/xml" -X GET \
"http://smartcredit.com/creditapp/xw5f45892"
```

**Example 10.17**

## Packaging Considerations

Task services have no specific packaging considerations beyond the resolution of dependencies towards composed services.

### SUMMARY OF KEY POINTS

- Task services can be decoupled from the underlying technology by utilizing agnostic service layers, instead of directly invoking specific Java APIs. They often cache state and contextual information across invocations of composed services.

- A REST task service can be modeled as a controller resource that coordinates the actions of multiple entity and utility services. Enforcing the hypermedia constraint allows the client to drive application state transitions through embedded resource links.

- For unit testing, composed Web services are temporarily replaced by local stubs, while REST service unit testing can use any HTTP utility library.

# Chapter 11

# Service Composition with Java

Decomposing a system into units of service-oriented logic and recomposing the units into new compounds of solution logic results in a higher degree of code reuse and greater flexibility in response to change. This chapter acts as a continuation of Chapter 10 to focus on the design and implementation considerations specific to service composition with Java.

## 11.1  Inside Service Compositions

The following sections highlight key service composition terms and concepts in preparation for the *Java Service Composition Design and Implementation* section.

### Service Composition Roles

A service invoked as part of a composition is a composition member, and a service that invokes other services as part of its processing is a composition controller. A service should ideally be a member of and built for more than one composition. As per the Service Composability principle, a service's composability is not an explicit design step or implementation detail but a manifestation of the extent to which service-orientation principles were applied during design, such as how reusable and autonomous the service is and whether or not it deals with standardized data types.

The composition controller sits on top of and invokes composition members in a defined sequence. Therefore, the composition controller must be aware of the context around individual service invocations, and may have to store state across invocations as well as provide transactional and/or security context. The composition members must be fully decoupled from the controller's service consumers, because the fact that a service composes other services must be hidden from service consumers, as per the Service Abstraction principle.

Within the composition logic, the controller must determine which protocol to use when synchronously or asynchronously invoking a composition member. Both the composition controller and member implemented in Java can be deployed into the same process, in which case service invocation becomes a local Java call. Beyond the composition controller and composition member, two additional roles are relevant to service composition:

- A composition initiator is the service consumer that triggers the execution of the composition.

- A composition sub-controller is a service that acts as a composition member but also delegates some or all of the processing to other services. This second composition becomes a sub-composition.

See Figure 11.1 for a visual illustration of a service composition hierarchy that includes a sub-controller.

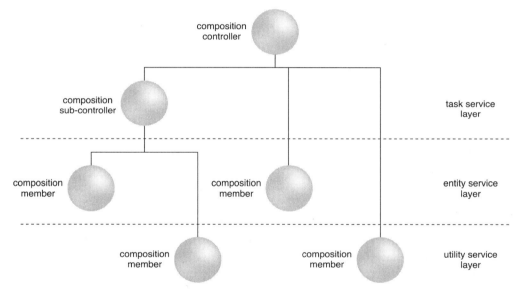

**Figure 11.1**

A service composition encompasses a composition controller and a composition sub-controller.

An entire chain of service compositions is possible, such as service sub-controllers invoking other service sub-controllers. However, the depth to which this can be done is often constrained by performance and other non-functional requirements.

## Compositions and MEPs

The interaction between two services often involves using a message exchange pattern (MEP). MEPs describe whether an interaction occurs synchronously or asynchronously or in the form of a request/response sequence. Individual MEPs are often limited to point-to-point interactions between a service consumer and a service.

In a given service composition, several different MEPs can exist. For example, if Service A invokes Service B as part of a composition, where Service A is the composition controller and Service B is a composition member, Service B can then invoke Services C and D, which makes Service B a composition sub-controller. The interactions between A and B and between B and C and D may use different MEPs, as shown in Figure 11.2.

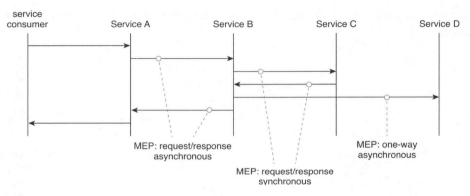

**Figure 11.2**
An invocation of Service A leads to the usage of several message exchange patterns within the service composition.

Messages that are part of such a service composition must be correlated somehow to identify which instance of a composition corresponds to each message. Differentiating messages from the composition instances is often a challenge when asynchronous messaging is used.

### Synchronous and Asynchronous Invocation

Services often separate their functional interface from the network invocation or binding, as is common for Web services in particular. While the functional interface may support what is needed for the composition, careful analysis of the supported binding is required.

Some services may only support an asynchronous invocation, which means that the request message is sent on a different thread than where the response message is received. The response message must be correlated with the request message, which often happens via a unique message identifier copied into the header of each message. Each participant in the asynchronous exchange agrees on the chosen mechanism. The invoked service copies the message ID of the incoming request message into the header of the outgoing response message.

The composition controller does not have to wait for the request to be processed by the composition member. Utilizing asynchronous invocation allows the composition controller to do other work in parallel until the response arrives. This can be useful in cases where several composition members are invoked simultaneously, because they perform work that does not require sequential execution.

For example, a task service is part of an order management system that offers a promised completion date for a new order based on availability of material in a number of warehouses. Each warehouse exposes a set of entity services that return that quantity of a certain material that is currently in stock. To calculate a completion date, the task service can send parallel requests to each warehouse for each of the required materials and collect all responses before running its calculation. Requests to each warehouse can be sent without waiting for the response, which improves the performance of the overall service. If offered by the warehouse services with the applicable correlation mechanism, the asynchronous invocation protocol is an appropriate design choice.

## Service Level Agreements (SLAs)

A composition controller's SLA is dependent on its composition members' SLAs. Any scheduled downtime of a composed service is also a scheduled downtime for the entire composition. Therefore, the SLA offered by the composition controller service is constrained by the SLAs of the composition members.

An existing service may be unsuitable in a composition because of incompatible SLAs, even though its functional interface meets the requirements. For example, if a service's minimum response time is longer than the minimum response time for the overall composition, than this service cannot be reused. Either a different service that offers better performance must be found, or the candidate service's owner can be pushed to improve its response time to the required level.

Some business-centric services may be need to be auditable down to individual messages, which means that no message can be lost during processing. If a potential composition member service can only be accessed over HTTP as the network protocol, messages can be lost, since HTTP is not a reliable transport. Therefore, various techniques can be applied to achieve different levels of reliability.

Service implementations based on SOAP and WS-* can benefit from the WS-ReliableMessaging standard to ensure reliable delivery of messages with various degrees of QoS support, such as at-most-once, at-least-once, exactly-once, or in-order delivery. REST services can resubmit a message until successful acknowledgement is received, which requires the message recipient to be capable of handling duplicate messages.

The weakest composition member defines the minimum support offered by the composition as a whole. The composition controller's SLA can be defined as the sum of all composition member SLAs. Note that this does not mean that all response times of composition member services are added together to calculate the expected response time of the composition. Remember that asynchronous, parallel invocations of services can shorten the processing time. To create the SLA for the composition, thoroughly examine the impact each composition member SLA will have individually, taking into consideration how each service's composed capability is invoked.

### SUMMARY OF KEY POINTS

- The main composition roles that services perform include composition controllers, which own and control the composition, and composition members, which are invoked as part of a composition.

- Within a service composition, individual service interactions can be based on different MEPs that can be incorporated into synchronous and asynchronous service activities.

- Service composition SLAs are derived from and dependent upon composition member SLAs.

## 11.2  Java Service Composition Design and Implementation

Service composition not only affects the overall runtime behavior of a particular service, but also the implementing, packaging, deploying, and testing of composed services. The following sections highlight a number of considerations and challenges.

### Composition Logic: Coding vs. Orchestration

Hand-coding service composition logic is common with task services. It provides a low barrier to entry; however, the long-term costs for complex service compositions can be high and pose the following challenges:

- A tight coupling is created between the composition controller and the composition members. Even minor changes to the invocation sequence results in a need to re-program the composing service.

- The composing service implementation can become highly complex. For example, if the task service must perform parallel queries or updates or asynchronous invocations, it may need to manage all the threading and/or parallel messaging itself. For long-running service compositions, programmatic composition logic may need to include routines for canceling service invocations, managing long-running conversational state, and performing conditional joins on parallel execution sequences.

- For complex transactional services, programmatic management of transactional integrity between various composition members may introduce additional complexity.

An alternative to hand-coding is to consider orchestration via the use of standards like WS-BPEL, which typically lead to the creation of *orchestrated* task services. With WS-BPEL, the sequence of interactions can be modified by making changes to the WS-BPEL flow rather than to the actual implementation code. The decision as to whether to incorporate orchestrated task services into service composition design is often dependent on the complexity and potential execution duration of service composition instances and service activities.

> **NOTE**
>
> This book does not cover orchestration in detail or the use of any high-level declarative language for the expression of service composition logic.

### REST Service Composition Considerations

In a REST service composition, the composition controller coordinates the actions of various member resources. New resources may be created, and existing resources may be updated or removed. This dynamic nature of the service composition results in potential changes to the member resources and their resource URIs.

The uniform contract constraint still applies to all member resources. The interaction between the composition controller and member resources will be restricted to the well-known HTTP verbs and/or a subset of those verbs as permitted by the resources themselves. The REST-style architecture characteristics also apply for all composition members. Each composition member will have its own media types (standard or custom), resource URIs that identifies the resources, and resource representations that may explicitly outline allowable resource transitions from a given resource state as per the hypermedia constraint.

For programmatic REST services, composition controllers have a choice of using various low-level HTTP-based Java APIs, such as the `HTTPURLConnection` or Apache `HttpClient` classes. However, the HTTP-based Java APIs do not deal with resources as an abstraction and have an RPC-centric focus based on request/response messages, which limits the usefulness of these APIs for building REST service consumers. Alternatively, the JAX-RS 2.0 Client API offers a set of Java APIs for communication with REST services irrespective of whether those services are implemented with the JAX-RS. The Client APIs provide resource-based abstractions and a more natural programming model centered on resources, URIs, and the uniform contract constraint. The JAX-RS client APIs can consume any Web service exposed over an HTTP protocol.

Under the covers, the client API implementation can use any low-level HTTP communication libraries. For example, the Jersey implementation provides a pluggable architecture where the application developer is free to choose any one of a number of different Java-based HTTP library implementations, such as JDK `HTTPURLConnection` or the Apache `HTTPClient` utilities. The JAX-RS 2.0 client programming model can be utilized to build REST service consumers, including composition controllers. With the JAX-RS client programming model, the central entity is a resource. The resource is modeled as a `javax.ws.rs.WebTarget` class that encapsulates a URI. The `WebTarget` resource class supports the fixed set of HTTP methods, and resource representations are modeled as Java types that may contain link relations to other `WebTarget` resources.

The starting point for coding a REST service consumer with JAX-RS is the `javax.ws.rs.client.Client` interface. A request is created based on the target, and the invocation is performed on the request as seen in Example 11.1.

```
Client c = ClientBuilder.newClient();
WebTarget order = c.target("http://com.soaj.restful/resources/order");
WebTarget invoice = c.target("http://com.soaj.restful/resources/
  invoice");
...
```

**Example 11.1**

The `request` method on the `WebTarget` interface allows media-type specification for the request, and returns an `Invocation.Builder` object in Example 11.2.

```
Invocation.Builder builder = order.request(MediaType.TEXT_PLAIN);
Invocation.Builder builder2 = invoice.request(MediaType.
  APPLICATION_XML);
```

**Example 11.2**

The `Invocation.Builder` object supports the HTTP methods. After the `Media` type is set, the request is invoked by calling the HTTP methods seen in Example 11.3.

```
String response = builder.get(String.class);
...
Invoice inv = new Invoice(); //Invoice is a JAXB bean
//call POST passing in the serialized inv via javax.ws.rs.client.
  Entity
String conirmationNumber = builder2.post(Entity.xml(inv), String.
  class);
```

**Example 11.3**

A POST is made to the `WebTarget` that accepts a media type of `application/xml`. In this case, the POST method takes an unmarshaled JAXB Invoice object. The implementation is flexible in handling different media types, and built-in content handlers manage the translation of media types and their Java counterparts.

The HTTP methods can be chained together to allow a fluent API style of programming where the sequence of calls from Example 11.3 can be replaced, as seen in Example 11.4.

```
String response = order.request(MediaType.TEXT_PLAIN).get(String.
  class);
```

**Example 11.4**

---

**NOTE**

For a more detailed exploration of REST service composition, read the following three chapters in the *SOA with REST: Principles, Patterns & Constraints for Building Enterprise Solutions with REST* series title:

- Chapter 11: Fundamental Service Composition with REST

- Chapter 12: Advanced Service Composition with REST

- Chapter 13: Service Composition with REST Case Study

## Composition Member Endpoints

For SOAP-based Web services, tooling is used to generate some form of code artifact that acts as a local representation of the remote service. For example, JAX-WS employs the wsimport tool to generate a client-side SEI, which is of type `javax.xml.ws.Service`. This class can be invoked like any other local Java class, and works with the underlying JAX-WS runtime to create an appropriate wire message to send out over the network.

A JAX-WS client-side proxy is usually obtained by calling one of the `Service.getPort()` methods defined in the generated SEI. The endpoint address of the used port is derived from the WSDL for the target service, and the location of this WSDL can be dynamically set. A default WSDL location is created when the code is first generated. The location of the WSDL and the endpoint address of the target service is either hardcoded in the proxy or set dynamically at runtime.

The resolution of the endpoint address used to invoke a service should be delegated to a registry that can change the endpoint address whenever a service is moved, without recompiling or reinstalling any code or restarting a server. While the resolution of endpoint address is true of any service consumer, extra care must be taken because a composition controller is eventually exposed as a service with potentially numerous service consumers. Composition member services can be invoked many times, and caching the endpoint information avoids having to perform a lookup every time. The exact endpoint used for a composition member depends on the context of the composition controller.

For example, an end user can have gold or silver status with a company that correlates to faster or slower service. A composition controller may have to select endpoints for its composition members based on the identity of the original caller. Most registries allow the endpoint address of a service to be queried based on more information than just the service name, such as information about caller identity. Determining which criteria affects the endpoint selection for composition members is part of the design process of a composition and should be documented accordingly.

For REST services, the composition controller resource can be looked up by service consumers via a well-known entry point or the URI of the controller resource. However, the controller resource must maintain a list of URIs for the composite member resources. A service registry can be used for storing REST service endpoint information, such as resource URIs, and can be used to look up such composition member endpoints. The need to store multiple resource URIs can be mitigated by the hypermedia constraint, where the composition controller can perform dynamic composition by navigating linked resource URIs and their associated link relations.

### Error Handling

Each service operation should define the possible fault messages that can occur. A composition controller must decide how to handle errors, both service-generated and infrastructure-based.

Invoking a number of other services can return any fault message defined by these services. The composition controller could copy all of the downstream fault messages into its own service contract and then pass fault messages to its own service consumers unchanged, although this method is not considered good practice. Copying faults into the service contract exposes details about composed services to the service consumer, which may run contrary to the objectives of the Service Abstraction principle.

Infrastructure errors can also cause problems with the invocation, such as when the network is down and a target service cannot be reached. An infrastructure error should not be modeled in the service contract of the target composition member. When a fault message is received from a downstream service invocation or when an infrastructure problem occurs, the composition controller must explicitly catch and transform error messages into the appropriate functional context. Rather than passing error messages through to its service consumers, the composition controller should capture the fact that an error has occurred in a way that makes sense to its own service consumer. Translating the error to the service consumer might include removing technical details of a message that may be appropriate to the service consumer of a utility service but not to the service consumer of a task service.

For SOAP-based Web services, a modeled fault in the `wsdl:operation` is mapped to a declared exception in the Java service endpoint interface. Any non-modeled errors are often mapped to a `javax.xml.ws.WebServiceException`, which is a subclass of `java.lang.RuntimeException`. Both types of errors can be caught by framing the invocation with a try/catch block. The error message can then transform to the appropriate format and throw the new exception type defined in the composition controller's WSDL.

For REST services, error handling is captured with HTTP response codes. Any REST-based composition member that fails to perform an expected operation should return an appropriate HTTP status code such as 500, which can also "bubble up" from the composition controller. Similar to fault translation for SOAP-based Web services, status code translations may be necessary in situations where the composition controller is unable to look up composition member resources, resulting in a 404 code. Rather than expose an implementation detail to the composite service consumer, the composition controller can choose to return the internal server error 500 status code.

The following case study examples illustrate how NovoBank and SmartCredit approach error handling for their respective services.

---

**CASE STUDY EXAMPLE**

An additional operation defined for the Process Customer Account service, named `sendCustomerNotification`, allows messages to be sent to the customer via e-mail. The E-Mail utility service processes the mail details, and uses the JavaMail API to send out messages.

In its first iteration, the E-Mail service in Example 11.5 does not define any fault message that can occur during the invocation of the `sendE-mail` operation.

```
<definitions xmlns="http://schemas.xmlsoap.org/wsdl/"
  xmlns:tns="http://e-mail.utility.services.novobank.com/"
  xmlns:xsd="http://www.w3.org/2001/XMLSchema"
  xmlns:soap="http://schemas.xmlsoap.org/wsdl/soap/"
  targetNamespace="http://e-mail.utility.services.novobank.com/"
  name="E-mailServiceService">
  <types>
    ...schema definition omitted here...
  </types>
  <message name="sendE-mail">
    <part name="parameters" element="tns:sendE-mail"/>
  </message>
  <message name="sendE-mailResponse">
    <part name="parameters" element="tns:sendE-mailResponse"/>
  </message>
  <portType name="E-mailService">
    <operation name="sendE-mail">
      <input message="tns:sendE-mail"/>
      <output message="tns:sendE-mailResponse"/>
    </operation>
  </portType>
  ...
</definitions>
```

**Example 11.5**

The E-Mail service implementation in Example 11.6 catches any errors that can occur during the invocation of the JavaMail interfaces, and then ignores them.

```
package com.novobank.services.utility.e-mail;
import java.util.Properties;
import javax.jws.WebService;
import javax.mail.Message;
import javax.mail.Session;
import javax.mail.Transport;
import javax.mail.internet.InternetAddress;
import javax.mail.internet.MimeMessage;
@WebService
public class E-mailService {
  public void sendE-mail(String e-mailAddress,
    String content) {
      try {
        Properties props =  new Properties();
        //Specify the desired SMTP server
        props.put("mail.smtp.host", "localhost");
        // create a new Session object
        Session session = Session.getInstance(props,null);
        // create a new MimeMessage object
        // (using the Session created above)
        Message message = new MimeMessage(session);
        message.setFrom(new InternetAddress(e-mailAddress));
        message.setRecipients(Message.RecipientType.TO,
          new InternetAddress[]
          { new InternetAddress(e-mailAddress) });
          message.setSubject("Customer Notification");
          message.setContent(content, "text/plain");
          Transport.send(message);
      }
    catch (Throwable t) {}
  }
}
```

**Example 11.6**

During the design of the Process Customer Account service's `sendCustomerNotifi-cation` operation, the NovoBank team decides to reuse or compose the E-Mail utility service. However, they discover that the service does not return any fault messages if the e-mail cannot be sent without the option to try again later. As error handling is required to ensure reliable message delivery, a request is made to update the interface of the E-Mail service to include a fault message.

The E-Mail service's updated WSDL definition is seen in Example 11.7.

```
<definitions xmlns="http://schemas.xmlsoap.org/wsdl/"
  xmlns:tns="http://e-mail.utility.services.novobank.com/"
  xmlns:xsd="http://www.w3.org/2001/XMLSchema"
  xmlns:soap="http://schemas.xmlsoap.org/wsdl/soap/"
  targetNamespace="http://e-mail.utility.services.novobank.com/"
  name="E-mailServiceService">
  <types>
    ...schema omitted here...
  </types>
  <message name="sendE-mail">
    <part name="parameters" element="tns:sendE-mail"/>
  </message>
  <message name="sendE-mailResponse">
    <part name="parameters" element="tns:sendE-mailResponse"/>
  </message>
  <message name="E-mailServiceException">
    <part name="fault" element="tns:E-mailServiceException"/>
  </message>
  <portType name="E-mailService">
    <operation name="sendE-mail">
      <input message="tns:sendE-mail"/>
      <output message="tns:sendE-mailResponse"/>
      <fault name="E-mailServiceException"
      message="tns:E-mailServiceException"/>
    </operation>
  </portType>
    ...binding omitted here...
</definitions>
```

**Example 11.7**

The implementation logic is also updated to reflect the change in the interface, and an exception indicating an error has occurred is thrown. The only part of the code that has changed is in the `catch()` block shown in Example 11.8.

```
package com.novobank.services.utility.e-mail;
import java.util.Properties;
import javax.jws.WebService;
import javax.mail.Message;
import javax.mail.Session;
import javax.mail.Transport;
import javax.mail.internet.InternetAddress;
import javax.mail.internet.MimeMessage;
@WebService
public class E-mailService {
```

```
  public void sendE-mail(String e-mailAddress, String content) {
    try {
      ...same code as before...
    } catch (Throwable t) {
      E-mailServiceException ex = new E-mailServiceException();
      ex.setOriginalMessage(t.getMessage());
      throw ex;
    }
  }
}
```

**Example 11.8**

Example 11.8 illustrates how the original exception message returned from the Java-Mail API is captured and stored in the new `Exception` object that is returned to the caller. The implementation of the `sendCustomerNotification` method in the Process Customer Account service is shown in Example 11.9.

```
package com.novobank.services.task.creditapproval;

import java.util.List;
import javax.ejb.Stateless;
import javax.jws.WebService;
import javax.xml.ws.WebServiceException;
import com.novobank.services.entity.account.Account;
import com.novobank.services.entity.account.AccountService;
import com.novobank.services.entity.account.AccountServiceService;
import com.novobank.services.entity.customer.Customer;
import com.novobank.services.entity.customer.CustomerService;
import com.novobank.services.entity.customer.CustomerServiceService;
import com.novobank.services.utility.e-mail.E-mailService;
import com.novobank.services.utility.e-mail.E-mailServiceService;
import com.novobank.services.utility.e-mail.E-mailServiceException_
Exception;
@WebService
@Stateless
public class ProcessCustomerAccountService implements
ProcessCustomerAccountRemote {
  ... retrieveCustomerAccountInfo method omitted ...
  public void sendCustomerNotification(String firstName, String
    lastName, String content) {
    // retrieve customer info
    CustomerService cs = new CustomerServiceService().
      getCustomerServicePort();
    Customer customer = cs.getCustomerByName(firstName, lastName);
```

```
   E-mailService es = new E-mailServiceService().
   getE-mailServicePort();
   try {
     es.sendE-mail(customer.getE-mailAddress(), content);
   } catch (E-mailServiceException_Exception x) {
     throw new WebServiceException(x.getFaultInfo()
       .getOriginalMessage());
   }
  }
}
```

**Example 11.9**

The Process Customer Account service implementation handles exceptions with the try/catch block.

The design team at NovoBank decides to map the fault defined on the E-Mail utility service as a technical error that is not mapped to a business-level fault on the Process Customer Account service. Instead, the error will be mapped to a `javax.xml.ws.WebServiceException` in the implementation, indicating that an infrastructure-level problem has occurred. The original exception message is preserved and can be used by a service consumer if necessary.

As defined in the JAX-WS specification, the original exception class `E-mailServiceException` is not exposed directly on the service interface, but wrapped into an additional exception class named `E-mailServiceException_Exception` which offers access to the fault message via the `getFaultInfo` method.

Note that the design team could also have decided that an explicit fault message was required on the `sendCustomerNotification` operation, identifying the error as an application-level problem as opposed to an infrastructure problem. Such design options are common when composing services, and may impact both the interface of the composition controller as well as the composition members.

Before calling the E-Mail utility service to send a message to the customer, the service composition first uses the Customer entity service to retrieve the customer's e-mail address, which performs a read operation on the customer data. In case the sending of the e-mail fails, there is no compensation required on the Customer service invocation. In other cases, additional processing can be necessary to compensate already executed processing in the event of a fault.

For a Credit Card Application service, the SmartCredit development team must use public credit score services offered by external credit agencies. For instant credit assessments, SmartCredit obtains credit scores from three independent credit agencies and calculates a combined score by applying a complex internal algorithm. All three external agencies offer public credit score services over a REST-based interface. SOA architects must build a composite REST service for reuse by other divisions of SmartCredit.

The composite REST service can perform the credit score lookups from external agencies, compute a combined score, and return the score to the caller. The implementation details of where raw credit scores are obtained from or how the combined score is calculated can be hidden from the internal service consumers. SmartCredit developers decide to build a hand-coded composition controller resource to perform the credit agency's REST service invocations and the combined score calculation. Rather than use low-level `HTTPURLConnection` or Apache `HttpClient` APIs, the development team employs the JAX-RS 2.0 Client API for its support of the resource-based programming model.

The composition controller resource offers a GET method to obtain the combined credit score as shown in Example 11.10.

```
GET smartcredit-internal/creditscore/555555555 HTTP/1.1
Host: smartcredit-internal.com

package com.smartcredit.credit.services;
  ...
import javax.ws.rs.core.MediaType;
import javax.ws.rs.client.*;
@Path("/smartcredit/internal/creditscore ")
public class CombinedCreditScoreResource {
  @GET
  @Path("{id})
  @Produces("text/plain")
  public int getCreditScore(
    @PathParam("id") String id) {
    Client c = ClientBuilder.newClient();

    //Get credit score from agency 1; identifier is part of the
      request URL
```

```
// GET /score/xxxxxxxx

WebTarget agency1 = c.target("https://agency1.com/score/"+id);
String agency1Score = agency1.request(MediaType.TEXT_PLAIN).
  get(String.class);
int score1 = Integer.parseInt(agency1Score);

//Get credit score from agency 2; uses a query parameter for
  specifying identifier number
//GET /creditscore?id=xxxxxxxx
//Note the usage of query params

WebTarget agency2 = c.target("https://agency2.com/score/").
  path("{id}");
String agency2Score = agency2.queryParam("id", id).
  request(MediaType.TEXT_PLAIN).get(String.class);
int score2 = Integer.parseInt(agency2Score);

//Get credit score from agency 3;
//...omitted for brevity

c.close(); //Client should be closed after each use
return calculateCombinedScore(score1, score2, score3);
}
private int calculateCombinedScore(int score1, int score2, int
  score3) {
  //Very complex calculation of a combined score
  ...
}
}
```

**Example 11.10**

Example 11.10 shows two ways of invoking a GET. The first credit agency's REST-based API expects the customer identifier to be part of the URL:

```
GET /creditscore/xxxxxxxxx
```

The second credit agency expects the id to be passed as a URI parameter:

```
GET /creditscore?id=xxxxxxxx
```

The client code constructs the appropriate `WebTarget` classes and attaches a URI parameter for the call to the second credit agency, which calls the GET method on the `Invocation.Builder` object returned by the `respose` method on the `WebTarget` class. For high availability, separate resource targets can be created for different services. The GET method passes in the type of response expected, such as a String obtaining the score.

Calls to the credit agencies are made in a serial fashion. An asynchronous approach allows work to continue until results are collected and ready. The JAX-RS 2.0 Client APIs support asynchronous calls via the `javax.rs.ws.core.Invocation.` `Builder.async` method. Control is immediately returned to the caller with a return type of `java.util.concurrent.Future<T>` object that encapsulates the result of the computation retrieved via the GET method on the `Future` object, as seen in Example 11.11.

```
WebTarget agency1 = c.target("https://agency1.com/score"+id);

Future<String> scoreFuture = agency1.request.(MediaType.TEXT_PLAIN).
  async().get(String.class);

//perform other useful computation here…
//When ready to retrieve score get it from the Future
String scoreStr = scoreFuture.get();
```

**Example 11.11**

Other forms of asynchronous communication are supported where callbacks are specified in asynchronous invocations and employed when the invocation succeeds or fails. More information on the other forms of asynchronous communication can be found in the JAX-RS documentation.

Even though the JAX-RS Client API offers powerful abstractions for such complex invocation patterns, performing such computations in code makes the code more complex and error-prone.

## Schema Type Reuse

During execution, a composition controller invokes a number of its composition members. With the exception of one-way operations, each composition member returns some data to the controller to calculate the result that the composition controller returns to its service consumer. There are many cases where the returned data can also be viewed as a composition, such as a composition of the members' response data.

For example, consider a composition member that is a entity service. Following the design and implementation practices for entity services established in Chapter 9, the service offers a business-relevant, shallow representation of the underlying data. A composition controller acts as the implementation for a task service that will later be used within a business process. The message entity exposed in the entity service contract will be useful as it remains unchanged within the context of the business process. Therefore, the service composition has no reason to redefine the respective message entity.

The message entity of one service can be wrapped into a larger message entity that includes data from other composition members. The composition controller aggregates the returned data from its members into one object that it returns to its clients. Reusing data returned unchanged from a composition member allows more efficient code to be written, and reduces the number of defined complex types in the schema. However, direct reuse may not be possible if the composition service interface is already fixed before the composition members are identified. Converter code must then handle the transformation between the data types used in composition members and the data types required for the composition controller.

---

### CASE STUDY EXAMPLE

NovoBank's Process Customer Account service composes the Customer and Account entity services. The `retrieveCustomerAccountInfo` operation returns data in a `CustomerAccountInfo` type, which is a wrapper around two message entity types defined by the reused Customer and Account entity services. The service design team examines the message entities returned from the two entity services and decides that they can be directly reused for the composition.

The XML schema definition for the `CustomerAccountInfo` type is already listed in Chapter 10, and Example 11.12 illustrates what the definition looks like in Java.

```
package com.novobank.services.task.creditapproval;

import java.util.List;
import com.novobank.services.entity.account.Account;
import com.novobank.services.entity.customer.Customer;

public class CustomerAccountInfo {
```

```
    private Customer customer;
    private List<Account> accounts;

    public Customer getCustomer() {
      return customer;
    }

    public void setCustomer(Customer customer) {
      this.customer = customer;
    }

    public List<Account> getAccounts() {
      return accounts;
    }

    public void setAccounts(List<Account> accounts) {
      this.accounts = accounts;
    }
}
```

**Example 11.12**

The code for the aggregated type is straightforward and no additional data transformation is required. A service consumer will see that the `Customer` and `Account` message entities are reused. The namespaces and package names indicate that the message entities are defined by the Customer and Account entity services. The Process Customer Account service interface exposes which services are composed internally.

Reusing composed data types reveals implementation details about a composition to its service consumers, such as the dependencies between the Process Customer Account service and Customer and Account entity services. Any change in the schema of the message entity for either of the entity services affects the service consumers of the task service. The following case study example illustrates how NovoBank manages the unwanted dependencies created in composition.

## CASE STUDY EXAMPLE

During a design review, the NovoBank team detects a dependency between service consumers of the Process Customer Account service and two underlying entity services. While the coupling increases reuse and simplifies the implementation of the Process Customer Account service, the team decides that such a coupling is overall undesirable. The Process Customer Account service interface is changed to hide the dependency in accordance with service-orientation design principles. The `Customer-AccountInfo` data type is changed, as shown in Example 11.13.

```xml
<xs:schema version="1.0" targetNamespace="http://creditapproval.
  task.services.novobank.com/" xmlns:tns="http://creditapproval.
  task.services.novobank.com/" xmlns:xs="http://www.w3.org/2001/
  XMLSchema">

  <xs:complexType name="customerAccountInfo">
    <xs:sequence>
      <xs:element name="accounts" type="tns:account" nillable="true"
        maxOccurs="unbounded" minOccurs="0"/>
      <xs:element name="customer" type="tns:customer" minOccurs="0"/>
    </xs:sequence>
  </xs:complexType>

  <xs:complexType name="account">
    <xs:sequence>
      <xs:element name="accountId"
        type="xs:string" minOccurs="0"/>
      <xs:element name="accountType"
        type="xs:string" minOccurs="0"/>
      <xs:element name="balance" type="xs:double"/>
    </xs:sequence>
  </xs:complexType>

  <xs:complexType name="customer">
    <xs:sequence>
      <xs:element name="customerId"
        type="xs:string" minOccurs="0"/>
      <xs:element name="e-mailAddress"
        type="xs:string" minOccurs="0"/>
      <xs:element name="firstName"
        type="xs:string" minOccurs="0"/>
      <xs:element name="lastName"
        type="xs:string" minOccurs="0"/>
```

```
        <xs:element name="streetAddresses"
          type="xs:string" nillable="true"
          maxOccurs="unbounded" minOccurs="0"/>
    </xs:sequence>
  </xs:complexType>
</xs:schema>
```

**Example 11.13**

The updated Process Customer Account schema changes the `Customer` and `Account` complex types to be locally defined in the same namespace as the `customerAccountInfo` complex type, no longer reusing the schema definitions from the other services.

The Process Customer Account service returns the locally defined types in its implementation by converting the data returned from the entity services into the appropriate local types. This conversion is handled by the classes named `CustomerConverter` and `AccountConverter`. Only the `CustomerConverter` source is listed in Example 11.14, since the `AccountConverter` is similar.

```
package com.novobank.services.task.creditapproval;

public class CustomerConverter {
  public com.novobank.services.task.creditapproval.Customer
    convert(com.novobank.services.entity.customer.Customer
    entityCustomer) {

    Customer c = new Customer();
    c.setCustomerId(entityCustomer.getCustomerId());
    c.setE-mailAddress(entityCustomer.getE-mailAddress());
    c.setFirstName(entityCustomer.getFirstName());
    c.setLastName(entityCustomer.getLastName());
    c.setStreetAddresses(entityCustomer.getStreetAddresses());
    return c;
  }
}
```

**Example 11.14**

The `converter` class performs a field-by-field transformation, which ensures that any changes to the underlying entity service's schema can be handled within the `CustomerConverter` without affecting service consumers. The field-by-field transformation creates the desired level of indirection between the services. (Note that besides using Java, there are alternative and potentially more efficient ways to implement this conversion.)

The only remaining change to make is in the `ProcessCustomerAccountSer-vice` class in Example 11.15, where the converters are invoked to perform the necessary conversion.

```
package com.novobank.services.task.creditapproval;

// import list omitted here
@WebService
@Stateless
public class ProcessCustomerAccountService implements
ProcessCustomerAccountRemote {
  private static final boolean isLogEnabled = true;
  protected CustomerConverter customerConverter = new
    CustomerConverter();
  protected AccountConverter  accountConverter = new
    AccountConverter();

  public CustomerAccountInfo retrieveCustomerAccountInfo(String
    firstName, String lastName) {

    // logging code as before, omitted here
    CustomerAccountInfo info = new CustomerAccountInfo();

    // retrieve customer info
    CustomerService cs = new zCustomerServiceService().
      getCustomerServicePort();
    Customer customer = cs.getCustomerByName(firstName, lastName);
    info.setCustomer(customerConverter.convert(customer));

    // retrieve account info
    AccountService as = new AccountServiceService().
      getAccountServicePort();
    List<com.novobank.services.entity.account.Account> entityAccounts
      = as.findAccountByCustomer(customer.getCustomerId());
    List<Account> localAccounts = new LinkedList<Account>();
    Iterator<com.novobank.services.entity.account.Account> i =
      entityAccounts.iterator();
      while(i.hasNext()) {
        Account a = accountConverter.convert(i.next());
        localAccounts.add(a);
```

```
    }
  info.setAccounts(localAccounts);
  return info;
 }

// other code as before, omitted here

}
```

**Example 11.15**

## Web-Based Services vs. Java Components

A Java-based service can generally be used in a variety of ways, all of which have already been described in previous chapters:

- *In-Process* – as a local Java class

- *In-Process* – as a stateless session EJB via its local interface

- *Cross-Process* – as a stateless session EJB via its remote interface (RMI/IIOP)

- *Cross-Process* – as a Web-based service via its service interface (SOAP or REST)

The choice of which mechanisms should be used in case of a service composition depends on a number of factors, all of which must be assessed during the design of the composition controller.

An in-process invocation is faster than crossing process boundaries or going across a network. When a service composition has non-functional requirements, support for extremely high-request loads, a large number of concurrent service consumers, and/or short response times may only be achievable by invoking composition members locally.

Developing in Java involves one language, which removes the need to create a language-neutral representation of parameters and return values. With Java, the use of a local stateless session EJB uses a local invocation model while taking advantage of the EJB container for instance pooling and transaction.

> **NOTE**
>
> Locally invoking a service has an additional side effect as parameters
> locally passed into the service are not copied to new object instances.
> Instead, parameters are passed by reference, and any manipulation of
> these instance references affects the Java code within the caller. Call-by-
> value semantics apply when calling a service remotely, which means that
> all parameters are copied and any changes to them are invisible to the
> calling application.

Invoking a composition member via its Java interface creates a tight coupling between the composition controller and composition member that is generally undesirable. The composition controller directly depends on Java artifacts from the composition member implementation, specifically on its Java interface and any related classes and interfaces. Any change in these artifacts can require a complete recompile of the composition controller implementation. The direct invocation model makes rerouting the request/ response message to insert additional processing for logging and auditing impossible.

Whether or not a Java interface is utilized instead of a Web service interface is a choice made based on non-functional requirements such as performance, and the necessity to support key service-orientation principles, such as Standardized Service Contract, Service Loose Coupling, and Service Abstraction, as well as associated design standards. Therefore, when considering the use of native Java interfaces, it is important to also consider the application of the Dual Protocols pattern to ensure that standardized access and communication are also supported within the service inventory.

Either way, it may be beneficial to implement the service logic within a stateless session EJB to add support for transactions, security, and other functionality offered by the Java EE application server environment. Employing an EJB to manage infrastructure-level functionality allows the developer to focus on implementing the business logic for the service.

Installing the service implementation logic on an application server achieves scalability of the service once its usage increases. Application servers can be clustered to offer load-balancing capabilities to spread client load across multiple instances of the same server, and expose several copies of the same service to service consumers. A Java EE application server has the ability to redirect service consumer requests from one server instance to another if a particular instance, or the server it runs on, is unavailable. Highly available services can remain active even in case of server hardware problems.

**CASE STUDY EXAMPLE**

To maintain the requests sent to the Process Customer Account service, the Novo-Bank IT team adds logging capabilities to the service implementation. After analyzing the portfolio of existing services, they find that the Generic Logger utility service fits their requirements. To preserve loose coupling between the composition controller (Process Customer Account service) and the composition member (Generic Logger service), it is decided that the utility service will be invoked over its Web service interface. The implementation for the `retrieveCustomerAccountInfo` operation is updated in Example 11.16.

```
package com.novobank.services.task.creditapproval;

import java.io.ByteArrayInputStream;
import java.util.List;
import javax.ejb.Stateless;
import javax.jws.WebService;
import javax.xml.parsers.DocumentBuilder;
import javax.xml.parsers.DocumentBuilderFactory;
import javax.xml.ws.WebServiceException;
import org.w3c.dom.Document;

import com.novobank.services.entity.account.Account;
import com.novobank.services.entity.account.AccountService;
import com.novobank.services.entity.account.AccountServiceService;
import com.novobank.services.entity.customer.Customer;
import com.novobank.services.entity.customer.CustomerService;
import com.novobank.services.entity.customer.CustomerServiceService;
import com.novobank.services.utility.GenericLogger;
import com.novobank.services.utility.GenericLoggerService;
import com.novobank.services.utility.Log;
import com.novobank.services.utility.e-mail.E-mailService;
import com.novobank.services.utility.e-mail.E-mailServiceService;
import com.novobank.services.utility.e-mail.E-mailServiceException_
Exception;

@WebService
@Stateless
public class ProcessCustomerAccountService implements
ProcessCustomerAccountRemote {
  private static final boolean isLogEnabled = true;
  public CustomerAccountInfo retrieveCustomerAccountInfo( String
    firstName, String lastName) {
```

```
    // log incoming request
    if (isLogEnabled) {
      try {
        GenericLogger logger =
          new GenericLoggerService().getGenericLoggerPort();
        // build an XML message to be logged
        StringBuilder sb = new StringBuilder();
        sb.append("<message>")
          .append("Account information requested for ")
          .append(firstName)
          .append(" ")
          .append(lastName)
          .append("</message>");
        DocumentBuilder db =
          DocumentBuilderFactory.newInstance()
          .newDocumentBuilder();
        Document d =
          db.parse(new ByteArrayInputStream(
        xmlString.getBytes()));
        Log log = new Log();
        log.setAny(d.getDocumentElement());
        logger.log(log);
      } catch (Exception x) {}
    }
    CustomerAccountInfo info = new CustomerAccountInfo();
    ... remaining code as listed before ...
}
```

**Example 11.16**

## Packaging, Testing and Deploying Composed Services

How a composition is packaged and installed into a runtime environment depends on how the composition members are invoked. If the composition members are invoked via a SOAP-based Web service interface, then the appropriate client-side artifacts should be generated from the service contract. An example is how the WSDL is generated via the wsimport tool. For REST services, the absence of a machine-readable service contract means there are no artifacts to be generated.

Even if the service invoked is developed in Java, never reuse any of the code or generated service interfaces directly from the service implementation. The client-side artifacts should all be generated for a particular service consumer, such as the composition controller, and packaged with its service implementation. Reusing code creates a level of coupling and dependency that should be avoided.

For SOAP-based Web services, the wsimport tool generates the Java service interface, JAXB-based classes representing the schema types referenced in the WSDL, and a number of other utility classes that depend on the exact JAX-WS implementation used. All of these artifacts can be packaged in a single utility JAR file and added to the classpath for development of the composition controller. Each composition member is represented by one JAR file. For final packaging, the utility JAR files can be added to the EAR file containing the entire composition implementation.

For REST services, the resource classes can be packaged inside a regular Web application WAR file. The JAX-RS implementation often provides a servlet or filter, such as in Jersey, that intercepts HTTP requests, performs request redirection to the JAX-RS resources, maps the HTTP methods to resource methods, and marshals/unmarshals resource method parameters to and from content in the HTTP request/response messages. The JAX-RS implementation servlet or filter is declared in the Web application's `web.xml` file.

---

### CASE STUDY EXAMPLE

After the Process Customer Account task service is complete, it composes the following composition members:

- Customer Entity Service

- Account Entity Service

- E-Mail Utility Service

- GenericLogger Utility Service

The generated code artifacts related to these services are packaged in separate JAR files that are added to the final, deployable EAR file as utility modules. In Java EE 5, the JAR files are put into the `/lib directory` within the EAR file and are automatically available to any other module within the application without requiring the creation of any deployment descriptors. Figure 11.3 provides an overview of the completed EAR file.

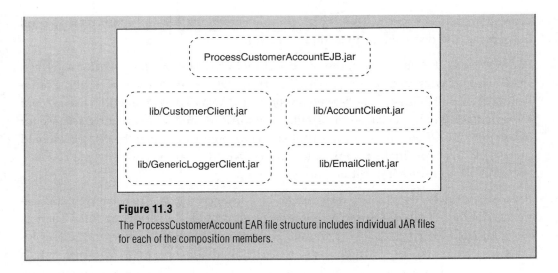

**Figure 11.3**
The ProcessCustomerAccount EAR file structure includes individual JAR files
for each of the composition members.

When a composition member is invoked using a Java call, either the entire composition member implementation can be packaged for local invocation, or the pieces required for a remote invocation can be selectively packaged. For example, a target composition member is invoked using the remote EJB interface and the appropriate client package containing all required artifacts packaged with the composition controller must be generated. Artifacts can be packed separately in a utility JAR file to avoid cluttering the code. References must be generated to the target EJB invoked in the composition's deployment descriptor or as annotations in the code. Packaging code artifacts that belong to different services into different JAR files keeps the services as separate as possible.

The techniques of creating local stubs for task services discussed in Chapter 10 equally apply to the composition members when testing a service composition. The composition controller code can be tested without requiring the invoked services to be available or even exist. Difficulties in tracking where and what has caused errors occur often when testing a distributed system, such as a service composition with many members. A transactional view of the system can help manage errors by adding trace points to the code that track the original request that was carried out when the trace information was written.

Traced messages must carry information that allows them to be properly correlated. The original request message often contains data forwarded to each composition member that can serve as the correlating element. For example, a customer ID is passed to a service composition for the invocation of each composition member, and all trace messages with the same customer ID belong to the same original request.

In cases where a correlating parameter does not exist, a message ID can be added to each message. The message ID is generated once in the composition controller and then passed with every message to each composition member. The creation and handling of the message ID should be delegated either to underlying middleware or to a separate component, such as an enterprise service bus.

For example, the JAX-WS defines the concept of handlers, which are invoked before a message is sent out and right after a message was received. Handlers enable the insertion and processing of message IDs to allow correlation of messages that belong to the same original transaction. Similarly, the JAX-RS implementations offer constructs called filters, which are inserted in the request/response chain and can be utilized to communicate such contextual information.

Test performance as early as possible, especially for service compositions, when the composition members are deployed in the same way as in the production environment. Early performance testing can reveal further changes to the way services are implemented and/or deployed, solely based on non-functional characteristics like response time or message throughput.

---

### CASE STUDY EXAMPLE

During integration testing of the Process Customer Account service, a significant gap is discovered between the test response times and the response documented as a non-functional requirement for the service. By analyzing and profiling the code, it is detected that calling the remote Generic Logger utility service for every request in the Process Customer Account service greatly increases the processing time. The Generic Logger utility service requires an XML document to be passed that also creates an additional burden on the processing time.

The IT team decides to change the code to use a local logging routine in Java called in-process, instead of remotely via the Web service. A static variable is left in place in the code for the remote call to be reactivated later, or in a different instance of the Process Customer Account service that carries lower performance requirements.

The updated `retrieveCustomerAccountInfo` method is seen in Example 11.17.

```
package com.novobank.services.task.creditapproval;

import java.io.ByteArrayInputStream;
import java.util.List;
import javax.ejb.Stateless;
import javax.jws.WebService;
import javax.xml.parsers.DocumentBuilder;
import javax.xml.parsers.DocumentBuilderFactory;
import javax.xml.ws.WebServiceException;
import org.w3c.dom.Document;

import com.novobank.services.entity.account.Account;
import com.novobank.services.entity.account.AccountService;
import com.novobank.services.entity.account.AccountServiceService;
import com.novobank.services.entity.customer.Customer;
import com.novobank.services.entity.customer.CustomerService;
import com.novobank.services.entity.customer.CustomerServiceService;
import com.novobank.services.utility.GenericLogger;
import com.novobank.services.utility.GenericLoggerService;
import com.novobank.services.utility.Log;
import com.novobank.services.utility.e-mail.E-mailService;
import com.novobank.services.utility.e-mail.E-mailServiceService;
import com.novobank.services.utility.e-mail.E-mailServiceException_
  Exception;

@WebService
@Stateless
public class ProcessCustomerAccountService implements
ProcessCustomerAccountRemote {
  private static final boolean isLogEnabled = false;
  private static final boolean isLocalLogEnabled = true;
  protected LocalJavaLogger localLogger =
    new LocalJavaLogger();
  protected CustomerConverter customerConverter =
    new CustomerConverter();
  protected AccountConverter accountConverter =
    new AccountConverter();

  public CustomerAccountInfo retrieveCustomerAccountInfo( String
    firstName, String lastName) {
    // log incoming request
    if (isLogEnabled) {
      try {
        GenericLogger logger =
          new GenericLoggerService().getGenericLoggerPort();
```

```
    // build an XML message to be logged
    StringBuilder sb = new StringBuilder();
    sb.append("<message>")
      .append("Account information requested for ")
      .append(firstName)
      .append(" ")
      .append(lastName)
      .append("</message>");
    DocumentBuilder db =
      DocumentBuilderFactory.newInstance()
      .newDocumentBuilder();
    Document d =
      db.parse(new ByteArrayInputStream(
      sb.toString().getBytes()));

    Log log = new Log();
    log.setAny(d.getDocumentElement());
    logger.log(log);
  } catch (Exception x) {}
}
if (isLocalLogEnabled) {
  localLogger.log("Account information requested for " +
    firstName + " " + lastName+".");
}
CustomerAccountInfo info = new CustomerAccountInfo();
  ... remaining code as listed before ...
}
```

**Example 11.17**

Use of the final static Boolean variables, `isLogEnabled` and `isLocalLogEnabled`, allows the logging code to be enabled/disabled by switching the Boolean between true and false.

Note that the `LocalJavaLogger` utility service (introduced in Chapter 8) uses the Java Logging API. With no Web service interface, the `LocalJavaLogger` utility service is accessed via local Java invocation only. The respective source code for this service must be added to the classpath of the invoking service.

Additional performance for service compositions can be achieved via regular tuning of both the code and the environment that it runs in. In some cases, an invocation of a remote Web service that normally results in a call being made over the network can be served from a local cache to avoid the remote call altogether by applying advanced caching mechanisms.

---

**SUMMARY OF KEY POINTS**

- There are distinct programming approaches when working with REST services and SOAP-based Web services.

- The decision to allow services to exist as Java components must be carefully assessed and use of the Dual Protocols pattern must be further considered.

- The service composition controller manages faults and errors that occur during processing, and maps them appropriately for its service consumers.

- Data types of composition members should never be exposed on the composition controller interface despite the achieved benefit of reduced complexity.

---

## 11.3 Service and Service Composition Performance Guidelines

Previous sections have already touched upon various performance-related considerations. This remaining section highlights a number of further guidelines that are applicable to services acting as composition controllers or composition members.

### Measuring Performance

When assessing the performance of a service composition, it is helpful to establish a set of baseline metrics that can be individually measured for each service, as well as collectively for the composition controller, on behalf of an entire service composition. The following are examples of common metrics that address runtime performance as well as reliability:

- *Response Time* – A service's response time is a measure of how quickly a response is returned to the caller. Stakeholders often outline their response expectations in the form of an SLA that states what the mean service response time or a percentile response time should be, such as "80% of the service invocations should return in less than three seconds." The service should maintain its desired level of SLAs when the system is under maximum expected load. The desired response times are commonly stated in the context of a peak concurrent load, such as "a service must return results within three seconds or less with 600 peak concurrent users using the system."

- *Throughput* – A service's throughput is the possible number of service requests served in a given time as expressed in units, such as a number of messages or service invocations in a given time interval. The SLA guarantees related to throughput may be expressed in terms of the system needing to support a specific number of service invocations in a given time window, such as 10,000 service invocations in one hour.

- *Resource Utilization* – An operational service consumes a certain amount of resources, such as memory, at the system level, or resources associated with managed environments like application servers, such as JVM threads, database connections, JVM heap memory, or a number of managed objects in a pool. Well-performing services exhibit a stable pattern of resource usage under expected load conditions. A stable pattern does not imply the resource consumption stays constant at a certain level, but indicates the trend does not fluctuate wildly under varying loads. Fluctuations in resource consumption could indicate instabilities within services or the system.

- *Capacity* – A service's capacity measures the maximum levels of load services can maintain. An in-depth capacity assessment measures how a service degrades in performance with increasing load. A well-designed and tuned service would experience gradual degradation in performance when load is increased beyond its projected capacity, but a sub-optimal service might experience severe degradation with temporary spikes in load beyond its expected capacity. Capacity planning tests are an important component of an overall scalability and performance testing initiative.

- *Availability* – Service availability means the percentage of time a service is available in a year. For example, an availability of five nines indicates the service is available 99.999% of the time during a year, which translates to approximately 5.26 minutes of downtime throughout the year. It is important to avoid guaranteeing the "four nines" (99.99% or 52.56 minutes of downtime) or the "three nines" (99.9% or 8.76 hours of downtime) of service availability before determining the realistic availability requirements of a service composing others.

## Testing Performance

Various types of testing are carried out to measure the performance and scalability characteristics of services and service compositions. In this section we highlight considerations specific to load testing, stress testing, and soak testing methods.

Performance testing measures different aspects of system behavior that can be corrected or tuned for optimization. Load testing of services is carried out during routine performance testing to simulate load on services and measure performance and stability characteristics. Gradually increasing the load determines how well the services and system comply with the SLAs as the load increases. Workload characterization is also considered during load testing. Workload characterization determines a realistic mix of service invocations.

For example, the peak operational hours in a typical retail banking IT system might experience a mix of 40% customer account inquiry, 30% debits, credits, and transfers, and 30% miscellaneous CRM operations. Before performing load tests, an appropriate workload characterization should be determined, and the load test profile should accurately reflect the workload seen in production. The performance SLAs of services must be captured in the same context, such as 90% of the customer account inquiry service invocations should return in no less than 3 seconds when the system is being used by 600 concurrent users (peak load), and the workload consists of 40% account inquiries, 30% update transactions, and 30% CRM services.

Stress testing ascertains what the breaking point of a service is, and how well the service behaves near the breaking point. Continuing to increase load on a system increases the response time and/or decreases the throughput. However, a buckle point occurs when the performance suffers a dramatic degradation to the point of rendering the system unusable. The operational goal is to ensure the system operates well below this buckle point, and can scale to meet the projected demand. Stress testing is documented in the service SLAs with a clear statement of the load limits the service can withstand and maintain acceptable performance.

Soak testing tracks the resource utilization patterns of services by subjecting them to normal load for extended durations, such as days and months. The system or services often exhibit resource leaks where used resources, such as memory, database connections, file handles, or open sockets, are not reclaimed or cleaned in a timely manner that can lead to the eventual starvation of resources. Systems can exhibit slow but gradual degradation of performance under normal load over days or weeks.

## Caching

Caching is an implementation technique to store service computation results in some form of volatile storage for return when the same information is requested. However, caching is also a significant architectural decision for performance-sensitive parts of the system. Stringent response time SLA requirements may be adversely affected by expensive processing, I/O latency, and excessive network round trips.

Caching unchanged or infrequently changed data spares the effort of repeatedly retrieving the same data from the source system, such as a database or ERP system. Reference data, such as country or currency codes, are commonly cached in read-only caches. To avoid a single point of failure and improve system availability, caches are often distributed across physical nodes. Keeping all copies of the caches in sync can be challenging.

Periodic cache refresh and notification techniques for cache invalidation can help maintain cache consistency across multiple cache nodes. However, building such caching utilities in-house is expensive and error-prone. Instead, open-source frameworks, such as Memcached, provide a distributed, in-memory object cache. Service implementations can use Memcached APIs to store and retrieve read-mostly objects from a distributed cache.

### Data Grids

Implementing a distributed read-write cache for frequently updated data is a challenge in software engineering compounded by the emergence of extreme transaction processing (XTP). Applications, such as realtime trading systems, generating large volumes of transactions, often encounter I/O bottlenecks because of excessive database reads/writes and the associated network and I/O costs. Besides high performance and scalability requirements, maintaining high levels of system availability are critical for such demanding services. In response, architectural patterns and software products have emerged that are collectively referred to as in-memory data grids.

An in-memory data grid provides a distributed read-write cache, and can effectively serve as the logical persistence layer for services to interact with the data grid to cache data. The data grid is responsible for synchronizing the data held in-memory with the persistence store, which can be a relational database, an ERP system, or any EIS system that provides integration APIs. The data grids write to the database or utilize the integration APIs to flush the data to the system in a synchronous (write-through) or asynchronous (write-behind) fashion.

The write-through approach has error handling and transaction rollback characteristics, in which cache updates can roll back in the event of a failure to write to the underlying store. If all the writes to the data in the persistent store are performed through the cache, the data in the cache will stay current. However, if persistent store data writes are performed through other channels, then the cache must refresh either periodically or by notification in the event of data updates happening via other mechanisms. Most data grid products allow registering notification listeners with persistent stores or back-end systems that can receive update event notifications and refresh the cache.

For services, implementations can plug into an in-memory data grid for data reads and writes offering better response times, scalability, and availability through a distributed set of nodes known as a cluster. The services and the service consumers can continue to function despite outages in the persistence layer. The data grid acts as the virtual persistence layer, which holds the information in memory across a cluster of nodes, receives updates, flushes, and synchronizes the data when the systems of record are brought back online.

Added complexity in the implementation results in managing what could be hundreds of cache nodes. The service implementations may require extensive use of proprietary data grid APIs. Careful design is necessary to keep the service business logic separate from the cache access code. The operations team should be trained in the administration and maintenance of data grids.

In-memory grids are not a replacement for disk-based transactional data systems such as databases, as the information is not persisted to disk or provided the same levels of transactional capabilities as relational databases. When performing multiple updates across different databases, a transaction management infrastructure and databases are required to handle data consistency and integrity issues.

*REST Caching*

Rather than requiring a service to use a caching library, the constraints of REST have promoted caching to an architectural construct. For example, the World Wide Web scaled because HTTP caching features have been successfully exploited by browsers, Web agents, proxy servers, and content delivery networks (CDN). Browsers cache Web content. Proxy servers and CDNs sit between and allow the content services and service consumers to intercept requests and provide content from their cache, rather than returning to the original server for the content. Proxy servers can perform the same role with REST services if the services are designed appropriately.

GET and HEAD requests are safe and idempotent, and make ideal candidates for caching the invocation results. The HTTP caching semantics provide fine-grained caching behavior that allows service designers to specify who is allowed to cache the results, how long a cache can remain valid, and what type of cache revalidation mechanism can be used. The HTTP 1.1 `Cache-Control` header specifies a number of directives that determine the exact caching behavior.

Some of the important directives include:

- `public` – Any entity in the request/response chain is allowed to cache the results, which allows proxy servers and CDNs to cache the results of a GET or HEAD invocation.

- `no-cache` – This directive indicates the response should not be cached.

- `max-age` – This directive determines the duration of the cache validity.

- `must-revalidate` – When this directive is present in the response, the cache must not use the entry after it becomes stale. Subsequent requests should be revalidated with the origin server.

A sample HTTP response with a `cache-control` directive is seen in Example 11.18.

```
HTTP/1.1 200 OK
Content-Type: application/xml
Cache-Control: public, max-age=600, must-revalidate
<Customer>
  ...
</Customer>
```

**Example 11.18**

The `Cache-Control` directive indicates the response can be cached by any intermediaries for ten-minute durations.

REST services can also support cache revalidation, which is often seen with conditional GETs. The service returns an `ETag` header that acts as a unique fingerprint of the response at a given time. The service caller is expected to store the `ETag` value, and can conditionally request cache revalidation by sending an `If-None-Match` header in a subsequent GET request that carries the stored `ETag` value. If the service has a fresher value of the cache, it will detect that the value in the `If-None-Match` request header does not match the latest `ETag` value and respond with a `200 OK` response with the new response and latest `ETag` value. If the content has not changed, the service returns a `304` `'Not Modified'` response, and the client can continue to use the cached result.

A typical cache exchange is illustrated in Example 11.19.

```
GET /customers/1234 HTTP/1.1
...
HTTP/1.1 200 OK
Content-Type: application/xml
Cache-Control: public, max-age=600
ETag: 123456789
<Customer>
  ...
</Customer>
```

**Example 11.19**

If the client issues a request within ten minutes, an intermediary, such as a proxy server, can return a cached result without going back to the origin server. After ten minutes, the client issues a conditional GET request, as seen in Example 11.20.

```
GET /customers/1234 HTTP/1.1
If-None-Match: "123456789"
And receives a modified response:
HTTP/1.1 200 OK
Content-Type: application/xml
Cache-Control: public, max-age=600
ETag: 785634892
<Customer>  '
  <!—a modified customer -->
</Customer>
```

**Example 11.20**

The response header `Last-Modified` and the request header `If-Modified-Since` serve similar revalidation purposes to `ETag` and `If-None-Match`. Exploring caching possibilities in a REST service design should be undertaken before the implementation phase. APIs, such as the JAX-RS, provide support for implementing caching constructs.

## Scaling Out Services with State

A stateless service can be deployed across multiple nodes. Requests to the services can be load balanced across the server farm. Some stateful services can still support a scale-out model by employing the State Repository pattern that assigns state management responsibilities to a dedicated storage, such as a database or file system. Such types of services refresh their state from the storage on every service request, which avoids storing state in memory and allows service requests to be appropriately load balanced.

Other types of stateful services, such as utility services, may need to maintain state information in memory, as per the Stateful Service pattern. In the absence of a centralized state repository, it becomes important to associate a service consumer with a specific service with the latest state information to ensure continuity of the conversational context. This "sticky" association breaks the load-balancing model, and has a negative effect on scalability.

The "sticky" association model introduces a single point of failure where an outage of the node hosting the stateful service results in a loss of availability. Infrastructure vendors mitigate this effect by introducing in-memory session replication where the state information held in memory is replicated to a secondary node. The secondary node acts as a backup when the primary node goes offline. However, in a typical application server deployment, this affects overall performance from replicating state changes across nodes that requires expensive broadcast message communications between nodes.

If there is a need to host large numbers of stateful services, consider the efficient support for maintaining cache consistencies offered by specialized solutions, such as in-memory data grids.

## Handling Failures

Services may fail at multiple points in a service invocation, which complicates failure handling. A service invocation can fail in the middle of the call or network failures between the caller and the service could leave the service consumer uncertain of whether the request was serviced or not. The call may have successfully processed, but the network might have had an outage before the results were returned to the caller.

The caller often cannot resubmit a request in the event of failure without undesirable side effects, such as processing a payment multiple times. Idempotency ensures invoking a service multiple times has the same effect as invoking it once, and service safety ensures no side effects occur even when a service is invoked multiple times. Safe methods, such as HTTP GETs, are appropriate candidates for request resubmission in the event of failures, but idempotent services may not be side effect-free. To prevent the side effects from being triggered multiple times, refrain from resubmitting a request to a non-idempotent service.

Recovery is a key consideration of failure handling. How does a service recover from a failure in the middle of a transactional update? Many business services update multiple transactional systems, such as databases, messaging systems, and third party-packaged applications. In such situations, a call may only have made partial updates before failing, and may compromise the system integrity in the absence of a transaction recovery infrastructure.

Implementing a distributed transaction recovery protocol is provided by infrastructure vendors. Without requiring assistance from the developer, transactional integrity is managed by sophisticated, distributed, transaction recovery mechanisms, such as XA. Popular distributed transaction management protocols are designed to handle failures. However, XA recovery adversely affects performance by requiring extensive checkpoint-based logging.

When an application server is responsible for managing transactional integrity for components, such as EJBs, the container starts and manages a distributed transaction that can involve multiple data sources. For a full XA recovery, all participants in the distributed transaction must support XA and offer an XA-based adapter, such as an XA-aware JDBC driver. Various XA optimizations offer a relaxed recovery protocol, which is still open to small windows of failure, for a less expensive transaction. However, distributed transaction recovery using a protocol, such as XA, involves locking resources. This is inadvisable and often impossible in a large, distributed environment without control over all systems.

Some advanced Web services standards, such as WS-AtomicTransaction, mimic XA recovery, but compensation-based approaches where undo actions are used to roll back failed updates offer a more scalable option. Manual reconciliations can also manage failures and recovery when the alternatives prove unsuitable.

## Parsing and Marshaling

This section considers different aspects of message parsing and marshaling/unmarshaling to illustrate how special handling can alleviate major performance problems in many situations, such as large message sizes, XML to Java marshaling and unmarshaling, and XML parsing.

Messages must often carry binary data, such as images, that can be substantial in size. A common practice is to Base64-encode the binary content and embed it in the message body, but this can result in poor performance as text-based serialization of binary data contributes an additional size bloat. The parser must perform unnecessary work to parse the entire payload, including the Base64-encoded content.

Instead, MTOM for SOAP-based Web services can be considered as a means of attaching binary data in a multipart MIME message. Attaching the binary data eliminates the size bloat and parsing overhead. Opaque data not requiring parsing or validation can be passed as attachments often in a compressed form. REST-style services can use MIME messages and attachments. The JAX-RS Jersey implementation facilitates construction and parsing of multipart messages. The JAX-RS implementation Jersey APIs help build multipart messages and submit them to the service. Example 11.21 uses Jersey 2.5.1 APIs for multipart support.

```
import javax.ws.rs.client.*;
import javax.ws.rs.client.WebTarget;
import org.glassfish.jersey.media.multipart.BodyPart;
import org.glassfish.jersey.media.multipart.MultiPart;
import javax.imageio.ImageIO;
import javax.ws.rs.core.MediaType;
import java.awt.image.BufferedImage;
import java.io.ByteArrayOutputStream;
import java.net.URL;

public class MultipartClient {
  public static void main(String[] args) throws Exception {
    ...//construct a claim JAXB object
    Claim cl = new Claim();
    cl.setType("CarInsurance");
    cl.setDescription("Accident claim");
    //other properties of claim…
    ByteArrayOutputStream bas = new ByteArrayOutputStream();
    URL url = new URL("file:///claims/iamges/accident-image.png");
    BufferedImage bi = ImageIO.read(url);
    ImageIO.write(bi, "png", bas);
    byte[] img = bas.toByteArray();

    // Construct a MultiPart with two body parts
    MultiPart multiPartEntity = new MultiPart().
      bodyPart(new BodyPart(cl, MediaType.APPLICATION_XML_TYPE)).
      bodyPart(new BodyPart(img, MediaType.
      APPLICATION_OCTET_STREAM_TYPE));
```

```
    // POST the request
    WebTarget target = ClientBuilder.newClient()
      .target("http://server/claim");
    Response response = target.request().post(Entity.
      entity(multiPartEntity, multipartEntity.getMediaType()));
    System.out.println("Response Status : " + response.
      getEntity(String.class));
  }
}
```

**Example 11.21**

In Example 11.21, the Jersey client multipart classes allow a multipart request to be constructed with a nested XML bodyPart that captures the details of a Claim object and an image of a vehicle. The org.glassfish.jersey.media.multipart.MultiPart class uses Builder to construct a multipart message with a chain of org.glassfish.jersey.media.multipart.BodyPart objects.

## SUMMARY OF KEY POINTS

- Service performance is about optimizing the service implementation and related architecture and design considerations within the context of service-orientation.

- Protocols, caching, message size management, transformation, failure handling, and parsing can be optimized to improve performance and reliability.

# Chapter 12

# ESB as SOA Infrastructure

A standard service development platform, such as a Web services stack or an API design and runtime stack, may no longer be enough to support the complex infrastructure requirements in a larger contemporary services ecosystem. In a heterogeneous environment, connecting applications together that use different communication protocols, message formats, or implementation technologies creates loosely coupled composite systems, requires building services out of existing assets, and warrants the delegation of system-level concerns to an infrastructure component.

System-level concerns include, but are not limited to:

- *Messaging* – to send and receive synchronous or asynchronous messages

- *Mediation* – to inspect, transform, or apply specific routing as part of message handling

- *Application Integration* – to connect disparate and heterogeneous applications

- *Service Composition* – to compose services from existing applications or a set of services, which include both REST and SOAP-based services

Although ESBs are not required for building SOA-based applications, they can be used to address a number of SOA infrastructural concerns. This chapter provides a basic overview of typical service infrastructure issues faced by IT organizations to illustrate how an ESB implements a combination of messaging, mediation, service hosting, and application integration techniques in support of service-orientation design principles.

| NOTE |
| --- |
| If you are already familiar with ESBs and their role within fundamental service infrastructures, you can skip this supplemental chapter. |

## 12.1 Basic Traditional Messaging Frameworks

Service consumers communicate with services via remote procedure calls, messaging, file exchange, or shared data in databases. For online applications, as opposed to batch applications that process data in bulk at pre-determined time intervals like in a monthly statement generation process, RPC and messaging are often the only viable options.

For example, messaging can be implemented using a message queuing technology, such as WebSphere MQ or ActiveMQ, but can also be realized using REST-style HTTP services. Therefore, messaging in this context means that the service consumer and service send each other self-describing messages.

Messaging can help applications achieve loose coupling. Basic messaging engines can be unsuccessful in meeting sophisticated message routing and transformation requirements. ESBs resolve this gap by acting as sophisticated messaging frameworks offering extensive support for configuration-driven message traffic management and transformation. For real-world applications, ESBs can be used as a messaging backbone.

### RPC vs. Messaging

Created in the 1980s, remote procedure calls are the foundation for more heavily used technologies, such as RMI/EJBs in Java. Application integration traditionally relied on RPC and messaging techniques. However, a large IT environment containing numerous applications reliant on an RPC model of integration can result in a spaghetti architecture where each application must know about the methods, method parameters, and return values of other applications. As the number of applications grows, the introduction of a new system means many of the other applications must change to interface with the new applications by calling another set of APIs.

In Figure 12.1, applications communicate with one another by calling APIs offered by other applications.

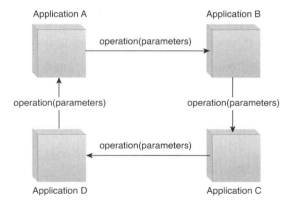

**Figure 12.1**
An RPC model of integration relies on applications that call APIs.

The RPC method of integration exposes a fine-grained API. Each application must know the API details of each of the service operations offered by other applications to ensure the right function calls are made, which results in various types of tight coupling between the applications.

### Technology Coupling

Applications communicating with one another via direct API calls are tightly bound at the technology level because of dependence on a common programming language, such as Java, or a specific application protocol, such as RMI or RMI/IIOP. In Figure 12.2, an EJB client calls an EJB service. Both are implemented on the Java

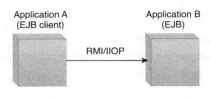

**Figure 12.2**
Technology coupling

platform with a tight degree of technology coupling. While a C++ application can use IIOP to communicate with a Java application, the scope of interoperability is limited by the widely varying nature of implementations.

### Spatial Coupling

Each application must be aware of the intimate details of other applications' API input parameters and return values. If any of these APIs change, the client applications must also change. In the absence of any infrastructure, service consumers are responsible for knowing

**Figure 12.3**
Spatial coupling

at which network node services are available, without location transparency.

If services move to a different network node, the client applications must also change. In Figure 12.3, an application calls another application to retrieve customer information.

### Temporal Coupling

In a blocking communication, the service consumer makes a service call and is blocked until a response is received from the service. If the service is unavailable due to a system outage, the service consumer is responsible for periodically retrying the service invocation until the

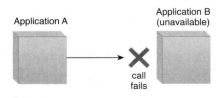

**Figure 12.4**
Temporal coupling

service is back online. In some situations, temporal coupling can be unavoidable due to the synchronous nature of the interaction. However, the service consumer can at times proceed and perform useful computation without waiting for the response while the original request is still being processed by the service. In Figure 12.4, the service consumer fails when the service is unavailable.

Applications can communicate with one another by sending and receiving messages rather than by calling APIs. A protocol is agreed upon by the service and the service consumer facilitating the transport for sending and receiving messages. Additionally, a message infrastructure or messaging engine can provide the backbone necessary for applications to communicate with each other.

Messaging styles include the point-to-point and publish/subscribe methods illustrated in Figure 12.5.

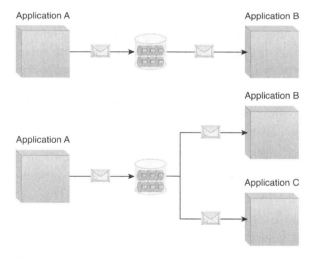

**Figure 12.5**
Messaging-style integration follows common models of messaging, such as point-to-point (top) and publish/subscribe (bottom).

Most message queuing infrastructures provide facilities for the message sender and message receiver to function regardless of one being offline, in a method known as guaranteed delivery.

The message sender can send a message to a destination that is accepted by the queue, and carry on with other actions regardless of whether the receiver is online. The queue will reliably deliver the message to the receiver irrespective of possible failures at the network or application level.

Message delivery is guaranteed only after the message has been delivered to the messaging queue and it has acknowledged the receipt of the message. The Asynchronous Queuing pattern captures this feature-set within the context of SOA.

The use of messaging queues minimizes many of the coupling-related problems associated with the RPC-centric integration model. When applied to the different types of coupling, the use of messaging produces the following results:

- Technology coupling is minimized since the message sender and message receiver rely on the messaging infrastructure, not each other. The dependency is transferred to the particular messaging queue(s) used to send and receive the messages.

- Temporal coupling is removed in truly asynchronous interactions, as messaging queues do not require the message sender and message receiver application to be running simultaneously.

- Spatial coupling is reduced, as applications can communicate with each other by sending documents as messages that no longer require intimate knowledge of the methods used by other applications.

    The document must still contain the correct data of the correct type, but how the document is interpreted by the receiving application is irrelevant to the message sender.

Figure 12.6 shows how applications implemented in different technologies can communicate with one another using messaging queues. Applications implemented in different technologies can communicate through messaging queues by exchanging documents as opposed to making method calls. The message sender application does not depend on the receiver application being operational at the time the message is sent. The message will be reliably delivered to the receiver when the receiving application comes back online.

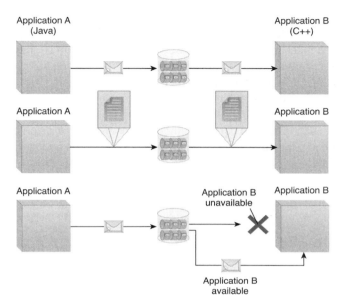

**Figure 12.6**
Messaging queues reduce technology coupling, temporal coupling, and spatial coupling between applications.

### *Message Producers and Message Consumers*

As messaging communication is unidirectional by nature, it is helpful to label applications with the message producer and message consumer roles when mapping message travel, irrespective of larger service composition activities.

In this section we'll use the term *message producer* to refer to an application that produces a message and directs it to an outgoing destination. Similarly, we'll use the term *message consumer* to refer to an application when it receives and processes the message at runtime. In a request/response MEP, the message producer issues a request message to the message consumer. The message consumer application then switches to the role of message producer to send back a response message.

Figure 12.7 illustrates these roles with both request/response and one-way MEPs.

---

**NOTE**

The terms message producer and message consumer can be mapped to the terms service consumer and service. However, using both sets of terms within the same scenario description can be confusing. Note also that when tracing message transmissions across multiple point-to-point branches, the terms *initial sender* and *ultimate receiver* are further helpful in identifying the service consumer that initiates the transmission of a message and the service that ultimately receives it at the end of the message path.

---

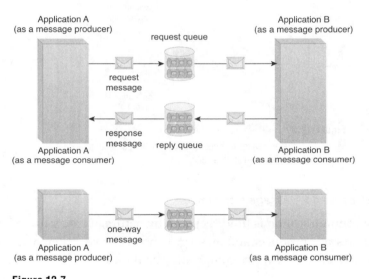

**Figure 12.7**

Applications assuming message producer and message consumer roles in request/response and one-way MEP scenarios.

---

**CASE STUDY EXAMPLE**

NovoBank already makes extensive use of a messaging infrastructure, WebSphere MQ. The Loans and Mortgage system is hosted on AS/400, and applications, such as Internet Banking, use the MQ messaging infrastructure to communicate with the AS/400-based back end. Different subsystems within the Loans and Mortgage application use different MQ queues to receive messages. The Internet Banking application components must be cognizant of all the different MQ queues in order to send their messages, as shown in Figure 12.8.

The current NovoBank messaging architecture is tightly coupled with the presentation-tier code that is directly exposed to low-level messaging infrastructure details. Any modification of the MQ deployment topology on the AS/400 system has an adverse impact on the channel application components. Introduction of new functional components on the back-end system require additional MQ queues in the messaging infrastructure, which further create additional work in the presentation tier.

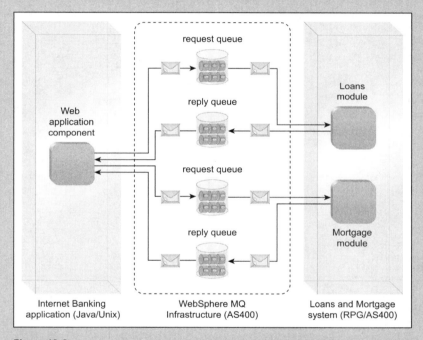

**Figure 12.8**
The current messaging architecture at NovoBank uses WebSphere MQ.

The proposed NovoBank messaging architecture is a loosely-coupled solution that offers greater flexibility and reusability. The Loans and Mortgage components running on AS/400 are wrapped in SOAP Web services that can be consumed from any banking channel application. Under the covers, the Web services will continue to utilize the current MQ infrastructure to communicate with the AS/400 system.

Without an advanced messaging infrastructure, the Web service implementations must still ensure that MQ messages are dispatched to the appropriate MQ queues on the AS400 system. To shield the Web service implementations from the internal MQ setup details on the AS/400 system, NovoBank architects and designers utilize the messaging infrastructure of an ESB. The service implementations in the ESB messaging infrastructure can communicate with a routing agent that handles the complexities of routing the messages to the appropriate MQ queues in the back-end system, as seen in Figure 12.9.

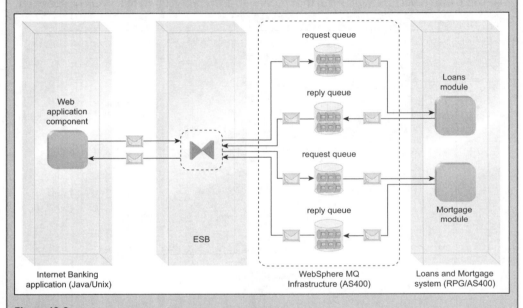

**Figure 12.9**
The future messaging architecture at NovoBank transforms data within an ESB.

## SUMMARY OF KEY POINTS

- An ESB can provide centralized message routing logic, such as the logic required to carry out content-based and context-based routing.

- An ESB can provide centralized transformation logic, such as the logic required to carry out data model and data format transformation, as well as protocol bridging.

- Intermediary logic established by an ESB can be centrally maintained using front-end tools.

## 12.2 Basic Service Messaging Frameworks

We will now take a look at simple ESB messaging functionality within the context of service interactions by comparing how common message processing and transformation functions can be carried out with and without an ESB middle tier.

### Basic Service Message Processing without ESBs

Designing messaging-based architectures is essential to establishing contemporary service-oriented architectures. This section addresses message routing and transformation processing for service-enabled, point-to-point messaging architectures that do not utilize a middle processing tier, as provided by an ESB. The subsequent *Basic Service Message Processing with ESBs* section provides the counterparts to the scenarios described in this section to highlight potential benefits of logic abstraction provided by an ESB. Figure 12.10 begins by showing a simple messaging architecture with a service consumer sending one-way messages to multiple services.

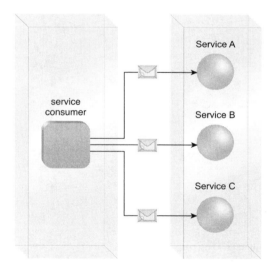

**Figure 12.10**

A basic messaging architecture involving one-way messaging between a single service consumer and three services. In order for the service consumer to successfully send each message, it must have logic that is coupled to each of the three service contracts.

*Message Routing without an ESB*

Each message producer is responsible for ensuring that the messages produced are directed at the appropriate recipient. Within a given message path, there may be service agents that automatically intercept and route messages or messages may be directed to services that themselves act as intermediaries and forward the message on further. To support the need for programs outside of the message producer to perform routing functions, messages can contain routing information within the message content. The routing of messages based on the contents of a message payload or message header is known as *content-based routing*.

Content-based routing, without the use of an ESB, requires that the routing logic be built into the message producer that generates the message with routing content (Figure 12.11). The result is an inflexible solution, as routing logic can often be subject to change, such as when it is based on business rules or other volatile conditions.

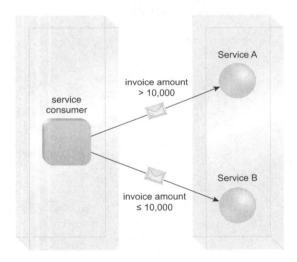

**Figure 12.11**

Content-based routing based on a business rule that determines the path of the message in relation to the value of the invoice document it contains. Because the messages are sent directly from the service consumer to the services, the routing logic needs to be embedded within the service consumer logic.

The routing of messages based on contextual information, such as the current workload on a particular system, is known as *context-based routing*. Similar to content-based routing, context-based routing logic is driven by rules and conditions that need to be embedded within the message producer if it is sending the messages directly to destination message consumers. As shown in Figure 12.12, this results in a comparably inflexible messaging architecture.

*Message Transformation without an ESB*

As already discussed during previous chapters, the need to carry out runtime transformation in order to overcome application or service disparity at the data model, protocol, or message format levels is sometimes unavoidable. When designing larger service inventories or when designing transformation points between disparate service inventories, the question as to where the actual transformation logic will reside needs to be carefully considered.

Figure 12.12 illustrates a seemingly simple approach whereby the transformation logic is embedded within the service consumer. The downside to this approach is that changes to the data, protocol, or format mapping that comprises the transformation logic will require direct programming updates to the service consumer logic. As with the aforementioned message routing approach, this results in a fragile messaging architecture.

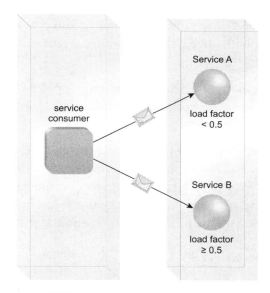

**Figure 12.12**

Context-based routing based on a runtime condition
that determines the path of the message in relation to the
value of the current load factor of a service. Because the
messages are sent directly from the service consumer to the
services, the routing logic needs to be embedded within the
service consumer logic.

## Basic Service Message Processing with ESBs

The next two sections provide corresponding architectures that demonstrate runtime message routing and transformation functionality with the use of ESBs.

### Message Routing with an ESB

The introduction of an ESB allows for message routing logic to be abstracted away from the service consumer into a middle tier in which routing functionality is established equivalent to the features resulting from the application of the Intermediate Routing pattern. This intermediary processing layer offers the following potential benefits:

- *Flexibility* – Service consumers do not require the details of the message destinations. The routing logic is moved the ESB's routing agent from where it is also maintained through the use of front-end tools.

- *Loose Coupling* – New services and message destinations can be incorporated into an existing architecture by configuring the routing agent to include additional targets and routing conditions without affecting any of the existing interactions.

The middle tier established by the introduction of an ESB provides intermediary routing logic that supports both content-based routing (Figure 12.14) and context-based routing (Figure 12.15).

ESBs provide a configuration framework where routing policies can often be specified either in a declarative manner, such as with XPath statements or XQuery expressions, or via pluggable custom components.

Although the figures depict the ESB in a separate box between the service consumer and service provider, the ESB is only logically separate. Depending on the implementation style, the ESB can also be co-located at the service consumer or service. This distinction is the delineating factor in viewing ESBs as either a technology or product or as a design pattern (as per the Enterprise Service Bus compound pattern).

### Message Transformation with an ESB

ESB messaging infrastructure provides intermediary transformation logic that can carry out the functionality established by the Service Broker compound pattern, which is comprised of the Data Model Transformation, Data Format Transformation, and Protocol Bridging patterns. Collectively, the feature-sets resulting from the application of these patterns provide the ability to carry out sophisticated runtime transformations that are centralized in the middle tier, from where they can also be centrally maintained via front-end tools.

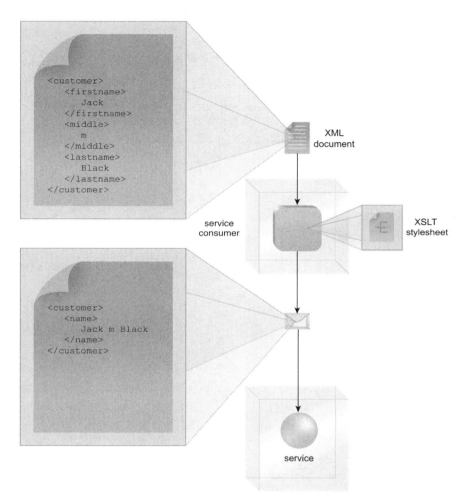

**Figure 12.13**

Exchanging message content based on different data models requires runtime transformation. In this case, the transformation logic is expressed in an XSLT stylesheet executed within the service consumer architecture on an XML document received from another source. The document contents are transformed and wrapped in a message format, prior to transmission to the service.

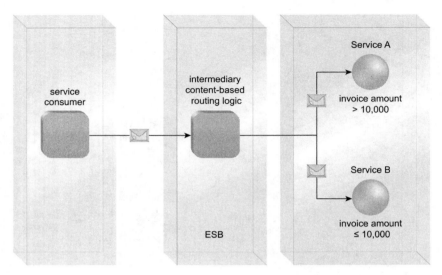

**Figure 12.14**
Content-based routing within an ESB.

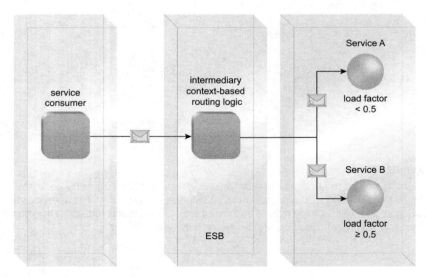

**Figure 12.15**
Context-based routing within an ESB.

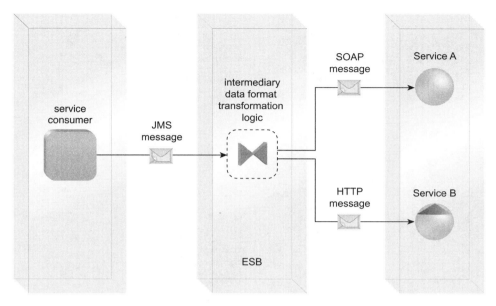

**Figure 12.16**

An ESB carrying out intermediary data format transformation logic is shown. A JMS message is converted into a SOAP message for Service A, which is a Web service. The same JMS message is converted into an HTTP message for Service B, which is a REST service.

Figure 12.16 shows how intermediary data format transformation logic provided by the ESB converts the format of one message into two others.

Figure 12.17 illustrates an ESB providing centralized transformation logic for the run-time conversion of message content structures from one data model to one of two other data models, as required to comply with the respective destination service contracts.

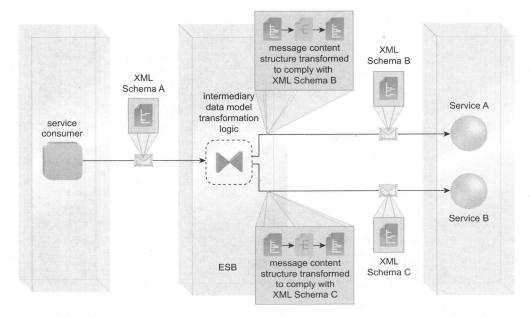

**Figure 12.17**
Message transformation with a canonical data model within an ESB minimizes the number of transformations required.

## SUMMARY OF KEY POINTS

- An ESB can provide centralized message routing logic, such as the logic required to carry out content-based and context-based routing.

- An ESB can provide centralized transformation logic, such as the logic required to carry out data model and data format transformation, as well as protocol bridging.

- Intermediary logic established by an ESB can be centrally maintained using front-end tools.

## 12.3 Common ESB Features Relevant to SOA

This next section highlights functions relevant to service processing and service-oriented architectures that are provided by various contemporary ESB products.

### Service Lookup and Invocation

A service consumer can select an appropriate service based on the information it retrieves from a service registry, such as functionality and quality of service. The service endpoint selection can be handled by an ESB mediation component which facilitates dynamic service selection.

The service endpoint selection can be handled by an ESB mediation component which facilitates dynamic service selection. If business rules change, the mediation component can change to select a different service endpoint rather than changing the service consumer. For example, an ESB mediation component can look up either a premium or regular subscription service based on the customer information obtained from the service consumer, as seen in Figure 12.18.

Service endpoint selection can at times be an even more dynamic process with intermediate steps, such as database lookups, performed to locate an appropriate service endpoint. Many ESB implementations offer a mechanism where a custom mediation component can be plugged to perform the necessary computation before a service endpoint is selected.

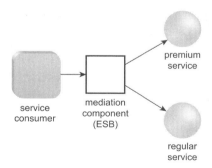

**Figure 12.18**

The ESB serves as a mediation component between a service and service consumer to help select an appropriate service endpoint.

**CASE STUDY EXAMPLE**

NovoBank plans to build a layer of business services to wrap and expose the existing legacy assets on the back-end systems as Web services. The Loans and Mortgage application system running on AS/400 is a candidate banking back-end system to become service-enabled. However, the increasing support required, maintenance costs, and lack of skilled resources on the AS/400 platform remain a concern for NovoBank's CIO.

The architects plan to build an architecture that allows NovoBank to migrate to a modern, off-the-shelf Loans and Mortgage system without any significant rewrite of the channel applications.

A degree of point-to-point coupling will remain between the back-end AS/400 system and channel applications with the proposed architecture if service consumers, such as the channel applications, communicate directly with the business services. Future introduction of a new back-end Loans and Mortgage system may require additional rework.

To avoid direct coupling, the architects use a service registry and ESB mediation component to facilitate and execute the service lookup respectively. Channel applications will interface with the mediation component that will in turn locate the appropriate service endpoint from the service registry. The service endpoints communicate with the current AS/400 system. However, the ESB mediation component can select appropriate service endpoints that communicate with any new systems that are later introduced, as seen in Figure 12.19.

Introduction of the ESB helps future-proof the architecture and insulate the service consumers from potential changes in the back-end system.

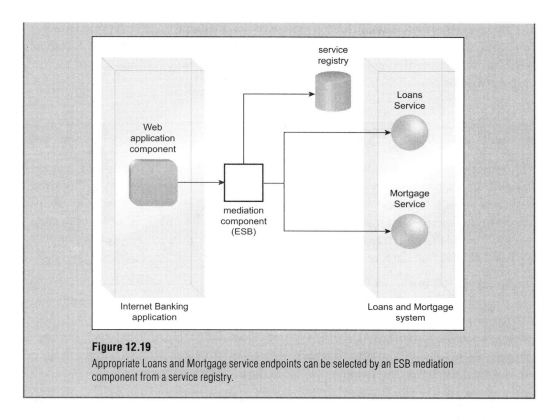

**Figure 12.19**
Appropriate Loans and Mortgage service endpoints can be selected by an ESB mediation component from a service registry.

## Service Processing

Generally, certain pre- and post-processing steps must occur before and after a business service is invoked. These steps are often unrelated to the core functionality offered by the service to handle non-functional aspects, such as auditing, security, and monitoring. The non-functional aspects are infrastructural in nature, and can be abstracted away from the core business logic of the service functions. For example, the service invocation pre-processing step of logging all service invocations for a premium service can be efficiently handled within a mediation component.

Sophisticated ESBs allow for a more general-purpose declarative composition of service pre-processors and post-processors, where they can be built to enhance a message processing cycle. The ESB can compose processors in a declarative fashion that allows for variation in the invocation sequence of the pre- and post-processing components by changing the configuration of the processors rather than the implementation code.

Examples of pre-processors include message enrichment, message encryption/decryption, and message de-duplication. Beyond providing the processors that developers must build. ESB mediation components facilitate an arbitrary composition of the processors in a declarative fashion.

---

### CASE STUDY EXAMPLE

In addition to reengineering the current IT architecture, the NovoBank IT team is attempting to improve the business value proposition of its IT systems by building systems capable of responding quickly and proactively to changing market conditions and customer interaction patterns. The marketing team would like to be able to identify high-value transactions on a checking account, such as deposits of over $10,000, to offer the customer a no-fee, high-interest savings account.

In the past, the introduction of new business rules meant excessive code changes in the back-end systems. Any changes to the business rules also corresponded to changes in the back-end system implementations. In some cases, these business rules were embedded in and coupled to the presentation-tier applications. However, implementing business rules in an ESB mediator component eliminates the coupling and distances changes to the business from the back-end systems.

The developers can build a mediation component that intercepts requests for all account transactions, identifies any checking account deposit transactions of over $10,000, and triggers a corresponding event in the CRM system that sends the new account offer to the appropriate customer.

As seen in Figure 12.20, separating the business rule pre- and post-processing in a separate mediation component provides the team with the flexibility to add a modern, sophisticated rules engine to navigate complex decision trees and make intelligent decisions.

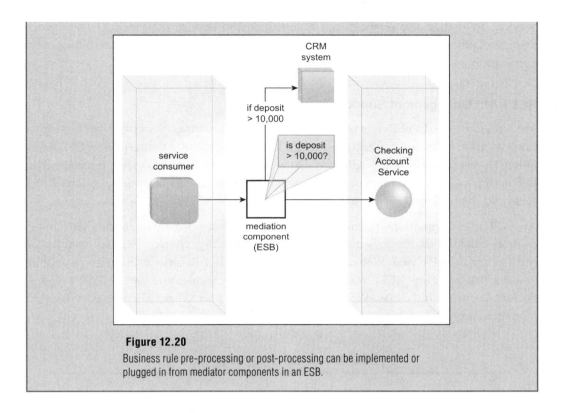

**Figure 12.20**

Business rule pre-processing or post-processing can be implemented or plugged in from mediator components in an ESB.

## Service Composition Support

ESB frameworks support service composition by offering out-of-the-box support for integrating technology artifacts from different platforms programming languages, such as Java, C#, and Ruby. An ESB integrates a pre-existing session EJB component to send a message to a messaging destination, which is similar for calling a POJO or scripting language-based component. ESBs can further provide features that help string together a variety of service composition resources through declarative configurations, such as a specialized a domain-specific language.

Commercial ESB vendors often offer a GUI tool to help developers create a service flow. In keeping with a contract-first development philosophy, it is still recommended to leverage these components as implementation artifacts with their own service contracts that are used in a declarative language.

The runtime may choose to use an optimized platform native communication protocol, such as an in-memory call to a POJO, rather than calling a SOAP-based or REST service. To realize the service flow at runtime, the service composition framework brings together all the infrastructure capabilities, such as messaging, mediation, and application integration features.

## REST API Management Support

Modern, lightweight ESBs can often act as a REST API management platform that functions as an enabler for connecting mobile Web applications to enterprise REST APIs. Often, these enterprise REST APIs are also wrappers over existing system interfaces. An ESB acting as an API management platform offers bridging capabilities between REST APIs and the back-end services.

An API management platform can mediate REST service interactions with interception capabilities for logging, auditing, and security checks, expose existing or third-party SOAP-based Web services as REST APIs for consumption from mobile devices (by bridging REST resources to existing services), and define API policies, such as security and SLAs. WSO2 is an example of a modern ESB product with API management features.

**SUMMARY OF KEY POINTS**

- ESB mediation components can provide service lookup and invocation features, as well as built-in processing features for services and service-based messaging.

- Contemporary ESBs can provide features that support service composition and API management.

# Part IV

# Appendices

# Appendix A

# Case Study Conclusion

The case study examples provided throughout the preceding chapters demonstrated the application of service-orientation design principles with Java services and technologies in a diverse variety of scenarios. This appendix summarizes and concludes the storylines of the two organizations originally established in Chapter 2.

## A.1 NovoBank

NovoBank has successfully completed the first roll-out of their next-generation banking system. The SOA architects at NovoBank were able to achieve the three main objectives of their transformation program as follows:

- *Improve Time-to-Market* – NovoBank was able to build a layer of business, utility, task, and entity services to help decouple their channel applications from the core legacy banking systems. With the availability of a reusable set of business services, enhancing existing channel applications is much easier than before. None of the channels are tightly coupled with any of the core systems. NovoBank was able to optimize their business processes and drive greater automation through the use of new orchestration services composed of different business, utility, and task services. The availability of different services affords the IT staff the ability to compose in different contexts in different business processes.

- *Reduce Operational Costs* – The technical costs of ongoing application maintenance or system integration efforts have been reduced by 20%. The bulk of cost savings were realized by leveraging the new services and avoiding one-off, custom developments in channel applications. However, the original target of 30% cost reduction in the IT maintenance budget was not met as some of the up-front costs of building out an SOA landscape and introducing SOA infrastructure solutions, such as ESBs, partially offset the cost reductions seen in routine maintenance efforts. However, it is expected that an economy of scale can be achieved with the services as more applications within other divisions in the bank begin using those services to avoid ground-up custom development.

However, along the way, NovoBank encountered the following challenges:

- *Emergence of Mobile Computing* – The proliferation of mobile devices, such as smartphones and tablets, made it imperative for NovoBank to introduce online banking applications. However, building applications to consume SOAP-based Web services was complicated. NovoBank IT staff realized they must build, at least in the short-to-medium term, REST API wrappers over their existing Web services that can be easily consumed by mobile applications. The architecture team is evaluating popular API management platforms to manage expansion in the mobile computing domain.

- *Complexity of the Industry Standard Models* – NovoBank standardized their canonical schema models on industrial financial messaging standards, but the complexity of the financial message schemas resulted in significant overheads during message parsing in their Web service implementations. In the end, NovoBank simplified the schema models to avoid unacceptable implementation and performance overheads.

## A.2 SmartCredit Co.

SmartCredit was successful in building a set of REST Web APIs allowing retail chain stores to submit credit card applications on behalf of their customers. Store clerks can submit the applications from different mobile devices using the mobile applications built for SmartCredit by a third-party contractor. The simplicity of the REST APIs and the ubiquity of the HTTP communications protocol and data formats (mostly JSON, some XML) have helped the mobile credit card application scale well. The widespread in-store usage has also led to an increase in business volume for the retail stores. The successful adoption of the applications and resulting business has been noticed by a competitive retail chain, which is in negotiations with SmartCredit to enter into a similar partnership.

Technical implementation considerations aside, the SmartCredit IT team followed the service design principles outlined in this book to ensure services are built modular, reusable, and lightweight to offer immediate value to a wide variety of service consumers. SmartCredit spent a significant amount of time building the REST service contracts by focusing on identifying the resources, the associated representations, the corresponding media-types, and the appropriate, semantically correct application of uniform interface HTTP operations on those resources. Even though the JAX-RS APIs proved to be an efficient tool to build REST APIs, the top-down design approach supported by SmartCredit was effective in the adoption of the APIs.

As with any other complex IT initiative, the implementation was not without challenges. SmartCredit made a conscious up-front decision not to make use of any custom media types, as they were initially skeptical of introducing additional coupling through non-standard media types. However, the impending partnership with another retail chain and the need to accommodate slightly different forms of credit applications with different resource schemas resulted in the need to introduce custom media types. Rather than using the generic `application/json` or `application/xml` media type, Smart-Credit is looking at using the following custom types:

- `application/vnd.com.smartcredit.creditapp+json`

- `application/vnd.com.smartcredit.creditapp+xml`

The custom media types will be able to communicate semantics about the resources in question and will help better enforce the service contract. SmartCredit will follow this approach for their next round of implementation.

# Appendix B

## Service-Orientation
## Principles Reference

This appendix provides profile tables for the eight design principles that are documented in *SOA Principles of Service Design*, a title that is part of this book series.

Every profile table contains the following sections:

- *Short Definition* – A concise, single-statement definition that establishes the fundamental purpose of the principle.

- *Long Definition* – A longer description of the principle that provides more detail as to what it is intended to accomplish.

- *Goals* – A list of specific design goals that are expected from the application of the principle. Essentially, this list provides the ultimate results of the principle's realization.

- *Design Characteristics* – A list of specific design characteristics that can be realized via the application of the principle. This provides some insight as to how the principle ends up shaping the service.

- *Implementation Requirements* – A list of common prerequisites for effectively applying the design principle. These can range from technology to organizational requirements.

Note that these tables provide only summarized content from the original publication. Information about service-orientation principles is also published online at SOAPrinciples.com and ServiceOrientation.com.

| Standardized Service Contract | |
| --- | --- |
| **Short Definition** | *"Services share standardized contracts."* |
| **Long Definition** | *"Services within the same service inventory are in compliance with the same contract design standards."* |
| **Goals** | • To enable services with a meaningful level of natural interoperability within the boundary of a service inventory. This reduces the need for data transformation because consistent data models are used for information exchange.<br><br>• To allow the purpose and capabilities of services to be more easily and intuitively understood. The consistency with which service functionality is expressed through service contracts increases interpretability and the overall predictability of service endpoints throughout a service inventory.<br><br>Note that these goals are further supported by other service-orientation principles as well. |
| **Design Characteristics** | • A service contract (comprised of a technical interface or one or more service description documents) is provided with the service.<br><br>• The service contract is standardized through the application of design standards. |
| **Implementation Requirements** | The fact that contracts need to be standardized can introduce significant implementation requirements to organizations that do not have a history of using standards.<br><br>For example:<br><br>• Design standards and conventions need to ideally be in place prior to the delivery of any service in order to ensure adequately scoped standardization. (For those organizations that have already produced ad-hoc Web services, retro-fitting strategies may need to be employed.)<br><br>• Formal processes need to be introduced to ensure that services are modeled and designed consistently, incorporating accepted design principles, conventions, and standards. |

- Because achieving standardized service contracts generally requires a "contract-first" approach to service-oriented design, the full application of this principle will often demand the use of development tools capable of importing a customized service contract without imposing changes.

- Appropriate skill-sets are required to carry out the modeling and design processes with the chosen tools. When working with Web services, the need for a high level of proficiency with XML schema and WSDL languages is practically unavoidable. WS-Policy expertise may also be required.

These and other requirements can add up to a noticeable transition effort that goes well beyond technology adoption.

**Table B.1**
A profile for the Standardized Service Contract principle

| Service Loose Coupling | |
| --- | --- |
| **Short Definition** | *"Services are loosely coupled."* |
| **Long Definition** | *"Service contracts impose low consumer coupling requirements and are themselves decoupled from their surrounding environment."* |
| **Goals** | By consistently fostering reduced coupling within and between services we are working toward a state where service contracts increase independence from their implementations and services are increasingly independent from each other. This promotes an environment in which services and their consumers can be adaptively evolved over time with minimal impact on each other. |
| **Design Characteristics** | • The existence of a service contract that is ideally decoupled from technology and implementation details.<br><br>• A functional service context that is not dependent on outside logic.<br><br>• Minimal consumer coupling requirements. |
| **Implementation Requirements** | • Loosely coupled services are typically required to perform more runtime processing than if they were more tightly coupled. As a result, data exchange in general can consume more runtime resources, especially during concurrent access and high usage scenarios.<br><br>• To achieve the right balance of coupling, while also supporting the other service-orientation principles that affect contract design, requires increased service contract design proficiency. |

**Table B.2**

A profile for the Service Loose Coupling principle

| Service Abstraction | |
|---|---|
| **Short Definition** | *"Non-essential service information is abstracted."* |
| **Long Definition** | *"Service contracts only contain essential information and information about services is limited to what is published in service contracts."* |
| **Goals** | Many of the other principles emphasize the need to publish *more* information in the service contract. The primary role of this principle is to keep the quantity and detail of contract content concise and balanced and prevent unnecessary access to additional service details. |
| **Design Characteristics** | • Services consistently abstract specific information about technology, logic, and function away from the outside world (the world outside of the service boundary).<br><br>• Services have contracts that concisely define interaction requirements and constraints and other required service meta details.<br><br>• Outside of what is documented in the service contract, information about a service is controlled or altogether hidden within a particular environment. |
| **Implementation Requirements** | The primary prerequisite to achieving the appropriate level of abstraction for each service is the level of service contract design skill applied. |

**Table B.3**

A profile for the Service Abstraction principle

| Service Reusability | |
| --- | --- |
| **Short Definition** | *"Services are reusable."* |
| **Long Definition** | *"Services contain and express agnostic logic and can be positioned as reusable enterprise resources."* |
| **Goals** | The goals behind Service Reusability are tied directly to some of the most strategic objectives of service-oriented computing:<br><br>• To allow for service logic to be repeatedly leveraged over time so as to achieve an increasingly high return on the initial investment of delivering the service.<br><br>• To increase business agility on an organizational level by enabling the rapid fulfillment of future business automation requirements through wide-scale service composition.<br><br>• To enable the realization of agnostic service models.<br><br>• To enable the creation of service inventories with a high percentage of agnostic services. |
| **Design Characteristics** | • *The service is defined by an agnostic functional context*—The logic encapsulated by the service is associated with a context that is sufficiently agnostic to any one usage scenario so as to be considered reusable.<br><br>• *The service logic is highly generic*—The logic encapsulated by the service is sufficiently generic, allowing it to facilitate numerous usage scenarios by different types of service consumers.<br><br>• *The service has a generic and extensible contract*—The service contract is flexible enough to process a range of input and output messages.<br><br>• *The service logic can be accessed concurrently*—Services are designed to facilitate simultaneous access by multiple consumer programs. |

| Implementation Requirements | From an implementation perspective, Service Reusability can be the most demanding of the principles we've covered so far. Below are common requirements for creating reusable services and supporting their long-term existence: |
|---|---|
| | • A scalable runtime hosting environment capable of high-to-extreme concurrent service usage. Once a service inventory is relatively mature, reusable services will find themselves in an increasingly large number of compositions. |
| | • A solid version control system to properly evolve contracts representing reusable services. |
| | • Service analysts and designers with a high degree of subject matter expertise who can ensure that the service boundary and contract accurately represent the service's reusable functional context. |
| | • A high level of service development and commercial software development expertise so as to structure the underlying logic into generic and potentially decomposable components and routines. |
| | These and other requirements place an emphasis on the appropriate staffing of the service delivery team, as well as the importance of a powerful and scalable hosting environment and supporting infrastructure. |

**Table B.4**

A profile for the Service Reusability principle

| Service Autonomy | |
|---|---|
| **Short Definition** | *"Services are autonomous."* |
| **Long Definition** | *"Services exercise a high level of control over their underlying runtime execution environment."* |
| **Goals** | • To increase a service's runtime reliability, performance, and predictability, especially when being reused and composed.<br><br>• To increase the amount of control a service has over its runtime environment.<br><br>By pursuing autonomous design and runtime environments, we are essentially aiming to increase post-implementation control over the service and the service's control over its own execution environment. |
| **Design Characteristics** | • Services have a contract that expresses a well-defined functional boundary that should not overlap with other services.<br><br>• Services are deployed in an environment over which they exercise a great deal (and preferably an exclusive level) of control.<br><br>• Service instances are hosted by an environment that accommodates high concurrency for scalability purposes. |
| **Implementation Requirements** | • A high level of control over how service logic is designed and developed. Depending on the level of autonomy being sought, this may also involve control over the supporting data models.<br><br>• A distributable deployment environment, so as to allow the service to be moved, isolated, or composed as required.<br><br>• An infrastructure capable of supporting desired autonomy levels. |

**Table B.5**

A profile for the Service Autonomy principle

| Service Statelessness | |
|---|---|
| **Short Definition** | *"Services minimize statefulness."* |
| **Long Definition** | *"Services minimize resource consumption by deferring the management of state information when necessary."* |
| **Goals** | • To increase service scalability.<br><br>• To support the design of agnostic service logic and improve the potential for service reuse. |
| **Design Characteristics** | What makes this somewhat of a unique principle is the fact that it is promoting a condition of the service that is temporary in nature. Depending on the service model and state deferral approach used, different types of design characteristics can be implemented. Some examples include:<br><br>• Highly business process-agnostic logic so that the service is not designed to retain state information for any specific parent business process.<br><br>• Less constrained service contracts so as to allow for the receipt and transmission of a wider range of state data at runtime.<br><br>• Increased amounts of interpretive programming routines capable of parsing a range of state information delivered by messages and responding to a range of corresponding action requests. |
| **Implementation Requirements** | Although state deferral can reduce the overall consumption of memory and system resources, services designed with state-lessness considerations can also introduce some performance demands associated with the runtime retrieval and interpretation of deferred state data.<br><br>Here is a short checklist of common requirements that can be used to assess the support of stateless service designs by vendor technologies and target deployment locations:<br><br>• The runtime environment should allow for a service to transition from an idle state to an active processing state in a highly efficient manner. |

- Enterprise-level or high-performance XML parsers and hardware accelerators (and SOAP processors) should be provided to allow services implemented as Web services to more efficiently parse larger message payloads with less performance constraints.

- The use of attachments may need to be supported by Web services to allow for messages to include bodies of payload data that do not undergo interface-level validation or translation to local formats.

The nature of the implementation support required by the average stateless service in an environment will depend on the state deferral approach used within the service-oriented architecture.

**Table B.6**

A profile for the Service Statelessness principle

| Service Discoverability | |
|---|---|
| **Short Definition** | *"Services are discoverable."* |
| **Long Definition** | *"Services are supplemented with communicative metadata by which they can be effectively discovered and interpreted."* |
| **Goals** | • Services are positioned as highly discoverable resources within the enterprise.<br><br>• The purpose and capabilities of each service are clearly expressed so that they can be interpreted by humans and software programs.<br><br>Achieving these goals requires foresight and a solid understanding of the nature of the service itself. Depending on the type of service model being designed, realizing this principle may require both business and technical expertise. |
| **Design Characteristics** | • Service contracts are equipped with appropriate metadata that will be correctly referenced when discovery queries are issued.<br><br>• Service contracts are further outfitted with additional meta information that clearly communicates their purpose and capabilities to humans.<br><br>• If a service registry exists, registry records are populated with the same attention to meta information as just described.<br><br>• If a service registry does not exist, service profile documents are authored to supplement the service contract and to form the basis for future registry records. (See Chapter 15 in *SOA Principles of Service Design* for more details about service profiles.) |

| Implementation Requirements | • The existence of design standards that govern the meta information used to make service contracts discoverable and interpretable, as well as guidelines for how and when service contracts should be further supplemented with annotations.<br><br>• The existence of design standards that establish a consistent means of recording service meta information outside of the contract. This information is either collected in a supplemental document in preparation for a service registry, or it is placed in the registry itself.<br><br>You may have noticed the absence of a service registry on the list of implementation requirements. As previously established, the goal of this principle is to implement design characteristics within the service, not within the architecture. |
|---|---|

**Table B.7**

A profile for the Service Discoverability principle

| Service Composability | |
|---|---|
| **Short Definition** | *"Services are composable."* |
| **Long Definition** | *"Services are effective composition participants, regardless of the size and complexity of the composition."* |
| **Goals** | When discussing the goals of Service Composability, pretty much all of the goals of Service Reusability apply. This is because service composition often turns out to be a form of service reuse. In fact, you may recall that one of the objectives we listed for the Service Reusability principle was to enable wide-scale service composition.<br><br>However, above and beyond simply attaining reuse, service composition provides the medium through which we can achieve what is often classified as the ultimate goal of service-oriented computing. By establishing an enterprise comprised of solution logic represented by an inventory of highly reusable services, we provide the means for a large extent of future business automation requirements to be fulfilled through…you guessed it: service composition. |
| **Design Characteristics for Composition Member Capabilities** | Ideally, every service capability (especially those providing reusable logic) is considered a potential composition member. This essentially means that the design characteristics already established by the Service Reusability principle are equally relevant to building effective composition members.<br><br>Additionally, there are two further characteristics emphasized by this principle:<br><br>• The service needs to possess a highly efficient execution environment. More so than being able to manage concurrency, the efficiency with which composition members perform their individual processing should be highly tuned.<br><br>• The service contract needs to be flexible so that it can facilitate different types of data exchange requirements for similar functions. This typically relates to the ability of the contract to exchange the same type of data at different levels of granularity.<br><br>The manner in which these qualities go beyond mere reuse has to do primarily with the service being capable of optimizing its runtime processing responsibilities in support of multiple, simultaneous compositions. |

| **Design Character- istics for Compo- sition Controller Capabilities** | Composition members will often also need to act as controllers or sub-controllers within different composition configurations. However, services designed as designated controllers are gener- ally alleviated from many of the high-performance demands placed on composition members. |
| --- | --- |
| | These types of services therefore have their own set of design characteristics: |
| | • The logic encapsulated by a designated controller will almost always be limited to a single business task. Typically, the task service model is used, resulting in the common characteristics of that model being applied to this type of service. |
| | • While designated controllers may be reusable, service reuse is not usually a primary design consideration. Therefore, the design characteristics fostered by Service Reusability are considered and applied where appropriate, but with less of the usual rigor applied to agnostic services. |
| | • Statelessness is not always as strictly emphasized on desig- nated controllers as with composition members. Depending on the state deferral options available by the surrounding architecture, designated controllers may sometimes need to be designed to remain fully stateful while the underlying compo- sition members carry out their respective parts of the overall task. |
| | Of course, any capability acting as a controller can become a member of a larger composition, which brings the previously listed composition member design characteristics into account as well. |

**Table B.8**

A profile for the Service Composability principle

# SOA Design Patterns Reference

This appendix provides profile tables for the patterns that are documented in *SOA Design Patterns* and *SOA with REST: Principles, Patterns & Constraints for Building Enterprise Solutions with REST,* both titles that are part of this book series.

Every profile table contains the following sections:

- *Requirement* – A requirement is a concise, single-sentence statement that presents the fundamental requirement addressed by the pattern in the form of a question. Every pattern description begins with this statement.

- *Icon* – Each pattern description is accompanied by an icon image that acts as a visual identifier. The icons are displayed together with the requirement statements in each pattern profile as well as on the inside book cover.

- *Problem* – The issue causing a problem and the effects of the problem. It is this problem for which the pattern is expected to provide a solution.

- *Solution* – This represents the design solution proposed by the pattern to solve the problem and fulfill the requirement.

- *Application* – This part is dedicated to describing how the pattern can be applied. It can include guidelines, implementation details, and sometimes even a suggested process.

- *Impacts* – This section highlights common consequences, costs, and requirements associated with the application of a pattern and may also provide alternatives that can be considered.

- *Principles* – References to related service-orientation principles.

- *Architecture* – References to related SOA architecture types (as described in *SOA Design Patterns*).

Note that these tables provide only summarized content from the original publication. All pattern profile tables in this book are also published online at SOAPatterns.org.

# Agnostic Capability

**By Thomas Erl**

*How can multi-purpose service logic be made effectively consumable and composable?*

| | |
|---|---|
| **Problem** | Service capabilities derived from specific concerns may not be useful to multiple service consumers, thereby reducing the reusability potential of the agnostic service. |
| **Solution** | Agnostic service logic is partitioned into a set of well-defined capabilities that address common concerns not specific to any one problem. Through subsequent analysis, the agnostic context of capabilities is further refined. |
| **Application** | Service capabilities are defined and iteratively refined through proven analysis and modeling processes. |
| **Impacts** | The definition of each service capability requires extra up-front analysis and design effort. |
| **Principles** | Standardized Service Contract, Service Reusability, Service Composability |
| **Architecture** | Service |

# Agnostic Context

**By Thomas Erl**

*How can multi-purpose service logic be positioned as an effective enterprise resource?*

| Problem | Multi-purpose logic grouped together with single-purpose logic results in programs with little or no reuse potential that introduce waste and redundancy into an enterprise. |
|---|---|
| Solution | Isolate logic that is not specific to one purpose into separate services with distinct agnostic contexts. |
| Application | Agnostic service contexts are defined by carrying out service-oriented analysis and service modeling processes. |
| Impacts | This pattern positions reusable solution logic at an enterprise level, potentially bringing with it increased design complexity and enterprise governance issues. |
| Principles | Service Reusability |
| Architecture | Service |

# Agnostic Sub-Controller

**By Thomas Erl**

*How can agnostic, cross-entity composition logic be separated, reused, and governed independently?*

| | |
|---|---|
| **Problem** | Service compositions are generally configured specific to a parent task, inhibiting reuse potential that may exist within a subset of the composition logic. |
| **Solution** | Reusable, cross-entity composition logic is abstracted or made accessible via an agnostic sub-controller capability, allowing that subset of the parent composition logic to be recomposed independently. |
| **Application** | A new agnostic service is created or a task service is appended with an agnostic sub-controller capability. |
| **Impacts** | The addition of a cross-entity, agnostic service can increase the size and complexity of compositions and the abstraction of agnostic cross-entity logic can violate modeling and design standards established by Service Layers. |
| **Principles** | Service Reusability, Service Composability |
| **Architecture** | Composition, Service |

# Asynchronous Queuing

By Mark Little, Thomas Rischbeck, Arnaud Simon

*How can a service and its consumers accommodate isolated failures and avoid unnecessarily locking resources?*

| | |
|---|---|
| **Problem** | When a service capability requires that consumers interact with it synchronously, it can inhibit performance and compromise reliability. |
| **Solution** | A service can exchange messages with its consumers via an intermediary buffer, allowing service and consumers to process messages independently by remaining temporally decoupled. |
| **Application** | Queuing technology needs to be incorporated into the surrounding architecture, and backup stores may also be required. |
| **Impacts** | There may be no acknowledgement of successful message delivery, and atomic transactions may not be possible. |
| **Principles** | Standardized Service Contract, Service Loose Coupling, Service Statelessness |
| **Architecture** | Inventory, Composition |

# Atomic Service Transaction
**By Thomas Erl**

*How can a transaction with rollback capability be propagated across messaging-based services?*

| Problem | When runtime activities that span multiple services fail, the parent business task is incomplete and actions performed and changes made up to that point may compromise the integrity of the underlying solution and architecture. |
|---|---|
| Solution | Runtime service activities can be wrapped in a transaction with a rollback feature that resets all actions and changes if the parent business task cannot be successfully completed. |
| Application | A transaction management system is made part of the inventory architecture and then used by those service compositions that require rollback features. |
| Impacts | Transacted service activities can consume more memory because of the requirement for each service to preserve its original state until it is notified to roll back or commit its changes. |
| Principles | Service Statelessness |
| Architecture | Inventory, Composition |

# Brokered Authentication

By Jason Hogg, Don Smith, Fred Chong, Tom Hollander, Wojtek Kozaczynski,
Larry Brader, Nelly Delgado, Dwayne Taylor, Lonnie Wall, Paul Slater,
Sajjad Nasir Imran, Pablo Cibraro, Ward Cunningham

*How can a service efficiently verify consumer credentials if*
*the consumer and service do not trust each other or if the consumer*
*requires access to multiple services?*

| | |
|---|---|
| **Problem** | Requiring the use of Direct Authentication can be impractical or even impossible when consumers and services do not trust each other or when consumers are required to access multiple services as part of the same runtime activity. |
| **Solution** | An authentication broker with a centralized identity store assumes the responsibility for authenticating the consumer and issuing a token that the consumer can use to access the service. |
| **Application** | An authentication broker product introduced into the inventory architecture carries out the intermediary authentication and issuance of temporary credentials using technologies such as X.509 certificates or Kerberos, SAML, or SecPAL tokens. |
| **Impacts** | This pattern can establish a potential single point of failure and a central breach point that, if compromised, could jeopardize an entire service inventory. |
| **Principles** | Service Composability |
| **Architecture** | Inventory, Composition, Service |

# Canonical Expression

**By Thomas Erl**

*How can service contracts be consistently understood and interpreted?*

| | |
|---|---|
| **Problem** | Service contracts may express similar capabilities in different ways, leading to inconsistency and risking misinterpretation. |
| **Solution** | Service contracts are standardized using naming conventions. |
| **Application** | Naming conventions are applied to service contracts as part of formal analysis and design processes. |
| **Impacts** | The use of global naming conventions introduces enterprise-wide standards that need to be consistently used and enforced. |
| **Principles** | Standardized Service Contract, Service Discoverability |
| **Architecture** | Enterprise, Inventory, Service |

# Canonical Protocol

**By Thomas Erl**

*How can services be designed to avoid protocol bridging?*

| | |
|---|---|
| **Problem** | Services that support different communication technologies compromise interoperability, limit the quantity of potential consumers, and introduce the need for undesirable protocol bridging measures. |
| **Solution** | The architecture establishes a single communications technology as the sole or primary medium by which services can interact. |
| **Application** | The communication protocols (including protocol versions) used within a service inventory boundary are standardized for all services. |
| **Impacts** | An inventory architecture in which communication protocols are standardized is subject to any limitations imposed by the communications technology. |
| **Principles** | Standardized Service Contract |
| **Architecture** | Inventory, Service |

# Canonical Resources

**By Thomas Erl**

*How can unnecessary infrastructure resource disparity be avoided?*

| | |
|---|---|
| **Problem** | Service implementations can unnecessarily introduce disparate infrastructure resources, thereby bloating the enterprise and resulting in increased governance burden. |
| **Solution** | The supporting infrastructure and architecture can be equipped with common resources and extensions that can be repeatedly utilized by different services. |
| **Application** | Enterprise design standards are defined to formalize the required use of standardized architectural resources. |
| **Impacts** | If this pattern leads to too much dependency on shared infrastructure resources, it can decrease the autonomy and mobility of services. |
| **Principles** | Service Autonomy |
| **Architecture** | Enterprise, Inventory |

# Canonical Schema
**By Thomas Erl**

*How can services be designed to avoid data model transformation?*

| | |
|---|---|
| **Problem** | Services with disparate models for similar data impose transformation requirements that increase development effort, design complexity, and runtime performance overhead. |
| **Solution** | Data models for common information sets are standardized across service contracts within an inventory boundary. |
| **Application** | Design standards are applied to schemas used by service contracts as part of a formal design process. |
| **Impacts** | Maintaining the standardization of contract schemas can introduce significant governance effort and cultural challenges. |
| **Principles** | Standardized Service Contract |
| **Architecture** | Inventory, Service |

# Canonical Schema Bus

**By Clemens Utschig-Utschig, Berthold Maier, Bernd Trops, Hajo Normann, Torsten Winterberg, Thomas Erl**

While Enterprise Service Bus provides a range of messaging-centric functions that help establish connectivity between different services and between services and resources they are required to encapsulate, it does not inherently enforce or advocate standardization.

Building upon the platform established by Enterprise Service Bus, this pattern positions entry points into the logic, data, and functions offered via the service bus environment as independently standardized service contracts.

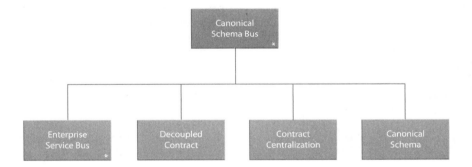

Canonical Schema Bus is comprised of the co-existent application of Enterprise Service Bus, Decoupled Contract, Contract Centralization, and Canonical Schema.

# Canonical Versioning
**By Thomas Erl**

v1 = v2

*How can service contracts within the same service inventory be versioned with minimal impact?*

| | |
|---|---|
| **Problem** | Service contracts within the same service inventory that are versioned differently will cause numerous interoperability and governance problems. |
| **Solution** | Service contract versioning rules and the expression of version information are standardized within a service inventory boundary. |
| **Application** | Governance and design standards are required to ensure consistent versioning of service contracts within the inventory boundary. |
| **Impacts** | The creation and enforcement of the required versioning standards introduce new governance demands. |
| **Principles** | Standardized Service Contract |
| **Architecture** | Service, Inventory |

# Capability Composition

**By Thomas Erl**

*How can a service capability solve a problem that requires logic
outside of the service boundary?*

| | |
|---|---|
| **Problem** | A capability may not be able to fulfill its processing requirements without adding logic that resides outside of its service's functional context, thereby compromising the integrity of the service context and risking service denormalization. |
| **Solution** | When requiring access to logic that falls outside of a service's boundary, capability logic within the service is designed to compose one or more capabilities in other services. |
| **Application** | The functionality encapsulated by a capability includes logic that can invoke other capabilities from other services. |
| **Impacts** | Carrying out composition logic requires external invocation, which adds performance overhead and decreases service autonomy. |
| **Principles** | All |
| **Architecture** | Inventory, Composition, Service |

# Capability Recomposition

**By Thomas Erl**

*How can the same capability be used to help solve multiple problems?*

| | |
|---|---|
| **Problem** | Using agnostic service logic to only solve a single problem is wasteful and does not leverage the logic's reuse potential. |
| **Solution** | Agnostic service capabilities can be designed to be repeatedly invoked in support of multiple compositions that solve multiple problems. |
| **Application** | Effective recomposition requires the coordinated, successful, and repeated application of several additional patterns. |
| **Impacts** | Repeated service composition demands existing and persistent standardization and governance. |
| **Principles** | All |
| **Architecture** | Inventory, Composition, Service |

# Compatible Change

**By David Orchard, Chris Riley**

*How can a service contract be modified without impacting consumers?*

| Problem | Changing an already-published service contract can impact and invalidate existing consumer programs. |
|---|---|
| Solution | Some changes to the service contract can be backwards-compatible, thereby avoiding negative consumer impacts. |
| Application | Service contract changes can be accommodated via extension or by the loosening of existing constraints or by applying Concurrent Contracts. |
| Impacts | Compatible changes still introduce versioning governance effort, and the technique of loosening constraints can lead to vague contract designs. |
| Principles | Standardized Service Contract, Service Loose Coupling |
| Architecture | Service |

# Compensating Service Transaction

By Clemens Utschig-Utschig, Berthold Maier, Bernd Trops, Hajo Normann,
Torsten Winterberg, Brian Loesgen, Mark Little

*How can composition runtime exceptions be consistently accommodated without requiring services to lock resources?*

| | |
|---|---|
| **Problem** | Whereas uncontrolled runtime exceptions can jeopardize a service composition, wrapping the composition in an atomic transaction can tie up too many resources, thereby negatively affecting performance and scalability. |
| **Solution** | Compensating routines are introduced, allowing runtime exceptions to be resolved with the opportunity for reduced resource locking and memory consumption. |
| **Application** | Compensation logic is pre-defined and implemented as part of the parent composition controller logic or via individual "undo" service capabilities. |
| **Impacts** | Unlike atomic transactions that are governed by specific rules, the use of compensation logic is open-ended and can vary in its actual effectiveness. |
| **Principles** | Service Loose Coupling |
| **Architecture** | Inventory, Composition |

# Composition Autonomy

**By Thomas Erl**

*How can compositions be implemented to minimize loss of autonomy?*

| | |
|---|---|
| **Problem** | Composition controller services naturally lose autonomy when delegating processing tasks to composed services, some of which may be shared across multiple compositions. |
| **Solution** | All composition participants can be isolated to maximize the autonomy of the composition as a whole. |
| **Application** | The agnostic member services of a composition are redundantly implemented in an isolated environment together with the task service. |
| **Impacts** | Increasing autonomy on a composition level results in increased infrastructure costs and governance responsibilities. |
| **Principles** | Service Autonomy, Service Reusability, Service Composability |
| **Architecture** | Composition |

# Concurrent Contracts

By Thomas Erl

*How can a service facilitate multi-consumer coupling requirements and abstraction concerns at the same time?*

| | |
|---|---|
| **Problem** | A service's contract may not be suitable for or applicable to all potential service consumers. |
| **Solution** | Multiple contracts can be created for a single service, each targeted at a specific type of consumer. |
| **Application** | This pattern is ideally applied together with Service Façade to support new contracts as required. |
| **Impacts** | Each new contract can effectively add a new service endpoint to an inventory, thereby increasing corresponding governance effort. |
| **Principles** | Standardized Service Contract, Service Loose Coupling, Service Reusability |
| **Architecture** | Service |

# Content Negotiation
By Raj Balasubramanian, David Booth, Thomas Erl

*How can a service capability accommodate service consumers with different data format or representation requirements?*

| | |
|---|---|
| **Problem** | Different service consumers may have differing requirements for how data provided by a given service capability needs to be formatted or represented. |
| **Solution** | Allow the service capability to support alternative formats and representations by providing a means by which consumer and service can "negotiate" data characteristics at runtime. |
| **Application** | The pattern is most commonly applied via HTTP media types that can define the format and/or representation of message data. The media type of the data is decoupled from the data itself, allowing the service to support a range of media types.<br><br>The consumer provides metadata in each request message to identify preferred and supported media types. The service attempts to accommodate preferences, but can also return the data in other supported media types when issuing the response message. |
| **Impacts** | Fewer service capabilities are needed to accommodate variation in service consumer requirements. Services are able to support old and new service consumer versions concurrently using the same service capabilities.<br><br>The complexity of cache implementations is increased, and requires that caching metadata indicate what metadata input to each request may affect which representation will be returned.<br><br>Requesting metadata that is not abstract enough can introduce consumer-to-service implementation coupling. |
| **Principles** | Standardized Service Contract, Service Loose Coupling |
| **Architecture** | Composition, Service |

# Contract Centralization

**By Thomas Erl**

*How can direct consumer-to-implementation coupling be avoided?*

| | |
|---|---|
| **Problem** | Consumer programs can be designed to access underlying service resources using different entry points, resulting in different forms of implementation dependencies that inhibit the service from evolving in response to change. |
| **Solution** | Access to service logic is limited to the service contract, forcing consumers to avoid implementation coupling. |
| **Application** | This pattern is realized through formal enterprise design standards and the targeted application of the Service Abstraction design principle. |
| **Impacts** | Forcing consumer programs to access service capabilities and resources via a central contract can impose performance overhead and requires on-going standardization effort. |
| **Principles** | Standardized Service Contract, Service Loose Coupling, Service Abstraction |
| **Architecture** | Composition, Service |

# Contract Denormalization

**By Thomas Erl**

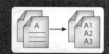

*How can a service contract facilitate consumer programs with differing data exchange requirements?*

| | |
|---|---|
| **Problem** | Services with strictly normalized contracts can impose unnecessary functional and performance demands on some consumer programs. |
| **Solution** | Service contracts can include a measured extent of denormalization, allowing multiple capabilities to redundantly express core functions in different ways for different types of consumer programs. |
| **Application** | The service contract is carefully extended with additional capabilities that provide functional variations of a primary capability. |
| **Impacts** | Overuse of this pattern on the same contract can dramatically increase its size, making it difficult to interpret and unwieldy to govern. |
| **Principles** | Standardized Service Contract, Service Loose Coupling |
| **Architecture** | Service |

# Cross-Domain Utility Layer
**By Thomas Erl**

*How can redundant utility logic be avoided across domain service inventories?*

| | |
|---|---|
| **Problem** | While domain service inventories may be required for independent business governance, they can impose unnecessary redundancy within utility service layers. |
| **Solution** | A common utility service layer can be established, spanning two or more domain service inventories. |
| **Application** | A common set of utility services needs to be defined and standardized in coordination with service inventory owners. |
| **Impacts** | Increased effort is required to coordinate and govern a cross-inventory utility service layer. |
| **Principles** | Service Reusability, Service Composability |
| **Architecture** | Enterprise, Inventory |

# Data Confidentiality

By Jason Hogg, Don Smith, Fred Chong, Tom Hollander, Wojtek Kozaczynski,
Larry Brader, Nelly Delgado, Dwayne Taylor, Lonnie Wall, Paul Slater,
Sajjad Nasir Imran, Pablo Cibraro, Ward Cunningham

*How can data within a message be protected so that it is not disclosed to unintended recipients while in transit?*

| | |
|---|---|
| **Problem** | Within service compositions, data is often required to pass through one or more intermediaries. Point-to-point security protocols, such as those frequently used at the transport layer, may allow messages containing sensitive information to be intercepted and viewed by such intermediaries. |
| **Solution** | The message contents are encrypted independently from the transport, ensuring that only intended recipients can access the protected data. |
| **Application** | A symmetric or asymmetric encryption and decryption algorithm, such as those specified in the XML-Encryption standard, is applied at the message level. |
| **Impacts** | This pattern may add runtime performance overhead associated with the required encryption and decryption of message data. The management of keys can further add to governance burden. |
| **Principles** | Service Composability |
| **Architecture** | Inventory, Composition, Service |

# Data Format Transformation
By Mark Little, Thomas Rischbeck, Arnaud Simon

*How can services interact with programs that communicate with different data formats?*

| | |
|---|---|
| **Problem** | A service may be incompatible with resources it needs to access due to data format disparity. Furthermore, a service consumer that communicates using a data format different from a target service will be incompatible and therefore unable to invoke the service. |
| **Solution** | Intermediary data format transformation logic needs to be introduced in order to dynamically translate one data format into another. |
| **Application** | This necessary transformation logic is incorporated by adding internal service logic, service agents, or a dedicated transformation service. |
| **Impacts** | The use of data format transformation logic inevitably adds development effort, design complexity, and performance overhead. |
| **Principles** | Standardized Service Contract, Service Loose Coupling |
| **Architecture** | Inventory, Composition, Service |

# Data Model Transformation
**By Thomas Erl**

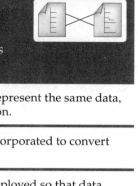

*How can services interoperate when using different data models for the same type of data?*

| | |
|---|---|
| **Problem** | Services may use incompatible schemas to represent the same data, hindering service interaction and composition. |
| **Solution** | A data transformation technology can be incorporated to convert data between disparate schema structures. |
| **Application** | Mapping logic needs to be developed and deployed so that data compliant to one data model can be dynamically converted to comply to a different data model. |
| **Impacts** | Data model transformation introduces development effort, design complexity, and runtime performance overhead, and overuse of this pattern can seriously inhibit service recomposition potential. |
| **Principles** | Standardized Service Contract, Service Reusability, Service Composability |
| **Architecture** | Inventory, Composition |

# Data Origin Authentication

By Jason Hogg, Don Smith, Fred Chong, Tom Hollander, Wojtek
Kozaczynski, Larry Brader, Nelly Delgado, Dwayne Taylor, Lonnie Wall,
Paul Slater, Sajjad Nasir Imran, Pablo Cibraro, Ward Cunningham

*How can a service verify that a message originates from a known*
*sender and that the message has not been tampered with in transit?*

| | |
|---|---|
| **Problem** | The intermediary processing layers generally required by service compositions can expose sensitive data when security is limited to point-to-point protocols, such as those used with transport-layer security. |
| **Solution** | A message can be digitally signed so that the recipient services can verify that it originated from the expected consumer and that it has not been tampered with during transit. |
| **Application** | A digital signature algorithm is applied to the message to provide "proof of origin," allowing sensitive message contents to be protected from tampering. This technology must be supported by both consumer and service. |
| **Impacts** | Use of cryptographic techniques can add to performance requirements and the choice of digital signing algorithm can affect the level of security actually achieved. |
| **Principles** | Service Composability |
| **Architecture** | Composition |

# Decomposed Capability

**By Thomas Erl**

*How can a service be designed to minimize the chances of capability logic deconstruction?*

| | |
|---|---|
| **Problem** | The decomposition of a service subsequent to its implementation can require the deconstruction of logic within capabilities, which can be disruptive and make the preservation of a service contract problematic. |
| **Solution** | Services prone to future decomposition can be equipped with a series of granular capabilities that more easily facilitate decomposition. |
| **Application** | Additional service modeling is carried out to define granular, more easily distributed capabilities. |
| **Impacts** | Until the service is eventually decomposed, it may be represented by a bloated contract that stays with it as long as proxy capabilities are supported. |
| **Principles** | Standardized Service Contract, Service Abstraction |
| **Architecture** | Service |

## Decoupled Contract
### By Thomas Erl

*How can a service express its capabilities independently of its implementation?*

| | |
|---|---|
| **Problem** | For a service to be positioned as an effective enterprise resource, it must be equipped with a technical contract that exists independently from its implementation yet still in alignment with other services. |
| **Solution** | The service contract is physically decoupled from its implementation. |
| **Application** | A service's technical interface is physically separated and subject to relevant service-orientation design principles. |
| **Impacts** | Service functionality is limited to the feature-set of the decoupled contract medium. |
| **Principles** | Standardized Service Contract, Service Loose Coupling |
| **Architecture** | Service |

# Direct Authentication

By Jason Hogg, Don Smith, Fred Chong, Tom Hollander, Wojtek Kozaczynski,
Larry Brader, Nelly Delgado, Dwayne Taylor, Lonnie Wall, Paul Slater,
Sajjad Nasir Imran, Pablo Cibraro, Ward Cunningham

*How can a service verify the credentials provided by a consumer?*

| | |
|---|---|
| **Problem** | Some of the capabilities offered by a service may be intended for specific groups of consumers or may involve the transmission of sensitive data. Attackers that access this data could use it to compromise the service or the IT enterprise itself. |
| **Solution** | Service capabilities require that consumers provide credentials that can be authenticated against an identity store. |
| **Application** | The service implementation is provided access to an identity store, allowing it to authenticate the consumer directly. |
| **Impacts** | Consumers must provide credentials compatible with the service's authentication logic. This pattern may lead to multiple identity stores, resulting in extra governance burden. |
| **Principles** | Service Composability |
| **Architecture** | Composition, Service |

# Distributed Capability

**By Thomas Erl**

*How can a service preserve its functional context while also fulfilling special capability processing requirements?*

| | |
|---|---|
| **Problem** | A capability that belongs within a service may have unique processing requirements that cannot be accommodated by the default service implementation, but separating capability logic from the service will compromise the integrity of the service context. |
| **Solution** | The underlying service logic is distributed, thereby allowing the implementation logic for a capability with unique processing requirements to be physically separated, while continuing to be represented by the same service contract. |
| **Application** | The logic is moved and intermediary processing is added to act as a liaison between the moved logic and the main service logic. |
| **Impacts** | The distribution of a capability's logic leads to performance overhead associated with remote communication and the need for new intermediate processing. |
| **Principles** | Standardized Service Contract, Service Autonomy |
| **Architecture** | Service |

# Domain Inventory

**By Thomas Erl**

*How can services be delivered to maximize recomposition when enterprise-wide standardization is not possible?*

| | |
|---|---|
| **Problem** | Establishing a single enterprise service inventory may be unmanageable for some enterprises, and attempts to do so may jeopardize the success of an SOA adoption as a whole. |
| **Solution** | Services can be grouped into manageable, domain-specific service inventories, each of which can be independently standardized, governed, and owned. |
| **Application** | Inventory domain boundaries need to be carefully established. |
| **Impacts** | Standardization disparity between domain service inventories imposes transformation requirements and reduces the overall benefit potential of the SOA adoption. |
| **Principles** | Standardized Service Contract, Service Abstraction, Service Composability |
| **Architecture** | Enterprise, Inventory |

# Dual Protocols

By Thomas Erl

*How can a service inventory overcome the limitations of its canonical protocol while still remaining standardized?*

| | |
|---|---|
| **Problem** | Canonical Protocol requires that all services conform to the use of the same communications technology; however, a single protocol may not be able to accommodate all service requirements, thereby introducing limitations. |
| **Solution** | The service inventory architecture is designed to support services based on primary and secondary protocols. |
| **Application** | Primary and secondary service levels are created and collectively represent the service endpoint layer. All services are subject to standard service-orientation design considerations and specific guidelines are followed to minimize the impact of not following Canonical Protocol. |
| **Impacts** | This pattern can lead to a convoluted inventory architecture, increased governance effort and expense, and (when poorly applied) an unhealthy dependence on Protocol Bridging. Because the endpoint layer is semi-federated, the quantity of potential consumers and reuse opportunities is decreased. |
| **Principles** | Standardized Service Contract, Service Loose Coupling, Service Abstraction, Service Autonomy, Service Composability |
| **Architecture** | Inventory, Service |

# Endpoint Redirection

By Raj Balasubramanian, David Booth, Thomas Erl

*How can consumers of a specific service endpoint adapt when the service endpoint changes or is removed?*

| | |
|---|---|
| **Problem** | Service endpoint identifiers include information that can change over time. It may not be possible to replace all references to an out-of-date endpoint, which can lead to the service consumer being unable to further interact with the service endpoint. |
| **Solution** | Automatically redirect service consumers that attempt to access out-of-date service endpoints to the current service endpoints. |
| **Application** | Include endpoint redirection as a feature of the service contract. When a service consumer attempts to invoke a stale service capability, return a redirection response. The service consumer follows the redirection instructions and retries the request on the new service capability. |
| | Redirections can be temporary or permanent. Permanent redirections are automatically recorded in the service consumer's configuration data to avoid subsequent requests to stale service capabilities. |
| | For services relying on resource identifiers to express capabilities, changes to identifiers amount to a change to the runtime-discovered service contract. Redirection is able to facilitate these changes. |
| **Impacts** | The service consumer needs to be developed with the logic required to process the redirection instructions. |
| | Explicit upgrades may be avoided entirely if permanent redirections are used. However, this can lead to wasteful runtime processing of repeated redirections that can be avoided by upgrading the service consumers. |
| | Returning redirection information to the consumer requires consumers to determine in advance how much to trust a redirection response. A service that has been compromised from a security perspective may cause the consumer to permanently change its identifiers to point to an invalid or malicious service. A misconfigured service can lead to similar disruption. Care may also need to be taken in order to avoid infinite redirection loops. |
| **Principles** | Service Loose Coupling |
| **Architecture** | Composition, Service |

# Enterprise Inventory

**By Thomas Erl**

*How can services be delivered to maximize recomposition?*

| | |
|---|---|
| **Problem** | Delivering services independently via different project teams across an enterprise establishes a constant risk of producing inconsistent service and architecture implementations, compromising recomposition opportunities. |
| **Solution** | Services for multiple solutions can be designed for delivery within a standardized, enterprise-wide inventory architecture wherein they can be freely and repeatedly recomposed. |
| **Application** | The enterprise service inventory is ideally modeled in advance, and enterprise-wide standards are applied to services delivered by different project teams. |
| **Impacts** | Significant up-front analysis is required to define an enterprise inventory blueprint and numerous organizational impacts result from the subsequent governance requirements. |
| **Principles** | Standardized Service Contract, Service Abstraction, Service Composability |
| **Architecture** | Enterprise, Inventory |

# Enterprise Service Bus
### By Thomas Erl, Mark Little, Thomas Rischbeck, Arnaud Simon

Enterprise Service Bus represents an environment designed to foster sophisticated interconnectivity between services. It establishes an intermediate layer of processing that can help overcome common problems associated with reliability, scalability, and communications disparity.

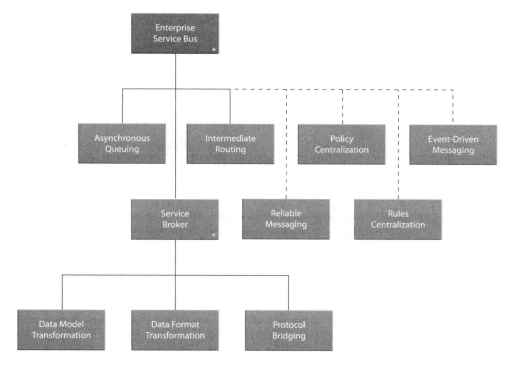

Enterprise Service Bus is fundamentally comprised of the co-existent application of Asynchronous Queuing, Intermediate Routing, and Service Broker, and can be further extended via Reliable Messaging, Policy Centralization, Rules Centralization, and Event-Driven Messaging.

# Entity Abstraction

**By Thomas Erl**

*How can agnostic business logic be separated, reused, and governed independently?*

| | |
|---|---|
| **Problem** | Bundling both process-agnostic and process-specific business logic into the same service eventually results in the creation of redundant agnostic business logic across multiple services. |
| **Solution** | An agnostic business service layer can be established, dedicated to services that base their functional context on existing business entities. |
| **Application** | Entity service contexts are derived from business entity models and then establish a logical layer that is modeled during the analysis phase. |
| **Impacts** | The core, business-centric nature of the services introduced by this pattern require extra modeling and design attention and their governance requirements can impose dramatic organizational changes. |
| **Principles** | Service Loose Coupling, Service Abstraction, Service Reusability, Service Composability |
| **Architecture** | Inventory, Composition, Service |

# Entity Linking

By Raj Balasubramanian, David Booth, Thomas Erl

*How can services expose the inherent relationships between business entities in order to support loosely-coupled composition?*

| | |
|---|---|
| **Problem** | Business entities have natural relationships, yet entity services are commonly designed autonomously with no indication of these relationships. Service consumers acting as composition controllers are commonly required to have entity linking logic hardcoded in order to work with entity relationships. This limits the composition controller to any additional links that may become relevant and further adds a governance burden to ensure that hardcoded entity linking logic is kept in synch with the business. |
| **Solution** | Services inform their consumers about the existence of related entities as part of the consumer's interactions with the services. |
| **Application** | Links are included in relevant response messages from the service. Service consumers are able to navigate from entity to entity by following these links, and accumulate further business knowledge along the way. This allows service consumers with little up-front entity linking logic to correctly compose entity services based on their relationships. |
| **Impacts** | Resource identifiers representing business entities need to remain relatively stable over the lifespan of the business entities they identify. Once an identifier is known it can be referred to in the future again by the same service consumers.<br><br>Links can be difficult to define if identifiers for business entities are specific to the services that own them. The application of Lightweight Endpoint can help achieve a uniform syntax for linked identifiers.<br><br>Links are not valuable if the service consumer is unable to access information about the linked entity. Therefore, the further application of Reusable Contract can ensure that service consumers are able to interact with linked entities. |
| **Principles** | Service Reusability, Service Abstraction, Service Composability |
| **Architecture** | Inventory, Service |

# Event-Driven Messaging

By Mark Little, Thomas Rischbeck, Arnaud Simon

*How can service consumers be automatically notified of runtime service events?*

| | |
|---|---|
| **Problem** | Events that occur within the functional boundary encapsulated by a service may be of relevance to service consumers, but without resorting to inefficient polling-based interaction, the consumer has no way of learning about these events. |
| **Solution** | The consumer establishes itself as a subscriber of the service. The service, in turn, automatically issues notifications of relevant events to this and any of its subscribers. |
| **Application** | A messaging framework is implemented capable of supporting the publish-and-subscribe MEP and associated complex event processing and tracking. |
| **Impacts** | Event-driven message exchanges cannot easily be incorporated as part of Atomic Service Transaction, and publisher/subscriber availability issues can arise. |
| **Principles** | Standardized Service Contract, Service Loose Coupling, Service Autonomy |
| **Architecture** | Inventory, Composition |

# Exception Shielding

By Jason Hogg, Don Smith, Fred Chong, Tom Hollander, Wojtek
Kozaczynski, Larry Brader, Nelly Delgado, Dwayne Taylor, Lonnie Wall,
Paul Slater, Sajjad Nasir Imran, Pablo Cibraro, Ward Cunningham

*How can a service prevent the disclosure of information about its internal implementation when an exception occurs?*

| | |
|---|---|
| **Problem** | Unfiltered exception data output by a service may contain internal implementation details that can compromise the security of the service and its surrounding environment. |
| **Solution** | Potentially unsafe exception data is "sanitized" by replacing it with exception data that is safe by design before it is made available to consumers. |
| **Application** | This pattern can be applied at design-time by reviewing and altering source code or at runtime by adding dynamic sanitization routines. |
| **Impacts** | Sanitized exception information can make the tracking of errors more difficult due to the lack of detail provided to consumers. |
| **Principles** | Service Abstraction |
| **Architecture** | Service |

# Federated Endpoint Layer
## By Thomas Erl

Federation is an important concept in service-oriented computing. It represents the desired state of the external, consumer-facing perspective of a service inventory, as expressed by the collective contracts of all the inventory's services.

The more federated and unified this collection of contracts (endpoints) is, the more easily and effectively the services can be repeatedly consumed and leveraged.

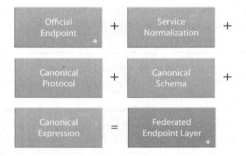

The joint application of Official Endpoint, Service Normalization, Canonical Protocol, Canonical Schema, and Canonical Expression results in Federated Endpoint Layer.

# File Gateway
By Satadru Roy

*How can service logic interact with legacy systems that can only share information by exchanging files?*

| | |
|---|---|
| **Problem** | Data records contained in flat files produced by a legacy system need to be processed individually by service logic, but legacy systems are not capable of directly invoking services.<br><br>Conversely, service logic may need to produce information for the legacy system, but building file creation and transfer functionality into the service can result in an inflexible design. |
| **Solution** | Intermediary two-way file processing logic is positioned between the legacy system and the service. |
| **Application** | For inbound data, the file gateway processing logic can detect file drops and leverage available broker features to perform Data Model Transformation and Data Format Transformation. On the outbound side, this logic intercepts information produced by services and packages them (with possible transformation) into new or existing files for consumption by the legacy system. |
| **Impacts** | The type of logic provided by this pattern is unsuitable when immediate replies are required by either service or legacy system. Deployment and governance of two-way file processing logic can further add to operational complexity and may require specialized administration skills. |
| **Principles** | Service Loose Coupling |
| **Architecture** | Service |

# Functional Decomposition

**By Thomas Erl**

*How can a large business problem be solved without having to build a standalone body of solution logic?*

| | |
|---|---|
| **Problem** | To solve a large, complex business problem a corresponding amount of solution logic needs to be created, resulting in a self-contained application with traditional governance and reusability constraints. |
| **Solution** | The large business problem can be broken down into a set of smaller, related problems, allowing the required solution logic to also be decomposed into a corresponding set of smaller, related solution logic units. |
| **Application** | Depending on the nature of the large problem, a service-oriented analysis process can be created to cleanly deconstruct it into smaller problems. |
| **Impacts** | The ownership of multiple smaller programs can result in increased design complexity and governance challenges. |
| **Principles** | n/a |
| **Architecture** | Service |

# Idempotent Capability

**By Cesare Pautasso, Herbjörn Wilhelmsen**

*How can a service capability safely accept multiple copies of the same message to handle communication failure?*

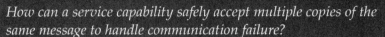

| | |
|---|---|
| **Problem** | Network and server hardware failure can lead to lost messages, resulting in cases where a service consumer receives no response to its request. Attempts to reissue the request message can lead to unpredictable or undesirable behavior when the service capability inadvertently receives multiple copies of the same request message. |
| **Solution** | Design service capabilities with idempotent logic that enables them to safely accept repeated message exchanges. |
| **Application** | Idempotency guarantees that repeated invocations of a service capability are safe and will have no negative effect. |
| | Idempotent capabilities are generally limited to read-only data retrieval and queries. For capabilities that do request changes to service state, their logic is generally based on "set," "put", or "delete" actions that have a post-condition that does not depend on the original state of the service. |
| | The design of an idempotent capability can include the use of a unique identifier with each request so that repeated requests (with the same identifier value) that have already been processed will be discarded or ignored by the service capability, rather than being processed again. |
| **Impacts** | The use of a unique identifier to define an idempotent capability requires session state to be reliably recorded by the service and preserved across server hardware failures. This can harm the scalability of the service, and may be further complicated if redundant service implementations are operating at different sites that experience network failures. |
| | Not all service capabilities can be idempotent. Potentially unsafe capabilities include those that need to perform "increment," "reverse" or "escalate" transition functions, where the post-execution condition is dependent upon the original state of the service. |
| **Principles** | Standardized Service Contract, Service Statelessness, Service Composability |
| **Architecture** | Inventory, Composition, Service |

# Intermediate Routing
By Mark Little, Thomas Rischbeck, Arnaud Simon

*How can dynamic runtime factors affect the path of a message?*

| | |
|---|---|
| **Problem** | The larger and more complex a service composition is, the more difficult it is to anticipate and design for all possible runtime scenarios in advance, especially with asynchronous, messaging-based communication. |
| **Solution** | Message paths can be dynamically determined through the use of intermediary routing logic. |
| **Application** | Various types of intermediary routing logic can be incorporated to create message paths based on message content or runtime factors. |
| **Impacts** | Dynamically determining a message path adds layers of processing logic and correspondingly can increase performance overhead. Also the use of multiple routing logic can result in overly complex service activities. |
| **Principles** | Service Loose Coupling, Service Reusability, Service Composability |
| **Architecture** | Composition |

# Inventory Endpoint

**By Thomas Erl**

*How can a service inventory be shielded from external access while still offering service capabilities to external consumers?*

| | |
|---|---|
| **Problem** | A group of services delivered for a specific inventory may provide capabilities that are useful to services outside of that inventory. However, for security and governance reasons, it may not be desirable to expose all services or all service capabilities to external consumers. |
| **Solution** | Abstract the relevant capabilities into an endpoint service that acts as a the official inventory entry point dedicated to a specific set of external consumers. |
| **Application** | The endpoint service can expose a contract with the same capabilities as its underlying services, but augmented with policies or other characteristics to accommodate external consumer interaction requirements. |
| **Impacts** | Endpoint services can increase the governance freedom of underlying services but can also increase governance effort by introducing redundant service logic and contracts into an inventory. |
| **Principles** | Standardized Service Contract, Service Loose Coupling, Service Abstraction |
| **Architecture** | Inventory |

# Legacy Wrapper
**By Thomas Erl, Satadru Roy**

*How can wrapper services with non-standard contracts be prevented from spreading indirect consumer-to-implementation coupling?*

| | |
|---|---|
| **Problem** | Wrapper services required to encapsulate legacy logic are often forced to introduce a non-standard service contract with high technology coupling requirements, resulting in a proliferation of implementation coupling throughout all service consumer programs. |
| **Solution** | The non-standard wrapper service can be replaced by or further wrapped with a standardized service contract that extracts, encapsulates, and possibly eliminates legacy technical details from the contract. |
| **Application** | A custom service contract and required service logic need to be developed to represent the proprietary legacy interface. |
| **Impacts** | The introduction of an additional service adds a layer of processing and associated performance overhead. |
| **Principles** | Standardized Service Contract, Service Loose Coupling, Service Abstraction |
| **Architecture** | Service |

# Lightweight Endpoint

By Raj Balasubramanian, Benjamin Carlyle, Thomas Erl, Cesare Pautasso

*How can lightweight units of business logic be positioned as effective reusable enterprise resources?*

| | |
|---|---|
| **Problem** | A service consumer that requires access to business entity information (such as data about an invoice) needs to maintain two identifiers: one for the service and another for the invoice itself. The business entity identifier may be unique only within the scope of the service contract, and the service consumer may be limited to using unnecessarily coarse-grained service capabilities pre-defined as part of the published service contract. This can result in wasteful data exchange and consumer-side processing. |
| **Solution** | Expose data and functionality associated with business entities as a series of granular, lightweight endpoints. Allow consumers to target those endpoints in order to optimize data exchange and consumer-side processing. |
| **Application** | A service contract needs to expose service capabilities that offer a range of functional granularity. Each of these "lightweight" capabilities is associated with a business entity. |
| **Impacts** | Finer-grained service capabilities can result in verbose resource identifiers that may impose a greater governance burden. |
| | Applying this pattern can lead to resource overlap in order for multiple service capabilities to offer access at multiple levels of granularity. For example, an invoice and properties of the invoice can be exposed as separate resources, even though they refer to a common set of underlying data or functionality. |
| | Greater effort may be required when applying Service Façade, when the facade relates functionality associated with granular resources to core service logic. |
| **Principles** | Standardized Service Contract, Service Loose Coupling, Service Abstraction, Service Composability |
| **Architecture** | Inventory, Service |

# Logic Centralization
By Thomas Erl

*How can the misuse of redundant service logic be avoided?*

| | |
|---|---|
| **Problem** | If agnostic services are not consistently reused, redundant functionality can be delivered in other services, resulting in problems associated with inventory denormalization and service ownership and governance. |
| **Solution** | Access to reusable functionality is limited to official agnostic services. |
| **Application** | Agnostic services need to be properly designed and governed, and their use must be enforced via enterprise standards. |
| **Impacts** | Organizational issues reminiscent of past reuse projects can raise obstacles to applying this pattern. |
| **Principles** | Service Reusability, Service Composability |
| **Architecture** | Inventory, Composition, Service |

# Message Screening

By Jason Hogg, Don Smith, Fred Chong, Tom Hollander ,Wojtek Kozaczynski, Larry Brader, Nelly Delgado, Dwayne Taylor, Lonnie Wall, Paul Slater, Sajjad Nasir Imran, Pablo Cibraro, Ward Cunningham

*How can a service be protected from malformed or malicious input?*

| | |
|---|---|
| **Problem** | An attacker can transmit messages with malicious or malformed content to a service, resulting in undesirable behavior. |
| **Solution** | The service is equipped or supplemented with special screening routines that assume that all input data is harmful until proven otherwise. |
| **Application** | When a service receives a message, it makes a number of checks to screen message content for harmful data. |
| **Impacts** | Extra runtime processing is required with each message exchange, and the screening logic requires additional, specialized routines to process binary message content, such as attachments. It may also not be possible to check for all possible forms of harmful content. |
| **Principles** | Standardized Service Contract |
| **Architecture** | Service |

# Messaging Metadata

**By Thomas Erl**

*How can services be designed to process activity-specific data at runtime?*

| | |
|---|---|
| **Problem** | Because messaging does not rely on a persistent connection between service and consumer, it is challenging for a service to gain access to the state data associated with an overall runtime activity. |
| **Solution** | Message contents can be supplemented with activity-specific metadata that can be interpreted and processed separately at runtime. |
| **Application** | This pattern requires a messaging framework that supports message headers or properties. |
| **Impacts** | The interpretation and processing of messaging metadata adds to runtime performance overhead and increases service activity design complexity. |
| **Principles** | Service Loose Coupling, Service Statelessness |
| **Architecture** | Composition |

# Metadata Centralization

**By Thomas Erl**

*How can service metadata be centrally published and governed?*

| | |
|---|---|
| **Problem** | Project teams, especially in larger enterprises, run the constant risk of building functionality that already exists or is already in development, resulting in wasted effort, service logic redundancy, and service inventory denormalization. |
| **Solution** | Service metadata can be centrally published in a service registry so as to provide a formal means of service registration and discovery. |
| **Application** | A private service registry needs to be positioned as a central part of an inventory architecture supported by formal processes for registration and discovery. |
| **Impacts** | The service registry product needs to be adequately mature and reliable, and its required use and maintenance needs to be incorporated into all service delivery and governance processes and methodologies. |
| **Principles** | Service Discoverability |
| **Architecture** | Enterprise, Inventory |

# Multi-Channel Endpoint

By Satadru Roy

*How can legacy logic fragmented and duplicated for different delivery channels be centrally consolidated?*

| | |
|---|---|
| **Problem** | Legacy systems custom-built for specific delivery channels (mobile phone, desktop, kiosk, etc.) result in redundancy and application silos when multiple channels need to be supported, thereby making these systems burdensome to govern and difficult to federate. |
| **Solution** | An intermediary service is designed to encapsulate channel-specific legacy systems and expose a single standardized contract for multiple channel-specific consumers. |
| **Application** | The service established by this pattern will require significant processing and workflow logic to support multiple channels while also coordinating interaction with multiple back-end legacy systems. |
| **Impacts** | The endpoint processing logic established by this pattern often introduces the need for infrastructure upgrades and orchestration-capable middleware and may turn into a performance bottleneck. |
| **Principles** | Service Loose Coupling, Service Reusability |
| **Architecture** | Service |

# Non-Agnostic Context

**By Thomas Erl**

*How can single-purpose service logic be positioned as an effective enterprise resource?*

| | |
|---|---|
| **Problem** | Non-agnostic logic that is not service-oriented can inhibit the effectiveness of service compositions that utilize agnostic services. |
| **Solution** | Non-agnostic solution logic suitable for service encapsulation can be located within services that reside as official members of a service inventory. |
| **Application** | A single-purpose functional service context is defined. |
| **Impacts** | Although they are not expected to provide reuse potential, non-agnostic services are still subject to the rigor of service-orientation. |
| **Principles** | Standardized Service Contract, Service Composability |
| **Architecture** | Service |

# Official Endpoint
By Thomas Erl

As important as it is to clearly differentiate Logic Centralization from Contract Centralization, it is equally important to understand how these two fundamental patterns can and should be used together.

Applying these two patterns to the same service realizes the Official Endpoint compound pattern. The repeated application of Official Endpoint supports the goal of establishing a federated layer of service endpoints, which is why this compound pattern is also a part of Federated Endpoint Layer.

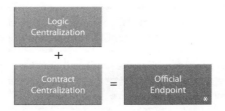

The joint application of Logic Centralization and Contract Centralization results in Official Endpoint.

# Orchestration
By Thomas Erl, Brian Loesgen

An orchestration platform is dedicated to the effective maintenance and execution of parent business process logic. Modern-day orchestration environments are especially expected to support sophisticated and complex service composition logic that can result in long-running runtime activities.

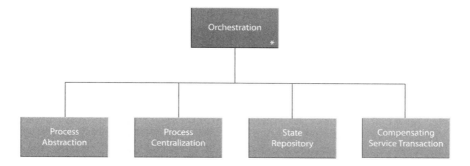

Orchestration is fundamentally comprised of the co-existent application of Process Abstraction, State Repository, Process Centralization, and Compensating Service Transaction, and can be further extended via Atomic Service Transaction, Rules Centralization, and Data Model Transformation.

# Partial State Deferral
By Thomas Erl

*How can services be designed to optimize resource consumption while still remaining stateful?*

| | |
|---|---|
| **Problem** | Service capabilities may be required to store and manage large amounts of state data, resulting in increased memory consumption and reduced scalability. |
| **Solution** | Even when services are required to remain stateful, a subset of their state data can be temporarily deferred. |
| **Application** | Various state management deferral options exist, depending on the surrounding architecture. |
| **Impacts** | Partial state management deferral can add to design complexity and bind a service to the architecture. |
| **Principles** | Service Statelessness |
| **Architecture** | Inventory, Service |

## Partial Validation

By David Orchard, Chris Riley

*How can unnecessary data validation be avoided?*

| | |
|---|---|
| **Problem** | The generic capabilities provided by agnostic services sometimes result in service contracts that impose unnecessary data and validation upon consumer programs. |
| **Solution** | A consumer program can be designed to only validate the relevant subset of the data and ignore the remainder. |
| **Application** | The application of this pattern is specific to the technology used for the consumer implementation. For example, with Web services, XPath can be used to filter out unnecessary data prior to validation. |
| **Impacts** | Extra design-time effort is required and the additional runtime data filtering-related logic can reduce the processing gains of avoiding unnecessary validation. |
| **Principles** | Standardized Service Contract, Service Loose Coupling |
| **Architecture** | Composition |

# Policy Centralization

**By Thomas Erl**

*How can policies be normalized and consistently enforced across multiple services?*

| | |
|---|---|
| **Problem** | Policies that apply to multiple services can introduce redundancy and inconsistency within service logic and contracts. |
| **Solution** | Global or domain-specific policies can be isolated and applied to multiple services. |
| **Application** | Up-front analysis effort specific to defining and establishing reusable policies is recommended, and an appropriate policy enforcement framework is required. |
| **Impacts** | Policy frameworks can introduce performance overhead and may impose dependencies on proprietary technologies. There is also the risk of conflict between centralized and service-specific policies. |
| **Principles** | Standardized Service Contracts, Service Loose Coupling, Service Abstraction |
| **Architecture** | Inventory, Service |

# Process Abstraction

**By Thomas Erl**

*How can non-agnostic process logic be separated and governed independently?*

| | |
|---|---|
| **Problem** | Grouping task-centric logic together with task-agnostic logic hinders the governance of the task-specific logic and the reuse of the agnostic logic. |
| **Solution** | A dedicated parent business process service layer is established to support governance independence and the positioning of task services as potential enterprise resources. |
| **Application** | Business process logic is typically filtered out after utility and entity services have been defined, allowing for the definition of task services that comprise this layer. |
| **Impacts** | In addition to the modeling and design considerations associated with creating task services, abstracting parent business process logic establishes an inherent dependency on carrying out that logic via the composition of other services. |
| **Principles** | Service Loose Coupling, Service Abstraction, Service Composability |
| **Architecture** | Inventory, Composition, Service |

# Process Centralization
**By Thomas Erl**

*How can abstracted business process logic be centrally governed?*

| Problem | When business process logic is distributed across independent service implementations, it can be problematic to extend and evolve. |
|---|---|
| Solution | Logic representing numerous business processes can be deployed and governed from a central location. |
| Application | Middleware platforms generally provide the necessary orchestration technologies to apply this pattern. |
| Impacts | Significant infrastructure and architectural changes are imposed when the required middleware is introduced. |
| Principles | Service Autonomy, Service Statelessness, Service Composability |
| Architecture | Inventory, Composition |

## Protocol Bridging

By Mark Little, Thomas Rischbeck, Arnaud Simon

*How can a service exchange data with consumers that use different communication protocols?*

| | |
|---|---|
| **Problem** | Services using different communication protocols or different versions of the same protocol cannot exchange data. |
| **Solution** | Bridging logic is introduced to enable communication between different communication protocols by dynamically converting one protocol to another at runtime. |
| **Application** | Instead of connecting directly to each other, consumer programs and services connect to a broker, which provides bridging logic that carries out the protocol conversion. |
| **Impacts** | Significant performance overhead can be imposed by bridging technologies, and their use can limit or eliminate the ability to incorporate reliability and transaction features. |
| **Principles** | Standardized Service Contract, Service Composability |
| **Architecture** | Inventory, Composition |

## Proxy Capability
By Thomas Erl

*How can a service subject to decomposition continue to support consumers affected by the decomposition?*

| | |
|---|---|
| **Problem** | If an established service needs to be decomposed into multiple services, its contract and its existing consumers can be impacted. |
| **Solution** | The original service contract is preserved, even if underlying capability logic is separated, by turning the established capability definition into a proxy. |
| **Application** | Façade logic needs to be introduced to relay requests and responses between the proxy and newly located capabilities. |
| **Impacts** | The practical solution provided by this pattern results in a measure of service denormalization. |
| **Principles** | Service Loose Coupling |
| **Architecture** | Service |

# Redundant Implementation
**By Thomas Erl**

*How can the reliability and availability of a service be increased?*

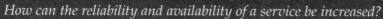

| | |
|---|---|
| **Problem** | A service that is being actively reused introduces a potential single point of failure that may jeopardize the reliability of all compositions in which it participates if an unexpected error condition occurs. |
| **Solution** | Reusable services can be deployed via redundant implementations or with failover support. |
| **Application** | The same service implementation is redundantly deployed or supported by infrastructure with redundancy features. |
| **Impacts** | Extra governance effort is required to keep all redundant implementations in sync. |
| **Principles** | Service Autonomy |
| **Architecture** | Service |

# Reliable Messaging

By Mark Little, Thomas Rischbeck, Arnaud Simon

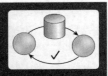

*How can services communicate reliably when implemented in an unreliable environment?*

| | |
|---|---|
| **Problem** | Service communication cannot be guaranteed when using unreliable messaging protocols or when dependent on an otherwise unreliable environment. |
| **Solution** | An intermediate reliability mechanism is introduced into the inventory architecture, ensuring that message delivery is guaranteed. |
| **Application** | Middleware, service agents, and data stores are deployed to track message deliveries, manage the issuance of acknowledgements, and persist messages during failure conditions. |
| **Impacts** | Using a reliability framework adds processing overhead that can affect service activity performance. It also increases composition design complexity and may not be compatible with Atomic Service Transaction. |
| **Principles** | Service Composability |
| **Architecture** | Inventory, Composition |

# Reusable Contract

**By Raj Balasubramanian, Benjamin Carlyle, Thomas Erl, Cesare Pautasso**

*How can service consumers compose services without having to couple themselves to service-specific contracts?*

| | |
|---|---|
| **Problem** | To access a service capability of a service with a service-specific contract, the service consumer must be designed to couple itself to the service contract. When the service contract changes, the service consumer may no longer be functional. To access a new version of the service contract, or to access other service contracts in order to compose other services, the service consumer must be subjected to additional development cycles, thereby incurring time, effort, and expense. |
| **Solution** | Limit tight coupling to a common, reusable technical contract that is shared by multiple services. The technical contract provides only generic, high-level functions that are less likely to be impacted when service logic changes. |
| **Application** | A reusable service contract can provide abstract and agnostic data exchange methods, none of which are related to a specific business function. Methods within a reusable contract are typically focused on types of data rather than on the business context of the data. |
| | The set of methods of the reusable contract is complemented by service-specific resource identifiers and media types to apply the context established by reusable methods to individual service capabilities. |
| | HTTP provides a reusable contract via generic methods, such as GET, PUT, and DELETE, that allow consumer programs to access Web-based resources by further providing resource identifiers. The combination of the resource identifier and the HTTP method and media type can comprise a service-specific capability. |
| | A reusable contract can also be created using a centralized WSDL definition, as long as the operations defined are sufficiently generic. |
| **Impacts** | Sharing the same contract across services increases the importance of getting the contract right, both initially and over the contract's lifetime. |
| | The reusable contract may still need to change if new services with new high-level functional requirements are introduced into the service inventory. |
| | The reusable contract can lack sufficient metadata to effectively enable a service to be discovered. Service-specific metadata may need to be maintained separately from the reusable contract definition to ensure that service consumers are able to select the correct service capability with which to interact. |
| **Principles** | Standardized Service Contract, Service Loose Coupling, Service Abstraction, Service Discoverability, Service Composability |
| **Architecture** | Inventory, Composition, Service |

# Rules Centralization

**By Thomas Erl**

*How can business rules be abstracted and centrally governed?*

| | |
|---|---|
| **Problem** | The same business rules may apply across different business services, leading to redundancy and governance challenges. |
| **Solution** | The storage and management of business rules are positioned within a dedicated architectural extension from where they can be centrally accessed and maintained. |
| **Application** | The use of a business rules management system or engine is employed and accessed via system agents or a dedicated service. |
| **Impacts** | Services are subjected to increased performance overhead, risk, and architectural dependency. |
| **Principles** | Service Reusability |
| **Architecture** | Inventory |

# Schema Centralization

**By Thomas Erl**

*How can service contracts be designed to avoid redundant data representation?*

| | |
|---|---|
| **Problem** | Different service contracts often need to express capabilities that process similar business documents or data sets, resulting in redundant schema content that is difficult to govern. |
| **Solution** | Select schemas that exist as physically separate parts of the service contract are shared across multiple contracts. |
| **Application** | Up-front analysis effort is required to establish a schema layer independent of and in support of the service layer. |
| **Impacts** | Governance of shared schemas becomes increasingly important as multiple services can form dependencies on the same schema definitions. |
| **Principles** | Standardized Service Contract, Service Loose Coupling |
| **Architecture** | Inventory, Service |

# Service Agent
**By Thomas Erl**

*How can event-driven logic be separated and governed independently?*

| | |
|---|---|
| **Problem** | Service compositions can become large and inefficient, especially when required to invoke granular capabilities across multiple services. |
| **Solution** | Event-driven logic can be deferred to event-driven programs that don't require explicit invocation, thereby reducing the size and performance strain of service compositions. |
| **Application** | Service agents can be designed to automatically respond to pre-defined conditions without invocation via a published contract. |
| **Impacts** | The complexity of composition logic increases when it is distributed across services, and event-driven agents and reliance on service agents can further tie an inventory architecture to proprietary vendor technology. |
| **Principles** | Service Loose Coupling, Service Reusability |
| **Architecture** | Inventory, Composition |

# Service Broker
### By Mark Little, Thomas Rischbeck, Arnaud Simon

Although all of the Service Broker patterns are used only out of necessity, establishing an environment capable of handling the three most common transformation requirements can add a great deal of flexibility to a service-oriented architecture implementation, and also has the added bonus of being able to perform more than one transformation function at the same time.

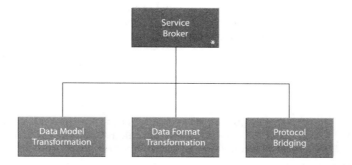

Service Broker is comprised of the co-existent application of Data Model Transformation, Data Format Transformation, and Protocol Bridging.

**Related Patterns in Other Catalogs**

Broker (Buschmann, Henney, Schmidt, Meunier, Rohnert, Sommerland, Stal)

**Related Service-Oriented Computing Goals**

Increased Intrinsic Interoperability, Increased Vendor Diversification Options, Reduced IT Burden

# Service Callback

By Anish Karmarkar

*How can a service communicate asynchronously with its consumers?*

| | |
|---|---|
| **Problem** | When a service needs to respond to a consumer request through the issuance of multiple messages or when service message processing requires a large amount of time, it is often not possible to communicate synchronously. |
| **Solution** | A service can require that consumers communicate with it asynchronously and provide a callback address to which the service can send response messages. |
| **Application** | A callback address generation and message correlation mechanism needs to be incorporated into the messaging framework and the overall inventory architecture. |
| **Impacts** | Asynchronous communication can introduce reliability concerns and can further require that surrounding infrastructure be upgraded to fully support the necessary callback correlation. |
| **Principles** | Standardized Service Contract, Service Loose Coupling, Service Composability |
| **Architecture** | Inventory, Service, Composition |

# Service Data Replication
By Thomas Erl

*How can service autonomy be preserved when services require access to shared data sources?*

| | |
|---|---|
| **Problem** | Service logic can be deployed in isolation to increase service autonomy, but services continue to lose autonomy when requiring access to shared data sources. |
| **Solution** | Services can have their own dedicated databases with replication to shared data sources. |
| **Application** | An additional database needs to be provided for the service and one or more replication channels need to be enabled between it and the shared data sources. |
| **Impacts** | This pattern results in additional infrastructure cost and demands, and an excess of replication channels can be difficult to manage. |
| **Principles** | Service Autonomy |
| **Architecture** | Inventory, Service |

# Service Decomposition
**By Thomas Erl**

*How can the granularity of a service be increased subsequent to its implementation?*

| | |
|---|---|
| **Problem** | Overly coarse-grained services can inhibit optimal composition design. |
| **Solution** | An already implemented coarse-grained service can be decomposed into two or more fine-grained services. |
| **Application** | The underlying service logic is restructured, and new service contracts are established. This pattern will likely require Proxy Capability to preserve the integrity of the original coarse-grained service contract. |
| **Impacts** | An increase in fine-grained services naturally leads to larger, more complex service composition designs. |
| **Principles** | Service Loose Coupling, Service Composability |
| **Architecture** | Service |

## Service Encapsulation
**By Thomas Erl**

*How can solution logic be made available as a resource of the enterprise?*

| | |
|---|---|
| **Problem** | Solution logic designed for a single application environment is typically limited in its potential to interoperate with or be leveraged by other parts of an enterprise. |
| **Solution** | Solution logic can be encapsulated by a service so that it is positioned as an enterprise resource capable of functioning beyond the boundary for which it is initially delivered. |
| **Application** | Solution logic suitable for service encapsulation needs to be identified. |
| **Impacts** | Service-encapsulated solution logic is subject to additional design and governance considerations. |
| **Principles** | n/a |
| **Architecture** | Service |

# Service Façade

**By Thomas Erl**

*How can a service accommodate changes to its contract or implementation while allowing the core service logic to evolve independently?*

| | |
|---|---|
| **Problem** | The coupling of the core service logic to contracts and implementation resources can inhibit its evolution and negatively impact service consumers. |
| **Solution** | A service façade component is used to abstract a part of the service architecture with negative coupling potential. |
| **Application** | A separate façade component is incorporated into the service design. |
| **Impacts** | The addition of the façade component introduces design effort and performance overhead. |
| **Principles** | Standardized Service Contract, Service Loose Coupling |
| **Architecture** | Service |

# Service Grid

**By David Chappell**

*How can deferred service state data be scaled and kept fault-tolerant?*

| | |
|---|---|
| **Problem** | State data deferred via State Repository or Stateful Services can be subject to performance bottlenecks and failure, especially when exposed to high-usage volumes. |
| **Solution** | State data is deferred to a collection of stateful system services that form a grid that provides high scalability and fault tolerance through memory replication and redundancy and supporting infrastructure. |
| **Application** | Grid technology is introduced into the enterprise or inventory architecture. |
| **Impacts** | This pattern can require a significant infrastructure upgrade and can correspondingly increase governance burden. |
| **Principles** | Service Statelessness |
| **Architecture** | Enterprise, Inventory, Service |

## Service Instance Routing

By Anish Karmarkar

*How can consumers contact and interact with service instances without the need for proprietary processing logic?*

| | |
|---|---|
| **Problem** | When required to repeatedly access a specific stateful service instance, consumers must rely on custom logic that more tightly couples them to the service. |
| **Solution** | The service provides an instance identifier along with its destination information in a standardized format that shields the consumer from having to resort to custom logic. |
| **Application** | The service is still required to provide custom logic to generate and manage instance identifiers, and both service and consumer require a common messaging infrastructure. |
| **Impacts** | This pattern can introduce the need for significant infrastructure upgrades and when misused can further lead to overly stateful messaging activities that can violate the Service Statelessness (418) principle. |
| **Principles** | Service Loose Coupling, Service Statelessness, Service Composability |
| **Architecture** | Inventory, Composition, Service |

# Service Layers
**By Thomas Erl**

*How can the services in an inventory be organized based on functional commonality?*

| Problem | Arbitrarily defining services delivered and governed by different project teams can lead to design inconsistency and inadvertent functional redundancy across a service inventory. |
|---|---|
| Solution | The inventory is structured into two or more logical service layers, each of which is responsible for abstracting logic based on a common functional type. |
| Application | Service models are chosen and then form the basis for service layers that establish modeling and design standards. |
| Impacts | The common costs and impacts associated with design standards and up-front analysis need to be accepted. |
| Principles | Service Reusability, Service Composability |
| Architecture | Inventory, Service |

# Service Messaging

**By Thomas Erl**

*How can services interoperate without forming persistent,*
*tightly coupled connections?*

| | |
|---|---|
| **Problem** | Services that depend on traditional remote communication protocols impose the need for persistent connections and tightly coupled data exchanges, increasing consumer dependencies and limiting service reuse potential. |
| **Solution** | Services can be designed to interact via a messaging-based technology, which removes the need for persistent connections and reduces coupling requirements. |
| **Application** | A messaging framework needs to be established, and services need to be designed to use it. |
| **Impacts** | Messaging technology brings with it QoS concerns such as reliable delivery, security, performance, and transactions. |
| **Principles** | Standardized Service Contract, Service Loose Coupling |
| **Architecture** | Inventory, Composition, Service |

# Service Normalization

**By Thomas Erl**

*How can a service inventory avoid redundant service logic?*

| | |
|---|---|
| **Problem** | When delivering services as part of a service inventory, there is a constant risk that services will be created with overlapping functional boundaries, making it difficult to enable wide-spread reuse. |
| **Solution** | The service inventory needs to be designed with an emphasis on service boundary alignment. |
| **Application** | Functional service boundaries are modeled as part of a formal analysis process and persist throughout inventory design and governance. |
| **Impacts** | Ensuring that service boundaries are and remain well-aligned introduces extra up-front analysis and on-going governance effort. |
| **Principles** | Service Autonomy |
| **Architecture** | Inventory, Service |

# Service Perimeter Guard

By Jason Hogg, Don Smith, Fred Chong, Tom Hollander, Wojtek Kozaczynski, Larry Brader, Nelly Delgado, Dwayne Taylor, Lonnie Wall, Paul Slater, Sajjad Nasir Imran, Pablo Cibraro, Ward Cunningham

*How can services that run in a private network be made available to external consumers without exposing internal resources?*

| | |
|---|---|
| **Problem** | External consumers that require access to one or more services in a private network can attack the service or use it to gain access to internal resources. |
| **Solution** | An intermediate service is established at the perimeter of the private network as a secure contact point for any external consumers that need to interact with internal services. |
| **Application** | The service is deployed in a perimeter network and is designed to work with existing firewall technologies so as to establish a secure bridging mechanism between external and internal networks. |
| **Impacts** | A perimeter service adds complexity and performance overhead as it establishes an intermediary processing layer for all external-to-internal communication. |
| **Principles** | Service Loose Coupling, Service Abstraction |
| **Architecture** | Service |

# Service Refactoring

**By Thomas Erl**

*How can a service be evolved without impacting existing consumers?*

| | |
|---|---|
| **Problem** | The logic or implementation technology of a service may become outdated or inadequate over time, but the service has become too entrenched to be replaced. |
| **Solution** | The service contract is preserved to maintain existing consumer dependencies, but the underlying service logic and/or implementation are refactored. |
| **Application** | Service logic and implementation technology are gradually improved or upgraded but must undergo additional testing. |
| **Impacts** | This pattern introduces governance effort, as well as risk associated with potentially negative side effects introduced by new logic or technology. |
| **Principles** | Standardized Service Contract, Service Loose Coupling, Service Abstraction |
| **Architecture** | Service |

# State Messaging

By Anish Karmarkar

*How can a service remain stateless while participating in stateful interactions?*

| | |
|---|---|
| **Problem** | When services are required to maintain state information in memory between message exchanges with consumers, their scalability can be compromised, and they can become a performance burden on the surrounding infrastructure. |
| **Solution** | Instead of retaining the state data in memory, its storage is temporarily delegated to messages. |
| **Application** | Depending on how this pattern is applied, both services and consumers may need to be designed to process message-based state data. |
| **Impacts** | This pattern may not be suitable for all forms of state data, and should messages be lost, any state information they carried may be lost as well. |
| **Principles** | Standardized Service Contract, Service Statelessness, Service Composability |
| **Architecture** | Composition, Service |

# State Repository
**By Thomas Erl**

*How can service state data be persisted for extended periods without consuming service runtime resources?*

| Problem | Large amounts of state data cached to support the activity within a running service composition can consume too much memory, especially for long-running activities, thereby decreasing scalability. |
|---|---|
| Solution | State data can be temporarily written to and then later retrieved from a dedicated state repository. |
| Application | A shared or dedicated repository is made available as part of the inventory or service architecture. |
| Impacts | The addition of required write and read functionality increases the service design complexity and can negatively affect performance. |
| Principles | Service Statelessness |
| Architecture | Inventory, Service |

# Stateful Services
By Thomas Erl

*How can service state data be persisted and managed without consuming service runtime resources?*

| | |
|---|---|
| **Problem** | State data associated with a particular service activity can impose a great deal of runtime state management responsibility upon service compositions, thereby reducing their scalability. |
| **Solution** | State data is managed and stored by intentionally stateful utility services. |
| **Application** | Stateful utility services provide in-memory state data storage and/or can maintain service activity context data. |
| **Impacts** | If not properly implemented, stateful utility services can become a performance bottleneck. |
| **Principles** | Service Statelessness |
| **Architecture** | Inventory, Service |

# Termination Notification

By David Orchard, Chris Riley

*How can the scheduled expiry of a service contract be communicated to consumer programs?*

| | |
|---|---|
| **Problem** | Consumer programs may be unaware of when a service or a service contract version is scheduled for retirement, thereby risking run-time failure. |
| **Solution** | Service contracts can be designed to express termination information for programmatic and human consumption. |
| **Application** | Service contracts can be extended with ignorable policy assertions or supplemented with human-readable annotations. |
| **Impacts** | The syntax and conventions used to express termination information must be understood by service consumers in order for this information to be effectively used. |
| **Principles** | Standardized Service Contract |
| **Architecture** | Composition, Service |

# Three-Layer Inventory
By Thomas Erl

This compound pattern is simply comprised of the combined application of the three service layer patterns. Three-Layer Inventory exists because the combined application of these three patterns results in common layers of abstraction that have been proven to complement and support each other by establishing services with flexible variations of agnostic and non-agnostic functional contexts.

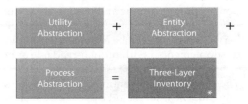

The joint application of Utility Abstraction, Entity Abstraction, and Process Abstraction results in Three-Layer Inventory.

# Trusted Subsystem

By Jason Hogg, Don Smith, Fred Chong, Tom Hollander, Wojtek
Kozaczynski, Larry Brader, Nelly Delgado, Dwayne Taylor, Lonnie Wall,
Paul Slater, Sajjad Nasir Imran, Pablo Cibraro, Ward Cunningham

*How can a consumer be prevented from circumventing a service
and directly accessing its resources?*

| | |
|---|---|
| **Problem** | A consumer that accesses back-end resources of a service directly can compromise the integrity of the resources and can further lead to undesirable forms of implementation coupling. |
| **Solution** | The service is designed to use its own credentials for authentication and authorization with back-end resources on behalf of consumers. |
| **Application** | Depending on the nature of the underlying resources, various design options and security technologies can be applied. |
| **Impacts** | If this type of service is compromised by attackers or unauthorized consumers, it can be exploited to gain access to a wide range of downstream resources. |
| **Principles** | Service Loose Coupling |
| **Architecture** | Service |

# UI Mediator

**By Clemens Utschig-Utschig, Berthold Maier,**
**Bernd Trops, Hajo Normann, Torsten Winterberg**

*How can a service-oriented solution provide a consistent,*
*interactive user experience?*

| | |
|---|---|
| **Problem** | Because the behavior of individual services can vary depending on their design, runtime usage, and the workload required to carry out a given capability, the consistency with which a service-oriented solution can respond to requests originating from a user-interface can fluctuate, leading to a poor user experience. |
| **Solution** | Establish mediator logic solely responsible for ensuring timely interaction and feedback with user-interfaces and presentation logic. |
| **Application** | A utility mediator service or service agent is positioned as the initial recipient of messages originating from the user-interface. This mediation logic responds in a timely and consistent manner regardless of the behavior of the underlying solution. |
| **Impacts** | The mediator logic establishes an additional layer of processing that can add to the required runtime processing. |
| **Principles** | Service Loose Coupling |
| **Architecture** | Composition |

# Uniform Contract
By Raj Balasubramanian, Benjamin Carlyle, Cesare Pautasso

Uniform Contract is a compound pattern comprised of the combined application of Reusable Contract, Lightweight Endpoint, and Entity Linking.

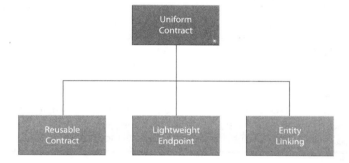

Uniform Contract is considered a specialized variation of Reusable Contract that is applied to all services within a given boundary (usually a service inventory). This compound pattern further requires that service functions are broken down to related individual resources, as per Lightweight Endpoint. It further enables links from one resource to another. Links are followed by service consumers to invoke the capabilities of each resource without foreknowledge of the service that exposes them, as per Entity Linking.

# Utility Abstraction

By Thomas Erl

*How can common non-business centric logic be separated, reused, and independently governed?*

| Problem | When non-business centric processing logic is packaged together with business-specific logic, it results in the redundant implementation of common utility functions across different services. |
|---|---|
| Solution | A service layer dedicated to utility processing is established, providing reusable utility services for use by other services in the inventory. |
| Application | The utility service model is incorporated into analysis and design processes in support of utility logic abstraction, and further steps are taken to define balanced service contexts. |
| Impacts | When utility logic is distributed across multiple services it can increase the size, complexity, and performance demands of compositions. |
| Principles | Service Loose Coupling, Service Abstraction, Service Reusability, Service Composability |
| Architecture | Inventory, Composition, Service |

# Validation Abstraction

**By Thomas Erl**

*How can service contracts be designed to more easily adapt to validation logic changes?*

| | |
|---|---|
| **Problem** | Service contracts that contain detailed validation constraints become more easily invalidated when the rules behind those constraints change. |
| **Solution** | Granular validation logic and rules can be abstracted away from the service contract, thereby decreasing constraint granularity and increasing the contract's potential longevity. |
| **Application** | Abstracted validation logic and rules need to be moved to the underlying service logic, a different service, a service agent, or elsewhere. |
| **Impacts** | This pattern can somewhat decentralize validation logic and can also complicate schema standardization. |
| **Principles** | Standardized Service Contract, Service Loose Coupling, Service Abstraction |
| **Architecture** | Service |

## Version Identification
By David Orchard, Chris Riley

*How can consumers be made aware of service contract version information?*

| Problem | When an already-published service contract is changed, unaware consumers will miss the opportunity to leverage the change or may be negatively impacted by the change. |
|---|---|
| Solution | Versioning information pertaining to compatible and incompatible changes can be expressed as part of the service contract, both for communication and enforcement purposes. |
| Application | With Web service contracts, version numbers can be incorporated into namespace values and as annotations. |
| Impacts | This pattern may require that version information be expressed with a proprietary vocabulary that needs to be understood by consumer designers in advance. |
| Principles | Standardized Service Contract |
| Architecture | Service |

# Appendix D

## The Annotated SOA Manifesto

The SOA Manifesto was authored and announced during the 2nd Annual International SOA Symposium in Rotterdam by a working group comprised of 17 experts and thought leaders from different organizations.

The original SOA Manifesto is published at www.soa-manifesto.org. You are encouraged to visit this site and enter your name on the *Become a Signatory* form to show your support for the values and principles declared in the manifesto.

Subsequent to the announcement of the SOA Manifesto, Thomas Erl authored an annotated version that supplements individual statements from the original manifesto with additional commentary and insights. The Annotated SOA Manifesto is published at www.soa-manifesto.com and has been further provided as a supplementary resource in this appendix.

## The Annotated SOA Manifesto

*Commentary and Insights about the SOA Manifesto from Thomas Erl*

**Service-orientation is a paradigm that frames what you do. Service-oriented architecture (SOA) is a type of architecture that results from applying service-orientation.**

From the beginning it was understood that this was to be a manifesto about two distinct yet closely related topics: the service-oriented architectural model and service-orientation, the paradigm through which the architecture is defined. The format of this manifesto was modeled after the Agile Manifesto, which limits content to concise statements that express ambitions, values, and guiding principles for realizing those ambitions and values. Such a manifesto is not a specification, a reference model, or even a white paper, and without an option to provide actual definitions, we decided to add this preamble in order to clarify how and why these terms are referenced in other parts of the manifesto document.

### We have been applying service-orientation...

The service-orientation paradigm is best viewed as a method or an approach for realizing a specific target state that is further defined by a set of strategic goals and benefits. When we apply service-orientation, we shape software programs and technology architecture in support of realizing this target state. This is what qualifies technology architecture as being service-oriented.

### ...to help organizations consistently deliver sustainable business value, with increased agility and cost-effectiveness...

This continuation of the preamble highlights some of the most prominent and commonly expected strategic benefits of service-oriented computing. Understanding these benefits helps shed some light on the aforementioned target state we intend to realize as a result of applying service-orientation.

Agility at a business level is comparable to an organization's responsiveness. The more easily and effectively an organization can respond to business change, the more efficient and successful it will be at adapting to the impacts of the change (and further leverage whatever benefits the change may bring about).

Service-orientation positions services as IT assets that are expected to provide repeated value over time that far exceeds the initial investment required for their delivery. Cost-effectiveness relates primarily to this expected return on investment. In many ways, an increase in cost-effectiveness goes hand-in-hand with an increase in agility; if there is more opportunity to reuse existing services, then there is generally less expense required to build new solutions.

"Sustainable" business value refers to the long-term goals of service-orientation to establish software programs as services with the inherent flexibility to be continually composed into new solution configurations and evolved to accommodate ever-changing business requirements.

### ...in line with changing business needs.

These last six words of the preamble are key to understanding the underlying philosophy of service-oriented computing. The need to accommodate business change on an on-going basis is foundational to service-orientation and considered a fundamental overarching strategic goal.

**Through our work we have come to prioritize:**

The upcoming statements establish a core set of values, each of which is expressed as a prioritization over something that is also considered of value. The intent of this value system is to address the hard choices that need to be made on a regular basis in order for the strategic goals and benefits of service-oriented computing to be consistently realized.

**Business value over technical strategy**

As stated previously, the need to accommodate business change is an overarching strategic goal. Therefore, the foundational quality of service-oriented architecture and of any software programs, solutions, and eco-systems that result from the adoption of service-orientation is that they are business-driven. It is not about technology determining the direction of the business, it is about the business vision dictating the utilization of technology.

This priority can have a profound ripple effect within the regions of an IT enterprise. It introduces changes to just about all parts of IT delivery lifecycles, from how we plan for and fund automation solutions, to how we build and govern them. All other values and principles in the manifesto, in one way or another, support the realization of this value.

**Strategic goals over project-specific benefits**

Historically, many IT projects focused solely on building applications designed specifically to automate business process requirements that were current at that time. This fulfilled immediate (tactical) needs, but as more of these single-purpose applications were delivered, it resulted in an IT enterprise filled with islands of logic and data referred to as application "silos." As new business requirements would emerge, either new silos were created or integration channels between silos were established. As yet more business change arose, integration channels had to be augmented, even more silos had to be created, and soon the IT enterprise landscape became convoluted and increasingly burdensome, expensive, and slow to evolve.

In many ways, service-orientation emerged in response to these problems. It is a paradigm that provides an alternative to project-specific, silo-based, and integrated application development by adamantly prioritizing the attainment of long-term, strategic business goals. The target state advocated by service-orientation does not have traditional application silos. And even when legacy resources and application silos exist in environments where service-orientation is adopted, the target state is one where they are harmonized to whatever extent feasible.

## Intrinsic interoperability over custom integration

For software programs to share data they need to be interoperable. If software programs are not designed to be compatible, they will likely not be interoperable. To enable interoperability between incompatible software programs requires that they be integrated. Integration is therefore the effort required to achieve interoperability between disparate software programs.

Although often necessary, customized integration can be expensive and time-consuming and can lead to fragile architectures that are burdensome to evolve. One of the goals of service-orientation is to minimize the need for customized integration by shaping software programs (within a given domain) so that they are natively compatible. This is a quality referred to as intrinsic interoperability. The service-orientation paradigm encompasses a set of specific design principles that are geared toward establishing intrinsic interoperability on several levels.

Intrinsic interoperability, as a characteristic of software programs that reside within a given domain, is key to realizing strategic benefits, such as increased cost-effectiveness and agility.

## Shared services over specific-purpose implementations

As just explained, service-orientation establishes a design approach comprised of a set of design principles. When applied to a meaningful extent, these principles shape a software program into a unit of service-oriented logic that can be legitimately referred to as a service.

Services are equipped with concrete characteristics (such as those that enable intrinsic interoperability) that directly support the previously described target state. One of these characteristics is the encapsulation of multi-purpose logic that can be shared and reused in support of the automation of different business processes.

A shared service establishes itself as an IT asset that can provide repeated business value while decreasing the expense and effort to deliver new automation solutions. While there is value in traditional, single-purpose applications that solve tactical business requirements, the use of shared services provides greater value in realizing strategic goals of service-oriented computing (which again include an increase in cost-effectiveness and agility).

## Flexibility over optimization

This is perhaps the broadest of the value prioritization statements and is best viewed as a guiding philosophy for how to better prioritize various considerations when delivering and evolving individual services and inventories of services.

Optimization primarily refers to the fulfillment of tactical gains by tuning a given application design or expediting its delivery to meet immediate needs. There is nothing undesirable about this, except that it can lead to the aforementioned silo-based environments when not properly prioritized in relation to fostering flexibility.

For example, the characteristic of flexibility goes beyond the ability for services to effectively (and intrinsically) share data. To be truly responsive to ever-changing business requirements, services must also be flexible in how they can be combined and aggregated into composite solutions. Unlike traditional distributed applications that often were relatively static despite the fact that they were componentized, service compositions need to be designed with a level of inherent flexibility that allows for constant augmentation. This means that when an existing business process changes or when a new business process is introduced, we need to be able to add, remove, and extend services within the composition architecture with minimal (integration) effort. This is why service composability is one of the key service-orientation design principles.

## Evolutionary refinement over pursuit of initial perfection

There is a common point of confusion when it comes to the term "agility" in relation to service-orientation. Some design approaches advocate the rapid delivery of software programs for immediate gains. This can be considered "tactical agility," as the focus is on tactical, short-term benefit. Service-orientation advocates the attainment of agility on an organizational or business level with the intention of empowering the organization, as a whole, to be responsive to change. This form of organizational agility can also be referred to as "strategic agility" because the emphasis is on longevity in that, with every software program we deliver, we want to work toward a target state that fosters agility with long-term strategic value.

For an IT enterprise to enable organizational agility, it must evolve in tandem with the business. We generally cannot predict how a business will need to evolve over time and therefore we cannot initially build the perfect services. At the same time, there is usually a wealth of knowledge that already exists within an organization's existing business intelligence that can be harvested during the analysis and modeling stages of SOA projects.

This information, together with service-orientation principles and proven methodologies, can help us identify and define a set of services that capture how the business exists and operates today while being sufficiently flexible to adapt to how the business changes over time.

**That is, while we value the items on the right, we value the items on the left more.**

By studying how these values are prioritized, we gain insight into what distinguishes service-orientation from other paradigms. This type of insight can benefit IT practitioners in several ways. For example, it can help establish fundamental criteria that we can use to determine how compatible service-orientation is for a given organization or IT enterprise. It can further help determine the extent to which service-orientation can or should be adopted.

An appreciation of the core values can also help us understand how challenging it may be to successfully carry out SOA projects within certain environments. For example, several of these prioritizations may clash head-on with established beliefs and preferences. In such a case, the benefits of service-orientation need to be weighed against the effort and impact their adoption may have (not just on technology, but also on the organization and IT culture).

The upcoming guiding principles were provided to help address many of these types of challenges.

**We follow these principles:**

So far, the manifesto has established an overall vision as well as a set of core values associated with the vision. The remainder of the declaration is comprised of a set of principles that are provided as guidance for adhering to the values and realizing the vision.

It's important to keep in mind that these are guiding principles specific to this manifesto. There is a separate set of established design principles that comprise the service-orientation design paradigm and there are many more documented practices and patterns specific to service-orientation and service-oriented architecture.

**Respect the social and power structure of the organization.**

One of the most common SOA pitfalls is approaching adoption as a technology-centric initiative. Doing so almost always leads to failure because we are simply not prepared for the inevitable organizational impacts.

The adoption of service-orientation is about transforming the way we automate business. However, regardless of what plans we may have for making this transformation effort happen, we must always begin with an understanding and an appreciation of the organization, its structure, its goals, and its culture.

The adoption of service-orientation is very much a human experience. It requires support from those in authority and then asks that an IT culture adopt a strategic, community-centric mindset. We must fully acknowledge and plan for this level of organizational change in order to receive the necessary long-term commitments required to achieve the target state of service-orientation.

These types of considerations not only help us determine how to best proceed with an SOA initiative, they further assist us in defining the most appropriate scope and approach for adoption.

**Recognize that SOA ultimately demands change on many levels.**

There's a saying that goes: "Success is being prepared for opportunity." Perhaps the number one lesson learned from SOA projects carried out so far is that we must fully comprehend and then plan and prepare for the volume and range of change that is brought about as a result of adopting service-orientation. Here are some examples.

Service-orientation changes how we build automation solutions by positioning software programs as IT assets with long-term, repeatable business value. An up-front investment is required to create an environment comprised of such assets and an ongoing commitment is required to maintain and leverage their value. So, right out of the gate, changes are required to how we fund, measure, and maintain systems within the IT enterprise.

Furthermore, because service-orientation introduces services that are positioned as resources of the enterprise, there will be changes in how we own different parts of systems and regulate their design and usage, not to mention changes to the infrastructure required to guarantee continuous scalability and reliability.

**The scope of SOA adoption can vary. Keep efforts manageable and within meaningful boundaries.**

A common myth has been that in order to realize the strategic goals of service-oriented computing, service-orientation must be adopted on an enterprise-wide basis. This means establishing and enforcing design and industry standards across the IT enterprise so as to create an enterprise-wide inventory of intrinsically interoperable services. While there is nothing wrong with this ideal, it is not a realistic goal for many organizations, especially those with larger IT enterprises.

The most appropriate scope for any given SOA adoption effort needs to be determined as a result of planning and analysis in conjunction with pragmatic considerations, such as the aforementioned impacts on organizational structures, areas of authority, and cultural changes that are brought about.

These types of factors help us determine a scope of adoption that is manageable. But for any adoption effort to result in an environment that progresses the IT enterprise toward the desired strategic target state, the scope must also be meaningful. In other words, it must be meaningfully cross-silo so that collections of services can be delivered in relation to each other within a pre-defined boundary. In other words, we want to create "continents of services," not the dreaded "islands of services."

This concept of building independently owned and governed service inventories within domains of the same IT enterprise reduces many of the risks that are commonly attributed to "big-bang" SOA projects and furthermore mitigates the impact of both organizational and technological changes (because the impact is limited to a segmented and managed scope). It is also an approach that allows for phased adoption where one domain service inventory can be established at a time.

**Products and standards alone will neither give you SOA nor apply the service-orientation paradigm for you.**

This principle addresses two separate but very much related myths. The first is that you can buy your way into SOA with modern technology products, and the second is the assumption that the adoption of industry standards (such as XML, WSDL, SCA, etc.) will naturally result in service-oriented technology architecture.

The vendor and industry standards communities have been credited with building modern service technology innovation upon non-proprietary frameworks and platforms. Everything from service virtualization to cloud computing and grid computing has helped advance the potential for building sophisticated and complex service-oriented solutions. However, none of these technologies are exclusive to SOA. You can just as easily build silo-based systems in the cloud as you can on your own private servers.

There is no such thing as "SOA in a box" because in order to achieve service-oriented technology architecture, service-orientation needs to be successfully applied; this, in turn, requires that everything we design and build be driven by the unique direction, vision, and requirements of the business.

**SOA can be realized through a variety of technologies and standards.**

Service-orientation is a technology-neutral and vendor-neutral paradigm. Service-oriented architecture is a technology-neutral and vendor neutral architectural model. Service-oriented computing can be viewed as a specialized form of distributed computing. Service-oriented solutions can therefore be built using just about any technologies and industry standards suitable for distributed computing.

While some technologies (especially those based on industry standards) can increase the potential of applying some service-orientation design principles, it is really the potential to fulfill business requirements that ultimately determines the most suitable choice of technologies and industry standards.

**Establish a uniform set of enterprise standards and policies based on industry, de facto, and community standards.**

Industry standards represent non-proprietary technology specifications that help establish, among other things, consistent baseline characteristics (such as transport, interface, message format, etc.) of technology architecture. However, the use of industry standards alone does not guarantee that services will be intrinsically interoperable.

For two software programs to be fully compatible, additional conventions (such as data models and policies) need to be adhered to. This is why IT enterprises must establish and enforce design standards. Failure to properly standardize and regulate the standardization of services within a given domain will begin to tear at the fabric of interoperability upon which the realization of many strategic benefits relies.

This principle not only advocates the use of enterprise design standards, it also reminds us that, whenever possible and feasible, custom design standards should be based upon and incorporate standards already in use by the industry and the community in general.

**Pursue uniformity on the outside while allowing diversity on the inside.**

Federation can be defined as the unification of a set of disparate entities. While allowing each entity to be independently governed on the inside, all agree to adhere to a common, unified front.

A fundamental part of service-oriented architecture is the introduction of a federated endpoint layer that abstracts service implementation details while publishing a set of endpoints that represent individual services within a given domain in a unified manner. Accomplishing this generally involves achieving unity based on a combination of industry and design standards. The consistency of this unity across services is key to realizing intrinsic interoperability.

A federated endpoint layer further helps increase opportunities to explore vendor-diversity options. For example, one service may need to be built upon a completely different platform than another. As long as these services maintain compatible endpoints, the governance of their respective implementations can remain independent. This not only highlights that services can be built using different implementation mediums (such as EJB, .NET, SOAP, REST, etc.), it also emphasizes that different intermediary platforms and technologies can be utilized together, as required.

Note that this type of diversity comes with a price. This principle does not advocate diversification itself—it simply recommends that we allow diversification when justified, so that "best-of-breed" technologies and platforms can be leveraged to maximize business requirements fulfillment.

**Identify services through collaboration with business and technology stakeholders.**

In order for technology solutions to be business-driven, the technology must be in sync with the business. Therefore, another goal of service-oriented computing is to align technology and business. The stage at which this alignment is initially accomplished is during the analysis and modeling processes that usually precede actual service development and delivery.

The critical ingredient to carrying out service-oriented analysis is to have both business and technology experts working hand-in-hand to identify and define candidate services. For example, business experts can help accurately define functional contexts pertaining to business-centric services, while technology experts can provide pragmatic input to ensure that the granularity and definition of conceptual services remains realistic in relation to their eventual implementation environments.

**Maximize service usage by considering the current and future scope of utilization.**

The extent of a given SOA project may be enterprise-wide or it may be limited to a domain of the enterprise. Whatever the scope, a pre-defined boundary is established to encompass an inventory of services that need to be conceptually modeled before they can be developed. By modeling multiple services in relation to each other we essentially establish a blueprint of the services we will eventually be building. This modeling exercise is critical when attempting to identify and define services that can be shared by different solutions.

There are various methodologies and approaches that can be used to carry out service-oriented analysis stages. However, a common thread among all of them is that the functional boundaries of services be normalized to avoid redundancy. Even then, normalized services do not necessarily make for highly reusable services. Other factors come into play, such as service granularity, autonomy, state management, scalability, composability, and the extent to which service logic is sufficiently generic so that it can be effectively reused.

These types of considerations guided by business and technology expertise provide the opportunity to define services that capture current utilization requirements while having the flexibility to adapt to future change.

**Verify that services satisfy business requirements and goals.**

As with anything, services can be misused. When growing and managing a portfolio of services, their usage and effectiveness at fulfilling business requirements need to be verified and measured. Modern tools provide various means of monitoring service usage, but there are intangibles that also need to be taken into consideration to ensure that services are not just used because they are available, but to verify that they are truly fulfilling business needs and meeting expectations.

This is especially true with shared services that shoulder multiple dependencies. Not only do shared services require adequate infrastructure to guarantee scalability and reliability for all of the solutions that reuse them, they also need to be designed and extended with great care to ensure their functional contexts are never skewed.

**Evolve services and their organization in response to real use.**

This guiding principle ties directly back to the "Evolutionary refinement over pursuit of initial perfection" value statement, as well as the overall goal of maintaining an alignment of business and technology.

We can never expect to rely on guesswork when it comes to determining service granularity, the range of functions that services need to perform, or how services will need to be organized into compositions. Based on whatever extent of analysis we are able to initially perform, a given service will be assigned a defined functional context and will contain one or more functional capabilities that likely involve it in one or more service compositions.

As real-world business requirements and circumstances change, the service may need to be augmented, extended, refactored, or perhaps even replaced. Service-orientation design principles build native flexibility into service architectures so that, as software programs, services are resilient and adaptive to change and to being changed in response to real-world usage.

**Separate the different aspects of a system that change at different rates.**

What makes monolithic and silo-based systems inflexible is that change can have a significant impact on their existing usage. This is why it is often easier to create new silo-based applications rather then augment or extend existing ones.

The rationale behind the separation of concerns (a commonly known software engineering theory) is that a larger problem can be more effectively solved when decomposed into a set of smaller problems or concerns. When applying service-orientation to the separation of concerns, we build corresponding units of solution logic that solve individual concerns, thereby allowing us to aggregate the units to solve the larger problem in addition to giving us the opportunity to aggregate them into different configurations in order to solve other problems.

Besides fostering service reusability, this approach introduces numerous layers of abstraction that help shield service-comprised systems from the impacts of change. This form of abstraction can exist at different levels. For example, if legacy resources encapsulated by one service need to be replaced, the impact of that change can be mitigated as long as the service is able to retain its original endpoint and functional behavior.

Another example is the separation of agnostic from non-agnostic logic. The former type of logic has high reuse potential if it is multi-purpose and less likely to change. Non-agnostic logic, on the other hand, typically represents the single-purpose parts of parent business process logic, which are often more volatile. Separating these respective logic types into different service layers further introduces abstraction that enables service reusability while shielding services, and any solutions that utilize them, from the impacts of change.

**Reduce implicit dependencies and publish all external dependencies to increase robustness and reduce the impact of change.**

One of the most well-known service-orientation design principles is that of service loose coupling. How a service architecture is internally structured and how services relate to programs that consume them (which can include other services) all comes down to dependencies that are formed on individually moving parts that are part of the service architecture.

Layers of abstraction help ease evolutionary change by localizing the impacts of the change to controlled regions. For example, within service architectures, service façades can be used to abstract parts of the implementation in order to minimize the reach of implementation dependencies.

On the other hand, published technical service contracts need to disclose the dependencies that service consumers must form in order to interact with services. By reducing internal dependencies that can affect these technical contracts when change does occur, we avoid proliferating the impact of those changes upon dependent service consumers.

**At every level of abstraction, organize each service around a cohesive and manageable unit of functionality.**

Each service requires a well-defined functional context that determines what logic does and does not belong within the service's functional boundary. Determining the scope and granularity of these functional service boundaries is one of the most critical responsibilities during the service delivery lifecycle.

Services with coarse functional granularity may be too inflexible to be effective, especially if they are expected to be reusable. On the other hand, overly fine grained services may tax an infrastructure in that service compositions will need to consist of increased quantities of composition members.

Determining the right balance of functional scope and granularity requires a combination of business and technology expertise, and further requires an understanding of how services within a given boundary relate to each other.

Many of the guiding principles described in this manifesto will help in making this determination in support of positioning each service as an IT asset capable of furthering an IT enterprise toward that target state whereby the strategic benefits of service-oriented computing are realized.

Ultimately, though, it will always be the attainment of real-world business value that dictates, from conception to delivery to repeated usage, the evolutionary path of any unit of service-oriented functionality.

*—Thomas Erl (November 22, 2009)*
*www.soa-manifesto.com*

# About the Authors

## Thomas Erl

Thomas Erl is a top-selling IT author, founder of Arcitura Education, editor of the *Service Technology Magazine,* and series editor of the *Prentice Hall Service Technology Series from Thomas Erl.* With more than 175,000 copies in print worldwide, his books have become international bestsellers and have been formally endorsed by senior members of major IT organizations, such as IBM, Microsoft, Oracle, Intel, Accenture, IEEE, HL7, MITRE, SAP, CISCO, HP, and many others. As CEO of Arcitura Education Inc. and in cooperation with CloudSchool.com™ and SOASchool.com®, Thomas has led the development of curricula for the internationally recognized Cloud Certified Professional (CCP) and SOA Certified Professional (SOACP) accreditation programs, which have established a series of formal, vendor-neutral industry certifications obtained by thousands of IT professionals around the world. Thomas has toured more than 20 countries as a speaker and instructor and regularly participates in international conferences, including Service Technology Symposium and Gartner events. More than 100 articles and interviews by Thomas have been published in numerous publications, including *The Wall Street Journal* and *CIO Magazine.*

## Andre Tost

Andre Tost works as a Senior Technical Staff Member and Software Architect in IBM's Software Group. He is currently helping to develop and evolve the new PureApplication System cloud platform. Previously, Andre spent 10 years as an SOA consultant for IBM, leading large SOA transformation projects with clients worldwide. His specific focus was on SOA governance and middleware integration using enterprise service bus technology. Andre has co-authored several technical books and has published many articles on SOA and related topics. He is also a frequent conference speaker. Originally from Germany, he now works and lives in Rochester, Minnesota. He likes to watch, coach and play soccer whenever his busy schedule allows. Andre has a degree in Electrical Engineering from Berufsakademie Stuttgart, Germany.

## Satadru Roy

Satadru Roy is a Consultant Architect who has designed and built large-scale, distributed systems using Java-based technologies for the last two decades. In that time he has worked as a product engineer and services consultant at Java infrastructure software vendors such as BEA Systems, Sun Microsystems, and Oracle Inc. He currently helps customers build mobile and cloud-hosted applications where he alternates between wearing architect and development manager hats, while his main areas of focus are API design and lightweight integration using agile development methodologies. Satadru is also immersing himself in the growing eco-system of the Scala platform and believes they will play increasingly important roles in future cloud and Big Data applications. He holds a Masters degree in Engineering from Indian Institure of Science.

## Philip Thomas

Phil Thomas is an IT Architect in IBM's Software Group. During his time in the technology sector, he has worked across industries and geographies with a range of organizations as a consultant on technology strategy and on the architecture, design, and implementation of a broad variety of solutions. His expertise spans a number of areas including Java/JEE, SOA, transaction processing systems, messaging/integration middleware, business process management, information management systems, and business analytics. He currently specializes in Big Data and analytics, based out of the UK. Prior to joining IBM in 2000, Phil trained as a physicist and holds a Ph.D. in experimental high-temperature superconductivity awarded by the University of Birmingham.

# About the Foreword Contributor

**Mark Little**

Dr. Mark Little is VP Engineering at Red Hat where he leads JBoss technical direction, research, and development. Prior to this he was the SOA Technical Development Manager and the Director of Standards. He was also the Chief Architect and Co-Founder at Arjuna Technologies, as well as a Distinguished Engineer at Hewlett Packard. He has worked in the area of reliable distributed systems since the mid-eighties. His Ph.D.f was on fault-tolerant distributed systems, replication, and transactions. He is currently also a professor at Newcastle University.

# About the Contributors

## Raj Balasubramanian

Raj Balasubramanian is a Senior Technical Staff Member and the product manager lead for the cloud services offering from Mobile First organization in IBM SWG. In this role, Raj manages and leads the delivery of mobile services in the cloud for IBM. He was previously a senior technologist on the Business Process Optimization (BPO) team within IBM Software Group, with a focus on delivering SOA, BPM, and cloud solutions across industries. Raj has taken on the role of Enterprise Architect, System Architect, and Solution Architect to meet the varied needs of the customer. He has published numerous articles on IBM DeveloperWorks and speaks at industry conferences on a variety of topics. His interests are in distributed systems, applying Web constructs to solution design, and using formal models and analytics to reason about large systems.

Previously in his IT career, he started by building enterprise systems using different technologies to solve business problems that includes Web technologies, SOA, BPM, and various machine learning techniques. He is also pursuing a Ph.D. in Computer Science at University of Texas at Austin. His official profile is on http://raj.balasubramanians.com, which links to his various personas.

## David Chou

David Chou is an architect at Microsoft, focused on collaborating with enterprises and organizations in areas such as cloud computing, SOA, Web, distributed systems, mobile apps, etc., and supporting decision-makers on defining evolutionary strategies in architecture. Drawing on experiences from his previous jobs at Sun Microsystems and Accenture, David enjoys helping customers create value from using objective and pragmatic approaches to define IT strategies, roadmaps, and solution architectures.

## Thomas Plunkett

Tom Plunkett is a principal consultant with Oracle and teaches graduate-level computer science courses for Virginia Tech. Tom also volunteers for the non-profit organization AtrocityWatch, where he is the Chief Data Officer and uses Big Data technologies to analyze social media to detect crimes against humanity. Tom is the author of several books and has given presentations at over fifty conferences.

Prior to joining Oracle, Tom practiced patent law with Fliesler Meyer in San Francisco, representing Oracle and other Silicon Valley companies. Tom has a B.A. and J.D. from George Mason University, an M.S. in Computer Science from Virginia Tech, and has taken graduate courses in Management Science and Engineering from Stanford University.

# Index

## A

abstraction. *See* Service Abstraction design principle

ACC (Applet and Application Client Container), 42

ACCEPT header, HTTP, 109-110

Agnostic Capability design pattern, 427

Agnostic Context design pattern, 428

agnostic functional contexts, 140

agnostic logic, defined, 31

Agnostic Sub-Controller design pattern, 429

annotated SOA Manifesto, 28, 38, 520-532

annotations

   defined, 54

   in JAX-RS standard, 125-129

   in JAX-WS standard, 113-115

APIs

   Java EE (Java Platform, Enterprise Edition), 49-59

      *JPA (Java Persistence API), 53-54*

      *JTA (Java Transactions API), 50-51*

   Java SE (Java Platform, Standard Edition), 46-49

      *JDBC (Java Database Connectivity), 49*

      *JNDI (Java Naming and Directory Interface), 48*

      *RMI (Remote Method Invocation), 46-47*

      *RMI over IIOP, 47-48*

**Applet and Application Client Container (ACC), 42**

# Arcitura
# Big Data School

## Vendor-Neutral Big Data Training & Certification

### 15 Course Modules • 15 Exams • 5 Certifications

The Big Data Science Certified Professional (BDSCP) program from the Arcitura Big Data Science School is dedicated to excellence in the fields of Big Data science, analysis, analytics, business intelligence, technology architecture, design and development, as well as governance. A collection of courses establishes a set of vendor-neutral industry certifications with different areas of specialization. Founded by best-selling author, Thomas Erl, this curriculum enables IT professionals to develop real-world Big Data science proficiency. Because of the vendor-neutral focus of the course materials, the skills acquired by attaining certifications are applicable to any vendor or open-source platform.

Certified Big Data Science Professional
Certified Big Data Scientist
Certified Big Data Engineer
Certified Big Data Architect
Certified Big Data Governance Specialist

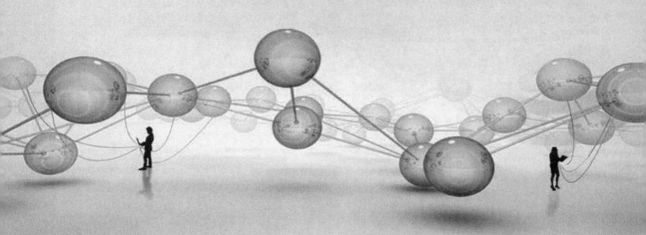

# Prentice Hall Service Technology Series from Thomas

*THE WORLD'S TOP-SELLING SERVICE TECHNOLOGY TITLES*

## ABOUT THE SERIES

The Prentice Hall Service Technology Series from Thomas Erl aims to provide the IT industry with a consistent level of unbiased, practical, and comprehensive guidance and instruction in the areas of service technology application and innovation. Each title in this book series is authored in relation to other titles so as to establish a library of complementary knowledge. Although the series covers a br spectrum of service technology-related topics, each title is authored in compliance with common language, vocabulary, and illustration conventions so as to enable readers to continually explore cross-topic research and education.

servicetechbooks.com/community

## ABOUT THE SERIES EDITOR

Thomas Erl is a best-selling IT author, the series editor of the Prentice Hall Service Technology Series from Thomas Erl, and the editor of the Service Technology Magazine. As CEO of Arcitura Education Inc. and in cooperation with CloudSchool.com™ and SOASchool.com®, Thomas has led the development of curricula for the internationally recognized SOA Certified Professional (SOACP) and Cloud Certified Professional (CCP) accreditation programs, which have established a series of formal, vendor-neutral industry certifications. Thomas has toured over 20 countries as a speaker and instructor. Over 100 articles and interviews by Thomas have been published in numerous publications, including the Wall Street Journal and CIO Magazine.

 |  |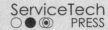

**informIT.com**
THE TRUSTED TECHNOLOGY LEARNING SOURCE

**PRENTICE HALL**

**ServiceTech** PRESS

**A Design Patterns**
Thomas Erl

N: 0136135161
rdcover, Full-Color,
5 pages

**SOA Governance:
Governing Shared
Services On-Premise
& in the Cloud**
by S. Bennett, T. Erl,
C. Gee, R. Laird,
A. T. Manes,
R. Schneider, L. Shuster,
A. Tost, C. Venable

ISBN: 0138156751
Hardcover, 675 pages

**SOA with REST:
Principles, Patterns &
Constraints for Building
Enterprise Solutions
with REST**
by Raj Balasubramanian,
Benjamin Carlyle,
Thomas Erl,
Cesare Pautasso

ISBN: 0137012519
Hardcover, 577 pages

**Cloud Computing:
Concepts, Technology
& Architecture**
by Thomas Erl,
Zaigham Mahmood,
Ricardo Puttini

ISBN: 9780133387520
Hardcover, 528 pages

**SOA with Java:
Realizing Service-Orientation
with Java Technologies**
by Thomas Erl,
Satadru Roy,
Philip Thomas,
Andre Tost

ISBN: 9780133859034

**rvice-Oriented
chitecture:
ield Guide to
egrating XML and
eb Services**
Thomas Erl

N: 0131428985
oerback, 534 pages

**Service-Oriented
Architecture:
Concepts, Technology
and Design**
by Thomas Erl

ISBN: 0131858580
Hardcover, 760 pages

**SOA Principles of
Service Design**
by Thomas Erl

ISBN: 0132344823
Hardcover, Full-Color,
573 pages

**Web Service Contract
Design and Versioning
for SOA**
by T. Erl, H. Haas,
A. Karmarkar, C. K. Liu,
D. Orchard, J. Pasley,
A. Tost, P. Walmsley,
U. Yalcinalp

ISBN: 013613517X
Hardcover, 826 pages

**SOA with .NET &
Windows Azure:
Realizing Service-
Orientation with the
Microsoft Platform**
by D. Chou, J. de
Vadoss, T. Erl, N. Gandhi
H. Kommalapati,
B. Loesgen, C. Schittko
H. Wilhelmsen, M. Williams

ISBN: 0131582313
Hardcover, 893 pages

**ming Soon:**
ervice Infrastructure: On-Premise & in the Cloud
Next Generation SOA: A Real-World Guide to the Modern Service-Enabled Enterprise
Cloud Computing Design Patterns

# FREE
## Online Edition

**Safari** Books Online

Your purchase of *SOA with Java* includes access to a free online edition for 45 days through the **Safari Books Online** subscription service. Nearly every Prentice Hall book is available online through **Safari Books Online**, along with thousands of books and videos from publishers such as Addison-Wesley Professional, Cisco Press, Exam Cram, IBM Press, O'Reilly Media, Que, Sams, and VMware Press.

**Safari Books Online** is a digital library providing searchable, on-demand access to thousands of technology, digital media, and professional development books and videos from leading publishers. With one monthly or yearly subscription price, you get unlimited access to learning tools and information on topics including mobile app and software development, tips and tricks on using your favorite gadgets, networking, project management, graphic design, and much more.

## Activate your FREE Online Edition at
## informit.com/safarifree

**STEP 1:**   Enter the coupon code: BMUFQGA.

**STEP 2:**   New Safari users, complete the brief registration form.
Safari subscribers, just log in.

If you have difficulty registering on Safari or accessing the online edition,
please e-mail customer-service@safaribooksonline.com

# SOA & Cloud Computing Training & Certification

## SOA Certified Professional (SOACP)

Content from this book and other series titles has been incorporated into the SOA Certified Professional (SOACP) program, an industry-recognized, vendor-neutral SOA certification curriculum developed by author Thomas Erl in cooperation with industry experts and academic communities and provided by SOASchool.com and training partners.

The SOA Certified Professional curriculum is comprised of a collection of 23 courses and labs that can be taken with or without formal testing and certification. Training can be delivered anywhere in the world by Certified Trainers. A comprehensive self-study program is available for remote, self-paced study, and exams can be taken world-wide via Prometric testing centers.

Dozens of public workshops are scheduled every quarter around the world by regional training partners.

All courses are reviewed and revised on a regular basis to stay in alignment with industry developments.

For more information, visit: **www.soaschool.com**

**www.soaworkshops.com** • **www.soaselfstudy.com**

## Cloud Certified Professional (CCP)

The Cloud Certified Professional (CCP) program, provided by CloudSchool.com, establishes a series of vendor-neutral industry certifications dedicated to areas of specialization in the field of cloud computing. Also founded by author Thomas Erl, this program exists independently from the SOASchool.com courses, while preserving consistency in terminology, conventions, and notation. This allows IT professionals to study cloud computing topics separately or in combination with SOA topics, as required.

The Cloud Certified Professional curriculum is comprised of 21 courses and labs, each of which has a corresponding Prometric exam. Private and public training workshops can be provided throughout the world by Certified Trainers. Self-study kits are further available for remote, self-paced study and in support of instructor-led workshops.

All courses are reviewed and revised on a regular basis to stay in alignment with industry developments.

For more information, visit: **www.cloudschool.com**

**www.cloudworkshops.com** • **www.cloudselfstudy.com**

---

SOASchool.com and CloudSchool.com exams offered world-wide through Prometric testing centers (www.prometric.com/arcitura)

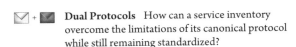 **Dual Protocols**   How can a service inventory overcome the limitations of its canonical protocol while still remaining standardized?

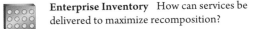 **Endpoint Redirection**   How can consumers of a specific service endpoint adapt when the service endpoint changes or is removed?

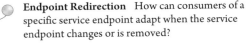 **Enterprise Inventory**   How can services be delivered to maximize recomposition?

**Enterprise Service Bus**

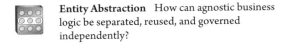 **Entity Abstraction**   How can agnostic business logic be separated, reused, and governed independently?

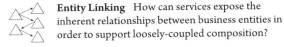 **Entity Linking**   How can services expose the inherent relationships between business entities in order to support loosely-coupled composition?

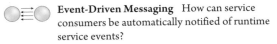 **Event-Driven Messaging**   How can service consumers be automatically notified of runtime service events?

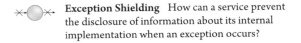 **Exception Shielding**   How can a service prevent the disclosure of information about its internal implementation when an exception occurs?

**Federated Endpoint Layer**

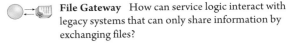 **File Gateway**   How can service logic interact with legacy systems that can only share information by exchanging files?

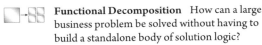 **Functional Decomposition**   How can a large business problem be solved without having to build a standalone body of solution logic?

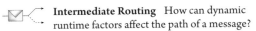 **Idempotent Capability**   How can a service capability safely accept multiple copies of the same message to handle communication failure?

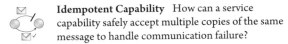 **Intermediate Routing**   How can dynamic runtime factors affect the path of a message?

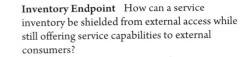 **Inventory Endpoint**   How can a service inventory be shielded from external access while still offering service capabilities to external consumers?

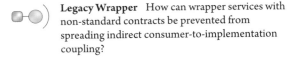 **Legacy Wrapper**   How can wrapper services with non-standard contracts be prevented from spreading indirect consumer-to-implementation coupling?

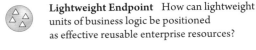 **Lightweight Endpoint**   How can lightweight units of business logic be positioned as effective reusable enterprise resources?

**Logic Centralization**   How can the misuse of redundant service logic be avoided?

  **Message Screening**   How can a service be protected from malformed or malicious input?

 **Messaging Metadata**   How can services be designed to process activity-specific data at runtime?

 **Metadata Centralization**   How can service metadata be centrally published and governed?

 **Multi-Channel Endpoint**   How can legacy logic fragmented and duplicated for different delivery channels be centrally consolidated?

 **Non-Agnostic Context**   How can single-purpose service logic be positioned as an effective enterprise resource?

**Official Endpoint**

**Orchestration**

 **Partial State Deferral**   How can services be designed to optimize resource consumption while still remaining stateful?

 **Partial Validation**   How can unnecessary data validation be avoided?

 **Policy Centralization**   How can policies be normalized and consistently enforced across multiple services?

 **Process Abstraction**   How can non-agnostic process logic be separated and governed independently?

 **Process Centralization**   How can abstracted business process logic be centrally governed?

 **Protocol Bridging**   How can a service exchange data with consumers that use different communication protocols?

 **Proxy Capability**   How can a service subject to decomposition continue to support consumers affected by the decomposition?

 **Redundant Implementation**   How can the reliability and availability of a service be increased?

**Reliable Messaging**   How can services communicate reliably when implemented in an unreliable environment?

 **Reusable Contract**   How can service consumers compose services without having to couple themselves to service-specific contracts?

**Rules Centralization**   How can business rules be abstracted and centrally governed?